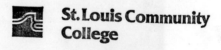

**charlie
chaplin**

charlie chaplin

THEODORE HUFF

ARNO PRESS & THE NEW YORK TIMES

New York · 1972

Reprint Edition 1972 by Arno Press Inc.

Manufactured in the United States of America

charlie chaplin

THEODORE HUFF

Henry Schuman New York

The author is indebted
to Joseph Cornell for
illustrations no. 37, 38, 46, 74, 86, 96, 112, 135;
to Herman G. Weinberg for no. 45, 47, 93, 97, 137, 138;
to Culver Service for no. 42;
to International News Photos for no. 147.
All other stills are from the private collection of the author.
For various favors the author wishes to thank
Harriet Freeman, Kent Munson, H. D. Waley, Tom Brandon,
Herman G. Weinberg, Charles Turner, James Card,
and the Theatre Collection of
the New York Public Library.

contents

i   the importance of Chaplin and his art   1

ii   childhood and stage career   10

iii   the Karno Company and tour of America   16

iv   the motion picture industry, December 1913, and a note on Mack Sennett   22

v   Chaplin at Keystone   28

vi   the Chaplin-Keystone films (1914)   35

vii   Essanay—the transitional period   46

viii $10,000 a week from Mutual   58

ix   the classic Mutual comedies   67

x   million-dollar contract and first marriage   84

xi   "A Dog's Life"—first masterpiece   95

xii   "Shoulder Arms"   101

xiii   two failures   109

xiv   Chaplin's method   116

xv   "The Kid"   124

xvi   Chaplin's 1921 trip abroad   135

xvii   new friends   148

xviii   two minor comedies   155

xix   "The Pilgrim"   162

xx   "A Woman of Paris"   168

xxi   "The Gold Rush"   187

xxii   Lita Grey—second marriage and divorce   199

xxiii   "The Circus"   208

xxiv   "City Lights"   218

xxv   Chaplin as a composer   235

xxvi   trip around the world; Paulette Goddard   242

xxvii   "Modern Times"   252

xxviii   "The Great Dictator"   262

xxix   law suits and another marriage   280

xxx   Chaplin and politics   287

xxxi   "Monsieur Verdoux"   293

postscript   308

an index to the films of Charles Chaplin   313

biographical sketches of the people
professionally associated with Chaplin   333

index   345

illustrations

following page 50

1 Chaplin in 1940.

2 Chaplin in his teens as a member of the music hall act "Casey's Court Circus."

3 Chaplin as he looked when he entered the movies.

4 The Sennett studio where Chaplin made his first comedies.

5 Mabel Normand, the leading comedienne at Keystone.

6 Scenes from "Making a Living," Chaplin's first film, before he adopted the tramp costume and make-up.

7 Frame enlargements from "Kid Auto Races at Venice," the short film in which Chaplin first wore his world-famous outfit.

8 A posed shot from "Kid Auto Races at Venice," showing director Henry Lehrman, Frank D. Williams at the camera, and Chaplin.

9 "Between Showers" with Chaplin and Ford Sterling.

10 Mack Swain obeying Sennett's oft repeated command, "Don't anticipate!" in "Laughing Gas."

11 Scenes from four Chaplin-Keystones: "Between Showers" (1), "Mabel's Busy Day" (2), "The Property Man" (3), "The Face on the Barroom Floor" (4).

12 Charlie welcomed (?) home by his wife (Phyllis Allen) in "The Rounders."

13 Charlie and Fatty Arbuckle create havoc in "The Rounders."

14 "The Rounders" end up in a sinking boat.

15 Three scenes from "Tillie's Punctured Romance" featuring Marie Dressler as Tillie, Chaplin as The City Slicker, and Mabel Normand as his partner in crime.

16 Leo White, Charlie, and Ben Turpin in "A Night Out."

17 A classic situation from "A Night Out."

18 Ben Turpin rescuing Charlie in "A Night Out."

19 Edna Purviance, Chaplin, and Turpin in "A Night Out."

20 Charlie ordered by his boss (Charles Insley) in the appropriately titled "Work."

21 After the explosion in "Work." The composite film "Triple Trouble" also ends with this scene.

22 Edna's stern father (Charles Insley) is deceived by the coy charm of Charlie disguised in "A Woman."

23 Close-up of Charlie in "A Woman."

24 Charlie as the janitor who adores the pretty stenographer (Edna Purviance) in "The Bank."

25 The janitor crushed when the stenographer tears up his note in "The Bank."

26 The end of the dream in "The Bank."

27 Charlie about to be shanghaied.

28 Charlie as a sailor in "Shanghaied."

29 Charlie as "Darn Hosiery" in his burlesque of "Carmen."

30 Charlie with Edna Purviance as Carmen in the famous burlesque.

31 Charlie becames bored in the middle of the duel in "Carmen."

following page 114

32 Chaplin with Thomas H. Ince, Mack Sennett and D. W. Griffith ca. 1916.

33 Charlie serenading Edna in "The Vagabond."

34 A scene from "One A.M.," the famous solo film.

35 The recalcitrant bed in "One A.M."

36 Eric Campbell, Charlie posing as Count Broko, and Edna Purviance as Miss Moneybags in "The Count."

37 and 38 Two scenes from the celebrated "The Pawnshop."

39 Charlie is puzzled by Edna disguised as a stagehand in "Behind the Screen."

40 Edna and Charlie in "The Rink."

41 One of the accidents in "The Rink."

42 Nijinsky and troupe visit the Chaplin studio in 1916 during the shooting of "Easy Street."

43 Charlie as a policeman in "Easy Street."

44 The little policeman asphyxiates the giant bully (Eric Campbell) in "Easy Street."

45, 46, 47, 48   Four scenes from "The Cure."

49 The arrival in the land of liberty, from "The Immigrant."

50 James T. Kelley, Eric Campbell, the broke Charlie, and Edna Purviance in "The Immigrant."

51, 52, 53, 54   Four scenes from "The Adventurer."

55 Douglas Fairbanks supporting Charlie and Mary Pickford (in costume for "Rebecca of Sunnybrook Farm"), 1917.

56 Charlie, Doug, and Mary clowning on the United Artists lot during the making of Miss Pickford's "Through the Back Door," 1921.

57 Mildred Harris in 1917 shortly before Chaplin met her.

58 Mildred Harris and Conrad Nagel in "Fool's Paradise," 1921.

59 Cecil B. DeMille directing Mildred Harris in "Fool's Paradise," 1921.

60 Charlie and "Scraps" in "A Dog's Life."

61 The happy ending of "A Dog's Life."

following page 178

62 to 69   Eight scenes from "Shoulder Arms."

70 The Hired Man and The Hardhearted Employer in "Sunnyside."

71 Charlie admires The Village Belle in "Sunnyside."

72 The dream ballet from "Sunnyside."

73 Chaplin and Jackie Coogan in "The Kid."

74 The Tramp and The Kid plying their trade.

75 The Policeman (Tom Wilson) is suspicious of The Tramp and The Kid.

76 The Tramp rescuing The Kid from the orphanage truck.

77 Chaplin directing Jackie Coogan.

78 Chaplin amusing Jackie Coogan between scenes.

79 Chaplin in 1921.

80 Portrait of Claire Windsor, 1922.

81 Claire Windsor in a Goldwyn picture of 1923.

82 Pola Negri, the tempestuous Polish actress.

83 Chaplin romping by the swimming pool of his Beverly Hills estate with Dinky Dean, son of his associate director Chuck Riesner.

84 "The Idle Class."

85 Edna Purviance believes the Tramp to be her husband in disguise.

86 Charlie and the foreman's daughter in "Pay Day."

87 Charlie's wife follows him on pay day.

88 Charlie believes he is riding a trolley home.

following page 210

89 Chaplin as The Pilgrim.

90 The new minister about to deliver his sermon on David and Goliath.

91 Edna Purviance and Adolphe Menjou in "A Woman of Paris."

92 Edna Purviance as Marie St. Clair.

93 Edna Purviance and Adolphe Menjou in "A Woman of Paris."

94 Edna Purviance, Carl Miller, and Adolphe Menjou in "A Woman of Paris."

95 Lydia Knott and Edna Purviance.

96 Chaplin directing Adolphe Menjou in "A Woman of Paris."

97 Chaplin directing "A Woman of Paris."

98 "The Gold Rush."

99 With Mack Swain in "The Gold Rush."

100 The Thanksgiving Dinner—eating the cooked shoe.

101 The Lone Prospector and the dancehall girl (Georgia Hale).

102 "The Gold Rush."

103 The dancehall girl ignores Charlie.

104 The New Year's Eve Dinner which Charlie celebrates alone.

105 Frame enlargements of the Roll Dance from "The Gold Rush."

106 Charlie gazing in at the festivities.

107 "The Gold Rush."

108 The cabin balancing on the edge of a cliff.
109 Georgia and Charlie in the final scene.
110 Chaplin directing "The Gold Rush."
111 Lita Grey signing contract to appear as Chaplin's leading lady.
112-115 Scenes from "The Circus."
116 Rex, the new tightrope walker, fascinates Merna Kennedy.
117 The substitute high-wire walker performs under difficulties.
118 The circus moves on.

following page 274

119-128 Scenes from "City Lights."
129 Chaplin playing his favorite instrument, the cello, during the scoring of "The Gold Rush," 1942.
130 "City Lights" themes.
131 London crowds greeting Chaplin, 1931.
132 Chaplin in 1931.
133 Chaplin with Bernard Shaw at the London opening of "City Lights."
134 "Modern Times."
135 With Chester Conklin in "Modern Times."
136 Charlie goes mad from the factory routine.
137 Charlie and the gamin (Paulette Goddard).
138 Henry Bergman is persuaded to give Charlie a job.
139 The finale of "Modern Times."
140 Chaplin as Adolph Hynkel in "The Great Dictator."
141 Hynkel with Napaloni (Jack Oakie).
142 The Jewish barber, who resembles Hynkel, gives Hannah (Paulette Goddard) a beauty treatment.
143 Hynkel embracing the world-globe.
144 Verdoux, the suave Bluebeard, preparing to "liquidate" his wife Lydia (Margaret Hoffman).
145 Verdoux with Annabella (Martha Raye).
146 Verdoux prepares to step out with the indestructible Annabella.
147 Verdoux's past catches up with him.
148 Chaplin with Mary Pickford and his wife, the former Oona O'Neill, at the premiere of "Monsieur Verdoux," 1947.

the importance of Chaplin and his art

Although he has made but three pictures in the last twenty years and many critics' thumbs went down on his last picture, Charles Chaplin was recently voted by members of the film industry the best actor of the past half century. Yet, this may be considered an understatement. Chaplin is more than an "actor"; he is a clown, in direct line of descent from the Commedia dell'arte; he is the twentieth-century counterpart of Arlequin and Grimaldi. Thanks partly to the universal nature of the film medium, he has made more people laugh than any other man who ever lived. And beyond this, he is a symbol of the age, the twentieth-century Everyman. In Gilbert Seldes' apt phrase, Chaplin was "destined by his genius to be the one universal man of modern times."

For over thirty-six years Chaplin has been the unquestioned King of Comedy. His films are shown continuously all over the world. Even his first comedies of 1914 to 1917 are still exhibited commercially, not as museum pieces or facetiously as "flicker flashbacks," but as modern entertainment—the only motion pictures of that period still to be so exhibited. It is estimated that three hundred million people have seen each Chaplin comedy.

Chaplin's role as the comic little vagabond, an underdog with profound and tragic overtones, has been appreciated in every part of the globe, in France as the beloved "Charlot," elsewhere as "Carlino," "Carlos,"

"Carlitos," etc. Anyone who could make such a lasting and universal impression is unquestionably deserving of a definitive study of his life and work.

More has been written on Chaplin than on any other film figure. Our foremost writers and intellectuals have vied in tributes to his art. Of those privileged to know him personally, numbers have given their impressions of his multifaceted personality. However, no one book—at least in English—has yet attempted a rounded study of both his career and his personal life.

It is obvious that a man's life affects and is affected by his work. In Chaplin particularly, his background, kaleidoscopic life, and the many people who played a part in it, have all left their mark on his screen creations.

Chaplin is an extremely complex personality. He is enigmatic about his birth, family background, childhood, and early youth. He let it be believed for many years, for reasons known only to himself, that he was born in Fontainebleau, France, when it has been established that London was his birthplace. The legends that grew around him may have been encouraged to grow. Individualistic, limited in formal education, making incredible sums of money in his middle twenties, spoiled by adulation, arrogant and selfish at times, anarchistic and unbound by love for any one country, a nonconformist in life as in his art, sometimes ruthless toward women—he was an inevitable target of criticism. For all his inexhaustible creative fecundity, his unique contribution to the world's gaiety, and his personal charm (the screen "Charlie" is in many ways a projection of his real self), we must face certain inexplicable aspects of his private life objectively. We must avoid whitewash, the better to understand him.

From his screen start in 1914, he was a richly rewarded hit comedian, and, from the start, he was also something more. His unique qualities were recognized at once.

Yet all he intended was to present a typical "Weary Willie." He did not realize that he was creating a mythical world figure any more than did the creators of Pierrot and Punchinello and Mickey Mouse. At the very outset he struck a rich vein of comedy, a vein that led deep into humanity and could therefore be appreciated and understood by all.

This was not entirely accidental. Both his extensive stage training as a pantomimist and his life experiences contributed to it. He himself has said, "Comedy must be real and true to life. My comedy is actual life with the slightest twist or exaggeration to bring out what it might be under certain circumstances. . . . I aimed exclusively at pleasing myself. For when I gave the subject thought, I became convinced it was the average man I tried to please. And was I not that average man?"

Chaplin himself is a composite, international type, a mixture of several nationalities. The tramp character he created could be of any country and of any time. In appearance he could be any age from twenty-five to fifty-five.

Costume and make-up, though mainly drawn from England before the First World War, spells shabby gentility and aspiring dignity in any language. This was Chaplin's own view, according to an interview with George P. West, in 1923, "That costume helps me to express my conception of the average man, of almost any man, of myself. The derby, too small, is a striving for dignity. The mustache is vanity. The tightly buttoned coat and the stick and his whole manner are a gesture toward gallantry and dash and 'front.' He is trying to meet the world bravely, to put up a bluff, and he knows that, too. He knows it so well that he can laugh at himself and pity himself a little." Almost anyone could identifiy himself with this screen character—especially the underdog and the "little man" buffeted by life.

Chaplin, then, worked out a common denominator of fun and feeling that accords with something in every age, class, and race of people the world over. Other comedians are typed as Irish, Dutch, Jewish, Broadway, Scotch, Negro, rubes, hillbillies, zanies, etc. Chaplin is universal and timeless. To the French he is a Frenchman; to the Japanese he is one of their own. To children he is the eternal mischievous boy. To the common, underprivileged, or little man, he is their champion who somehow manages to outwit Mr. Big. To esthetes he is the dreamer ever searching for beauty in an often ugly and cruel world—the conscience of the world. In women he appeals to their maternal instinct. For Freudians he personifies our frustrations. To left-wingers, his comedies "protest against the crushing of the individual by social forces."

However, according to Robert E. Sherwood, a motion-picture critic before he became a playwright and biographer, "Charlie Chaplin is a great artist, an inspired tragedian—and everything else that the intellectuals say he is—but there can never be any doubt of the fact that he is fundamentally a clown; and it is when he is being most broadly, vulgarly, crudely funny that he approaches true genius."

These endlessly various interpretations have kept the Chaplin legend eternally green and have led each new generation to rediscoveries of the secrets of his art. Each finds in Chaplin what he brings to him—as with all great art.

One of Chaplin's greatest assets is his deep understanding of human nature—again an outcome of his own circumstances which compelled first-hand knowledge of life and close observation of people at an early age. As stated in an early article ("What People Laugh At," *American Magazine,* November 1918, ghost-written by Rob Wagner), "There is no mystery connected with 'making people laugh.' All I have ever done is to keep my eyes open and my brain alert for any facts or incidents that I could use in my business. I have studied human nature, because without a knowledge of it I could not do my work."

Elsewhere Chaplin said: "I have aimed in all my comedies at satirizing the human race. . . . The human race I prefer to think of as an underworld of the gods. When the gods go slumming they visit the earth. You see, my respect for the human race is not one hundred per cent."

His own physical stature made it natural for him to personify the little fellow, maladjusted to his environment and kicked about by life. If he had been three inches taller, Chaplin himself has remarked, it would have been impossible for him to portray this part. He arouses our sympathy as well as our laughter, as he portrays this tragi-comic figure of the tramp-underdog, harassed by poverty, the law, and his own handicaps—in Chaplin's own words again, "forever seeking romance, but his feet won't let him." Sometimes this character wins a temporary victory as David did over Goliath, by sheer wit and agility, both sharpened on the whetstone of life. Usually, however, he loses, yet with a shrug he ends up—a solitary figure—wandering hopefully up the eternal road to further adventure.

People pity and love this gallant figure who smiles through hardships, who desperately maintains his dignity and self-respect under the most trying circumstances. "I began to look upon humor," said Chaplin, "as a kind of gentle and benevolent custodian of the mind which prevents one from being overwhelmed by the apparent seriousness of life. It finds compensation in misfortune." A philosophy, teaching the sweetness of adversity, runs through all the amusing but penetrating studies of life Chaplin has given us.

It is a historic fact, with which Chaplin himself agrees, that the children of America first discovered him. They began imitating the funny little man with the big feet. "I am here today," announced the cardboard cut-out figure set up before theatres. It was enough to draw the kids of the whole neighborhood.

Not until the end of 1914, with the release of "Tillie's Punctured Romance," (the full-length comedy with Marie Dressler), did Chaplin's name become widely known. By 1915 he had become and was to remain the most popular figure in motion pictures. Children and grown-ups of almost all classes succumbed to the "Chaplin craze."

Middle-class elders, alone, held out. Ministers and teachers complained of Chaplin's "vulgarity"—objecting particularly to his "drunk act." Their complaints continued as late as 1921 when "The Kid" was shown, but without effect on the box-office. By 1925 he was an accepted tradition, already a legend, although periodically criticized for his not-so-"private" life.

As early as 1916, the intellectuals began to discover Chaplin. Except for some perceptive critics in the fan and trade magazines, Mrs. Fiske, the actress, seems to have been the first notable to write of him seriously. In *Harper's Weekly* of May 6, 1916, she called him "an extraordinary artist, as well as a comic genius," spoke of his "inexhaustible imagination" and "unfailing precision of a perfect technique." She also likened the mimic's vulgar buffoonery to a similar quality found in the broad comedy of such masters as Aristophanes, Plautus, Shakespeare, and Rabelais.

Louis Delluc, pioneer French film critic, who wrote glowingly of the new art of the cinema in general, compared Chaplin to Nijinski, "an inventor in his art as Nijinski in his." In a small volume offering a detailed, though esoteric, interpretation of the comedian, Élie

Faure in 1922 hailed Chaplin as a poetic creator of myths and symbols who "conceives the universe in its totality and translates it in terms of the moving picture." He also emphasized Chaplin's creation of a "cineplastic" art and his kinship with Shakespeare in the humanization of man's conflict with fate. Gilbert Seldes, in his "Seven Lively Arts," gave an enthusiastic and detailed analysis of Chaplin's technique and screen character.

The author of "Limehouse Nights," Thomas Burke, a Londoner with a background similar to Chaplin's, writes of his friend's personality with perhaps more understanding than anyone. Burke claims that this man, who has "brought the whole civilized and uncivilized world together in warm laughter and delight," and "the first man in the history of the world of whom it can be truly and literally said that he is world-famous," is "unknowable. . . . It is almost impossible to locate him. . . . He is first and last an actor, possessed by this, that, and the other. He lives only in a role, and without it he is lost. . . . He can be anything you expect him to be, and anything you don't expect him to be."

Impelled by a fierce vitality and exuberant spirit, he can be a stimulating talker. "With a few elementary facts upon a highly technical subject," his receptive and retentive mind can so work upon them that he can carry on a discussion with an expert on that subject in such a way as to make that expert consider him an authority, too. . . . In private life he is selfish, self-centered, erratic, moody and vaguely dissatisfied with life. But somehow he has "been able to fuse the remnants of wistfulness and simplicity he has into a work of art." Burke feels that the quality of "goodness" in Charlie is that of the typical Cockney. "His appeal is to the meek, and the meek, though they have not yet inherited the earth, make the bulk of its people."

Waldo Frank, probing for the wellsprings of Chaplin's

art, found a "mysticism" in the artist's personal character. Max Eastman, who has known Chaplin since 1919, writes, "His life is filled to the brim with what most lives consist of yearning after—wealth and fame and creative play and beautiful women—but he does not know how to enjoy any one of the four . . ." and is "in the depths of his heart humble, a poor boy who had no opportunities and is eager to learn." Eastman also feels that he has fallen short of his potentialities; he would have gone much further could he have let himself go intellectually, poetically, and financially.

Alexander Woollcott rhapsodized over Chaplin as "the foremost artist of the world. . . . His like has not passed this way before and we shall not see his like again." Even Winston Churchill, calling the silent movies "everybody's language," referred glowingly to several Chaplin films and analyzed his pantomimic art. And the greatest playwright of our time, the late Bernard Shaw, named Chaplin "the only genius developed in motion pictures."

More recent critics have continued to heap adulation upon Chaplin. There are some who feel that this adulation from the intellectuals has had an adverse effect on Chaplin—turned him from comedy and emotion to fields beyond his depth. Chaplin had once characterized himself as "only a little nickel comedian. . . . All I ask is to make people laugh." Later, however, he began to see himself as an intellectual, a thinker able to help change the world.

Chaplin has been vehemently attacked for his so-called politics and his private life. But he is indifferent to criticism and ignores it. As Burke observes, "He does not serve the press or critics. He serves the people." Hence he has never bothered to explain his views or actions—even why he has never become a citizen of the country which alone could have given him such wealth.

On his position in motion pictures, however, James Agee in *Life* Magazine (1949) sums it up: "Of all the comedians he worked most deeply and most shrewdly within a realization of what a human being is, and is up against. The Tramp is as centrally representative of humanity, as many-sided and as mysterious as Hamlet, and it seems unlikely that any dancer or actor can ever have excelled him in eloquence, variety or poignancy of motion. . . . The finest pantomime, the deepest emotion, the richest and most poignant poetry are in Chaplin's work."

childhood and stage career

Charles Spencer Chaplin was born on April
16, 1889, in London, England, just about the time
that Thomas A. Edison in far-off America had finally succeeded in developing motion pictures. Date and birth-
places are certain but otherwise there is considerable
mystery surrounding the event. The name Charles Chaplin does not appear in the records of Somerset House,
where all English births are recorded, suggesting that
Chaplin might not be his real name.

His father, bearing the same name, came of an Anglicized French Jewish family. His mother Hannah (last
name unknown) was said to be of Spanish and Irish origin. Both parents were vaudevillians. His mother had
run away from home at sixteen. Under the stage name of
Lily Harley she sang and danced in various troupes, including Gilbert and Sullivan companies. Chaplin senior,
billed as a "topical vocalist," was famous in the music
halls of the eighties for his baritone voice. He had appeared on the Continent and once in New York, singing
descriptive ballads.

One of Charles' half-brothers, Sidney, four years his
senior, was the son of a former marriage of Hannah's to
Sidney Hawkes, a Jewish bookmaker. After her divorce
from Hawkes, Sidney entered her new household and
also took the Chaplin name. The two other half-brothers

of Charles, Guy and Wheeler Dryden, were brought up by their father.

Despite their touring of England and the Continent, the elder Chaplins were always hard up. When money came in, the father drank it up.

Young Charles was taught to jig and sing as soon as he could toddle. He was barely two or three years old when his mother was already boasting about his acting. At parties, after their own performances, his parent would pull Charles out of bed, stand him on the table and have him recite for the group. He could mimic everyone he saw and sing all the songs.

At five, Charles had his stage premiere, replacing his mother who was suddenly taken ill. His father pushed him onto the stage and ordered him to sing an old coster song, "Jack Jones." Charlie overcame his terror and sang with all his might, was showered with coins, and kept repeating the song until dragged off by his father.

His parents drifted apart, reducing Charles to a dismal childhood in London's Kennington slum. The death of his father followed soon afterwards. He died of alcoholism in St. Thomas' Hospital. His mother's recurring ill health, not helped by her hardships, wrecked her stage career.

Sid and Charles were sent to the Hanwell Residential School, variously described in publicity stories as an orphanage and a poorhouse. Sid left for sea shortly after and Charles spent a lonely and unhappy year or two at Hanwell. He would creep off by himself to daydream of riches and grandeur. His mother's health improved and she took her children back, supporting them by sewing blouses.

Charles was about seven years old when he joined a music-hall act called "The Eight Lancashire Lads," doing clog dancing and mimicry. When the troupe was engaged to impersonate cats and dogs in the pantomime "Puss in

Boots," Charles, in a dog make-up, brought down the house with some unrehearsed bits of sniffing and other "dog business." The act, on tour, lasted a year and a half. When it closed, Charles was sent to Hern Boys College near London for two years, while Sidney went to a school in Surrey to study for the sea. This was all the schooling Chaplin had.

He credited his mother with the major part of his education. Her powers of observation were uncanny. She could tell by a man's gait, the condition of his shoes, the expression on his face, and the fact that he entered a bake shop, that he had had a fight with his wife and left without breakfast. Whenever checked, her window-side observations would be corroborated. Her habit of studying people passed on to her son.

However, her mind began to fail. One day Charles returned to an empty home. He was told that "they" had taken his mother away. He was left all alone. Sidney had sailed off to Africa.

Before he secured another stage job he lived like a Dickens waif on the London streets. Some of these experiences have been preserved in "The Kid." He appears to have fed himself as a chore boy in Covent Garden market by dancing in the streets, selling paper boats, as a lather boy in a barber shop, and so on. His bedroom was the market or the park.

When Sidney returned from Africa with a little money saved and presents for his mother, she was unable to recognize her sons. Sidney, the businessman of the family, then conducted Charles around the theatrical agencies.

It is extremely difficult to establish the exact chronology of Chaplin's stage appearances since many were outside London. However, it is recorded that he played in "Giddy Ostend" at the London Hippodrome on January 15, 1900. He would then have been ten years old. He toured the provinces as the boy hero of an anglicized version of "From Rags to Riches," a typical Alger story dramatized by Charles A. Taylor. Joseph Stanley and Laurette Taylor starred in the American version.

The play, of the "East Lynne" School, reflected both Charlie's actual life and his dream life. A street waif to the last act, he then reunites his scattered family and wins a fortune, Young Chaplin received fine notices for his performance. He became quite a cocky young actor, enjoyed the life, dressed nattily, and sported a cane.

His temporary prosperity enabled him to place his mother in a convalescent home. She was never to regain her sanity, despite the best of care.

There were three years of touring in "Sherlock Holmes," with H. A. Saintsbury in the lead and Chaplin as Billy the office boy. The role of the crafty young rascal who understands his master perfectly was a natural for the young Cockney. Among other roles, he played Sammy the newsboy in Saintsbury's "Jim, the Romance of Cocaine" (or "Jim, the Romance of a Cockney"?) and one of the wolves in the first production of "Peter Pan" at the Duke of York's Theatre, London, December 27, 1904. Chaplin was now a well-known boy actor for whom a brilliant future was predicted. He was popular with stage folk, who enjoyed his imitations of Sir Herbert Beerbohm Tree and other stage notables.

When William Gillette, the original American star of "Sherlock Holmes," visited London, he added a curtain-raiser to the featured play, "Clarice." The one-acter was called "The Painful Predicament of Sherlock Holmes." For this Chaplin was hired by the American impresario, Charles Frohman, to resume the role of Billy. It opened on October 3, 1905, at the Duke of York's Theatre. In the two companies were a number of stage celebrities. Supporting Gillette in "Clarice" was the beautiful Marie Doro, later to star in American movies, and Lucille La Verne, American character actress of "Sun Up" fame. In the curtain-raiser Irene Vanbrugh was the leading lady.

Marie Doro was one of Charlie's first crushes. He worshipped her from afar.

One evening King Edward saw the performances, with Queen Alexandra and the King of Greece. The actors were ordered not to look at the royal box, but Charlie could not resist the temptation. There was an awful stillness in the audience until a chuckle from King Edward broke the silence. Chaplin was scolded, but exultant that he had succeeded in amusing royalty.

Chaplin had expected to be invited to America with the Gillette company, but from the great and awesome Gillette he received only a pat on the shoulder. A lean period followed during his "awkward age." He found work in a glass factory, but lasted only one day. He burned his hand and could not stand the extreme heat. He got occasional bookings in burlesque. One was with "The Ten Looneys;" and as a single "turn" he was billed as "Sam Cohen, the Jewish Comedian."

But soon he had a long engagement in "Casey's Court Circus," a skit in which youngsters wore grown-ups' hats and trousers and impersonated public favorites. Charles considered it a comedown after his appearances on the legitimate stage. His part was to impersonate Dr. Walford Bodie, a patent-medicine faker and "electrical wizard," then a London sensation.

Studying the real Dr. Bodie, Chaplin ignored his manager's directions. In a dignified entrance, perfectly aping his model, he hung his cane on his arm by the wrong end and it clattered to the stage. Startled, he stooped and his high silk hat bounced off. Its paper wadding dropped out, and when he put the hat on, it settled over his ears. Pushing the hat back, he then spoke his lines. This bit of "business" brought bursts of laughter.

He also scored in a burlesque of Fred Sisnette's "Turpin's Ride to York."

During the run of "Casey's Court Circus" Chaplin gradually gave up his ambition of becoming a dramatic actor and concentrated on comedy. Once, while playing in the Channel Islands, he found that his jokes were not getting over because, as he soon discovered, the natives knew little English. He resorted to pantomime and got the desired laughs. From this he learned the power of pantomime which became the major element in his art.

Meanwhile, Sidney Chaplin, too, had gone on the stage as a member of the Fred Karno Company. He spoke to Karno about his younger brother and when Charlie was about seventeen he became a member of this famous pantomime group. He remained with it until 1913, when, during an American tour, the movies signed him.

the Karno Company and tour of America

As an apprentice in the Karno Company, Chaplin learned the traditional English pantomime together with sure-fire gags, comedy routines, and other time-honored devices. In Karno's acts all the forms and traditions of theatrical entertainment were preserved— acrobatics, juggling, tumbling, miming, broad slapstick, song, dance, and burlesque.

The titles of some of the famous Karno music-hall skits give a clue to their type of comedy: "Hilarity," "Jail Birds," "Early Birds," "Mumming Birds" (called "A Night in an English Music Hall" in this country), "The New Woman's Club," "His Majesty's Guests," "A Tragedy of Errors," "The Dandy Thieves," "Home from Home," "The Thirsty First," "The Casuals," "Saturday to Monday." Their characters were drunks coming home, bicycle snatchers, poolroom sharks, punch-drunk boxers, music hall hams, magicians, and so on.

English pantomime was famous for its rhythm even in knockabout action. The English clown was celebrated for his impassive style as well as his dexterity. It was a splendid training ground for Chaplin, and Karno took an interest in the little actor with the curly black hair and the sad eyes.

Chaplin's first big part was in "The Football Match," in which he burlesqued a melodramatic villain. His costume was a slouch hat, a voluminous black cape in which his slight figure was almost lost, and a little black mustache. His stage mission was to tempt "Stiffy the Goalkeeper" (played by Harry Welden) to throw the game. The inducements included a bribe but also alcoholic refreshment labeled "training oil."

When Karno offered Chaplin the lead in "Jimmy the Fearless," Chaplin hesitated, perhaps through lack of confidence. The part was given to another bright young comedian named Arthur Stanley Jefferson (later to become famous on the screen as Stan Laurel of Laurel and Hardy.) Both young actors were reminiscent of the celebrated Dan Leo. The forte of all three was to preserve a touch of pathos even in their most boisterous action. Chaplin regretted his decision, but got the part later when Karno moved Jefferson elsewhere.

"Jimmy the Fearless" was a boy who should have got home hours ago. When he eventually returned, he informed his questioning parents that he had been out with "a bit o' skirt," which earned him a scolding from his mother. Left alone with his supper and a candle, Jimmy starts to read a "penny dreadful," falls asleep, and dreams himself into incredible feats of valor. He triumphs over a Wild West gang, rescues beautiful maidens, and acquires great wealth. Just as he wins the consent of a beautiful maiden, he wakes up, and the skit ends with the father giving Jimmy a strapping.

This was the germ of some of the later Chaplin movies. "A Night in the Show," "One A.M.," and other Chaplin films revive some of the Karno turns. To this rich early background and experience Chaplin was to add a profusion of comic inventions and a rare subtlety and originality of presentation. But the lessons of this period were not forgotten.

Chaplin stepped up in the world in other ways. His apartment in Glenshore Mansions was furnished with "Turkish carpets and red lights." He also went through his first love pangs. The story has received considerable elaboration—and from Chaplin himself—but the following appear to be the facts. The girl was Hetty Kelly, an actress too, and sister of a colleague of Chaplin's called Sonny Kelly. Later, as Arthur Kelly, he became foreign manager of United Artists and then vice-president.

Chaplin was then nineteen and a dude—but a shy one. At Kennington Gate he would wait with fluttering heart for the adored one to step off the street car. On park benches and in corners of little tea houses he dreamed of a future with her. The affair was hardly more than a boy-and-girl flirtation, for Hetty did not take him too seriously. She made a rich marriage in England while Chaplin was making a fortune in America. Nevertheless it was probably her image that spurred him to win fame and wealth there.

Chaplin was never to forget the enchantment of this first love. Some believe he was always looking for another Hetty in his numerous girl friends. The idealistic and romantic love he usually portrays on the screen had its source in this unrequited episode to which he paid a more direct tribute, some years later, in a song entitled "There's Always Someone You Can't Forget." On his 1921 visit to England, he was stunned when he received word of her death.

With the Karno company, Chaplin also toured the Continent, and appeared in Paris at the Folies-Bergères. Karno later recalled that Chaplin was a preoccupied and taciturn traveler, staring out of the train windows while his companions played cards. He lived frugally and had an understandable aversion to alcohol, which had brought such tragedy to his family.

Between 1910 and 1913 Chaplin toured the United States extensively in Karno's second company. Its most popular act was "A Night in an English Music Hall."

However, it was not in this skit, as is usually recorded,

but in another called "The Wow Wows," that he made his American debut on October 3, 1910, at the Colonial Theatre in New York. His act was part of a typical variety show including a dog turn, a quick-change artist, acrobats, and ballad singers. "The Wow Wows" burlesqued a secret-society initiation in a summer camp. According to *Variety*, "Chaplin is typically English, the sort of comedian that American audiences seem to like, although unaccustomed to. His manner is quiet and easy and he goes about his work in a devil-may-care manner. . . ." With prophetic understatement *Variety* concluded, "Chaplin will do all right for America."

There is, further, this choice note from the *Brooklyn Eagle* of October 18, 1910, to dispel any idea that Karno's was a minor company and that Chaplin, before his screen career, went unnoticed: "Charles Chaplin, leading comedian of Karno's Comedians, which are playing at the Orpheum Theatre, this week, is being extensively entertained by the British residents of Brooklyn. The members of the St. George Society and the Usonas are among those who have arranged affairs for Mr. Chaplin and his confreres." To theatre devotees in England, indeed, Chaplin had been known since his boyhood.

In the more popular "A Night in an English Music Hall," Chaplin played the part originated by Billy Reeves, star of the first company, and often played in England by Sid Chaplin. The setting was an average English music hall—with boxes and audience as well as the stage itself. Typical music-hall "turns" were presented on the stage within the stage. Chaplin, playing a drunken "swell" in evening clothes, kept half-falling out of his box, annoying the performers and the audience alike. He finished on the stage itself in a wrestling match with the "Terrible Turk." With the popularity of this act, a similar one, called "A Night in a London Club," was put on, in which Chaplin again played the lead.

Alf Reeves managed Karno's touring second company. In 1918 he became business manager for Chaplin when the latter launched out as an independent movie producer. Other Karno notables followed Chaplin into the movies: Billy Reeves (star of Karno's first company and brother of Alf), Billie Ritchie, Jimmy Aubrey ("The Terrible Turk"), Stan Laurel (Chaplin's understudy on the tour), Billy Armstrong, Albert Austin, and others.

There are many apocryphal stories concerning Chaplin's entry into films. The facts are less colorful. The first phase, perhaps, was a discussion Chaplin once had with Reeves about buying a camera to record his acts. He then had the naïve belief that movies were shot all at one time, without changes of angles, cutting, etc.

In August 1912, during a trip home, Chaplin watched an English newsreel being made of the Carnival of Flowers on the island of Jersey off the English coast. Chaplin's attention was drawn by the crowd around the camera and the laughter and mock applause it was directing at an obtrusive official who kept moving into the camera foreground and striking a pose. For Chaplin the crowd's reaction struck a prophetic note, setting him to further thought and discussion of movies with his brother Sid.

Virtually everyone associated with Chaplin in his early film days claims credit for discovering or developing him. The Sullivan and Considine Circuit on the Pacific coast, which was included in his tour, often brought him to Los Angeles. At the Empress Theatre in Spring Street he was seen by the movie people and was well known to them long before he joined their ranks.

Mack Sennett was among his admirers. During the middle of 1913, Ford Sterling, Sennett's chief Keystone comedy star, was threatening to quit unless he got more money. Consequently, when Chaplin was suggested to

Sennett, he readily agreed to sign him as a potential replacement.

Careful examination of evidence indicates that Adam Kessel of Kessel and Baumann, owners of the New York Motion Picture Company, whose holdings included Kay Bee, Broncho, Domino, and the Keystone films, was the man responsible for the actual signing. On May 12, 1913, while playing in Philadelphia at the Nixon Theatre, Alf Reeves received a telegram: "Is Charlie Chapman with your company? Have him call Saturday our office Putnam Bldg. Kessel and Baumann."

Chaplin, then receiving $50 a week on the stage, went to see Kessel in New York. After some hesitation over his chances in moving pictures, about which he knew little, he was finally won over by the then unbelievable offer of a year's contract at $150 a week.

Chaplin's bookings with Karno did not permit him to leave the troupe until November 28, 1913, at which time he played his last performance at the Empress Theatre in Kansas City. He then left immediately for California, filled with fears and doubts about the future of films and his part in them.

the motion picture industry, December 1913, and a note on Mack Sennett

December 1913, when Chaplin entered motion pictures, was a period of change and chaos like the shift to sound films in the summer of 1928. It was marked by competition from abroad, the rise of new companies springing up to meet the competition with feature-length pictures in place of the standard two-reelers, and an influx of screen adaptations of plays, and of actors from the stage, amounting almost to a migration of Broadway to Hollywood. In these changes old production companies passed out of existence and the screen industry's originators and founders were thrust into the shade!

Although American films were technically in advance of the foreign output, they were shorter and less imposing. In France, theatre celebrities like Sarah Bernhardt were appearing before the camera in versions of their stage successes. Italy was producing almost two-hour-long spectacles like "Quo Vadis," "The Last Days of Pompeii," and "Cabiria."

This competition forced American companies to change their policies and re-gear their production. Adolph Zukor formed the Famous Players Company and signed world-famous stage stars to make feature-length pictures based on famous plays. He was followed by others. As they forged ahead, older companies like Edison,

Biograph, Vitagraph, Kalem, Selig, Essanay, Lubin, and the Universal group, fell behind, some temporarily, some to vanish.

What was being produced in America in December 1913? The leading American director, D. W. Griffith, who had left Biograph, had finished his first feature for Reliance and was starting work on "The Escape," after which he was to set off to California to begin "The Birth of a Nation." Thomas H. Ince was still turning out two-reel westerns and dramas for the New York Motion Picture Company; but he had made one feature, "The Battle of Gettysburg," and was soon to start "Typhoon" and "The Wrath of the Gods," starring the Japanese actor Sessue Hayakawa. Herbert Brenon was in Bermuda, directing Annette Kellerman in "Neptune's Daughter" for the Imp Company, a Universal subsidiary. John Barrymore, still a light comedian, was doing "An American Citizen" for Famous Players, for whom Mary Pickford was then making "Hearts Adrift." Vitagraph was starting "A Million Bid" with Anita Stewart. Cecil B. De Mille, Jesse Lasky, and Sam Goldwyn were producing their first picture, "The Squaw Man." (In De Mille publicity releases, this has been claimed as the first feature made in America. Actually thirty or forty features had preceded it.)

The introductory episode of Selig's "The Adventures of Kathleen," the first American screen serial, properly so-called, came out that month, soon to be followed by Pathé's "The Perils of Pauline" with Pearl White, Thanhouser's "The Million Dollar Mystery," and others. These serials and Chaplin's first pictures appeared about the same time, providing a film feast for youngsters not equaled since.

In the big 1913–1914 change-over, actors and actresses, as we have seen, swarmed into the films from the stage. Most failed to adapt themselves to the new medium, but the migration continued until the failure of the Triangle Company, and Goldwyn's fiasco in 1917.

Some of the younger picture performers, more adaptable to new conditions, survived the change-over. Most of the first-generation players, however, among them Florence Turner, Maurice Costello, Florence Lawrence, Arthur Johnson, Mary Fuller, etc., gradually faded from the scene, along with the original producers and inventors whose demise we have already noted.

Comedy, a neglected stepchild of the industry, was less affected. Comedy was then dominated by Mack Sennett of Keystone, who relied on lively slapstick and a company of picturesque clowns headed by Ford Sterling, Mabel Normand, and Fatty Arbuckle. Vitagraph, more polite in its humor, featured John Bunny, who remained the leading screen comic from 1910 until his death in 1915. The middle-aged, rotund, and good-natured Bunny was usually teamed with skinny, old-maidish Flora Finch and young, dimpled Lillian Walker. Sydney Drew, uncle of the Barrymores, was another member of the company, though not yet paired with his wife in their later popular series. There were several minor comedians who, like Broncho Billy, were known by their screen names and appeared in weekly "series": Alkali Ike (Augustus Carney), Slippery Slim (Victor Potel), Swedie (Wallace Beery), etc.

Foremost among the European comedians was France's Max Linder, who had been making comedies since 1905 for Pathé and had developed a world following. Both in style and subject matter, he anticipated Chaplin who acknowledged later that he learned much from him. Among other French comedians were Rigadin (his real name was Charles Prince) who was also known as Whiffles in England, Moritz in Germany, Tartufini in Italy; André Deed, of the Gribouille series; Onésime, and others. These, not too well known in America, were mostly buffoons in the circus and vaudeville tradition, exaggerated in make-up and in acting style. Germany's contribution in that period consisted of several light comedians from the stage, of whom the most popular was Ernst Lubitsch, playing bumptious young Yiddish clerks in comedies whose appeal was virtually limited to German audiences.

Chaplin came at the psychological moment; the screen was ripe for him.

A Note on Mack Sennett

The Keystone studio, where Chaplin made his first movies, was located at 1712 Allesandro Street, Glendale, California. From the summer of 1912 on, its presiding genius was the colorful and fabulous Mack Sennett, a Canadian by birth and then in his thirties. Sennett had learned movie technique from D. W. Griffith who had directed him in comedies for the Biograph Company from 1908 to 1912. The sequence of his career had been boiler-maker to chorus boy to comedian to director.

Sennett is rightly called the father of American film comedy. Despite some influences from early French farce and trick pictures, his wild action, slapstick, play upon physical disaster, inspired nonsense, and burlesque of every convention and institution, sacred or otherwise, is indigenously American. He assembled a wonderful troupe of clowns; he originated the hilarious Keystone cops and the eye-magnetizing bathing beauties, along with the flying custard pie, and fantastic gags often involving trick camera work.

Among the stars Sennett introduced or developed were Ford Sterling, Mabel Normand, Fatty Arbuckle, Mack

Swain, Marie Dressler, Tom and Edgar Kennedy, Charlie Murray, Slim Summerville, Hank Mann, Charley Chase, Louise Fazenda, Polly Moran, Gloria Swanson, Raymond Griffith, Phyllis Haver, Marie Prevost, Billy Bevan, Harry Gribbon, Harry Langdon, Sally Eilers, Carole Lombard. In the early sound days he introduced Bing Crosby after three major studios had pronounced him unsuited for motion pictures. He also rescued W. C. Fields from oblivion.

Some of his directors—Roy Del Ruth, Eddie Kline, and Mal St. Clair—carry on his tradition, and his influence remains visible in animated cartoons, the satires of René Clair, the comedies of the Marx Brothers, in "screwball" comedies of the "Nothing Sacred" school, in some of the Capra films, and in the work of Preston Sturges. But if he had contributed nothing else, Sennett would be sure of a place in history as the man who ushered Chaplin to his movie debut and gave him his first lessons in screen comedy.

A rough and uneducated Irishman, Sennett had an intuitive knowledge of what would make people laugh. If a scene made him laugh, it stayed in the picture; if not, it was cut out or reshot. He had a genius for the ridiculous. His taste was an accurate barometer of the average. His fast-paced humor and slapstick provided the relief of the belly laugh for unnumbered millions.

The universality of his pictures came from their direct visual appeal and their simple images. Beneath the surface humor of appearance and situation, there was often a wry commentary on the conventions and hypocrisies of life and manners. A circus origin was clear in many of his comic gags; others derived from burlesque and vaudeville. There were elemental jokes that had rocked audiences for centuries: the humor of physical deformity, ludicrous costumes, horseplay, the comedy of undress, the fall of dignity, the risible accident and disaster. Sennett had filled them out with the enormous new powers of the screen—the fast motion of the "under-cranked" camera, the fantasy made possible by trick cutting, double printing, and the like.

Though serving different ends, Sennett made good use of what he had learned from Griffith. He adopted the Griffith camera technique and editing, known to the trade then as "Biograph editing." This called for frequent changes of angle, inserted close-ups of people and objects, for emphasis and expression, short scenes, cutbacks, and parallel action. This last device was not limited to horsemen rescuing a damsel. In ordinary action, editing it to essentials and cross-cutting, a simultaneous effect was created with a resulting heightening of tempo. Though many of the Keystones lacked story or logic, they at least had beauty of pace. Sometimes they had technical brilliance.

In his best comedies, the gags were thrown at the audience at race-track tempo, one nudging the other, leaving no time or space for analysis or second impressions. The Sennett style was a blend of lunatic fantasy, preposterous physical types, exaggerated costumes and make-up, whirlwind pace, violent action, and zany gags. His films were improvisations—"shot on the cuff," and on the spot—a laundry, a restaurant, the park, anywhere. Chaplin was to adopt many of his methods.

After violent action, a comedy would be resolved by and culminate in a wild chase. This often resembled ballet in its movements and staging, though, of course, a cinematic chase had qualities impossible in any other medium. Sennett's chase as an end in itself was borrowed by the English comedian after he left Keystone. From the Sennett bag of tricks Chaplin also borrowed the "breakaway" bottles and vases (made of resin and plaster), the custard pie (usually made of blackberries for photographic reasons), and other slapstick devices.

V

Chaplin at Keystone

Chaplin arrived at the Keystone studio in December 1913. The studio itself was hardly more than an open platform with the sun diffused by muslin sheets hung above. Lights were seldom used as yet—although the Keystone photography was, as a rule, clear and bright. Several pictures were made simultaneously on the same stage. It was absolute bedlam.

The leading Keystone comedian was Ford Sterling, using a Dutch make-up. He was discontented with his reported $200 a week salary and on the point of quitting to form his own company. Other comedians were the beautiful and vivacious Mabel Normand, rotund Roscoe "Fatty" Arbuckle and his wife Minta Durfee, the giant Mack Swain (known as "Ambrose"), meek little Chester Conklin ("Walrus") with his droopy mustache, the blond juvenile Harry McCoy, the veteran character actress Alice Davenport of the famous theatrical family, the tall and husky Phyllis Allen, Sennett himself usually playing a "rube," and, in minor parts, many who were later to become more famous: Edgar Kennedy, Charlie Murray, Al St. John, Hank Mann, Slim Summerville, Charlie Chase, and others.

Chaplin was to have difficulty fitting into this school. The speed and violence bewildered him. The style of acting, as exemplified by Sterling, was one of rush and exaggerated movement and gesture. Chaplin was used to a slower, subtler, and more individual pantomime.

Sennett and the others were surprised to find him so young, only twenty-four years of age. He had played much older parts on the stage. He also had to contend with jealousy on the part of the stars who had worked hard to establish themselves in this new field. Mabel Normand, calling him "that Englisher so-and-so," thought he looked like a "package mis-sent," and refused to go on with him in his first film.

The new English actor was assigned to a dressing room with the huge-bodied Arbuckle and Swain, to whom he was no competitive threat; and they proved friendly. For his first film the director assigned was Henry ("Pathé") Lehrman (so nicknamed by D. W. Griffith after he had bluffed his way into a job at Biograph, claiming experience in French films). In this first film Chaplin did not wear his famous tramp costume. He appeared in a long frock coat, high silk hat, drooping walrus mustache, and a monocle—much the same get-up he had used in "A Night in an English Music Hall." His first leading lady was Virginia Kirtely, a girl with a slight resemblance to Blanche Sweet. After hardly a year at Keystone, she vanished into obscurity.

Chaplin and his first director clashed frequently. Lehrman tried to force the frenzied Keystone style upon him. Chaplin wanted a slower and more deliberate pace, more suited to his subtleties. Chaplin, not yet acclimated to motion-picture technique, did not understand "filmic geography," "filmic time," and cutting. For example, after making a scene on one location the camera was moved two blocks away and around a corner to film an earlier scene. Asked to look at a girl he couldn't possibly see from this position, Chaplin objected. He did not realize that when the film was pieced together there would be perfect illusion.

According to reports, Sennett gave the newcomer the
severest call-down ever heard on the Keystone lot. Chaplin remained doggedly silent and went on acting his own
way. Sennett feared that he had a "lemon." Others who
acknowledged his talent thought it was not for the
screen. Nevertheless, though he appeared to be something of a misfit and kept to himself, the quiet and serious Englishman soon became personally popular. One
reason was that he taught them how to do falls without
hurting themselves.

When Sennett saw a screening of the first Chaplin
film, he was sure it would be a flop. Kessel and
Baumann groaned at their mistake in hiring him. Mabel
Normand, however, realized that the newcomer had something and predicted he would go places.

When "Making a Living" was released February 2,
1914, it did not do badly. Of the new English comedian,
variously referred to as Chapman, Chatlin, and Edgar
English during the first few months (Keystone did not
run a cast of characters on the screen) the *Moving Picture World* wrote, "The clever player who takes the part
of a sharper . . . is a comedian of the first water."
Many, however, did not think him as funny as Ford
Sterling. The screen character and costume that would
really put Chaplin over was yet to come.

Chaplin hit on his world-famous costume by accident.

It was Sennett's custom to place his actors, whenever
possible, in the foreground of races and parades. Hearing
that there was to be a children's auto race at Venice, the
Los Angeles seaside resort, Sennett despatched Lehrman
and Chaplin to the scene for a short "filler." For the
film, eventually called "Kid Auto Races at Venice,"
Chaplin was told to go on in a funny costume. He put
one together from what he saw around him—oversize
pants belonging to Arbuckle, size-14 shoes belonging to
Ford Sterling (each placed on the wrong foot so they

would stay on Chaplin's small feet), a tight-fitting coat,
a derby that was a size too small (belonging to Minta
Durfee's father), a bamboo cane, and the small "tooth-
brush" mustache (cut down from one of Mack
Swain's).

A prop camera was set up in front of the real camera.
Chaplin made a nuisance of himself running out on the
race track and getting in the way of the camera that
was supposedly filming the races. He used a splayed,
shuffling walk. In this, then new, and later world-famous
costume and gait, he collided and brawled with the
cameraman and the cops who tried to get him out of the
way.

Legend has it that the film was made in forty-five
minutes. A "split reel" (500 feet or less), it was released on the same reel with an early, factual-educational
short entitled "Olives and Their Oil."

Mabel Normand was making a comedy called "Mabel's
Strange Predicament." Sennett, feeling that it needed
pepping up, called for the Englishman with whom Mabel
was now willing to appear. Lehrman was directing and
again had trouble with the new actor. Sennett took over
and wisely turned Chaplin loose to see what he could
do.

The picture was one of those hotel mix-up farces.
Nonchalantly, Charlie shuffles into the lobby in his new
costume and gait, to use the telephone. He discovers to
his dismay that he has no nickel. Mabel enters with a
dog on a leash. Charlie gets mixed up with the dog,
trips over the leash, falls, and gets his hand caught in a
cuspidor. All the while, and all through a scolding by
the hotel clerk, he preserves the utmost dignity. The
scene runs longer than the customary few feet Sennett
usually allowed for such action.

The actors and prop men on the sidelines began to
applaud and roar with laughter. Sterling, watching the

scene, turned away brokenhearted, realizing that his throne was tottering. After two more pictures, Sterling left Sennett in February, to form his own company. Lehrman also left to form the L-Ko (Lehrman Knock-Out) Company which made outright imitations of the Keystone pictures. Sterling was to return to Sennett after Chaplin left him.

In this third film Chaplin also introduced another famous mannerism. Running, he turned a sharp corner and skidded, holding one foot straight out and balancing on the other while looking back and clutching his hat.

Chaplin made a new comedy every week. His correct name was mentioned for the first time by the *Moving Picture World* in its notice of "Caught in a Cabaret" (April 27, 1914), which film was announced as the first of a new series. Chaplin was catching on. The *Dramatic Mirror,* the same month, acclaimed him as "second to none."

Sennett soon realized that it would be best to give Chaplin a free hand in story and style. Beginning with "Caught in the Rain," his thirteenth film, Chaplin wrote and directed all his pictures, blending the Keystone style and his own with great skill. He may be said to have welded his stage-comedy training and his uniquely attractive personality to the Sennett cinematic method.

Chaplin's screen character (not fully developed during this first year) was built in part, on his pantomime training with the Karno Company. Even the costume had Karno relatives. Fred Kitchen, for instance, also used large shoes and loose trousers. More important still, in its origin, were his memories of London street types, especially an old man who minded horses.

Last but not least was the influence of Max Linder, the pioneer French screen comic. Linder projected a similar personality and wore a similar make-up, but more on the "dude" side with a high silk hat and dapper

clothes. Chaplin himself once called Linder his teacher.
A number of his comedies, such as "The Rink" and
"Sunnyside," were similar in subject matter to Linder's.
After Chaplin left Essanay, Linder was brought over
from France to replace him, but did not quite "go over."
A relapse from war injuries sent him back to France
where he later committed suicide.

Chaplin's costume personifies shabby gentility—the
fallen aristocrat at grips with poverty. The cane is a
symbol of attempted dignity, the pert mustache a sign
of vanity. Although Chaplin used the same costume
(with a few exceptions) for almost his entire career, or
for about twenty-five years, it is interesting to note a
slight evolution. The trousers become less baggy, the
coat a little neater, and the mustache a little trimmer
through the years.

Although Charlie and Mabel Normand were at first at
odds, especially when Mabel was given the directorial
reins in some of the early comedies, eventually their
frictions wore away and they became warm personal
friends. They appeared as a team in several of the Keystones. In addition to her beauty and her vivacity, Mabel
Normand was gifted with a natural instinct for pantomime. She invented little gestures and original business
which she put over in an apparently spontaneous manner.

A colorful personality, once described by Jim Tully as
"vivid as summer lightning, beautiful as dawn, and as
natural as both," her final years were clouded with tragedy. She had the misfortune to have been the last-
known person to have seen the murdered director,
William D. Taylor.

Chaplin remembered her with gratitude for her generosity and her geniality. Hers was the only dressing
room equipped with a little stove. In the rainy season
everyone gathered there with the informal camaraderie

of genuine troupers. She and Chaplin often discussed their work and life. Mabel also acted as liaison between him and "Moike" (as she called her boy friend, Mack Sennett) in discussion of raises and other delicate ·matters. Chaplin is also reported to have received valuable camera-acting tips from her. If so, "Keystone Mabel," in turn, made use of some Chaplinesque bits in her greatest success, "Mickey" (1918). In fact, the silent screen's greatest comedienne was often called the female Chaplin. In private life she had some of the same gifts of mimicry and repartee. She joked even on her death bed. "A very remarkable girl," was Chaplin's obituary.

Almost all the Keystone players of this 1914 period went on to fame and fortune, but none to such heights as Chaplin reached—he whom several of them had predicted would prove unsuited to films.

the Chaplin-Keystone films (1914)

In his year at Keystone Chaplin made thirty-five films—a rate of one a week, except for a feature, which took fourteen weeks. They were improvised on the spot and filled with slapstick and knockabout action. They do not compare with Chaplin's later and more polished works, but they have spontaneous charm and are interesting for the first appearance of the characteristic Chaplin traits. They also merit a place in history for introducing him to the world and for teaching him the rudiments of motion-picture technique.

In these Keystones Chaplin's costume became fixed and his style almost perfected but the wonderful sympathetic "Charlie" had not yet emerged. Instead he appears as a basically unsympathetic, though engaging, character—a sharper, a heel, an annoying blunderer, a thief, an obnoxious drunk, who is cruel, sometimes to the point of sadism. Not until the next year at Essanay does the real "Charlie" appear.

The Keystone plots—if you could call them that—were no more than a hook on which to hang a succession of comic incidents. Sometimes the hook would be a locale —a park, a restaurant, a bakery, a dentist's office, the backstage of a theatre, a race track; sometimes a trade— janitor, piano mover, waiter, property man, boxing referee, etc. Each would suggest comic bits of business. In that way the film would take shape. When the action got too involved, or the fun possibilities had been exhausted, violence would resolve the problem—a melee with the Keystone cops, a comic brawl, an explosion, a ducking in a lake, or the water-hose treatment.

Many of the comedies are motivated around rivalry for a girl, with the fumbling Chester Conklin or the mammoth Mack Swain. Drunken flirtations recur among the episdoes, ending in hilarious altercations with enraged husbands.

The backstage of movie studios and theatres furnish the background for three or four films, with Chaplin in the role of the blundering actor or "helper." In some Keystones Chaplin, playing a waiter or bandit, poses as a nobleman at ritzy gatherings, the final comic business hinging on his exposure. Two deal with the trials of married life. As was customary with Mack Sennett, several were located at races or other public events.

Chaplin's famous stage "drunk act" was repeated in several of the films; it was the feature of "The Rounders," where he is teamed with Fatty Arbuckle. The influence of the Karno Pantomime acts, in many of these early Keystones, has already been noted. On the other hand, Chaplin hit on new ideas and situations from which germinated ideas used in his later, more finished, comedies.

It seemed enough at that time to rely on the Chaplin mannerisms: the shuffling walk, the swinging and juggling and poking of the cane, the vertical raising of the derby, the wiggling of the mustache as smiles bared his prominent teeth, the one-footed hopping around corners, the resting of his foot on laps, etc. These sparked the brawls and falls, the slapstick, the stunts, the chases, the mix-ups, the burlesque, of the typical Keystone fare.

The brawls often involved real roughhouse, with bricks and mallets, kicks and pin-sticking, and ducking into ponds. Chaplin was a master of acrobatic falls. He would raise a foot, miss the step and fall on his face; and a slippery floor and he would inevitably meet. Autos would knock him down; stairs would seem to fold under him. In "His Favorite Pastime," following a woman up-stairs while drunk, he somersaults over the banister and lands upright on a sofa where he continues to puff on his cigarette as if nothing had happened.

Even the Keystone pie sometimes appeared on the Chaplin menu. Although considered today a staple of the era, pie throwing appears in only a couple of the Chaplin-Keystones. Pies spatter faces in the finish of "Caught in a Cabaret." In "Dough and Dynamite," wads of dough and flour bags fly through the air. In this film, we get what is to become a classic situation—Chaplin ducking and the boss' face receiving the missile instead.

Slapstick and violence marked many of the others. In "The Rounders," Chaplin and Arbuckle seek sleep in a restaurant, using as a cover a tablecloth that happens to be loaded with dishes. In "His Trysting Place," Mabel Normand, as Chaplin's wife, breaks an ironing board over his head. In the earlier "Mabel at the Wheel," she falls off the rear of Charlie's motorcycle into the mud. In a fall in "Laughing Gas," Charlie pulls a lady's skirt off, revealing her stylish bloomers. And in "The Property Man" Charlie makes an old prop man carry a heavy trunk, kicks the man in the face, sits on the trunk when the oldster collapses under it. All these incidents were sure-fire laugh-getters at that time.

Chases were not as frequent in the Chaplin films as in other Keystones, but there is a good example in his first film, "Making a Living," where he appears as a "sharper." After stealing a camera from his benefactor-rival, Charlie tries to escape through traffic. He is pursued upstairs, into a lady's bedroom, where the rival, wrestling under covers with the woman whom he believes to be Chaplin, is caught by the irate husband. After further chase and a melee with the cops, Chaplin arrives at the newspaper office in time to scoop his rival. In "The Masquerader," the blundering actor is chased by the angry director and others around the studio and through various sets until he lands in a well.

In the Chaplin-Keystones, there are also elements of burlesque. "The Property Man" provides amusing caricatures of vaudeville stereotypes—the sister song-and-dance act, the strong-man turn, the old-fashioned melodramatic "sketch." In "The Masquerader," there is similar kidding of the movies. "The Face on the Bar-room Floor," though not entirely a success, richly travesties in places the bathos of that unmitigated tear-jerker. In "His Prehistoric Past," Charlie, as Weakchin, burlesques the current faddist interest in the stone age. Garbed in a tiger skin and a derby, he flirts with grass-skirted maidens and wields clubs.

Most interesting in the Keystones are those tricks and stunts, not yet full-blown "gags," which were prophetic of the brilliant comedy touches to come later. In his very first film Chaplin, as the impoverished Englishman, begs money from Lehrman. Offered a coin, he refuses it as too small, but snatches it as Lehrman is returning it to his pocket. In the same film, applying for a newspaper job, Charlie keeps slapping the editor's knee. When the editor moves his knee, Charlie, missing it, pulls it back. Ordered out, he rises, and his cuff slides down his cane and is deftly retrieved.

In "A Film Johnny," Charlie, swinging his cane, pops the director and lights his cigarette by firing a revolver at the tip. In the end, after a general soaking with a fire hose, he twists his ear and water jets out of his mouth. In "Twenty Minutes of Love," seeing a couple kissing on a park bench, Charlie embraces a tree.

In "Caught in a Cabaret," where he impersonates a

duke, he flirts with Mabel at a garden party and nearly exposes himself when he crosses his legs, revealing a hole in the sole of his shoe. He retrieves the situation by hanging his hat on the toe. In "The Property Man," he tears a piece of cloth whenever the "strong man" bends, causing the performer to worry about possible rips in his pants. Appearing for only three minutes in Arbuckle's "The Knockout," Chaplin is an officious referee who gets caught between the fighters and gets their blows. In "The Rounders," he enrages a bald man by striking a match on his pate.

In "Dough and Dynamite," largely made up of typical Keystone slapstick, Chaplin interjects a clever bit, making doughnuts by forming bracelets of dough around his wrist, then deftly slipping his hand out. In "The New Janitor," leaning over to pick up a pistol, Charlie points the revolver between his legs at an approaching crook, straightens up by stepping over his hands while continuing to cover the crook. In "Those Love Pangs," Charlie lounges crosslegged in a movie theatre and gesticulates with his feet as if they were hands. At a lunch counter in "His Trysting Place," the whiskers of a neighboring diner serve him as a napkin. At the end of "His Prehistoric Past," as Charlie is hit over the head by the king of the tribe, the scene changes to a park bench with a policeman flourishing his club over the awakening Charlie.

Despite the crudity of the Chaplin-Keystones, such comic flashes make them worth seeing and studying.

All more or less of the same pattern and style, it is difficult to pick the outstanding ones. However, though not one of the hits, "Making a Living" stands out today for its wry comments on "success." To illustrate go-getter ethics, Chaplin, who has just begged and gotten money from a news photographer, makes love to his benefactor's girl and scoops him by stealing his camera.

Other films have other special points of interest. We can see Chaplin himself, without make-up, in "Tango Tangles," an impromptu film taken in a real dancehall at a tango contest. In "A Busy Day" and "The Masquerader" there is another costume break, with Chaplin impersonating a woman, a "battle-ax" type of wife in the former and a coy actress in the latter. "Dough and Dynamite" was generally considered his first big hit as a director of his own films. It began, as "Those Love Pangs," with Charlie and Chester, as bakers and rivals in love. The bakery sequence turned out so funny it was released separately as a second film.

"Getting Acquainted," although not as well known as some others, has some unusual qualities. At first glance, this picture, set in a park, appears to be just another marital mix-up. Analysis shows it to be filled with amazingly clever and fast-paced bits of business. Charlie, married to the buxom Phyllis Allen, Mabel Normand and her husband Mack Swain, Edgar Kennedy the policeman, a mysterious "Turk," and other characters, dance a veritable comic ballet until Charlie is yanked away by his husky and jealous wife. "The Rounders," with Chaplin and Arbuckle as homecoming drunks pursued by their wives, is marked by clever teamwork and amuses average audiences of today more than most others.

The best known of all the thirty-five films Chaplin made for Sennett is, of course, the six-reel "Tillie's Punctured Romance," the first feature-length comedy. It starred Marie Dressler, brought from the stage in the general movement of the period. Though Chaplin supported Marie Dressler who got the star billing, it was this film, released late in 1914, that made his name widely known to the general public. It was a free-swinging adaptation of Marie Dressler's stage success "Tillie's Nightmare," in which she sang the hilarious "Heaven Will Protect the Working Girl."

Begun in April 1914, the picture took fourteen weeks
to shoot. With sumptuous staging and the support of the
whole Keystone troupe, "Tillie's Punctured Romance"
was a decided hit. Robust, aimed at a wide audience,
healthily vulgar, filled with earthy American humor, it
entertained millions, though with today's diminished appetite for kicks and falls it may seem overexuberant.
Even some contemporary critics objected to it as a mere
Keystone anthology. They counted "at least seventeen
punctures in Tillie's Romance." But it is more than mere
slapstick. It is a smart take-off of the old city slicker-
country maiden cliché, adding some pointed thrusts at
the "high society" of the period.

The beginning of the picture betrays its stage origin,
but it becomes more cinematic toward the end. At
times the lips move in simulated "soliloquies" and
"asides" that are actually pantomimed to the audience.
Along about the middle of 1914, this device—a hang-
over from the stage and until then common in Sennett's
and some other films—disappeared as the actors developed
techniques more appropriate to the silent medium. Later
it may be noticed that Chaplin seldom moves his mouth,
relying on pantomime and action alone.

Marie Dressler's acting is extremely broad as compared with her later work—and she was never noted as
a restrained performer. This, again, may be laid to her
stage training. But such qualities were then in vogue;
her gyrations and grimaces brought down the house.
(Parenthetically it may be noted that Marie Dressler,
in spite of sequels to this picture made for other companies, never again attained outstanding success until
"Anna Christie," the talkie of 1930. Then she became
one of the top attractions of all time.)

"Tillie's Punctured Romance" opens with Charlie, a
city slicker, sporting a genuine "villain" mustache of two

small tufts, testing the countryside for easy pickings. He is hit by a brick tossed by the hulking farm lass in innocent roughhousing with her dog. Contritely she hauls the injured man into the farm house. Her father gives him a drink. While he turns to transact some business, Charlie picks up a bill and fans himself when caught with it. That embarrassment safely past, he ferrets out where the old man hides his money.

As Tillie skips coyly through the garden, Charlie follows. There is a fetching sequence on a high fence where coquetry is combined with maintaining a precarious balance. Charlie's alluring descriptions of life in the city seduce her into stealing the money and running away with him.

In the city Tillie, in a dress of preposterous cut and volume and a hat topped with an unfashionable but conspicuous bird, has hairbreadth escapes through traffic on Charlie's guiding arm. They are spied by Mabel, his partner in love and crime, who proceeds to knock him down. Tender Tillie lifts him up—by the hair—and drags him away when a policeman comes on the scene. Mabel tries her arts, she smiles coquettishly, drops her muff, and, when the cop proves no gallant and fails to pick it up, she makes a face after him.

In a cafe Tillie reacts to strong drink by frantic dancing—with strangers and solo. When she slips, five men are not enough to lift her. At Mabel's nudging, Charlie takes care of Tillie's pocketbook for her and he and Mabel make a getaway. Tillie, after some tomboyish play with the police, which they fail to appreciate, lands in jail. A wealthy uncle secures her release but sternly refuses to see her.

While Charlie and Mabel are spending Tillie's money, they go to a restaurant where Tillie has taken a job as a waitress. Recognizing her deceiver, Tillie drops her tray on him as she faints. Meanwhile her rich uncle, while on a mountain-climbing expedition, slips and is lost in a snow crevasse.

Charlie and Mabel are at their ease on a park bench, Charlie reading his paper, Mabel toying with a lorgnette, when Charlie sees the headline, "Farmer's Daughter Inherits Millions." As he steals away, Mabel "feels" his absence. Turning corners sharply at right angles, Charlie hurries to the restaurant, knocking people over in his haste to get the startled Tillie to a minister. After some fancy fumbling, including the substitution of a telephone book for the Bible, he succeeds in marrying the reluctant girl. Returning to the restaurant, Tillie becomes ponderously kittenish, pounds her husband with kisses, and yanks him inside. When lawyers come to inform her that she has inherited three million dollars, she staggers, then pausing with tongue in cheek, looks significantly at her wedding ring. Charlie smiles sheepishly; Tillie gives him a scolding, but when he puts on a weeping act forgives him and bear-hugs him.

The newlyweds go off to a rococo mansion, their new home. In the overdecorated hall, butlers with powdered wigs stand at attention. Charlie hangs his hat and cane on the stiff arm of one of them while Tillie slouches against another. Neither of the flunkies so much as twitches. One of these human statues comes to life, at last, when Charlie flicks cigarette ashes into his face. Tillie scolds both butlers, but when she and Charlie attempt a dignified exit, Charlie spoils it by tripping on a tiger rug. The complications multiply when Mabel secures a job as a maid in order to be near her former sweetheart.

An elaborate ball given to mark the entrance of the couple into high society provides opportunities for hilarious travesty. Two solo dancers perform the tango à la Irene and Vernon Castle, the leading stars of the time in ballroom dancing turns. Tillie in a fantastic "harem gown" and Charlie in full dress make a grand entrance. Tillie, leading her small partner by the neck, goes into a frenzied tango, varied by kicks, trips, splits, whirls, and falls. In a side room Charlie is confronted by Mabel. They go through a sequence of quarreling and making up.

Tillie, discovering them embracing in an alcove, goes berserk, firing pastry at them, most of the shots finding targets on other guests. She reaches a climax when she finds a pistol. Charlie takes refuge in a big vase. Mabel under a rug. Tillie, swinging a cane, breaks the vase, and is choking Charlie just as the uncle, who had been rescued and revived, returns home. The "apparition" terrifies Tillie. He orders them all out of the house.

"Tillie rich and Tillie poor are two different things." Charlie now turns to Mabel—with Tillie at their heels. The uncle has called the police who come skidding into the station, knocking each other into a heap, then skidding out.

The wild chase culminates on a pier off which a police car, congested with cops, knocks Tillie, itself, and its contents into the ocean. Another kind of cops, water police, dash to the scene with collisions and capsizing lifeboats. Tillie is fished out and deposited on the pier where, as Mabel also spurns him, she expresses final disillusionment with Charlie, hands him back his ring, and declares "He ain't no good to neither of us." While the two women console each other, Charlie meets this turn of events with a philosophical shrug before the cops drag him off.

"Tillie's Punctured Romance" is still running today in various cut-up, sixteen-millimeter versions. An abridged, thirty-five-millimeter has dubbed-in music and sound effects. Since it reached the screen a little ahead of "The Birth of a Nation," which also receives occasional commercial revivals, "Tillie" may be said to be the oldest "living" feature picture.

To cash in on Chaplin's popularity his Keystone pictures were frequently reissued under new titles to deceive the public into believing they were new films. Some thus acquired as many as four aliases. Hence the confusion about the number of films and their titles. A complete and accurate list will be found in the index. They were also cut and spliced into a composite thirty-reel serial called "The Perils of Patrick," burlesquing, with the help of subtitles, the adventure serials of the period.

Unfortunately, the Keystone films have passed through many and sometimes mutilating hands. When Sennett went to Paramount in 1917, he relinquished the name Keystone as well as the film rights. Many of the Keystones, and particularly the Chaplins, have been added with extraneous subtitles to "pep them up" and lengthen their playing time. The original films contained only a few, amusingly succinct titles; the padding process resulted in a profusion of anachronistic, overdecorated and tasteless titles.

Another reason for this retitling is that the original negatives were packed in small rolls and, for the needs of the international market of silent pictures, the English titles were not permanently inserted in the negatives. Titles were photographed from cards with black letters on white backgrounds and the negatives were spliced direct into positive prints. Many title cards were misplaced and retitling was frequently necessary. Rarely does one come across an unmutilated Keystone original. These titles are done in a style similar to Biograph titles; the word Keystone, lettered in an arc, appears in the upper left corner and a circular border encloses the main title. The name of the picture above and two Keystone trademarks in the lower corners with "Part One" or "Part Two" between, are found on the interior subtitles. This elaborate use of trade-marks was a precaution against duping.

Essanay—the transitional period

Realizing the value of his now world-famous new star, Mack Sennett tried to hold him with an offer of four hundred a week. Chaplin's counterdemand, on the advice of friends, was seven hundred and fifty. Sennett, to his subsequent regret, turned it down.

In the meantime he did his best to keep agents from other companies away from Chaplin. No strangers were admitted into the guarded studio. According to one story, Sennett's vigilance was put to naught by an Essanay agent who got to Charlie by hiring out as a cowboy extra on the Keystone lot. To Essanay the comedian upped his demand to $1250 a week, which was accepted.

On January 2, 1915, it was announced that Chaplin had signed with Essanay at some ten times his Keystone salary.

Essanay was founded in 1907, its name an adaptation of the initials S. & A. S was for George K. Spoor, inventor-producer, and A for G. M. Anderson, America's first "star," better known as "Broncho Billy." The company folded in 1917-1918, when the Sherman antitrust laws were invoked against the Motion Picture Patents Company, the monopoly group headed by Edison, who claimed exclusive rights to certain patents. The active Essanay Company would now be virtually forgotten but for Chaplin's year with them.

At Essanay's main studio in Chicago, at 1333 Argyle Street, Chaplin made but one film, "His New Job." Then, because of the cold climate, he moved to the firm's California studio at Niles near San Francisco. (A glimpse of its little glass-covered stage may be seen in "The Champion.") Five comedies were made at Niles.

After finishing "The Tramp," Chaplin moved farther south to Los Angeles, arriving on April 8, 1915. For a few weeks he worked at the Bradbury mansion studio, at 147 North Hill Street, whose exterior was used in "Work." In the middle of May, he moved to a larger studio, the old Majestic on Fairview Avenue, just outside the downtown Los Angeles business center.

The fourteen Chaplin-Essanay films, made during 1915, were a transition from the Keystone charades to the polished Mutual series of 1916-1917. Though Chaplin has never forgotten, nor entirely abandoned, the lessons in slapstick and cinematic comedy he learned from Sennett, by 1915 he was creatively pretty much on his own. His earlier films had been shot in a day or two, or a week at most, and improvised on the spot; now he took more time and care. Three weeks were spent on "The Tramp" alone. And though Chaplin never used a shooting script until the sound era, preferring to improvise from a rough outline, the Essanays are well constructed over a more developed plot and show more restraint than his previous efforts.

In his acting Chaplin slowed his pace a bit, depending more on subtle pantomime. He experimented with new effects or renovated his old tricks by original twists. The two-reelers of this period cost from twelve hundred to fifteen hundred dollars each.

In the Keystones, in keeping with the Sennett style, much of the comedy depended on fantastic practical jokes, incongruities, collapses of dignity, the furious chase, and the varied properties of slapstick. In his Essanay series, Chaplin introduced other elements—pathos, satire, comic transpositions, genuine gags, surprise twists, fantasy and irony.

Some of the earlier Essanays continue on the Keystone track: "A Night Out"—adventures of a pair of drunks—is an expansion of "Caught in the Rain" and "The Rounders"; "In the Park"—a flirtatious tramp in a chase by a policeman—is virtually a remake of "Twenty Minutes of Love" and other "park" pictures (see Index); "The Champion"—a ring story—is similar to "The Knockout" in much of its business, though the approach has been subtilized: "The Jitney Elopement"—a chase film featuring the Ford car, a favorite target of contemporary humor; "By the Sea"—beach brawls and flirtations; "Work"—paperhangers messing up a house; 'A Woman"—a new female impersonation; and "Shanghaied"—comic roughhouse on shipboard. All are in the Keystone slapstick and knockabout tradition. "A Night in the Show" goes back even further to Chaplin's old Karno vaudeville skit, "A Night in an English Music-Hall."

Yet in his very first 1915 film, "His New Job," Chaplin introduced *satire*. The Keystones had frequently burlesqued contemporary fashions and morals. "His New Job" was real satire. The movies themselves and the making of stars were mercilessly kidded. Ham actors, aspiring actresses, producers, directors, and prop men all came in for jibes.

The film opens with Charlie getting a prop man's job at the Lockstone Studio. Chance wins Charlie an actor's part. Appearing as a romantic military hero, he is weighed down by the huge fur shako on his head and quite submerged in his comic-opera uniform. Blundering through a farewell with the statuesque leading lady, he gets into trouble with a swaying column. Then, driving the director frantic, he unwittingly kneels on the actress' long train and pulls off her skirt as she marches grandly upstairs. It is likely that in some scenes Chaplin was burlesquing Francis X. Bushman, Essanay's drama lead and the romantic idol of the day.

"Carmen" was a satire not only of the opera, but more particularly of the Cecil De Mille movie version starring Geraldine Farrar and Wallace Reid and the competing Fox version starring Theda Bara, both released that year. The sets and much of the action directly travestied the De Mille picture.

By general agreement "The Tramp," released April 11, 1915, is ranked as the first Chaplin classic. It remains one of his most important pictures, the first in which he injects a clear note of *pathos,* so important in most of his later films. This comedy ventured on a "sad" ending, unheard of in those days.

As the tramp, Charlie saves a girl from a robber gang. He is rewarded with a job on her father's farm. The crooks return to rob the farmer. Charlie routs them, but is shot in the leg. Nursed by the girl, he is supremely happy until the girl's handsome sweetheart arrives. Sadly Charlie scribbles a note of farewell, ties up his little bundle, and goes on his vagabonding way. In the fade-out scene we see him, back to the camera, starting dejectedly down the long road. Suddenly he pauses, shrugs philosophically, flips his heels, and ambles jauntily toward the horizon, as the scene irises out. Many variations of this ending were to be used.

Pathos also appears in "The Bank." Charlie, the janitor, is dissolved in distant adoration of a beautiful stenographer. Outside her office he holds his hand over his heart, blows a kiss toward her in mock-heroic fashion, turns and bumps into the door he has just closed. Next she breaks his heart by tossing out an expensive bouquet he has sent her and tearing up the accompanying love note. In his corner he dreams up a bank robbery in which he emerges as hero, capturing the robbers and freeing the girl. As he embraces her, the dream fades, and he wakes up to find himself kissing his mop. Catching sight of the stenographer and her cashier sweetheart in affectionate embrace, he kicks away the wilted bouquet and ambles back to the vault.

In later years Chaplin remarked, "I dislike tragedy. Life is sad enough. I only use pathos as a means of effecting beauty, for so much of the tragic is in all beauty."

Another new note, introduced in this period, was the *comic transposition*. In "A Night Out" Charlie, undressing in drunken confusion, puts his cane to bed, tries to pour himself a glass of water out of the telephone, "hangs" his trousers out of the window, uses tooth-paste to polish his shoes, and so forth. In "The Tramp" he tries to milk a cow by "pumping" her tail and uses a small watering can on a row of orchard trees. In "Police" he approaches an oven door as if it were a safe and opens it by working the "combination" on the knob. The "Carmen" duel is successively transformed into a dance, a billiard game, and a wrestling match. These oblique transmutations of objects or movements were carried to a climax in the famous alarm-clock scene in "The Pawnshop" (1916); but perhaps the most famous example is the Thanksgiving dinner in "The Gold Rush" (1925), where Charlie sucks every last bit of nourishment from a boiled shoe.

Closely related to the comic transpositions are the little notes of *fantasy* inserted into realistic scenes. In "A Night Out," as the drunken Charlie is being dragged along the sidewalk by Ben Turpin, his partner of the evening, he daintily plucks flowers in the bordering grass and inhales their fragrance as if he were floating dreamily in a boat among waterlilies. In "Work" the tilt of the camera exaggerates the slope of a hill up which Charlie drags his boss, seated on a heavily laden wagon

Chaplin in 1940.

2   Chaplin in his teens as a member of the music
hall act "Casey's Court Circus."

3 Chaplin as he looked when he entered the movies.

5 Mabel Normand, the leading comedienne at Keystone.

4 The Sennett studio where Chaplin made his first comedies. The open air stages are covered with sheets to diffuse the sunlight. The mission style entrance was featured in many a Keystone film.

6　Scenes from "Making a Living," Chaplin's first film, before he adopted the tramp costume and make-up.

chapter **V**

7 Frame enlargements from "Kid Auto Races at Venice," the short film in which Chaplin first wore his world-famous outfit.

8 A posed shot from "Kid Auto Races at Venice," showing director Henry Lehrman, Frank D. Williams at the camera, and Chaplin.

9 "Between Showers" with Chaplin and Ford Sterling. Chester Conklin and Emma Clifton in the background.

10 Mack Swain obeying Sennett's oft-repeated command, "Don't anticipate!" in "Laughing Gas."

11   Scenes from four Chaplin-Keystones: "Between Showers" (*a*), "Mabel's Busy Day" (*b*), "The Property Man" (*c*), "The Face on the Barroom Floor" (*d*).

12 Charlie welcomed (?) home by his wife (Phyllis Allen) in
"The Rounders."

13 Charlie and Fatty Arbuckle create havoc in "The Rounders."

14 The Rounders end up in a
    sinking boat.
15 Three scenes from "Tillie's
    Punctured Romance" featur-
    ing Marie Dressler as Tillie,
    Chaplin as the City Slicker,.
    and Mabel Normand as his
    partner in crime.

16 Leo White, Charlie, and Ben Turpin in "A Night Out."
17 A classic situation from "A Night Out."
18 Ben Turpin rescuing Charlie in "A Night Out."
19 Edna Purviance, Chaplin, and Turpin in "A Night Out."

20 Charlie ordered by his boss (Charles Insley) in the appropriately titled "Work."

21 After the explosion in "Work." The composite film "Triple Trouble" also ends with this scene.

22 Edna's stern father (Charles Insley) is deceived by the coy
charm of Charlie disguised in "A Woman."

23 Close-up of Charlie in "A Woman."

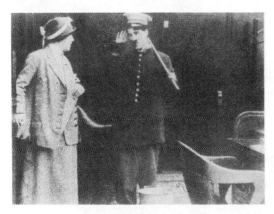

24   Charlie as the janitor who adores the pretty stenographer (Edna Purviance) in "The Bank."

25   The janitor crushed when the stenographer tears up his note in "The Bank."

26   The end of the dream in "The Bank."

27 Charlie about to be shanghaied.
28 Charlie as a sailor in "Shanghaied."

29 Charlie as Darn Hosiery in his burlesque of "Carmen."

30 Charlie with Edna Purviance as Carmen in the famous burlesque.

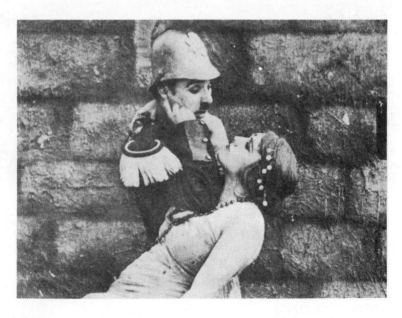

chapter **VII** cont.

31   Charlie becomes bored in the middle of the duel in "Carmen."

which, in a previous scene, he had pulled through heavy traffic as if he were a truck horse.

In the same picture, amidst violent slapstick with buckets of paste, Charlie puts a lampshade on a small nude statue to provide it with a skirt. As we are about to scoff at his prudery, he peeks under the lampshade like a naughty schoolboy (a wonderful illustration of the roots of obscenity) and manipulates the lampshade to make the statue do "bumps" and "grinds." Throughout he wears an expression of disarming casualness.

In "Carmen" soldiers ramming a heavy courtyard door detach it from its hinges. The smugglers behind it continue to "hold" and the door is juggled all around the courtyard—the sort of grotesquerie later copied in cartoons.

Then came the *gag*, which became the foundation of American screen comedy in its classic era, in the twenties, after pie-throwing and the chase had gone out. (Pie-throwing, though this is seldom realized, was considered old-fashioned as early as 1918. In a press interview Sennett himself spoke patronizingly of the "old days" when pie-throwing was popular. "Speed, pretty girls and spectacular effects" had become the Sennett formula in 1918.)

The Chaplin gag, perhaps, was an accommodation to his short stature. This called for the use of his wits in encounters with giants—like David with Goliath. It was a clever trick or comic stunt, not necessarily "legitimate," invented to overcome superior force.

Thus, in "The Champion," before getting a job as a sparring partner, Charlie picks up a horseshoe, the symbol of good luck—and makes sure of the luck by slipping it inside his boxing glove. Later, as Charlie is being worsted, he calls his faithful dog to the rescue, which the animal accomplishes by holding the bruiser back by the seat of the pants so Charlie can deliver the knockout. Incidentally, "The Champion," the third Essanay, seems to have been the first Chaplin film to be referred to by name—instead of merely "the latest Chaplin."

In his female impersonation in "A Woman" Charlie keeps losing his "falsies"—a pincushion—as he flirts coyly with his sweetheart's father. A preoccupied salesman in "The Bank" allows the janitor to feel his pulse and, when requested, sticks out his tongue on which Charlie proceeds to moisten a stamp for a letter. "Shanghaied" employs the old gag, perhaps not original with Chaplin, of keeping a tray of dishes upright through falls and somersaults on the violently rocking ship.

A good sample of the popular "substitution" gag occurs in "A Night at the Show," when Charlie, flirting with a girl in the audience, finds himself holding hands with her husband. In "Police," Charlie picks the pocket of the crook who is holding him up and goes through *his* pockets. Then there is the "unconscious" gag. In "The Bank" every time Charlie, shouldering a mop, turns around, he swats somebody in the face. Harold Lloyd built his career on such gags and scores of other comedians were to use similar stunts and tricks for comic effect throughout the twenties.

The Chaplin-Essanays are rich in surprise *twists*. In the opening scene of "The Bank" Charlie makes an officious entrance into an imposing bank, opens a spacious vault— and brings out his mop and pail and his janitor's coat and hat. In "A Night Out" he flirts with a veiled woman —only to uncover a preposterously homely face. A variation of one of his pet tricks appears in the little impromptu comedy "By the Sea." Tossing a banana skin in the air he bats at it with the wrong foot, slips on the skin and falls, all in one unbroken "ballet" movement.

As a variation Chaplin sometimes turned to straight acting. The last scene of "Carmen"—the plea to the girl to come back to him—is played completely straight. Receiving a mocking refusal, he stabs her, lowers her gently to the ground, bends over her, kisses her, stabs himself, and falls dead over her prostrate form. But when the toreador enters and discovers them, Charlie's rear end suddenly revives: a spasmodic kick sends the toreador out of the scene, and the "dead" couple spring to life. In a final closeup Charlie mockingly demonstrates that the murder dagger is a fake—a collapsing toy.

Unfortunately "Carmen" was tampered with after Chaplin left Essanay, as was "Police," which he made about the same time. Chaplin had intended to release "Carmen" in December 1915 as a two-reeler. But the company, which he had left in the meantime, used discarded material and added new scenes to pad it into a four-reeler, which was released on April 22, 1916. A sub-plot, using Ben Turpin in scenes with the gypsies, was shot, independently of the main story, and was crosscut with the original film, Chaplin and Turpin never meeting. Most audiences, consequently, found "Carmen" repetitious, monotonous, and somewhat confusing, especially when the star was absent. Justifiably Chaplin sued Essanay for tampering with the film.

A new note, *irony*, makes its appearance in the Essanay films. It is marked in "Police" which begins with Charlie's release from prison ("Once again the cruel, cruel world"). He meets a reformer, who pleads, "Let me help you go straight." Charlie, overcome, wipes his streaming eyes on the reformer's beard as the latter looks heavenward. Later, when Charlie sees a drunkard leaning against a telephone pole with a watch dangling from his vest pocket, he remembers the reformer's words and resists the temptation, only to see the watch gone after the reformer has stopped to deliver a temperance lecture. Needless to say Charlie resists all subsequent "reformers."

Later he meets an old cell-mate and agrees to team up with him in a robbery. But they are discovered by a pretty girl who offers them food and tries to persuade

Charlie to "go straight." Charlie, suspicious of "do-good-ers," keeps an eye on his pockets. When the police arrive, the girl protects the chivalrous Charlie by pretending that he is her husband. Then she gives him a dollar and sends him on his way. Charlie wanders in blissful redemption down the road until the inevitable cop appears and the old chase resumes.

In its original form, "Police" would compare with the best of his two-reelers. Its comments on life and society are bitingly perceptive. But, like "Carmen," it was tampered with after Chaplin left Essanay. One whole sequence was removed to help "pad" another film.

Chaplin made only fourteen films for Essanay, but a fifteenth, "Triple Trouble," was released by the company in August 1918, as "a new Chaplin comedy," held back by them. Actually it was patched together from bits extracted from "Police," "Work," and an unfinished feature titled "Life" (which Chaplin abandoned because of the demand for short comedies) and non-Chaplin scenes directed by Leo White, in 1918. The patchwork was pulled into some unity by ingenious cutting, the use of doubles, and subtitles to give it a 1918 flavor. The plot concerns a janitor who works in the house of an inventor from whom German diplomats are trying to obtain a formula. It ends in a melee at the inventor's house, with Charlie and everyone else vaporized in an explosion.

The film is a study in movie "magic." Edna Purviance, in 1915, throws a wet rag out a door; it hits Leo White in 1918, and he tosses it back to the cook in 1915! In several scenes the cook, the butler, and the thief change faces as doubles step in, and at one point hands purporting to be Chaplin's dump a garbage can over a fence. The exteriors are plainly Chicago in wintertime.

In the flophouse Charlie assumes an odd sleeping posture. He has his head at the foot of the bed, and his

shoes are held up by his hands. The neighboring sleeper
is a miser. As he counts his money he is confused in his
count by the sight of a wiggling finger poking through a
hole in a shoe and, on investigating, he gets a jab in the
face. Here we find the germ of the camouflaged tree sequence in "Shoulder Arms" (1918). Its coin-swallowing-
and-rattling business was to be used again in "The Great
Dictator" (1940); and other bits from this scene were to
serve again, in fuller development, in "The Kid"
(1921), "The Gold Rush" (1925), and later films.

During his Essanay period, Chaplin assembled a supporting group of players and technicians who were to
stick with him through the years. Gloria Swanson, then
an extra in the Chicago studio, very nearly became his
leading lady. However, she resembled Chaplin too much
in stature, coloring, and certain aspects of personality to
be a perfect foil. She may be glimpsed in the bit part of
a stenographer in "His New Job," though she receives no
billing and though she denies she ever played with Chaplin!

At a party soon after his arrival back in California,
Chaplin met Edna Purviance. She came from Nevada
(born 1894), and was the daughter of a miner. She was
then a stenographer, with neither stage nor screen experience. Chaplin molded her to his needs. She was physically
and temperamentally a perfect foil for Chaplin. Her
classic blonde beauty contrasted with his brunette cast;
her stature was just tall enough and her figure just
Junoesque enough to make him appear even slighter than
he is; and her placidity set off his volatile style. After
some difficult coaching, she became a perfect partner for
him, supplying the romantic interest, and was always able
to turn on the right mixture of surprise and amusement
at Charlie's everlasting blunders. With marvelous econ-

omy of means, rare for the period, Chaplin taught her to suggest a wide range of emotions.

Edna Purviance became Chaplin's leading lady without signing a contract. Over a period of nine years she played in thirty-five of his films. Away from the studio she and Chaplin became inseparable and the "gossip columnists" assumed imminent bridals. Even after Chaplin's sudden marriage to Mildred Harris in 1918, Edna continued to work for him, turning down offers for fifteen times the hundred dollars a week she received from the Chaplin Company. Chaplin rewarded her loyalty by making a dramatic actress of her in "A Woman of Paris" (1923). Today she is on his pension roll.

Cross-eyed Ben Turpin, an Essanay veteran, proved an excellent butt for Charlie. Leo White, specializing in the "excitable Frenchman," was also picked up at the Chicago studio and became a Chaplin "regular." White was a graduate from the musical-comedy stage (for several years he supported Fritzi Scheff in "Mlle. Modiste"). The giant Bud Jamieson's only training had been amateur magic when Chaplin met him in San Francisco and added him to his troupe. Detectives later became Jamieson's specialty and he was to continue sleuthing through countless sound films.

Others in the company included Billy Armstrong, an English player from the Karno Company, who turned in his best performance in "The Bank," John Rand, a one-time circus performer, Marta Golden, who did character types, Paddy McGuire, Charles Insley, Carl Stockdale, Ernest Van Pelt, Charlotte Mineau, and James T. Kelley. A number of them were to be with Chaplin for a quarter of a century. Wesley Ruggles, now a prominent director, played small parts for Chaplin at Essanay. Rollie Totheroh, who began as Chaplin's cameraman in 1915, has continued with him up to "Monsieur Verdoux" (1947).

When Chaplin completed his year at Essanay he was unquestionably the top figure in the motion picture industry—after only two years on the screen! The Essanay Company cleared well over a million on the Chaplin series.

The pictures have passed through many hands and have been duped, retitled, and revived, time after time. Original Essanay prints can be identified by a bordered opening title with two Indian-head trademarks and the name, "Essanay," in back-slanting letters, in between. The original interior subtitles are undecorated.

Many Essanays, in a more or less mutilated state, are still in circulation in "sound" prints. In the version of "The Bank," now being shown, cuts in the cashier's part obscure the entire motivation. Similarly, in the "Tramp," Charlie seems merely to fall off the fence instead of being shot, and so on.

An entire generation has been given a distorted view of Chaplin's early genius through the slipshod handling of these classics. Unfortunately the original negatives were not preserved.

The Essanay films are unequal in quality and technique. Artificial lights were used in the Chicago film and occasionally, to boost the daylight, in Essanay's Niles studio. The photography is uneven in some of the remaining pictures. In the Essanays, however, we have the beginnings of Chaplin's art. In virtually every one of the Essanays some bit or idea appears that was to come to fuller flowering in his later works. In this year at Essanay the immortal and world-famous character of the Tramp—the tragi-comic vagabond so perfectly symbolizing the universal underdog—came into being. It is possibly the most significant artistic archetype of this century.

$10,000 a week from Mutual

At the end of 1915 other companies began
bidding for Chaplin. To continue with Essanay, Spoor offered him a profit-sharing contract, guaranteeing a minimum of $500,000. Chaplin was about to accept when his
brother Sidney, who had quit acting for the time to become his business manager, announced that Charlie was
worth more: Instructing Edna Purviance and other associates to stand watch to see that he did not accept the
Essanay offer, Sidney went off to New York to sound out
the other companies. Charlie soon followed him.

For Chaplin the period of negotiations was an almost
continual fete. Offers poured in for stage appearances.
Once, at a benefit concert at the old Hippodrome (February 20, 1916), Chaplin led the famous Sousa's band.
His conducting, according to George Canham who was
there, drew only perfunctory applause, but when, on his
third curtain call, he executed a few steps of his famous
walk, pandemonium broke loose. The experience led
Chaplin to the resolution to stick to pictures thereafter
(and, in truth, he has seldom appeared before the public
in any other medium).

On February 26, 1916, Chaplin signed with the Mutual Company where John R. Freuler was at the helm.
His salary, which received world-wide publicity, was
$10,000 a week, with a bonus of $150,000—totaling
$670,000 a year. Once again, he had signed a contract for

ten times his salary of the previous year—an incredible
amount of money for a young man of twenty-six who, less
than three years before, had been an obscure vaude-
villian.

His great and sudden wealth had curiously little effect
on him as a person and no effect on him as an artist. His
remark, after the signing, is said to have been "Well,
I've got this much if they never give me another cent.
Guess I'll go and buy a whole dozen neckties."

A new studio, The Lone Star, was built at 1025 Lillian Way, Hollywood, and opened March 27, 1916.
More time and effort went into the Mutual pictures. For
instance, 90,000 feet were shot to provide the 1,809 feet
of the two-reel "The Immigrant," roughly the same footage as was exposed for the twelve-reel "The Birth of a
Nation." (But at that time, Griffith, after many rehearsals,
seldom shot a scene more than once.) Five hundred
prints of the Mutual comedies were distributed, a large
number compared to the hundred and fifty to two hundred prints for a hit picture today.

Counting in Chaplin's salary, the cost of each Mutual
approximated one hundred thousand dollars which
topped the average cost for features at the time. Theatres
which paid fifty dollars a day for the Mutuals when first
issued paid four times that price for the same pictures six
or seven years later. In 1925 Terry Ramsaye estimated
that the cinema theatres of the world had already paid
five millions in film rentals for these pictures and the
public had spent twenty-five millions at the box offices!

There was much "dumping" of the old Chaplin comedies by the illegal process of making a new negative from
a positive print. When the prints of the Sennett and
Essanay comedies wore out they were replaced by "boot-
leg" duped prints re-imported from abroad. Some idea of
the traffic in Chaplin films may be gained from the records of the little Crystal Hall on 14th Street in New

York. From 1914 to 1923, when the theatre burned down, Chaplin was on its screen continuously except for one week when the management tried out an imitator, with disastrous results.

Because of the extra care he gave them Chaplin's twelve Mutual two-reelers took eighteen months to complete, half a year longer than anticipated. They show decided progress all around. Chaplin was more sure of what he was after. Each of the new films was an entity in itself, with clear plots and definite themes. They had satire, irony, surprise, pathos—all the elements he had introduced in the best Essanays, but more surely executed. Where there was slapstick it grew naturally out of the picture, it was not dragged in. The sets were more elaborate, the photography improved.

For the first few films Totheroh worked with William C. Foster. Diffused sunlight was still used in interiors but a couple of Klieg broadlights were used to boost a dark corner in "The Floorwalker" set, and in the police-station scenes of "Easy Street," which may have been shot during the rainy season. The moving camera is used to follow the two dancing couples in "The Count." It was also used for Chaplin's encounter with the tough in "Easy Street." "Truck backs" also appear in "The Vagabond" and "The Cure." (In the twenties many critics mistakenly credited the Germans with the invention of the moving camera, forgetting that it had been used in the Italian spectacle, "Cabiria" (1914) and in the Griffith films, notably "Intolerance.") The photography in the Mutuals has remarkable clarity, especially in good prints.

Many of Chaplin's supporting actors moved over with him from Essanay to Mutual. From "stooges" they advanced to more fully developed characters. A real "ensemble" was built up, each actor with a personality of his own. Edna Purviance continued as leading lady; John Rand came and stayed on with Chaplin; but Leo White,

a year later, left him to join Billy West, Chaplin's
leading imitator.

A new recruit was Eric Campbell, the giant "heavy,"
who came from the D'Oyly Carte Gilbert and Sullivan
Company, as his Mikado-like make-up suggests. He distinguished himself in "Easy Street." He died in an auto
accident in December 1917, just as he was about to
launch an independent career. Tall, lean, curly-haired Albert Austin, who distinguished himself in "Behind the
Screen," was a Karno alumnus who had played with
Chaplin in "A Night in an English Music-Hall." He was
to have a hand, acting or directing, in almost all subsequent Chaplin films.

The short, stout Henry Bergman came on as both actor
and assistant director. Since Chaplin both directs and acts,
he needs another's view when he is before the camera.
Through the years, until his death in 1946, "Uncle" Bergman remained Chaplin's closest assistant. Between pictures he operated a Hollywood Cafe called "Henry's."
Lloyd Bacon, now a prominent director, played juvenile
leads, and Leota Bryan played second feminine leads. As
assistant scenario writers, later called "gagmen," Chaplin
had Vincent Bryan, a skit and song writer, and Maverick
Terrill.

Early in 1916 Chaplin sued Essanay for tampering with
"Carmen," to be met with a countersuit for six hundred
thousand dollars for alleged contract violations—not completing the stipulated number of pictures.

Chaplin still lived in a small room in the old Stowell
Hotel in Spring Street in downtown Los Angeles. Outside of his work he was pretty much of a lone wolf, avoid-
ing the places where the movie crowd congregated, and
wandering at night through the poorer quarters of the
town. Julian Eltinge, the noted female impersonator, then
making films for Lasky, and a Hofbrau House habitué
along with William Farnum, Raymond Hitchcock, and

other transplanted Broadwayites, is said to have introduced Chaplin into that set.

He brought Chaplin to a party an Englishwoman friend was giving, and at which Geraldine Farrar and Sir Beerbohm Tree, both of whom were making films, were guests. This was followed by a party at Sunset Inn, overlooking the sea, at Santa Monica, where Beerbohm Tree and his daughter Iris, and Mrs. William K. Vanderbilt were fellow guests. Mrs. Vanderbilt puffed at a long, gold cigarette holder, violating a Santa Monica ordinance against women smoking in public. The mayor and chief of police were unimpressed when the owner of the Inn identified the lawbreaker as Mrs. Vanderbilt; but when he identified her little fellow guest as Charlie Chaplin, all was forgiven.

Eltinge urged Chaplin to move to a better district, and in the fall of 1916, he took rooms in the Los Angeles Athletic Club. His brother persuaded him to buy an automobile, a Locomobile, and hire a secretary, Tom Harrington. The latter, in turn, hired the Japanese, Kono, as chauffeur.

Kono was to remain with Chaplin for eighteen years as his "man-Friday"—combination chauffeur, valet, private secretary, and bodyguard. For years people had to deal with Chaplin through the shrewd little Japanese, who earned his employer's trust by loyal and sensitive attendance. It was Paulette Goddard, wanting to "take over" herself, who finally caused Kono's downfall. As chauffeur Kono would call for Tom Harrington just before nine each morning, drive him to the Los Angeles Stock Exchange where he left Harrington to transact business for the boss, turn back to the Athletic Club to pick up Charlie, go on to the Engstrom Hotel for Miss Purviance, and deliver them both to the studio at about ten.

Chaplin continued to be Svengali to the Trilby of Edna

Purviance, supplementing her natural endowments of beauty and charm with expressiveness and style. They continued to be the best of friends. Around Hollywood they would be seen arm in arm; and inevitably their names were linked. Edna, the eternal mother type, ministered to Chaplin's needs, was playful when he was in the mood, consolatory when he was depressed. She was his adviser for many years. Her phlegmatic temperament remained unruffled by his wildest moods. She is said to have been able to do more with him than any other girl. Those who knew them thought she would have made him an ideal mate; but their close and serene companionship failed to reach that consummation. More troubled loves were to come to Chaplin.

1916-1917 saw the steady rise of Chaplin's fame. World-famous figures visited his studios, musicians, opera stars, and stage celebrities, among them Paderewski, Leopold Godowsky, Nellie Melba, and Harry Lauder. Numbers of intellectuals, following the lead of Mrs. Fiske, began writing serious appreciations of his art. The war, too, according to some, boosted his popularity. His pictures, old and new, did much to cheer the British and French at the battle lines and in the hospitals, and on the home front as well.

An anecdote, illustrating the international spread of his fame among fellow artists, is told by Dorothy Gish, who during her "black wig" period (1918-1921), was often called the female Chaplin. She accompanied Chaplin to the Nijinski ballet when it visited Los Angeles, in 1916. Catching sight of Chaplin in the audience the dancers stopped the show, invited him backstage, and made the audience wait a half hour, while each member of the company, in turn, embraced him. Later the entire troupe visited him at the studio during the showing of "Easy Street." Such adulation was enough to turn anyone's head and it is to Chaplin's credit that, instead of unbalancing him, it seemed to strengthen his self-assurance and spur him to greater achievements.

There were endless "fake" Chaplin pictures during this period. His old issues were revived under new titles to mislead the public. Spurious "new" Chaplins were turned out by using a few clips and close-ups from old Chaplin prints and adding scenes done by imitators. Most of them burlesqued some popular feature of the day. Among them were "The Fall of the Rummy-Nuffs," "The Dishonor System," "One Law for Both," "Charlie in a Harem," "Charlie Chaplin in 'A Son of the Gods.'" This last combined Chaplin shots and footage from the Fox-Kellerman fantasy "A Daughter of the Gods," making Chaplin appear to be cavorting among mermaids. Such retitling and rehashing of the Chaplin films is not unknown today! 1915-1918 was also the era of Chaplin impersonation contests, Chaplin toys, and Chaplin show numbers. There was even a Chaplin animated cartoon and Chaplin caricatures in the papers.

Foremost among the many imitators of Chaplin was Billy West who flourished during 1917-1918, making pictures for the King Bee Company. His was unashamed aping of every Chaplin detail of costume, gesture, and movement. West, a Russian-born actor who had appeared in minor films, was supported by Oliver ("Babe") Hardy, Ethel Teare, and later Leo White, lured from the Chaplin Company. Billie Ritchie, from the Karno Company, Bobbie Dunn, Ray Hughes, and Charles Amador were other formidable imitators. Amador, a Mexican, eventually adopted the name Charles Aplin. None of these imitators succeeded in holding the public, for, while it was not too difficult to imitate Chaplin's mannerisms and gags, it was impossible to simulate the more delicate pantomime and the personality the great comedian had created. However, Chaplin sued "Charles Aplin" and won a judgment in 1925, decreeing his costume and gait to be his private property.

The imitations spread abroad. France had a "Monsieur Jack" and André Séchan; Germany a Charlie Kaplin and Ernst Bosser. In fact, most of the comedians of the time copied Chaplin and borrowed his gags.

By his own admission, Harold Lloyd imitated Chaplin in his Lonesome Duke character which he played, from 1915 to 1917, in hundreds of short comedies. Although costume and make-up were not an exact copy, rather the opposite, the pants being tight instead of floppy and the mustache turned up instead of down, the whole conception was Chaplinesque. It was not till 1917 that Lloyd put on his horn-rimmed glasses and became the typical small-town American youth.

1916-1917 were Chaplin's most fertile years, his most sustained creative period. With ripened art he now made twelve almost perfect comedies in eighteen months. All his early techniques were matured and performed with precision and dexterity. These comedies laid the foundation for his later period—several of the little Mutuals were prototypes of his features—and he was to borrow and build on them for the rest of his career. From a study of these comedies, still being revived and arousing hilarity, one can get the essence of Chaplin.

The Mutuals have passed through many hands. When the company went bankrupt in 1919, the Chaplins were acquired by the Clark-Cornelius firm, which held them until 1922 when they were sold to a "Chaplin Classics" company. In 1925 they were obtained by the Export and Import Company which controlled the rights until 1932 when they were purchased by the R.K.O.–Van Beuren Corporation. This firm added music and sound effects under the supervision of Gene Rodemich, and there was some cutting and sub-title changes or deletions. Subtitles, in original Mutual prints, including the conversational titles, have an enlarged and illuminated initial boxed in a rectangle with a floral background.

Unfortunately, although some of the added music is not bad, R.K.O.–Van Beuren overdid the sound effects, with sliding whistles, ratchets, and other noisemakers borrowed from the modern cartoon technique. They also committed the artistic sin of adding the human voice on occasions. This further compels running the pictures at higher sound speed of twenty-four frames a second, when they were taken at sixteen per second (or less, since Chaplin often undercranked, to get special effects). This sometimes hurries and blurs the action.

The Mutuals are now owned by Guaranteed Pictures and are put out in combinations of four or six, as "Chaplin Festivals." Sixteen-millimeter prints are distributed by Brandon Films. With each new handling, the negatives have suffered some further cuts or damages. Nor are Chaplin films alone in meeting this fate. It is unfortunate that the original negatives of these and many other great films have not been preserved. Worn and duped prints give little idea of the quality of the original.

The Chaplin-Mutual films cannot be lumped together. Each is a distinctive creation and must be reviewed separately.

the classic Mutual comedies

The idea for his first Mutual comedy came to Chaplin while visiting a New York department store. Going up an escalator, he saw a nervous man slip, and at once grasped the comic possibilities of the moving staircase. On his return to Hollywood he ordered a department-store set built and wrote a comedy around it —"The Floorwalker," released May 15, 1916.

Except for some clever gags and more elaborate properties, this first Mutual comedy stays in the slapstick tradition.

Charlie enters, picks up an artificial limb (which he is told is not for sale), knocks over boxes with his cane, mismanages the drinking fountain from which he emerges, his face adrip, and is worsted in his first bout with the moving staircase. About to kick a clerk he changes his mind when a store detective appears, and stoops to brush off his pants.

Upstairs the floorwalker double-crosses the manager with whom he was to abscond with the store receipts, hits him over the head, and goes off with all the loot. In the anteroom he encounters Charlie who is almost his double in appearance.

Imagining they are looking in a mirror, their hands touch, they scratch their heads together and raise and lower their arms in unison (ancestor of the similar stunt in the Marx Brothers' "Duck Soup," years later).

The confusion ends when Charlie notices that the other is carrying a satchel instead of a cane.

The floorwalker bribes Charlie to change places with him only to fall into the cop's hands and get a billy over the head as Charlie, just in time, doffs his derby. When Charlie picks up the satchel of money he gets a scare as a dummy's hand falls on it.

The stunned manager comes to and rushes at Charlie but stops as the detectives turn to see and his lunge changes to an affable handshake with the surprised Charlie. But the assault resumes upstairs where Charlie's efforts to fend off his assailant with some exquisite ballet steps go unappreciated. He is picked up by the neck and given a shaking. Managing to slip out of the other's grip Charlie dives under his legs and a minor chase goes into a major one as the police swarm in.

The chase proceeds down the "up" escalator. Charlie slipping when he reaches bottom is pulled up again. Then another mechanical monster, the store elevator, joins in the free-for-all. It cracks the crooked store manager on the head and brings the comedy to an end.

The "Floorwalker's" mirror and ballet scenes are its high points.

"The Fireman" is perhaps the least interesting of the Mutuals since it depends most on violence and slapstick. But it is redeemed by several outstanding touches to which George Jean Nathan, no lover of the movies, has paid tribute.

Fireman Charlie, still abed, mistakes a drill bell for a fire alarm, slides down the pole and upsets the whole fire company by driving the engine out, single-handed. The tough fire chief administers heavy-handed punishment. Ordered to serve breakfast, the coffee and cream for which are extracted from the engine boiler, Charlie's

clumsiness earns him some more knock-down punishment.

As he lies prostrate, the chief becomes remorseful and
lifts him up. Charlie kicks him into a bucket of water,
shins up the pole, and resorts to prayer as he sees the
chief working his way up after him. Charlie is saved by
the timely entrance of the chief's sweetheart and her
father, who takes him aside to whisper, "Let my house
burn. I'll get the insurance. You wed my daughter."

Later when an alarm interrupts Charlie and another
fireman at a game of checkers Charlie stuffs a handkerchief in the bell as a silencer. When the owner of the
burning house calls, Charlie nonchalantly picks up the
phone, shrugs as he confuses his pipe and the earpiece,
and ends by ripping out the telephone wire. The frantic
owner storms into the firehouse and falls, sobbing, on
Charlie's shoulder. Charlie, moved, also begins yelling
"Help! Fire!" Handing the owner a book to relax with,
he goes to fetch the captain from the girl's house.

Back at the firehouse the fire victim pores over the
book, absentmindedly looks up, recalls the fire, and starts
raving again. Upstairs the firemen jump out of bed, rush
out of the camera frame, to return, immediately, in uniform. The engine strews men and equipment all along
the road. Before the burning house the men go into a
musical comedy fire drill, passing axes from left to right
shoulder and executing dance steps.

Meanwhile the insurance-hungry father sets his house
afire, unwittingly trapping his daughter on the third
floor. Frantic, he hunts for the firemen, finally locating
them at the other fire. Charlie, on the driver's seat, rides
like the wind, only to lose most of the engine turning a
sharp corner. Little is left except the seat when he arrives at the fire; but he makes up for it by climbing up
the face of the building to make a heroic rescue.

"The Vagabond," on the other hand, is almost straight drama. This unique little picture is a prototype of "The Kid" and "The Circus." It has many enthusiasts though others find the emotional scenes awkward. They feel that Chaplin, as a director, was then not quite up to the effects he was to get so masterfully later on. Nevertheless "The Vagabond," in which Chaplin ventures into a new realm, is an important picture.

It opens with a shot of Charlie's familiar feet under the swinging door of a saloon. He is playing a violin but yields to a competing German brass band. Moving over to the free lunch, he switches signs so that an old Jew can help himself to some ham. Then he passes the hat, ostensibly for the brass band. He is caught and chased away.

Out in the country he plays for a pathetic gypsy drudge weeping over a washtub. As his tempo rises in a rhythmic gypsy number, the girl's rubbing speeds up until the tub upsets. Charlie bows like a maestro taking curtain calls, but gets no applause from the brutal chief who chases him and gives the girl a beating. From a refuge in a tree Charlie fells the pursuing gypsies, one by one, and makes an escape with the girl in the gypsies' wagon. Camping out happily, Charlie washes the girl's hair in a bucket, uses a hammer to open eggs, executes offending flies by making his pocket their death chamber. An artist meets the girl and paints her portrait. "His romance fading," Charlie makes pathetic competitive attempts at drawing but cannot wake the girl out of her dream of the handsome artist.

Taking first prize at an exhibition, the portrait is publicized. In it the girl's wealthy mother recognizes her daughter, abducted as an infant. "That birth mark—my child!" Arriving at Charlie's camp to claim her daughter the mother acknowledges Charlie's existence with a shoulder-high society handshake. Charlie refuses a money reward and bids the girl a fond goodbye. Watching the auto drive off Charlie tries unsuccessfully to perk up by flipping his heels, then disconsolately leans against the wagon.

Seated between the artist and her mother, the girl undergoes "the awakening of the real love," has the car turned back, flings her arms around Charlie, and pulls him into the automobile. This ending supplanted another in which the despairing Charlie, saved from a watery suicide by a homely farm woman (played by Phyllis Allen), plunges in again after one look at his rescuer.

"One A.M.," which came next, was also an experimental departure from previous practice. Unlike "The Tramp" it provides no model for later films. In it, except for a brief passage with a taxi driver, Chaplin appears alone. "One A.M.," however, is a rare piece of virtuosity, a tour de force in which Chaplin successfully holds the screen with pantomime alone for two reels. Though some of the comic business, especially with the folding bed, is rather repetitious, most people find this picture very choice. Chaplin himself evidently did not think too highly of it. He never gave it the compliment of imitating it. And he is reported to have remarked, "One more film like that and it will be goodbye Charlie."

Yet "One A.M." ranks with Chaplin's cleverest pictures. In full evening dress and high silk hat Charlie returns, after a night out, to a nightmarish home cluttered with stuffed animals and other horrors. Above the double staircase swings a huge pendulum. The walls are covered with a livid, striped wallpaper. The whole has an almost surrealist—or delirium tremens—look.

Charlie skids on rugs, shrinks from the stuffed animals, chases a drink around a revolving table, pours liquor into a bottomless decanter, is knocked down one staircase by the pendulum and is cascaded down the other, rolled inside the stair carpet, climbs a teetering rubber clothes tree, and ducks under the pendulum to get into the bed-room.

Here he presses a button to bring out a folding bed but it sticks halfway, then catching him in it, spins him into the closet. Several other attempts end in bringing the bed down on his head. Finally settled in it he leans over to pick up a cigarette, only to have the bed shed him and retire back into the wall.

At later attempts to mount it the bed bucks like a colt under his first saddle, pins him to the wall, then flops down and turns over. Suddenly the bed falls out right side up. Charlie dives into it only to have it collapse. Giving up, Charlie retires to the bathroom. After a mis-hap under the shower he finally succeeds in making his bed in the tub.

Throughout it all he maintains the utmost dignity. This draws more laughs than if he had played the hilari-ous drunk.

"The Count" marks a return to more standard comedy. An expansion of, but also, in a sense, a regression to earlier manners, this picture is marked by fast action, slapstick, and clever pantomime.

It begins with blundering Charlie being fired by his huge boss, a tailor. Finding a note from Count Broko regretting his inability to attend a reception given by Miss Moneybags, the tailor decides to impersonate the count. At the Moneybags mansion, he encounters Charlie who is visiting the servants' quarters. Riding up the dumb-waiter his head appears between two curtains and he is at first taken for a painting by his startled ex-boss. With the aid of some crushing nudges, against which Charlie uses a tall chair as a shield, the tailor persuades Charlie not to expose him and to join in the imposture by posing as his secretary.

Subsequent funny business includes Charlie's inter-

ruption of the tailor's noisy ingurgitation of soup long
enough to hear Miss Moneybags' questions, his parlor
magic with the tailor's disappearing spaghetti, cascades of
stolen silver when he is slapped on the back, and his
quick recovery by a peek under the tailor's vest and ad-
ministering a scolding to him. Other comic business follows on the slippery dance floor, including splits and ele-
vations from the floor after a fall by hooking his cane on
the chandelier, undercover exchanges of kicks with his
obese rival, coyly flirting his cane at a harem-costumed
girl with a wiggling rear, then spearing, instead, a roast
fowl which he forward-passes to the butler, and "driving"
gobs of icing off a large cake upon the other guests.

The comedy reaches its climax with the arrival of the
genuine Count Broko. In the ensuing chase Charlie slides
among the dancers, where his feet churn in one spot like
a stalled locomotive. It winds up in the arrest of the
tailor, and Charlie's escape and fadeout running up a
sidewalk.

"The Pawnshop," which followed "The Count," is a
little masterpiece. It contains all of Chaplin's choicest ingredients: irony, pity, fantasy, and comic transpositions.
Chaplin demonstrates his genius for comic invention by
overcoming the handicaps of the restricted locale and ex-
tracting humor out of everything in it. The slapstick world
obliquely reflects life but makes no attempt at realism.
Here Charlie takes advantage of the suspension of reality
for some marvelously imaginative touches, by fantastic
distortion of the familiar.

The story is simple. Its humor turns on a comic rivalry
with another clerk, encounters with eccentric customers,
and the foiling of a robbery. The comic business used in
their development is extraordinary.

With his rival helpless between two steps of the step-
ladder they are carrying, Charlie "boxes" him. When a

cop arrives, he dances innocently back into the store, past the boss and out again. On top of the ladder Charlie "shoe polishes" one of the golden balls after bouncing it on the rival's head. In an attempt to clean an inaccessible sign he tips the ladder and goes through a magnificent balancing act before the ladder falls. Rising, Charlie's first thought is to see if his watch is still running.

Another bout with the clerk exhausts the boss's patience. Fired, Charlie pleads for his job, pantomiming that he has six children. The boss has his hands clasped behind his back but Charlie manages a farewell handshake. As the boss relents Charlie catapults upon him in gratitude. Immediately after, the wrestle with the rival clerk resumes. Charlie is giving his enemy a beating when the boss's daughter enters. Charlie drops down and pretends to be the victim, getting her consolation while his rival gets the scolding. When her consoling hand strays off, he hauls it back. Taken to the kitchen, he is further consoled with a home-baked doughnut so heavy that he uses it for dumbbell exercises, and it breaks the plate it is dropped on. Other comic business includes passing a plate, a cup, and his hands through a dry-wringer; a flash-length impersonation with a lei made of dough around his neck, strumming a ladle ukulele, and a show of innocent preoccupation by passing dough through the wringer to make pie crust when the boss's sudden entrance interrupts another altercation.

Into the shop staggers an old man—the broken-down-Shakespearean-actor type. With quivering emotion and tragic gestures he offers his wedding ring for pawn. Charlie, reduced to tears, can find only a ten-dollar bill in the register. Told to keep the ring, the old man puts the bill in his mouth, pulls out a big wad of money, and counts the change over to Charlie. As he exits Charlie blinks and slaps his face with a hammer. Next follows a typical transmutation. A rope on the floor defies all of Charlie's attempts to sweep it up. He tries straightening it, then does a tight-rope walk on it with all the teetering and panic of making one's way across a chasm.

Deservedly the most famous passage in "The Pawn-shop" is the alarm-clock scene. The ailing timepiece is brought in. Charlie puts a stethoscope to it, taps it like a doctor examining a lung, raps it as if testing porcelain, snaps his thumb on the bell, starts drilling with an auger, opens it with a can-opener, takes a significant sniff at its insides; then, with the telephone mouthpiece in his eye like a jeweler's magnifying glass, he examines it, oils it, uses dental forceps for some necessary extraction, taps it with a plumber's hammer, listens for noises, then pulls out the spring, measures it like ribbon, snips off lengths with a plier, then empties the remaining contents on the counter, where he stops the worm-like wriggling of the springs by squirts of oil. Finally sweeping the debris into the puzzled customer's hat, he solemnly shakes his head. (The scene is photographed in two long takes of several hundred feet each, separated by a two-foot flash of the customer's face.)

The final robbery scene is practically a ballet. As the thief backs out with the jewels, Charlie steps out of a trunk with a rolling pin, fells the robber, bows circus-fashion, embraces the girl, and delivers a back kick at his rival—all in one continuous movement.

"Behind the Screen," not as well known as some other Mutuals, is an amusing satire on Keystone slapstick. The setting is a movie studio. The comedy department re-hearses "a new idea"—which turns out to be pie-throwing —at which one of the actors quits in disgust over "this highbrow stuff." Much of its comic business repeats the older "Property Man," but in reverse. Charlie is David, the stage hand Goliath's assistant. He does all the heavy work, while the loafing Goliath takes all the credit.

Charlie carries eleven chairs at a time, and looks like a porcupine. With all the concentration of a hairdresser he combs a bear rug, applies a hair tonic, gives it a finger massage, parts its front hair, and hot-towels its face. At lunch hour, in defense against a comrade partaking of onions, Charlie clears the air with a bellows and dons a helmet, opening the visor just long enough to stuff bread in his mouth. Following the onions the stagehand goes to work on a meaty bone, an end of which projects into Charlie's face. Charlie, sandwiching his end between lids of bread, stealthily munches away. When caught, he imitates a dog.

Other comic business includes a miscuing which plunges Goliath, director, and leading lady down a trapdoor: a strike of stagehands, indignant over having been scolded for napping; by-play with a screen-struck girl in a stagehand's disguise, very convincing until Charlie spies her long hair; and double-entendres as Goliath catches her and Charlie kissing. The giant dances about skittishly, pinches their cheeks, and exits with a soubrette kick. Shortly afterwards the comedy director (wearing a long beard and smoked glasses) offers Charlie a job as an actor. Charlie, in his comedy role, ducks too successfully, and his boss and dignified actors on a neighboring set are hit with juicy pies. There is a chase, whose tempo increases until there is an explosion set by the vengeful strikers. Amid the collapsing sets Charlie and the girl kiss in the final close-up, where Charlie, flouting another convention, winks at his camera audience. (Chaplin often looks directly at the camera for intimate effects.)

Chaplin's next Mutual, "The Rink," a popular and fast-moving comedy, exhibits his agility and grace. In this picture he is a waiter who spends his lunch hours at the roller-skating rink. At one skating session, spinning around gracefully, he observes Edna being annoyed by the flirtatious Mr. Stout, whom he upsets in what starts a general scramble. Later Mr. Stout and Edna, Mrs. Stout and *her* partner in flirtation, and Charlie (posing as Sir Cecil Seltzer) all turn up unexpectedly at a skating party. Consternation follows. The ensuing action rings in every variety of fall, every species of mayhem, and ends in a grand chase in which Charlie makes his escape by hooking his cane on an automobile rear and being towed to safety.

The fast but delightfully graceful action is flavored with delicious comic bits. In one scene he mixes drinks to a wonderfully apposite "shimmy" rhythm; in another he unknowingly places a broiler cover over a live cat which he serves to the startled diner. (Imitations and variations of this gag have been legion). Then there is his super-gallant kissing of Edna's hand; his dashing party entrance, shoulders aslant and flicking ashes into his hat; his hat tipping by pressures against the wall. (It would be hard to say who invented this gag which was often later worked by W. C. Fields.) Other prime comedy bits occur in the melee when, falling upon Mrs. Stout (played by Henry Bergman), Charlie decorously pulls down her skirt; and his attempts to retain his balance by rotating his hands like an electric fan.

"Easy Street," released in January 1917, is the most famous of the Chaplin Mutuals. Though not as hilariously funny as some, it has the most cleverly worked-out story, in which some have read social criticism and others a satire on puritanism. Charlie, a derelict, wanders into a Mission. Reformed by the minister and the angelic organ player, his first act is to return the collection box he had stolen.

Gang war on Easy Street, the toughest section of the city, rises to a crescendo, with policemen carried back on stretchers, like soldiers from a battlefield. Help is needed and Charlie gets a job on the force. The very first day on his beat he encounters the leading gangster, whose appearance alone is enough to clear the street. The giant bully and the new cop size each other up. Charlie, at the alarm box, nervously tries to put in a call with the bully listening in. To deceive him, Charlie "plays" the receiver like a musical instrument and "looks through" it like an eyeglass. When the bully picks it up to take a look, Charlie gets in a lick with his club. As the sneering bully bends his head for more futile blows, Charlie tries to pacify him. In another display of his strength, the bully bends the gaslight lamp-post. Climbing quickly on his back, Charlie fits the lamp over the bully's face to anesthetize him. With all the finesse of a physician, he feels the bully's pulse and turns on more gas.

The Easy Streeters are awed by the new policeman while regulars on the force continue to cringe before a neighboring kid. Other funny business includes Charlie's catching a poor woman stealing a ham—and then, overcome by her sobs, "borrowing" vegetables from a neighboring stand to round out her dinner. For thanks he receives a flowerpot dropped on his head from above. Dispensing charity with Edna, he visits a couple with ten small children all in one slum room. Eyeing the puny father Charlie feels his muscle and pins his badge on him. He then strews cornflakes before the children as if they were chickens in a barnyard.

Pursued by the bully, who has broken jail, Charlie finally subdues him by dropping a stove on his head. In another scene Edna is trapped in a dive and Charlie thrown down a manhole into the same room. Their plight seems hopeless when a dope fiend knocks Charlie on his hypodermic needle. The accidental injection produces superman results. He KO's the attacker, spins around and embraces Edna; then, with flying leaps, subdues the mob that hems them in.

The subtitle, "Love Backed by Force; Forgiveness Sweet, Bring Hope and Peace, to Easy Street," introduces the closing scene. The reformed Easy Streeters, including the bully and his wife in their Sunday best, walking sedately to the new Mission with Charlie and Edna joining in the procession.

"The Cure" is probably the funniest of the Mutuals, interlacing fast and hilarious action with subtle pantomime and agile grace. At times it resembles a ballet laid in a sanitarium. Charlie in a light coat and straw hat is wheeled to the spring to take the water cure. The first comic sequence is a mixup in a revolving door with a gouty man whose tender foot is caught. Charlie is given a shove and they go round and round unable to "get off." This is followed by a muscle-feeling sequence in which a pretty nurse is involved. Urged by an attendant to feel his muscle as proof of the effects of the water cure, Charlie also feels the nurse's muscle. Then considering leg muscles as important to feel as arm muscles, he reaches toward the girl—but playfully feels his shoe instead. In another scene Charlie spills his spa water—and blames the puddle on a toy dog.

The gouty man, who happens to wear a fantastic beard, reappears and starts a flirtation with Edna. Charlie, seated between them, mistakes the handwavings and the winks as meant for him. As he turns a love seat, spilling the giant on the floor, he is ordered out—until Edna intercedes for him.

Upstairs the bearded bellhop has been sampling Charlie's trunkful of liquor. The head of the institution orders another drunken bellhop to dispose of Charlie's liquor supply. He carries out the order by tossing the bottles into the spa whose waters then impart unexpected powers.

In a steamroom sequence Charlie assumes statuesque

poses each time the gouty man opens the curtain, finally dancing out daintily on his toes into the pool. In the massage room Charlie, watching a patient being pounded, raises the masseur's arm and proclaims him "the winner!" When his time comes, Charlie turns the treatment into a slippery wrestling match.

Pepped up by the spiked "water," two male invalids chase Edna whom Charlie rescues by deft use of his cane; then gallantly moves one of the "bodies" so that Edna may pass. A sampling of the water has its effects on him. He rests his foot on Edna's lap, sends the gouty man head-first into the pool, gets caught again in the revolving door, which sends him spinning around (photographed in fast motion) until he falls into the pool. Next morning Edna explains as he holds an ice cake on his head. After Charlie vows to reform, the couple stroll forward—to his last ducking in the pool.

"The Immigrant" is another Chaplin triumph which compares favorably with any of his later works. Sentiment and social satire are adroitly worked into the story. The entire last half is cleverly constructed around an elusive coin, in one of the longest variations on a single comedy incident ever portrayed on the screen, yet so skillfully managed that every moment seems natural and spontaneous. Slower paced than the other Mutuals, "The Immigrant" has drama in the comedy and comedy in the drama.

On a rocking ocean liner, jammed with immigrants, we first see Charlie from the rear, leaning over the rail. His head is down and his shoulders quiver in an apparent spasm of *mal de mer*. Then, with a sudden turn forward, he triumphantly displays a large fish he has just hooked. The next scene is dinner on the violently rocking boat, with the passengers tossed from one end of the

room to the other, and soup plates sliding from person
to person as each helps himself in turn.

To comfort two weeping women, mother and daughter,
who have just been robbed by a gambler, Charlie slips
his crap winnings in the girl's pocket. The suspicious
purser catches him as he is tempted to retain a bill or
two. But the girl, finding the money, frees him and gives
him tearful thanks. "The arrival in the Land of Liberty."
As the ship passes the Statue of Liberty, the passengers
are shoved and roped in like cattle, and Charlie takes a
quizzical second look at the statue.

Ashore, "Later—hungry and broke," he picks up a
coin, which slips through his torn pocket. He enters a
restaurant, where a bullying waiter orders him to remove his hat, which Charlie finally does by making it
bounce up into the air. Then he pantomimes musical
fruit (beans), which he delicately masticates one by one.

Suddenly he spies the girl sitting alone across the
aisle. He hugs her and leads her over to his table.
Clasping her hands, he discovers she is clutching a black-
bordered handkerchief and so learns of her mother's
death. With a look of infinite sympathy he lowers her
hand. After a poignant pause their spirits revive. Offi-
ciously Charlie orders food for Edna. As they eat, six
waiters manhandle a customer who, Charlie is informed,
"was ten cents short." Just then he discovers his own
loss. An old tramp who has picked up the coin, enters.
He hands it to the waiter, who drops it to the floor and
steps on it. As he turns, it is deftly covered by Charlie's
foot. The waiter, securing the coin, bites it and finds it
to be counterfeit.

The slumped and despairing Charlie is given another
lease on life when an artist, there in search of unusual
models, takes an interest in the couple. When Charlie's
bill is presented he and the artist wrestle for it with ex-

aggerated Alphonse and Gaston courtesy. The artist gives
way too soon and Charlie is stuck with the bill. He gets
out of this dilemma by putting his check over the tip
left by the artist. Outside the restaurant Charlie asks
for and receives an advance of a couple of dollars from
the artist. He promptly puts the money to use at a "marriage license" bureau, across whose threshold he carries
the coyly protesting girl.

"The Adventurer," the last and perhaps the most popular of the famous Mutuals, was photographed at and
near Santa Monica in July 1917. It is old-time screen
comedy at its best and most typical—all wild chases, slapstick, and clever pantomime.

Charlie, an escaped convict, emerges from the sand
into a guard's rifle. He does a "double take" and buries
his head again. As the guard dozes, he scales a cliff with
lightning rapidity (fast-motion photography), only to
bump into other guards, whom he eludes with miracu-
lous agility, sliding eel-like under their legs. In a borrowed bathing suit he rescues two women from drowning
along with the hulking but cowardly suitor of the
younger woman. The two women invite Charlie, "the
gallant sportsman," to stay over at their house. Waking
next morning in striped pajamas that flash a frightening
reminder of his prison garb, he receives another chilling
reminder as he touches the brass bars of the bed.

Downstairs a ritzy party is in progress. Charlie, thirsty
for more refreshment, bumps his empty glass into another guest's full one, thus refilling his own, and apologizes grandly for the apparent collision. There is another
reminder of his past when the butler uncorks a bottle.
Charlie puts up his hands—then nonchalantly covers the
gesture by smoothing his hair. Joining dancers upstairs,
Charlie takes Edna to a balcony where they eat ice-
cream. Charlie has a mishap with his portion, drop-

ping the ball down his pants front. By his facial expression one follows its path downward. It lands on the bare back of the mother below. As it slides down her fashionable decolleté, the screaming woman slaps the man with her who tries to reach for the icy lump.

Prison guards arrive. During the chase up and down stairs Charlie, donning a lampshade, "freezes" as the guards rush by. Pinning the jealous suitor between sliding doors, Charlie leaps over the balcony. He kisses Edna's hand and apologizes. As a guard grabs him he introduces him politely to Edna; the guard lets go to shake her hand—and Charlie takes off again.

million-dollar contract and first marriage

Toward the end of his Mutual contract, Chaplin was offered a million dollars by the same company, for another series of twelve. Monetarily this was a better offer than the one he accepted since the million dollars was offered him clear, as straight salary, and Mutual was to bear all production costs. He signed, instead, with the newly formed First National Circuit (J. D. Williams, President) because he was given greater range and freedom in the making of his pictures.

The contract received world-wide publicity. It gave him a million dollars, plus a $15,000 bonus for signing, for eight pictures to be made within eighteen months. They were not to run under 1600 feet. If they ran over 2300 feet, he was to receive a proportionate increase and other financial inducements.

But Chaplin was now to be his own producer and bear the costs. He was to make the films in his own studio for the new releasing company, which had been formed partly to combat Adolf Zukor's domination of the industry with his powerful Paramount organization. First National was to advance $125,000 to make each negative, the sum including Chaplin's salary. Should the picture run longer than two reels, First National was to advance $15,000 for each additional reel. First National was also to defray the cost of prints, advertising, and other incidentals. Distribution costs were figured at thirty per cent of total rentals. After all costs had been recouped, Charlie and First National were to divide the profits equally.

On finishing his last Mutual, "The Adventurer," Chaplin took a much-needed vacation in Hawaii. He was accompanied by his secretary, Tom Harrington, Edna Purviance, and Rob Wagner, a professor of Art and Greek and author of "Film Folk." Wagner hoped to do a biography of Chaplin during the trip but had to be content with a few articles. Chaplin's vacation was rather brief. A little golf at which he was mediocre, a few plunges into the surf at Waikiki, and he had had enough. He was restless to get back to work.

On his return to Hollywood in October, he and his brother broke ground for a new studio at the corner of La Brea and Sunset Boulevard. The five-acre lot on which it was located was then on the outskirts of Hollywood and more than a mile beyond the studio section. Today the site straddles the center of Hollywood, a block from Grauman's Chinese Theatre. Purchased for $34,000, it is now worth over a million. Its La Brea Avenue front is camouflaged as a row of English cottages. A residence and tennis court face Sunset Boulevard. The studio itself faces south on De Longpre Avenue. For some years the stage was an open-air platform with girders supporting diffusers. Roofed over in the twenties, it is today a modern, sound-proof studio. All Chaplin's pictures since 1918 have been made here.

As a precaution against the swarm of imitators and the flood of revivals, his First National films carry his signature on the opening title with the statement, "None genuine without this signature." This opening title is usually decorated with a drawing. The subtitles have a chain border with the First National trade-mark below.

Chaplin announced that the new series would concentrate on character. They show a marked advance in every respect. More time was spent on each picture. Scenes were worked at till they were perfected. There was constant experimenting. The Chaplin screen character becomes gentler; the supporting characters are less caricatured; settings and action are more realistic. For various reasons the eight films of the First National Series took five years to make. They include some of Chaplin's greatest and most popular works along with some failures. Only three, "A Dog's Life," "Shoulder Arms," and "Sunnyside," were filmed in the first eighteen months.

The First Nationals were made with virtually the same company he had assembled for the Mutuals. Sid Chaplin appeared in several; and, among other additions, was "Chuck" Riesner, arrived from vaudeville to serve both as actor and associate director.

Soon after America entered the war, thousands of letters poured into the studio demanding that Chaplin enlist. A considerable number came from England, for he was still a British subject. Reflecting the war hysteria many were abusive and threatening. White feathers were enclosed in some of the envelopes from abroad. An examination establishing that Chaplin did not meet the army's physical requirements (he is five feet four and then weighed 130 pounds), was not sufficient to counteract the hysteria. As late as 1921, when he visited England, it was still simmering. Responsible notables, including a minister, pointed out Chaplin's value in sustaining morale. Had he done military services an Allied army would have gained an indifferent soldier but would have lost an invaluable morale booster. His films cheered many millions on both the battle and the home fronts. Undoubtedly, the envy inevitably incited by fame and money partly accounted for the persistent attacks.

After completing his first film for the new company, Chaplin put in two months touring for the Third Liberty Loan. With him were Douglas Fairbanks and Mary

Pickford. On April 8, 1918, a crowd approaching thirty
thousand packed the streets around the Sub-Treasury
building at Wall Street to hear him speak from its steps.
The exuberant "Doug" led the ovation by hoisting Chaplin on his shoulders. After being received in the White
House by President Wilson, himself a movie "fan," Chaplin danced with Marie Dressler before more than
sixty-five thousand delirious Washington residents, many
of whom bought bonds on the spot.

Touring the South by himself, Chaplin helped swell
bond sales in Dixie. One incident in this campaign
proved unpleasant though amusing. In New Orleans a
former Secretary of the Treasury, also on tour in the
bond drive, insisted on having his name printed above
that of a "vulgar movie actor." The issue was settled by
arranging separate appearances, Chaplin in the afternoon
and the dignitary at night. The "vulgar" movie actor
drew an audience of forty thousand; the dignitary drew
four hundred. Soon after, Chaplin, tiring of the tour,
physically, mentally, or both, canceled the remaining
schedule and returned to Hollywood. For his contribution he did not go entirely unrewarded. His visits to
training camps, during the tour, provided the material
for "Shoulder Arms."

An additional contribution (made also by other prominent movie figures), was a propaganda short made for
and donated to the government for its Liberty Loan
drives. It was distributed in the fall of 1918 without
rental charge to all theatres in the United States. It was
called "The Bond" and it explained itself as follows:
"There are different kinds of Bonds: the Bond of Friendship; the Bond of Love; the Marriage Bond; and most
important of all—the Liberty Bond." It is rather interesting for its technique and characteristic Chaplin touches.
In each skit simple, white, stylized properties were set up
against a black drop. In one allegorical scene Edna

Purviance appeared as the Statue of Liberty; in other scenes she led Charlie to the altar. Charlie performed in character, hanging his cane on the prop moon, and a little cupid's arrows bind him and Edna together.

In the summer of 1918, as he was starting "Shoulder Arms," Chaplin met Mildred Harris at a party. She was then sixteen years old and had been acting since her tenth year at the Ince studio where her mother was wardrobe mistress. She had appeared in a few Griffith-Triangle films, and was now with Universal. At Universal Lois Weber, one of Hollywood's few women directors, had written and directed such sensational "problem" pictures as "Hypocrites," featuring allegory in the nude, and "Where Are My Children," a birth-control drama with Tyrone Power, Sr. She had starred Mildred in a series of somewhat milder "woman-angle" films: "For Husbands Only," "The Price of a Good Time," "Borrowed Clothes," etc.

Chaplin's infatuation with the young blue-eyed blonde began at their first meeting. It was natural that the girl's head should be turned by the attentions of the screen's richest and best-known actor who, at twenty-nine, was physically extremely attractive as well. According to her later statements, Chaplin was "wonderful" and "so fatherly" and "acted to me as though I had been a mere child." She was living with her mother at the time, in the Cadillac hotel in Venice (California).

When the affair took on a serious cast Mildred's mother expressed objections to their marriage, which she wanted deferred until her daughter was a little older. Chaplin used to sit in his car for hours outside the Universal studio waiting for her appearance. One day Griffith, seeing them together, exclaimed, "Mildred, why don't you marry Charlie? He'd make a nice husband for you"; and turning to Chaplin, "Charlie, wouldn't she make a

wonderful wife for you?" Mildred said she did not want
to marry until she was twenty-two or twenty-three.
Charlie said she was silly but when she asked him when
he planned to marry he replied, "Never." Suddenly, however, they married (October 23, 1918), at the home of
Rev. James Myers in Los Angeles. It took Hollywood,
the world, and even intimate friends, by surprise. No
importance had been attached to their comparatively
few public appearances together.

After a honeymoon of a week at Catalina Island the
couple settled in their new home at 2000 De Mille
Drive in the hilly Lachman Park section of north Hollywood. Marjorie Daw, a young actress who grew up with
Mildred, described the new home in a newspaper article
as a "symphony in lavender and ivory, exquisite in
every detail." "I intend to have a happy home," Mildred
is quoted as saying, "and realize that the trouble with
most love affairs is that romance dies out after marriage
and is supplanted by commonplace things. I determined
that this should never be." In the couple's plans, a trip
around the world, "with not so much as a movie camera
in sight," was to follow two years of work.

Belying a namby-pamby appearance, Mildred proved
to be headstrong. In January 1919 we find her "agitated"
because her employers failed to accord financial recognition to the added value of her new name (she was now
billed as Mildred Harris Chaplin). She refused to continue working and her doctor ordered her to the mountains for a rest.

A son was born in the summer of 1919, a malformed
baby who lived but three days. For a time the mother's
life was also despaired of. They buried the child in a
Hollywood cemetery under the simple inscription, "The
Little Mouse," the mother's name for him. Chaplin later
told a friend that the undertaker had fixed a little prop

smile on its face although the baby had never smiled. He was to remember the infant much longer than the mother who gave it birth.

Mildred was to complain that Chaplin's love for her died together with their baby. According to some of Chaplin's intimates, however, his love had died before their marriage. They had little in common. The rather shallow child-wife could not comprehend her more complex husband. She tried to domesticate him into an average husband, little understanding his devotion to his work. There were long periods of silence between them. Chaplin leased another house at 674 South Oxford Drive, near Wilshire Boulevard, for his wife, and then soon left to take quarters at his club. The failure of the marriage had been foreseeable from the start.

Early in 1920, several months after the separation, charges and countercharges began to appear in the press. Chaplin was declared "cruel" and was accused of desertion and nonsupport. "He humiliated me before my servants," Mildred pouted. "Isn't that cruelty?" Chaplin pointed to fifty thousand dollars in canceled checks as proof that he had not neglected her. That sum, she replied, covered household expenses for their entire married life. "I do not want a divorce, neither do I want Mr. Chaplin's money, but I must have support." Next she blamed her unhappiness on a woman acquaintance of Chaplin's before the marriage. Should Chaplin bring suit for divorce, she intimated that she would contest the action with a countersuit, naming a co-respondent. "There is another woman back of all this," she charged with tears in her eyes. "I still love Charlie to death," but she protested that she did not want to hold an unwilling man.

On April 8, 1920, the papers reported fisticuffs between Chaplin and Louis B. Mayer, who was by now producing the Harris pictures in addition to the Anita

Stewart films. The encounter was at the Alexandria Hotel where Mayer, in a party of twelve including Miss Stewart, and Chaplin, in a smaller group, sat at nearby tables. Notes were exchanged and the two men met in the lobby. There was a heated discussion between them over terms offered for settlement that Miss Harris—and apparently Mayer—considered niggardly. "Take off your glasses," Chaplin ordered. Mayer did so and Chaplin hit him in the face. Mayer returned the blow and Chaplin went down. Friends and hotel employees intervened. Jack Pickford took Chaplin in charge and sent him home. "I only did what any man would have done," was Mayer's smug description of his "protection" of a commercial property.

Chaplin continued to avoid his wife. Mildred is said to have often waited, huddled in her parked car at a corner past which Kono drove her husband to the Athletic Club in Los Angeles, hoping for a glimpse or a word from him. At the suggestion of her friend, Anita Stewart, she tried arousing his jealousy. It was arranged to have George Stewart, Anita's brother, dine several nights a week at Mildred's home.

The effect of this news on Chaplin was opposite to what was intended. Hopeful of learning the worst, to use as evidence for a divorce, Charlie and Kono, on three successive nights, tiptoed to the house to eavesdrop. They were disappointed to find nothing amiss. The spying ended when a detective chased them. Later, when Chaplin learned of a party given by Mildred on a chartered yacht, he hopefully plied its captain with liquor. Again he met with disappointment. The captain reported a most decorous evening; no one drunk; dancing to a victrola; and early to bed, the women in one cabin, the men in another.

August 1920 finally saw announcements of Miss Harris's suit for divorce accompanied by sensational accusations. "My allegations of cruelty refer to mental cruelty. Charlie did not beat me, but caused me to suffer great mental anguish by his neglect. I never knew where he was or what he was doing. He married me, and as soon as he married me he forgot all about me. He economized in caring for me when ill and preached economy even to and including the funeral arrangements. When I was able to leave the hospital and go home he would not go home with me." She charged that she bought clothes for her husband with her own money; and that her mother had darned and patched Chaplin's socks and pajamas. "Like all artists, Charlie loved bloom and life and youth. During the months before the baby came he was fretful and irritable—and when it did, he didn't seem interested in looking out for me."

Chaplin refused to reply to such "foolish charges." "We were not happy and I did what I thought was right by offering a generous settlement. She wouldn't take it. I'm not going to fight the case."

Chaplin's lawyer, Arthur Wright, warned that his wife could attach all his assets and might claim a share of company property. "The Kid," his most ambitious film up to that time, was on the verge of completion. At this point Chaplin's finances were in a depleted state. His Liberty Loan tour, domestic troubles, and other interruptions had slowed down his output. Payment of a judgment awarded to Essanay for alleged breach of contract, government taxes, and his three-hundred-thousand-dollar investment in "The Kid" had left his bank balance marginal.

One night Chaplin woke Kono and announced that they had to get "The Kid" out of the state. With the negative stuffed in an old suitcase they hurriedly drove by back roads and through desert heat to Salt Lake City, Utah. The laws of this state secured them from legal pro-

ceedings instituted in California. Arriving at a hotel un-
shaven, dirty, and with only a few cents between them,
they were at first refused a room, the clerk informing
them no cheap rooms were available. Telegraphing
brought money and clothes.

Chaplin's identity was revealed. He was reported to be
"resting." According to one rumor he was "through" and
was seeking another tenant for his studio. Chaplin announced that he would not contest the divorce provided
Miss Harris withdrew an order restraining him from
selling his latest picture. A reasonable financial settlement was finally made out of court. Miss Harris received
$100,000 and a share of community property. The divorce
was granted November 19, 1920.

Chaplin shipped "The Kid" to New York, and followed to put it in final shape for launching there. He
stayed at the Ritz Carlton, registering under his middle
name, Spencer, and savoring New York's night life.

The Chaplin marriage and divorce had been unfortunate, but thousands of marital mixups outside of Hollywood were no less unfortunate. However, as in the case
of the Pickford-Fairbanks divorces and marriage and the
Arbuckle and Taylor tragedies of the following year, the
newspapers dwelt luridly on the details.

No doubt much of what Miss Harris charged was true.
Chaplin is notorious for his moods. Sometimes he would
lock himself in his room for days, writing. He might retire to play his cello for hours or go out on long walks,
alone, until four in the morning. How could a rather
conventional young girl understand or suit such a husband? How could she grasp that his long silences were in
part symptoms of their mismating? That a man might be
so engrossed in his work seems never to have been
grasped by this simple, bewildered girl. The experience
must have affected Chaplin too; reporters commented on
his graying hair.

To finish the Harris saga, her last days of glory after the Mayer pictures were in De Mille's "Fool's Paradise" (1921). From this she slipped down through roles in minor films to the status of an "extra." Hers was the type of beauty which blossoms in the teens. She matured into a rather commonplace woman. She filed a petition for bankruptcy in 1922. The following year she married Everett T. MacGovern, a Florida real estate man by whom she had a son. After divorcing him she secured a few minor parts in the talkies, then went into vaudeville. In 1936 she married William P. Fleckenstein, a vaudeville producer. Finally she appeared in burlesque, not in strip tease but as a singer "fully gowned." One of her turns was a Greta Garbo imitation. In 1944, at the age of forty-one, she died of pneumonia after an operation, an unfortunate end to a rather unfortunate career.

"A Dog's Life"—first masterpiece

Chaplin's opening First National film, "A Dog's Life," was his best up to that time, his· first real masterpiece. The techniques he had been experimenting with and perfecting, these four years, were now applied with complete mastery; and his style was at the ripening point of fullness and flavor. Its special quality of the commingling smile and sigh characterized the picture throughout, instead of in flashes as in the previous "The Tramp," "The Vagabond," and "The Immigrant." Pathos is now emphasized in the three-reel "A Dog's Life." It is a prototype of his great features, "The Gold Rush" and "City Lights."

The treatment is realistic; caricature is sparing. In fact, "A Dog's Life" is conceived and played almost as straight drama. Its story line is firm and logical. It has suspense and clear plot resolutions. Its mixture of pathos and laughter derives from ingenuities and surprises in poignant situations, as Chaplin leads a "dog's life" almost literally, as well as figuratively.

Delluc, the French critic, acclaims "this pieta" as the cinema's "first complete work of art." (The Griffith classics, however, had not yet reached France when this was written.) Profound philosophy and social satire have been seen in "A Dog's Life" by other critics. The general parallel between the vagabond's life and the dog's life is made powerfully specific in the daring juxtaposition of the frantic scene in the employment office and the dog fight. Curiously enough, its (perfectly logical) happy ending—along with the omission of the cane—keeps "A Dog's Life" from being the most typical of Chaplin's pictures.

The gags and comedy routines in "A Dog's Life" are classic. The scene in the employment office, with Charlie always missing out, is pure ballet and extraordinary for its precision. Hilarious and beautifully timed, also, is the surreptitious cake-devouring scene at the lunch stand. Sidney Chaplin's pantomime here, as the proprietor, equals his brother's. The "puppet" sequence where Chaplin from behind a curtain, by deft manipulations of his hands under the arms of a knocked-out crook, continues negotiations with his partner, is outstanding. Incidentally, this gag has been much imitated. Harold Lloyd worked a variation of it in "The Freshman" (1925) and years later Laurel and Hardy repeated it in "Chumps at Oxford" (1940). Whether Chaplin invented it or it originated in circus clowning, this was its first screen use—and its most effective use, the camera facilitating its closest and most intimate presentation.

"A Dog's Life" has not been seen for many years. All Chaplin's films made since 1918 are his property and are revived at his choice and he has withheld this one. Duped prints cannot be shown legally. A few shots from this little gem of 1918 were used in King Vidor's "Cynara" (1932) with Ronald Colman, in a sequence showing theatregoers in England during World War I being entertained by Chaplin.

As the sun rises over the city, we see a tramp asleep beside a fence in a vacant lot. It is cold in the dawn breeze, and to stop the "draught" he stuffs a handkerchief in a knot-hole. "Scraps," a "thoroughbred mongrel," leading a similarly vagrant existence, is asleep in a basket by an ashcan. A hot-dog vendor sets up his stand on the other side of the fence. The smell awakens

Charlie, who serves himself a free lunch, through a hole in the fence.

He is about to begin eating when he sees a cop's face glaring over the back fence. Hastily Charlie returns the food. The cop tries to coax him out but Charlie resists the blandishments. When the cop enters from behind, Charlie eludes him by rolling through a gap under the fence into the street. When the cop returns to the street, Charlie rolls back into the lot. From there he reaches out to untie the policeman's shoe laces and stick him with a pin. After having exhausted the cop, as he thinks, by rolling in and out, he considers himself safe, raises to take a circus bow, only to have his outstretched hand touch the badge of another cop and his expression changes radically. However, he manages to escape.

Outside an employment office Charlie sees an offer of brewery jobs and rushes in, only to be knocked down and shoved off the bench by competing jobhunters. As the office is opened and a call is given, Charlie rushes forward but is shouldered from one window, and then from the other, just as he reaches each. He dashes madly back and forth only to miss out every time. Finally, just as he gets a place before a window, it shuts in his face. He skids into the clerk who comes out to rub off the blackboard. No more jobs.

Scraps, who also lives in dread of the big district cop, comes upon some food in the middle of the street. Immediately other dogs rush in from all sides to grab for it. Charlie, sitting disconsolately by the curb, fastidiously sifting trash, notes the growing looseness of his trousers. His attention drawn to the predicament of Scraps, he joins the dog fight, lifts up the victim, and runs down the street pursued by the howling animals. The melee causes a small riot with screaming women running in all directions and pushcarts tipping over. Though one attacking dog, fastening onto his coattail, gets away with a considerable section of his pants, Charlie and Scraps emerge victorious. Resting on a doorstep Charlie is licked by the affectionate mongrel. When Scraps fails to get at the milk in a half-filled bottle that Charlie finds nearby, Charlie helps out by dunking the dog's tail.

As a team, Charlie and Scraps feed better than when alone. They saunter over to a food stand dispensing freshly made cakes and sausages. Charlie engages the proprietor's attention—and Scraps swipes a string of sausages. Charlie then attends to his own needs wolfing cakes down whole at each turn of the proprietor's back. The proprietor becomes suspicious as the cakes vanish and he sees the dog licking his chops. When he is finally caught Charlie pretends to be brushing flies off the plate. As he is about to make away with the last cake, he sees the cop watching him through the back window. Replacing the cake, Charlie ducks off and the cop is smacked with a big wurst intended to down the fugitive.

At night Charlie seeks shelter in the Green Lantern Cafe—"a tender spot in the Tenderloin." Hiding Scraps in his baggy pants, Charlie threads his way through wildly dancing couples, the dog's tail wagging out of a hole in his trousers. At a stop near the orchestra, the wagging tail beats the drum to the mystification of the drummer. "A new singer sings an old song." A simple country girl, seeking a career, comes out on the stage and her drunken auditors applaud her awkward and nervous performance by crying into their beer.

With a forlorn smile to Charlie, the girl awakens new life in him. He leads the girl, who is starved for kindness, out on the dance floor, only to come to grief on a large wad of chewing gum. Charlie's struggles to free himself is a wonderful passage of pulls and falls, hilariously complicated by the towing dog. Further comic business follows upon a collision with the diminutive partner of a fat lady equipped with an elastic muff which he snaps, getting into an altercation with her puny escort. He dances away to a table, and when the bartender comes up plays innocent before a half-empty glass. Unable to produce cash, however, he gets the "bum's rush" through the front door.

In the next sequence a pair of crooks, after "rolling" a rich drunk, seek a hiding place for the loot to evade the police. They bury the stolen wallet in Charlie's bedroom—the vacant lot to which Charlie returns to sleep with Scraps as his pillow. The crooks then go on to the Green Lantern to celebrate. One of them shows an interest in Edna, who repulses him. The boss, anxious about his customers' good will, fires the girl. Edna, coming out of her dressing room with her suitcase, asks the boss for her pay, is refused, and falls weeping on the table.

Meanwhile Scraps, foraging for food, digs up the wallet. Fortified by this wealth Charlie returns to the Green Lantern. He suffers a minor defeat trying to roll a cigarette in "tough guy" style. He sees the weeping Edna and learns that she has been fired. After a shrug he assumes the arrogance of a rich man in his orders to the waiter. He is observed by the crooks showing off the wallet. "We will settle down in the country," he tells Edna and pantomimes a happy future with marriage, a home, and no less than five little ones. The crooks put a rough end to that dream and once more Charlie finds himself in the gutter.

After Edna picks him up and dusts him off, Charlie steals back in an effort to regain what he considers his property. Crawling behind the bar, he takes a position next to the curtained booth where the two crooks are again celebrating. Charlie pulls out a mallet from under his hat, draws the curtains, and comes down with the mallet on the head of one of the crooks. Charlie promptly slips his own arms through the stunned man's coat from behind, gestures to the other man to keep quiet, lifts a glass, and holds his hand out for his share of the money. Each time the stunned man comes to,

Charlie stiffens him again with a poke in the jaw. Pocketing his part of the swag, Charlie strokes the victim's
mustache, rubs his hands as drinks are poured, and goes
through other lavish puppetry. Finally Charlie motions
the other crook closer and gives him the bottle on the
head. As the two crooks collapse on the table, Charlie
enters through the curtain and retrieves the wallet.

Wriggling back behind the bar, he is caught between
the legs of the bartender who pulls him up by the hair.
Once more the wallet changes hands. In the meanwhile
the two crooks revive. The wallet passes like a basketball,
from hand to hand, with Charlie finally snatching it and
dashing out.

There is a chase and wild shooting, with the lunch
wagon the scene and the suffering owner, whose hat is
shot off, as chief victim. He and Charlie pop up and
down behind the counter together and alternately.
Charlie tests the situation by raising a plate which is
promptly punctured with bullets. As the crooks storm
the wagon and choke Charlie, his faithful dog makes off
with the fallen wallet. The melee ends with the crooks in
the cop's hands, the counterman adorned with a beautiful black eye and his dishes neatly drilled through—and
Charlie off with Scraps and Edna, and the wallet, headed
for a new life.

"When dreams come true." The camera irises in on the
interior of a picturesque little farm. In the cottage Edna
prepares tea at the fireplace. Out in a large field the
straw-hatted Charlie is planting a long furrow, digging
little holes with his finger and inserting a seed in each
hole, one at a time. His wife calls. Gathering up his fork
and rake, he enters and the couple kiss playfully. Then
he carries her on his back to a basket by the fire; they
kiss and sigh as they look fondly down. The camera tilts
to reveal a litter of puppies, and Scraps, the proud
parent.

XII

"Shoulder Arms"

"Shoulder Arms" won phenomenal popularity
in 1918–1919 and during frequent revivals in the twenties. Until "The Gold Rush" was released, "Shoulder
Arms" was generally considered Chaplin's masterwork.
And even then many Chaplin connoisseurs preferred the
older picture because of its faster pace and more compact
humor. Filmed in mid-1918, during a crucial period of
World War I, Chaplin's friends advised him to withhold
its release for fear that its satirical thrusts at army life
and the war, and other audacious touches, might be
deemed in "bad taste." "Shoulder Arms" was finally, and
with considerable trepidation, released on October 20,
1918, three weeks before the armistice. Cautious trade-
magazine writers hastened to assure the public that
" 'Shoulder Arms' does not detract from the dignity of
soldiering" and "never oversteps to the point of ridicul-
ing the service." Their worries proved groundless. There
was no adverse criticism and its unprecedented world-
wide success made motion-picture history.

"Shoulder Arms" is an unusual mixture of realism and
fantasy, flavored with Chaplin's characteristic touches of
slapstick, satire, irony, and pathos. Its opening distils the
essence of the average man's reaction to soldiering—the
regimentation, the hardships, the wry humor, the home-
sickness, the suffering. Its touches of slapstick and burlesque merely relieve the utter realism of the approach.

Without any bombast, flag-waving, or stimulation of ha-treds, "Shoulder Arms," although a comedy, provides a truer picture of World War I—thanks to Chaplin's sharp observation and oblique approach—than more ambitious "epics" of the period. It is Everyman at war and, in the words of Jean Cocteau, "It moves like a drumroll."

After the realistic opening, the irony and satire sharpen. Touches of fantasy are introduced: the under-water berths in the trench; the use of the enemy's marks-men to open bottles, by holding them up as targets; the opening and closing of a door that stands in a diswalled ruin; etc. Gradually the fantasy intensifies pushing cre-dulity to the limit, to parallel the insanity of war—pushes until the bubble bursts.

Its scenes became the talk of the time. Few pictures before or since have been so widely discussed so that even people who missed the film were acquainted with its major episodes. Particularly talked about were the sequence in the flooded trench; the business with the limburger-cheese "grenade"; Chaplin's vicarious enjoy-ment, over a comrade's shoulder, of a letter from home; the tree-camouflage sequence; the simple and eloquent "Poor France" scene of the dejected girl in the doorway of her ruined home; the stars-and-stripes pantomimed by which Charlie identified himself to the girl; and the fantastic capture of the Kaiser. The picture influenced many other films. The mail scene, with its genuine pa-thos, was borrowed direct in "The Big Parade" of 1925.

Technically, too, the picture was an advance over Chap-lin's previous work. As in "A Dog's Life" lights are some-times used for effects, not merely for illumination on dark days. There are advances in cutting, double exposure by split screen, iris effects, etc.

Five reels were planned but the picture was cut down to three. Existing stills indicate the elimination of se-quences showing Chaplin as a family man with three kids, his induction into the army, and the subsequent feteing of Charlie by Allied leaders. In that sequence Poincaré was among the speakers eulogizing him and the King of England was shown snipping a button off his uniform as a souvenir. Cut down to three reels, the film's pace and impact were magnified.

It is impossible to designate a "best" Chaplin. Motion pictures, like other creations, look different in each period through changes in intellectual and emotional climates. Today, perhaps, "Shoulder Arms" might seem sketchy and hurried in its effects and some of its humor might seem dated. Nevertheless, it is sure of a place among Chaplin's masterworks and in the art of all time.

In the first scene Charlie is a member of "the awkward squad" in a training camp. We see him at drill and the sergeant ordering "Put those feet in!" Trying to obey the drill commands, Charlie tangles himself up as the rest of the squad march off. He catches up with the others, to go into a sequence of in-turning and out-turning of his toes accompanied by barked commands. At dismissal Charlie hops to his tent to fall exhausted on his cot. (Fade out.)

"Over There." Iris in on trench. Charlie staggers in under knapsacks, rifle, blankets, household utensils, etc. Tapping an officer on the shoulder for directions, he walks forward (moving camera) to a sign labeled: "Broadway and Rotten Row." The new recruit is put through an inspection by a sergeant who gets his fingers caught in provident Charlie's rat trap. With his billowing equipment he gets stuck in the dugout door and is helped through, finally, by a boot from the sergeant. His first act, when he reaches his quarters, is to hang up a nutmeg grater to scratch his back on, the "cooties" having already "occupied" him.

The scene shifts to the enemy trenches where a pint-size, goose-stepping German officer carries on an inspection, consisting mainly of kicks. Back in Charlie's trench, he and the sergeant enjoy "a quiet lunch" during a shelling. Charlie is told to make himself at home as his helmet bounces around with the detonations.

Later Charlie is standing guard in pouring rain, dreaming of home. In a split screen effect we see, on the left, a New York street scene dissolving to a bartender serving drinks. As Charlie smiles, the vision fades back to the muddy trench. The guard is changed, and the miserable soldier marches to his bed and lies down—all in rhythm.

A postman brings "news from home." Charlie rushes forward, only to hear everybody's name called but his own. Sitting on his bunk, he leans disconsolately on his elbow. As Sid and another soldier open food packages, Charlie, refusing snacks offered by his buddies, nibbles the cheese in his trap. Sauntering outside, moodily he looks over the shoulder of a man reading a letter and reacts vicariously as if it were his own, smiling when the other man smiles, or registering concern. He leans forward for a closer look, smiles again—until the soldier glares and moves away.

The mailman returns, "This must be yours." Charlie frantically opens his package—to extract dog biscuit and limburger cheese. Protecting himself with a gas mask, he tosses the cheese like a grenade across No Man's Land into the enemy trenches. It lands on the face of the little German officer just as he is toasting their early arrival in Paris.

"Bedtime" finds the little dugout half filled with water. Only the sergeant's head and his feet, with a frog perched on one of them, show above the water. Charlie lifts his pillow out of the water, to fluff it before he lies down, then pulls the sopping blanket over him. The sergeant's snoring is so effective that when Charlie scoops water over to his open mouth, a geyser results. Splashing back at him, the sergeant orders him to "Stop rocking the boat!" A lighted candle comes floating by and Charlie blows it, like a little sailboat, toward Sid's protruding toes, and plays innocent when the hotfooted man awakes. Charlie hunts a more comfortable spot at the other end of the bunk only to have his head submerge. With the help of a phonograph horn as a breathing tube he settles down to a submarine snooze.

As zero hour approaches next morning Charlie finds that his identification tag is number 13. Pulling a mirror out of his pocket he primps as a means of bracing his courage. Ordered "over the top," Charlie rushes heroically up the ladder which hurtles him back into the mud.

"13 not so unlucky." He is next seen herding a line of captured Germans, among them the little officer, whom Charlie takes in his lap for a spanking. This earns him the admiration of a huge German soldier, who shakes his hand. Asked how he captured them, Charlie makes the now classic reply, "I surrounded them."

"Poor France." Iris in on a dejected, shawled French girl sitting in the doorway of her shattered home. At another explosion, she lowers her head into her hands. Iris out.

Charlie and the sergeant, "Two of a kind," indulge in a little sharpshooting from within their trench. To open a bottle Charlie holds it up in the range of obliging enemy snipers who shoot off the top. A cigarette is lit in the same manner. Charlie chalks his tally of hits as if he were merely trapshooting or playing billiards. When, peering over the top, his helmet is shot off, he erases the last mark. Then he fires at an unseen airplane. His eyes follow it down to a "crash"—and another mark appears on his scoreboard. There is a call for volunteers and Charlie outstrips his pal. When told "You may never return," he magnanimously yields his place, but the sergeant as magnanimously refuses—and Charlie receives the congratulations and farewells.

"Within the enemy's lines," Charlie is camouflaged as a tree trunk, his arms simulating branches, his eyes peering cautiously through a hole. The moving tree scratches its "rear" with one of its branches. It "freezes" stiffly as a squad of Germans march by. Three Germans camp near by. Hunting firewood, one approaches with an axe. He is about to chop Charlie down when he gets a poke in the rear. On another attempt he gets a knock over the head. A second soldier, puzzled, comes to investigate and is flattened alongside his comrade. The third suffers the same fate.

Meanwhile the sergeant, performing "more heroic work," is caught telephoning back to his line. About to be shot, he is saved by the Charlie-tree. Then a heavy German chases the moving tree into the woods. The confused German shoots a real tree, then finds his gun butt against the false tree, which gives him a poke before it steps off the stump on which it has mounted. Through the thickly wooded forest, the Charlie tree zigzags around the real trees, pursued by the fat German who bayonets numerous trees trying to locate the spy who becomes "invisible" at will. The camouflage is so perfect that not only the German but the audience is continually being fooled. Charlie finally escapes through a sewer pipe, in which his stout pursuer gets stuck.

Next Charlie enters through the door of the French girl's wrecked home and carefully closes it, although the walls are gone. Ascending to the second floor, open to the sky, he pulls down the shade of the remaining window frame and drops on the bed. The girl enters and, believing the sleeping man to be wounded, begins to soothe him, while Charlie steals sly glances at her. When she discovers him to be undamaged, she asks, "Parlez-vous français?" He shakes his head, and the girl becomes alarmed. Whereupon Charlie makes a German mustache gesture, points to himself and shakes his head. The girl is relieved. Displaying his uniform, he says, "Me American soldier," but she does not understand. He makes an "eagle" with his hands, but she still does not understand. Then he picks up a brick, hits his head, points to "stars," "draws" stripes, and waves his hand like a bandleader. The girl smiles and salutes the "sammy" who kisses her hand.

Germans arrive below. The girl denies hiding an American, but Charlie, upstairs, breaks a pitcher against the bed. Then he bids a mock farewell to the girl and makes an imposing but nervous descent. Disarming an officer, Charlie escapes as the remains of the house collapse on the enemy. The girl is arrested for aiding the Allies.

In his flight Charlie stumbles on the enemy headquarters where the girl is held. Climbing down the chimney and out of the fireplace he arms himself with a hot poker and chases into a closet an officer who is menacing the girl. As troops line up outside, Charlie applies the poker to a German descending the chimney.

"The Kaiser Visits the Front." Charlie dashes into the closet as the Kaiser enters and asks the Crown Prince where the officer is. Charlie emerges buttoning up the uniform he has just borrowed from the locked-in officer. To the girl he exclaims "Ja!" Charlie and the girl pass through the line of soldiers outside. Though he jumps when they put their rifles at ease, he exhibits his nonchalance by scratching a match on the Kaiser's automobile, to the great annoyance of the chauffeur.

"His pal captured again," Charlie pulls the sergeant to one side and reveals himself, while pretending to rough-house him. Ordering the soldiers away, Charlie gets a chance kick from the goose-steppers and returns one. Observing that the chauffeur has seen them greeting and embracing each other, the pals continue the bogus pun-

ishment performance. They then gag the suspicious chauffeur and lead the footman off at the point of a gun.

Thanks to "prompt action" the three allies, Charlie,
Sid, and the French girl, are now all in German uni-
forms. Charlie now outranks the sergeant whom he orders
on when the latter kisses the girl's hand. While the
gagged Germans struggle to loosen their bonds, the girl's
cap is pulled down and a mustache is painted on her
face with grease from the hub-cap. Kissing Charlie, she
leaves a smudge on his cheek.

"The Capture." The Kaiser and the Crown Prince enter the car and Charlie drives on at full speed. Word is
telegraphed ahead by the sergeant to the Allies. The
speeding car almost runs over two men. Then cheers and
embraces as Charlie arrives "bringing home the bacon."

"Peace on earth, good will to all mankind." Charlie is
carried about on his buddies' shoulders. The scene of
jubilation irises out and into the tent in the training
camp where two soldiers shake and bounce Charlie to
wake him. The "hero" scratches his head as the iris
closes.

two failures

On top of Chaplin's personal unhappiness in 1919 the two films he produced that year, "Sunnyside" and "A Day's Pleasure," were generally considered failures. But after the enormous success of "A Dog's Life" and "Shoulder Arms," almost any picture would have seemed an anticlimax.

In "Sunnyside" Chaplin experimented with a change of pace; in "A Day's Pleasure" he returned to tried-and-true comedy formulas. Neither picture has been revived in many years. "Sunnyside," however, would probably delight today's audiences, used to the mature Chaplin; and "A Day's Pleasure" would be rated with the better Essanays.

In 1919, however, the two films got a panning from both press and public. *Photoplay Magazine,* the screen's most influential journal at that time, and then presided over by the truculent James Quirk, pleaded editorially for Chaplin to "come back." Said Quirk, " 'Sunnyside' was anything but sunny; 'A Day's Pleasure' certainly not pleasure." Again the hint that the "Chaplin craze" was dying—this time for good, if he did not return to "comedy."

During 1919–1920, when only these two short Chaplin films appeared, his position was further endangered by the more regular output of rising rivals like Harold Lloyd, Larry Semon, Buster Keaton, and the unfadingly popular Fatty Arbuckle. After several years of his Lonesome Luke series, Lloyd had hit upon his tortoise-shell-"glass" character. In glasses and a pale make-up, he typified the small-town American boy whose earnestness and persistence overcame impossible obstacles. In these two years he made a dozen delightful comedies, filled with clever gags, among them "Captain Kidd's Kids," "Haunted Spooks," and "High and Dizzy."

Larry Semon offered entertaining stunts and acrobatics in "The Grocery Clerk," "The Fly Cop," and other pictures. And Buster Keaton returned from army service, to make a popular series featuring his "frozen faced," otherworldly zany, that included "Convict 13" and "The Scarecrow." Arbuckle's broad burlesque proved so successful in shorts that, in 1920, he ventured into features making "The Round Up" and "The Life of the Party." However, with "The Kid," in 1921, Chaplin made his "come back."

"Sunnyside," neither comedy nor drama, is a gentle pastoral idyl containing little of the old slapstick. The Chaplin screen character was becoming more complex and his emotions more refined. Now he receives the kicks without retaliation. Satire was also intended, with the rural, Charles Ray type of films, popular at that time, as its butt. Although the story had a flawlessly logical construction and a polished production, movie audiences (in general) sat back through most of it, wondering when a laugh was in order.

Its highlight is, of course, Charlie's ballet with the nymphs in the delightful dream sequence which, by itself, is enough to make the picture memorable. On its subsequent release in Europe, "Sunnyside" evoked rhapsodies from Delluc and other French critics, who raved over its poetry, its lyricism, its deft touch. The dream sequence was compared to paintings of Corot. Even in the United States, the film was not without influence. The cow-herding scene introduced a new comedy situation—

something huge, beast or machine, getting out of the control of its simple-minded attendant. Keaton, Laurel and Hardy, Langdon, and others were to take it over in later films.

The tone of "Sunnyside," laid "some few years back," is set by the rural backgrounds. It begins with an iris in on the steeple of a small church and opens up to reveal the quiet little country town of Sunnyside. It boasts a real hotel appropriately named "Evergreen," from the verdant crop of grass in the lobby. The Hired Man is the all-in-one staff for the combination hotel and farm. The Hardhearted Boss is a slavedriver though professing to be a pious pillar of the church. Overwork and underpay is his principle. He drives the poor drudge to the point of exhaustion. Charlie goes to bed with his clothes on, to lose no time getting to work in the morning. His day starts at 4 A.M. and finishes at midnight. Oversleeping on this particular typical day, he moves his shoes on the floor to give the impression that he is already up. He fails to evade punishment, is kicked out of bed and gets a tongue-lashing.

To make it possible for him to do all his chores Charlie uses a wonderful array of home-made labor-saving devices. With the cow in the kitchen he is able to milk her directly into the coffee cups; he holds a hen over a frying pan so she can lay a fried egg. When he waits on table, the same day, he gets his pan in a tangle with the boss and draws further punishment.

Charlie's sole solace in his twenty-four-hour day is his quite hopeless love for Edna, the Village Belle, the neighboring farmer's daughter. Sugar dribbles on the counter as, in a dreamy daze, he serves her. Half out of pity, she tolerates his attentions.

One Sunday afternoon, driving the cows home from pasture, visions of his fair lady hold him spellbound at a fork in the road while the herd strays off. The moving camera follows the herd along the country lane and, through focusing on Charlie's funny walk, the low back-lighting casts shadows and fringing radiance, a pictur-esque rather than comic effect.

Charlie has no luck getting the cows back in forma-tion. He adds to his troubles by mistaking the back of a certain stout citizen for one of his strays.

One of the cows straggles into the church as the miserly boss is addressing a meeting. Charlie's hilarious efforts to coax the cow out fail and the wrathful boss threatens dire revenge. Finally Charlie jumps on the animal's back and steers her out, but for a longer and wilder ride than he intended, the cow making it impos-sible for him to dismount.

It is the ungovernable cow herself who attends to the dismounting. She bucks and Charlie sails overboard into a brook. Knocked unconscious, Charlie is the beneficiary of a dream rescue by a bevy of beautiful wood nymphs—four lovely, bare-limbed maidens in filmy Greek costumes. They perform a sylvan dance in the pastoral woodland setting.

Charlie joins them, twisting his hair into a Pan coiffure and piping through a daisy. Charmingly he burlesques the classic Greek dance à la Ballet Russe, with Nijinskite leaps and grotesque poses. Parts of it are virtually straight ballet which is danced with notable grace.

But even in dreams bad luck pursues Charlie. He stumbles into a bed of cactus—which accelerated his tempo, giving his dancing a delirous bacchanalian effect. His efforts to remove the prickles while maintaining his bland smile and keeping in step with his lovely partners, are richly amusing. The dance over, Charlie resumes his place in a flower bed where the maidens tend him. But, alas, the dream fades; Charlie regains consciousness; and the fair maidens bulge out into worldly creatures, headed by the vengeful boss, who pull him out of the brook with a rope.

Charlie visits Edna at her home and listens enraptured as she plays a parlor organ. Occasional sour notes do not bother him, but the arrival of her father sends him running.

Once more the somnolent village is disturbed—this time by an automobile accident in front of the hotel. A handsome city stranger is spilled out of his car in front of the hotel and is carried in for repairs. There is an amusing bit as the village doctor goes to work with Charlie imitating him. The convalescent City Slicker now starts a flirtation with the Village Belle to while away the time. Edna, in hair ribbons and in her Sunday best, is so smitten by the newcomer's dashing lovemaking, his stylish clothes, and his automobile, that she loses all awareness of her hired-man swain. Coming up with a bunch of flowers and peering through the window, Charlie sees her yielding to the slicker's blandishments. Charlie vividly pantomimes his disappointment with a woebegone expression and a crushing of the bouquet so hopefully gathered. As he leaves dejection virtually oozes from his dragging walk and drooping shoulders.

The despondent hired man, as his last hope, resolves to outdo the city slicker in elegance. Old socks over his shoes serve as spats; a candle in his cane competes with his rival's fancy stick which sports a concealed cigarette lighter. The result only produces ridicule from the other "rubes" and a definite break on the part of Edna. In jealous despair he is about to hurl himself before a passing auto when a blow by his boss awakes him and he finds he has been dreaming again. The City Slicker is departing; Charlie, escorting him to his auto, receives a big tip. Once again he is left in possession of the fair country maid, with the chastening knowledge that his unhappiness came from his own want of faith.

"A Day's Pleasure" is in an entirely different mood. A departure from the style of the last three films, it is a simple, realistic piece, recounting the mishaps of a family holiday outing—the sort of thing W.C. Fields later did on the stage and in his early sound films. It was made quickly for laughs alone and as such is successful, though at the time it was considered too mild and slow-paced for the Chaplin public. Much is made of the comedy device of repetition: A gag will be repeated over and over, the audience anticipating what is going to happen and laughing with the thrill of recognition— only to be pleasantly shocked with a surprise variation. Examples of this are the Ford car whose motor stops when it shouldn't, the folding chair with which Charlie patiently struggles, unfolding it only to have it collapse under him each time (a gag borrowed by Keaton and others). Perhaps some of these gags were overworked and the seasick scenes may be in bad taste, but the picture certainly has rewarding passages. The scene where Chaplin and the cop are stuck in the tar is particularly amusing.

Charlie, his wife, and two kids (dressed as miniature junior Chaplins) set out for a day of recreation in the family jalopy—a model-T Ford, of course. There is the usual trouble starting the motor of the stubborn "flivver." With each turn of the crank, mother and children bounce and shake. The auto out-shimmies the shimmy (the shuddering dance that was the ballroom rage of the period). When Charlie gets the motor running, every time he puts his foot on the running board the motor stops.

At last the car starts and does well up to its arrival at a busy intersection. Mistaking the traffic signals Charlie is about to turn when the cop bawls him out and sends him back. Waiting meekly at the head of a line of cars he stays motionless when the cop signals him to start and starts at the stop signal. Sent back once more the car stalls and traffic piles up behind it.

32 Chaplin with Thomas H. Ince, Mack Sennett and D. W. Griffith *ca.* 1916.

33 Charlie serenading Edna in "The Vagabond."

34 A scene from "One A.M.," the famous solo film.
35 The recalcitrant bed in "One A.M."

36 Eric Campbell, Charlie posing as Count Broko, and Edna Purviance as Miss Moneybags in "The Count."

37 and 38 Two scenes from the celebrated "The Pawnshop."

39 Charlie is puzzled by Edna disguised as a stage-
    hand in "Behind the Screen."
40 Edna and Charlie in "The Rink."
41 One of the accidents in "The Rink."

42 Nijinsky and troupe visit the Chaplin studio in 1916 during the shooting of "Easy Street." The famous dancer appears next to Chaplin. Others in the picture are Pierre Monteux, Lydia Lopokova, Richard Herndon, Eric Campbell and Edna Purviance.

chapter **VIII** cont.

chapter IX

43 Charlie as a policeman in "Easy Street."
44 The little policeman asphyxiates the giant bully
    (Eric Campbell) in "Easy Street."

45   47
46   48   Four scenes from "The Cure."

49 The arrival in the land of liberty, from "The Immigrant."
50 James T. Kelley, Eric Campbell, the broke Charlie, and Edna
Purviance in "The Immigrant."

5¹ 53
5² 54 Four scenes from "The Adventurer."

55 Douglas Fairbanks supporting Charlie and Mary Pickford (in costume for "Rebecca of Sunnybrook Farm"), 1917.

apter X

56 Charlie, Doug, and Mary clowning on the United Artists lot
during the making of Miss Pickford's "Through the Back
Door," 1921.

57 Mildred Harris in 1917 shortly before Chaplin
met her.

58   Mildred Harris and Conrad Nagel in "Fool's Paradise," 1921.

59 Cecil B. DeMille directing Mildred Harris in "Fool's Paradise," 1921.

60   Charlie and Scraps in "A Dog's Life."

61   The happy ending of "A Dog's Life."

chapter **XI**

The general mixup is complicated by the dropping of a crate from a truck upon the heads of two prosperous-looking passengers in an expensive car; and still more by the spilling of a barrel of hot tar by careless repairmen in front of the family automobile.

The usual cop-and-driver altercation is enlivened by the precarious angles at which Charlie and the two policemen, stuck in the tar, carry on the debate. One of the traffic cops unwittingly disposes of his partner by lifting a sewer cover with his tarry shoe. Suddenly the flivver tears loose and the family rides off triumphantly.

The next scene is on an excursion boat. On a last-minute errand off the boat Charlie returns just as she is pulling away. He gets aboard by using another unfortunate as a gangplank—a stout lady suspended by her hands and toes between wharf and boat.

Back on deck he gets the dance fever as a Negro jazz band plays a lively tune. But after a few steps with his wife the boat interrupts with a dance of its own as it enters rough water. Charlie, seasick, is tormented by a persistent buttered popcorn salesman.

All the passengers now feel the effect of the rocking boat. Charlie's tortures are intensified by the suggestive glissandos of the trombone player. Driven beyond endurance he grabs and pitches the offending instrument overboard. There follows the folding-chair gag. Patiently and persistently he tries to undo the contraption. No matter how he arranges it the chair collapses beneath him. After repeated trials he disgustedly sends it overboard after the trombone.

A violent lurch of the boat sends Charlie into the lap of a stout lady whose equally hefty husband has gone for a drink of water. Returning to find a stranger in his wife's lap he picks a fight from which Charlie eventually emerges the surprised victor; and the family disembarks after its day of dubious "pleasure."

Chaplin's method

By now Chaplin's method of working had crystallized and his films were the full artistic expression of a single mind. The basis of his technique had been derived, as we have noted, from D. W. Griffith via Mack Sennett: the reliance upon improvisation on the set instead of a written script, photographing scenes from many angles and retaking if necessary, narrative and dialogue in terms of action and pictorial effects, the use of revealing pantomime or what Griffith termed "attitudes," building up of effects through editing, etc.

Chaplin saw "The Birth of a Nation" nearly every week during its long Los Angeles run. Such scenes as the homecoming of the Little Colonel (where only the arm of the mother is shown reaching out and drawing her wounded son into the door of their damaged home) left their mark on cinematic expression. In his last years Griffith proudly repeated Charlie's comment that the couple of dead bodies in this film had been far more telling than the whole abattoir in "Gone With the Wind."

The inspiration for Chaplin's comedies came from incidents or characters observed in everyday life. A visit to a department store suggested "The Floorwalker"; observation of firehouse routines led to "The Fireman"; meeting Jackie Coogan inspired "The Kid"; encounters during his trip around the world furnished ideas for "Modern Times"; etc. All his films are built on real backgrounds or people, with the slight twists which render them funny or pathetic.

Working independently in his own studio and not under the rigid routine of a large corporation, operating on a small overhead and with no five-thousand-a-week salaries, Chaplin could afford to take his time and work according to his mood. With only a rudimentary idea in his head he concocted the story as he went along. Some pictures changed completely in the course of production. He improvised a scene or a series of gags, then discussed the results the next day in the projection room. A bit might be used or all of it might be reshot; or the whole project might be scrapped and some other idea substituted.

Since overrehearsing sometimes causes stilted action, Chaplin photographed scenes over and over in his striving for perfection. In "The Count" he is said to have spent three weeks on the scene where, dancing with the heroine, he kicks his former boss and whirls the girl around as his giant rival tries to retaliate. A simple effect in appearance—yet it involved hiring a band, learning certain dance steps, perfecting certain facial expressions, timing the action with the moving camera, etc.

In "A Woman of Paris" many scenes were shot fifty times—and one difficult scene went to over two hundred takes. Adolphe Menjou, in his book "It Took Nine Tailors," describes the shooting of a kiss in that picture. In his case the kiss had to show passion, yet avoid any indication that he was in love; in Edna Purviance's case it had to appear that it was not repulsive to her yet to show that she was unhappy. The two had to go through about a hundred kisses before Chaplin was satisfied.

In "City Lights" the meeting of the blind flower girl and the tramp took months before the variation that satisfied Chaplin was reached. The scene had to reveal both why the girl believed the tramp to be a millionaire and how he discovered her to be blind. Chaplin would screen the scene for friends or visiting correspondents and ask them what they saw. If something did not get across clearly, he would groan and reshoot it.

Directorial methods vary. In marked contrast was the working method of King Vidor in the silent era. Two of the outstanding scenes in "The Big Parade" (the touching shellhole scene where John Gilbert encounters the dying German soldier and the delightful scene where he teaches Renée Adorée to chew gum) were shot once without even a rehearsal! Of course, in the silent days, it was possible to shout instructions to the actor while the camera turned. But even so, these two scenes, noted for their spontaneity and naturalness, had rather complicated business and each was about five minutes in length. In the talkie era the late W. S. Van Dyke was known as a "one take" director; but he usually handled experienced actors repeating their familiar characterizations.

Methods vary. There are the perfectionist directors like Chaplin, Griffith, Lubitsch, and von Stroheim, who impress their own personalities on the actors. There are the others who, because their personality jibes with the picture being made, are able to keep actors in the proper mood. And there are those who merely yell "Action!" "Camera!" and "Cut!"

For his short, eighteen-hundred-feet comedies, Chaplin thought nothing of shooting from thirty to ninety thousand feet of film. For his features he often shot half a million feet to get eight reels. His shorts took much longer than was then customary and many of his features were a year or more in the making. Only the world-wide popularity of his pictures permitted such extravagance.

Before shooting a picture, or sometimes in the midst of one, Chaplin could go off for a few days' peaceful fishing at Catalina Island and mull over ideas. On his return he could confer with his little "clique," Al Reeves, his tactful and kindly business manager being the main spoke in the wheel whose hub was Chaplin. Then there was loyal Henry Bergman whose two interests in life were Chaplin and his restaurant. Laughing when the master laughed and brooding when the master brooded—Chaplin once cracked, "He'd kiss me if I'd let him." Besides old reliables from his stage days, technical experts, "stooges," and court jesters, Chaplin would hire bright young men like Monta Bell and Eddie Sutherland for a picture or two. If one of the "clique" had an idea or suggestion to make, he was careful to let the boss think it was his own, the usual device being to say: "I was just thinking of that gag you told me about, Charlie—it's a good one. . . ."

Once the idea was lodged in Chaplin's mind, he was impatient to start work and, as soon as the sets were ready, plunged in with his tireless energy. Chaplin's arrival in his car for the day's work, at least in the early days, was the signal for considerable ceremony on the part of the staff—the deference accorded a king. Eddie Sutherland, an assistant director in the mid-twenties, claimed he could tell the boss's mood by the clothes he arrived in. A dark green suit evidenced a heavy mood— trouble ahead. A blue suit with pin stripes was the sign of a good mood—a good day when he was approachable and some fine scenes could be expected to be made. A gray suit signaled an in-between mood.

The staff and players had to feel their way until a definite mood developed. Often Chaplin would be late or would disappear for days, sometimes for solitude in figuring out some angle in the picture. But his staff would turn up regularly at nine and wait until they were certain the boss was not coming.

During the actual shooting Chaplin allowed few visitors on the set. The people who worked for him guarded the details like military secrets. Chaplin often shot so that not even the players knew what the story was about. This secrecy was made necessary by the lifting of his gags by other comedians who reached the screen with them before his own picture was finished.

Through the years Chaplin's hunt for new ideas has kept him tense and anxious. As early as 1915 he feared loss of his fame. In moments of depression he has exclaimed, "I must get back to work—but I don't feel like it. I don't feel funny. Think—think of it: if I never could be funny again!" In dull spells he would tell himself, "You're through. You've lost your creative streak for good!" But a couple of days in bed mulling over the problem would bring a solution. As he once told Max Eastman, "There's no use just sitting down and waiting for inspiration. You've got to play along. The main thing you've got to do is preserve your vitality. A couple of days of complete rest and solitude helps. Not seeing anybody. I even conserve my emotions. 'I'm not going to get excited about anybody or anything,' I say, 'until I get this gag worked out.' I go along that way, living a quiet, righteous life, and then I stay out late one night and have a couple of drinks—perhaps all night—and the next morning the reserve pours out. But you've got to have that reserve. Dissipation is no use except as a release. You've been damming it up inside of you, and all of a sudden you say: 'Oh, there it is!' And then you go to work."

In an early interview Chaplin said of comedy: "It is really a serious study, although it must not be taken seriously. . . . To make a comedy a success there must be an ease, a spontaneity in the acting that cannot be associated with seriousness. . . . Even in slapstick there is an art. If one man hits another in a certain way at exactly the right psychological moment, it is funny. If he does it a moment too late, it misses the mark." It also matters who is the recipient of slapstick action. In the classic ice-cream gag of "The Adventurer," the first laugh comes from Chaplin's embarrassment over his predicament; the second, and bigger laugh, comes when the ice cream slips down the bare back of a dignified, dowager-like woman; the third, topping laugh, when the shrieking woman turns and slaps the man reaching down her back to remove the cold lump.

In this simple incident Chaplin showed his insights into human nature. One is the human tendency to experience, by empathy, the emotions projected by actors. We all know that ice cream is cold, therefore we can shiver with the woman. Another is the delight the average person takes in seeing the rich and the pompous get the worst of things—since a large proportion of the people in the world are poor and secretly resent the wealthy. As Chaplin points out, "If I had dropped the ice cream, for example, on a scrubwoman's neck, instead of getting laughs, sympathy would have been aroused for the woman. Also, because a scrubwoman has no dignity to lose, that point would not have been funny."

As for the comedian's own characterization and style, he feels that a comedian must be sincere even in falling down stairs. "People want the truth. . . . You must give them truth in comedy." His use of the contrast of his size with that of other people or objects, his surprise twists, and other devices have already been described. One human trait that he plays on as much as anything else is that it strikes people funny when a dignified person is placed in an undignified or embarrassing position.

"Even funnier," Chaplin writes in the early article, "What People Laugh At," "than the man who has been made ridiculous, however, is the man who, having had something funny happen to him, refuses to admit that anything out of the way has happened, and attempts to maintain his dignity. Perhaps the best example is the intoxicated man who, though his tongue and walk give him away, attempts in a dignified manner to convince you that he is quite sober. He is much funnier than the man who, wildly hilarious, is frankly drunk and doesn't care a whoop who knows it. . . . For that reason, all my pictures are built around the idea of getting me into trouble and so giving me the chance to be desperately serious in my attempt to appear as a normal little gentleman. That is why, no matter how desperate the predicament is, I am always very much in earnest about clutching my cane, straightening my derby hat, and fixing my tie, even though I have just landed on my head."

Chaplin's direction of others was also individual. Most of his actors had been his collaborators for years and knew his methods. He usually had them rehearse their parts separately. He himself played every character in every one of his pictures, to show the actors, men and women, exactly how he wanted them to do a character or a scene. And he accompanied each actor's miming with a running commentary of suggestions, criticism, or encouragement.

He was always on guard against overemphasis, always calling for restraint. Parenthetically, standards for "restraint" have varied through the years. Our upper lips seem to have become stiffer and our faces to reveal progressively less inner emotion. This is one reason why the heavy emoting in some old motion pictures often seems strange. From the beginning Chaplin, realizing the intimacy of the screen close-up, sought to avoid the stage style. "Don't *act!*" was one of his favorite admonitions. "I don't want any of the conventional business of the usual cinema traitor. Just get yourself used to the idea that you're a rascal who isn't an out-and-out bad one, but simply hasn't got any moral sense. Don't put on that savage look. And above all, don't *act!*"

In later years his favorite expression was, "Don't sell it. Remember they're peeking at you." According to

Menjou, he repeated this line often during the production of "A Woman of Paris"—a line which sums up the difference between stage and screen acting. At any bad or overacted bit he would say, "They're peeking at you!" Another pet line: "Think the scene! I don't care what you do with your hands or feet. If you think the scene, it will get over."

After shooting was completed, Chaplin edited the film himself with the aid of a cutter. Robinson relates that he took four days and nights cutting "The Immigrant," and went without sleep. Chaplin, like Griffith, then "tried it out on the dog," at one of the local theatres, without any preliminary advertising. If a sequence missed fire, or laughter didn't appear at the expected place, retakes were in order.

Chaplin's films are indeed one-man jobs—producing, writing, directing, acting, editing, and later, musical arrangement. He even officiated as hairdresser in "The Great Dictator," feeling that he could arrange Paulette Goddard's hair to simulate a scrubwoman's better than a professional hairdresser.

Nearly every significant milestone of the screen has been the work of one man. Witness the films of Griffith, von Stroheim, Eisenstein, and, in recent times, Sturges and Welles (at least his first effort). Hollywood, however, prefers the factory method of many "experts" assembling their products, instead of one man's work, as leading to more certain box-office returns. In recent years, with the necessity of putting the dialogue on paper before shooting and with the unionization of technicians, Chaplin encountered difficulty working by inspiration, when and as long as he pleased, without regard to time or expense. In his two talkies he tried, with qualified success, to work in his old manner. However, his remaining seventy-odd films were made with his own unconventional methods.

"The Kid"

"The Kid," released February 6, 1921, was Chaplin's first feature-length picture (if we except "Tillie's Punctured Romance" which had not been produced by him). It was his first film in more than a year and it ran six reels. A meeting with the five-year-old Jackie Coogan was its inspiration. Tradition has it that the boy winked at him in a hotel lobby. Jackie's parents were in vaudeville, and he had appeared on the stage with his dancer father, before he was two. When Chaplin saw him he was appearing, with his father, in Annette Kellerman's act at the Los Angeles Orpheum Theatre. In this act the tot did a take off on the dignified David Warfield. Around this youngster with the mischievous brown eyes, Chaplin began building a story which was virtually a chapter out of his own life in the London slums. Even the garret room in the film is said to have been modeled after one in which he had lived with his mother.

In the fall of 1919 Chaplin used Jackie Coogan as an extra in some of the crowd scenes of "A Day's Pleasure," to accustom him to the camera. After finishing "A Day's Pleasure," Chaplin set to work on "The Kid." As it developed the story demanded more than the planned footage. Most of 1920 was spent shooting the film, a time coinciding with the Harris divorce suit. Chaplin's investment came to $300,000, a sum much larger than he had spent on any previous picture; and over a half a million feet of film was exposed.

The scene in which Jackie makes pancakes and Chaplin rises from his bed in the suddenly improvised blanket-lounging robe, is said to have taken two weeks and fifty thousand feet of film to shoot. Even counting in the fact that two cameras were used (one negative was for Europe), this is exceptional footage for a scene scarcely a minute in length. But perfect timing and precision were desired and achieved.

Jackie Coogan was an unusually bright youngster and had had some acting experience, but he still required careful training for the demanding scenes he had to perform before the camera. The training itself called for patience, tact, and the infinite charm Chaplin was capable of. Jackie came to adore his mentor and the affection is communicated on the screen. Possessed of a decided personality—the kind that registers well—the child acquired an unfailing ease before the camera.

When the picture was completed, Chaplin felt that it deserved more money from First National than the $15,000 per extra reel above the two stipulated in the contract, a sum which would not have covered production costs. Negotiations were prolonged, and finally, after the flight to Utah to keep his wife from attaching the picture, Chaplin showed the film before the company's directors in New York. They viewed it in silence and professed to see nothing exceptional in it. To them it was merely a comedy stretched out beyond the customary two reels. One official declared coldly he had not found a single interesting or moving sequence in the film! Chaplin sarcastically replied that if he thought it would improve the film, he would add a train wreck or an explosion.

Fully cognizant of the value of his picture Chaplin persisted until he won out. First National gave him $600,000 for "The Kid" and the company's earnings from it exceeded any of their other films' income. The film grossed about $2,500,000. Sharing seventy-thirty on the gross, Chaplin himself profited well over a million.

"The Kid" was an overwhelming critical as well as box-office success. Critics hailed it as equal to, "in some ways better" than, or almost as good as "Shoulder Arms," for many years the critical yardstick for Chaplin films. Here and there critics, or some self-elected representatives of the public, found two or three scenes "vulgar" or in "bad taste." Audiences, in general, welcomed it for something refreshingly different which they found both entertaining and heartwarming—though some few missed the old Chaplin knockabout clowning.

With "The Kid," after his comparatively long screen absence and his two "failures," Chaplin regained and strengthened his position.

"The Kid" is almost straight drama and Chaplin is more the dramatic actor and less the clown than ever before. The laughs rise mostly from situation and pantomime rather than slapstick and horseplay. The plot is well worked out and the dramatic situations are handled realistically in the manner foreshadowed by "The Vagabond" and "A Dog's Life." No characters are played as caricatures with the exception of the Bully.

Jackie Coogan made a great personal hit and was hailed as the best child actor yet seen on the screen. Endowed with naturally expressive features and profiting from Chaplin's coaching, he became adept in screen pantomime, playing his light scenes with Chaplinesque zest and the emotional scenes with wonderful feeling. For this film Jackie Coogan deserves equal honors with the star; each scene together belongs equally to both. In fact, his performance here was not equaled until Jackie Cooper's "Skippy" (1931). "The Kid" launched Jackie Coogan on a phenomenally successful career. "Peck's Bad Boy," "Trouble," "Oliver Twist," "Circus Days," "Long Live the King," and the rest earned millions for his parents. Only Shirley Temple, in the thirties, achieved comparable popularity. When he reached his teens Coogan lost his "cuteness." After a spotty adult career, he tried vaudeville for which he wore a toupee and is now reported to be part-owner of a kitchen-ventilator company. But his amazing performance in his first film will never be forgotten.

"The Kid" is characterized by genuine pathos—a "picture with a smile—perhaps a tear." A single misstep might have made it mawkish but no such misstep was made. Some touches remind one of Griffith, whom Chaplin admired. There is a similar simplicity in statement, a similar emotional intensity, a similar use of symbolism. One or two scenes have the feeling of "Broken Blossoms." The constructed sets, supplemented by Los Angeles' own back alleys, achieve a rather "Londonish" look.

The two "offensive" scenes sometimes objected to were those where Chaplin peeps under the infant's blanket to investigate its sex, and the humanly handled episode of the moist baby. Certain other of the early scenes, instead, might be considered tasteless or banal: the dissolving from the unmarried mother to a painting of Christ carrying the cross; or her standing in front of a church with the stained-glass window lighting up and haloing her head; or the symbolism at the wedding where, in a heart-shaped iris close-up, rose petals fallen from a young bride's bouquet are stepped on by the elderly husband; or the symbolical book, entitled "The Past," opening on the page "Regrets"; or some flowery titles, typical of the period, mentioning "The Crucible of Sorrow," etc.

Direction and acting, on the whole, are very fine, Edna Purviance's first emotional scenes however, seemed rather stilted even at the time of first release. The photography, although clear, is not up to the best work of the period. Chaplin was still using an open-air stage, with daylight "boosted," now and then, by a few banks of lights. No use was made of backlighting, by now commonplace in Hollywood, leaving some of the interiors flat in appearance. On the other hand the dissolve from the sleeping tramp to the "heaven" scene is perfect, the actor not appearing to move an inch while the scene changes around him.

"The Kid" also had the distinction of criticism from one of the immortals of our time. When Chaplin met James M. Barrie, the noted novelist and playwright declared the "heaven" scene superfluous (did he feel the flying scenes invasions of his territory?). He also considered the footage allotted to the mother and to her meeting with the father, excessive. Chaplin, understanding that Barrie was paying him a subtle compliment by his severely critical discussion of dramatic construction with him, was flattered by his interest. But he was not too overawed to disagree, and argued his reasons for including those scenes.

Whatever minor faults it may possess, "The Kid" remains one of Chaplin's masterworks and one of the best remembered and most loved of all motion pictures.

"The Kid" opens with the Woman ("Her only sin was motherhood") leaving a charity hospital with her baby in her arms. A nurse smiles cynically as an attendant shuts the gates. The Man, an artist, is shown in his studio. Studying his painting he carelessly knocks a small photograph of the Woman off the mantelpiece into the fire.

Wandering about aimlessly the distraught mother stops at a church, watching a sad young bride descend with an elderly husband. Stopping at a handsome limousine she scribbles a note, "Please love and care for this infant child," leaves the baby in the back seat and hurries away. The car is stolen, and when the thieves, stopping in a slum district, discover the baby, they leave it beside a refuse can in an alley.

Here a shabby but debonair Tramp appears, taking his morning promenade. As he ambles forward swinging his cane, he ducks cascades of garbage from windows above. Suavely he removes his fingerless gloves and, opening a sardine-can cigarette case, he picks out a butt. About to put his gloves in his pocket, he gives them a disparaging glance and tosses them into a refuse can. The baby's cries bring him to the bundle near by. Glancing up at a window, he lifts the baby and places it in a carriage with another infant, but the angry mother denies that it is hers and the Tramp is forced to take back the bundle. About to return it to the carriage, a cop passes and he hastily picks the baby up again. He asks an old man to hold the infant while he fixes his shoe—then runs off and hides in a shed. The old man places the bundle once more in the carriage and the woman, finding it there, blames the Tramp and beats him with her umbrella. The cop, summoned to the scene, forces him to take the baby once more. The Tramp, sitting on the curb, wonders whether to toss his burden down the manhole. Glancing at the baby, he finds the note.

Meanwhile the distraught mother contemplates suicide off a high bridge. A child, wandering from its nurse, tugs at her feet. Her maternal instincts suddenly obliterate thoughts of disgrace and death. Running back to the house in front of which the auto was parked she faints on the doorstep on learning that the car was stolen.

In the Tramp's slum garret the baby swings in a home-made hammock with a nursing bottle contrived from a coffee pot suspended from a string. As he cuts up cloth into diapers, he makes faces at the baby. Patting the bottom of the hammock, he has to wipe his hand. To provide against similar mishaps he carves a hole in the seat of a chair, places the chair under the hammock and a spittoon under the chair.

Five years pass. We see the Kid sitting on the curb manicuring his nails with all the aplomb of his foster father. Upstairs there is an inspection of his hands and ears before the Tramp and the Kid go out on their day's work. The Kid's part is to throw stones at a window and run. The Tramp, as an itinerant glazier, "happens by" after the accident and is hired to repair the damage. About to make another throw, the Kid's hand contacts a burly policeman right behind him. Pretending to be juggling the stone, the Kid tosses it to the ground and runs off. The cop's suspicions deepen when he sees the Tramp at work. The Tramp asks a dollar for his job but, noticing the cop, returns it to the woman. While the cop watches the Kid tries to join his father who keeps kicking him away as if he were a barking puppy. In a long rear shot we see them trailed by the cop, whom they finally shake by a dash around a corner.

On "Job 13," the Tramp, with his arm innocently around a woman's waist, disposes her so that she can view his handicraft. The woman scolds him and he doffs his hat in apology, but maneuvers himself into the crook of her arm as she leans on the window sill—and then playfully taunts her. She laughingly pokes him with her elbow and he is about to return the poke with his trowel as the cop enters his house. Grabbed around the neck from behind, the Tramp first thinks it is the woman. Discovering his mistake, a chase follows up back alleys. The Tramp and the Kid manage to elude the policeman. In their room they have a banquet at which the Kid daintily uses a "finger" bowl after demolishing his sizable pile of fodder.

Meanwhile the mother has risen to heights as an opera singer. Material success, however, has not extinguished her maternal instinct. As a substitute satisfaction she dispenses charity in the slums. She gives a toy to the Kid without recognizing him as her child. "The world welcomes fame." At a reception the opera singer meets the Man again. Emotionally upset, she leaves friends and admirers. Alone, on a balcony outside, the Man joins her. A symbolic book entitled "The Past" opens on the page "Regrets." There is no reconciliation.

Back in the slum garret the Kid is making pancakes while the Tramp, smoking, takes his ease in bed. The boy orders him to get up. Stretching, he registers surprise as his foot appears through a hole in the blanket. Sticking his head through the hole the Tramp conjures a lounging robe out of the ragged blanket in which he rises, inserts his feet into his shoes and proceeds to the table in state. Dividing the cakes evenly the two say Grace and dive in. Lessons in the most advantageous uses of a knife enliven the meal.

Out in the street a tough boy grabs the Kid's toy. Between "rounds" of the ensuing fight the Tramp coaches the Kid where to hit and kick. The Bully, brother of the tough kid, struts in cuffing an onlooker out of his way. The Tramp backs out but the Bully warns: "If your kid beats mine, I'll beat you." The Tramp declares the other boy, who is taking a beating, "the winner." The Bully goes after the protesting Tramp, stopping to knock a hole in a brick wall and bend a lamppost to display his strength. Finally he pulls the tramp out of the window he has taken refuge in. Just then the opera star enters and pleads with the men to stop fighting. They shake hands before the woman. But the Tramp, taking advantage of the intercession, slyly bats the Bully over the head with a brick. He contrives to duck and hit the Bully until the tough is reeling.

The Woman, carrying the Kid in her arms, meets the "father" and tells him he must call a doctor. The doctor examines the boy and advises that the "child must have proper care and attention"—which is beyond the Tramp's capacity. Sadly the Tramp sits beside the boy and feels his pulse. After a period of convalescence, we see the boy sitting up in bed reading the *Police Gazette* while his father prepares a mustard plaster.

The doctor, who on the first visit had discovered that the Kid is not the Tramp's son, has reported the case. A truck marked County Orphan Asylum stops at the door. Officials enter the garret room to take the Kid away. Lifted to the door the Kid cries out and the Tramp runs to him. The Kid and the Tramp resist. As the Tramp is overpowered the Kid cries in a corner, then snatches a hammer and zestfully uses it on the heads of the men. Charlie tosses a bowl to help out.

With the aid of a cop the Kid is finally forced into the van. While the boy is crying for his "Daddy" the Tramp escapes up the skylight and balances along the roof cornices with the cop in pursuit. The two meet at the top of a gable where the cop is pushed down. Seeing the orphanage van below the Tramp takes a short cut over the rooftops to a shed from which he jumps into the rear of the truck. He tosses out the orphanage official.

When the truck stops the driver is startled to see the Kid and his foster father in a tearful embrace. The Tramp chases the driver, keeping him running by jumping up and down in one spot in pretended pursuit. By now the doctor has shown the mother the note and she realizes the Kid is her lost son.

At night the Tramp and the Kid retire to a flophouse. The Tramp has difficulty finding a dime to pay the tough proprietor. He opens a window and admits the Kid who hides under the blanket. As the Tramp stands by the bed, a "sleep-walking," snake-like, pickpocket hand (from the neighboring bed back of him) searches all four of the Tramp's pockets. A dime is discovered in one and the

Tramp bats his eyelashes in surprise. He then places the mysterious hand back in his pockets in the hope of finding more, angering his odd neighbor.

Getting into bed, the Tramp kisses the Kid who gets out to say his prayers. The suspicious proprietor investigates as the boy hides under the bed and the Tramp prays soulfully. With an engaging smile at the proprietor, he lifts his feet up so the Kid can jump under the blanket. Amazed at the height of the Tramp's "knees" the owner lingers until the ruse is uncovered. He demands more money.

The proprietor, reading an announcement of a reward by the mother for the lost boy, recognizes the Kid from the printed description. As we watch the Tramp and the Kid sleeping, their reflexes jumping in comical unison, the flophouse owner picks up the boy and takes him to the police station. The Tramp wakes to find the boy gone. He calls out "Jack!" No answer, he tears the blankets off the rows of men, causing hilarious hubbub. The Tramp wanders the streets searching for the boy till dawn.

Arriving at the police station, the mother tearfully embraces the sad-faced little boy. Meanwhile, back in front of his slum dwelling, the exhausted Tramp falls asleep on the doorstep and dreams his way into the famous burlesque heaven.

The slum court is transformed into a veritable Fairyland. Everything is an immaculate white and festooned with flowers. Angel wings have sprouted on the inhabitants' shoulders. Food and drinks are free. The Bully flies in playing a harp and dancing. The Kid wakes his father who cannot believe his eyes. Even a little dog goes winging by. The Tramp, too, receives wings with which he skims across the length of the court.

But, sliding past a napping watchman, "Sin Creeps In." Three devils enter paradise and trouble begins. One devil appears behind the Bully's young wife and instigates her to flirt with the Tramp who keeps playing his harp innocently until a devil goes to work on him too. Then, as the flirtatious girl shows her ankle, the Tramp "dives" after her. With another devil prompting the Bully to take offense as his wife accepts the other man's kisses, a fight ensues. Angel feathers start flying. As the Tramp takes to flight, the Policeman shoots him down, and leans over to pick him up.

The Tramp wakes on his doorstep under the cop's shaking. He is collared and led around the corner and into a waiting automobile. Wonder, fear, and astonishment play across his face as the car drives up to a large mansion. He is escorted to the door. The Kid and his newly found mother greet him warmly. The policeman shakes hands with him and leaves. The mother invites him in, and the picture fades out as the Tramp is being escorted into the house.

Chaplin's 1921 trip abroad

Following "The Kid," Chaplin produced the two-reel "The Idle Class," in the spring of 1921. Desiring to finish his First National contract for eight pictures he spent three months preparing the script and a month building the sets of the next film. At last, on a day in August 1921, everything was ready. Actors on the set at eight in the morning, cameras and lights in position— but no Chaplin. Shortly after noon he arrived in a highly nervous state. Carl Robinson was called by Sidney into the office, where Chaplin was pacing up and down. Suddenly Charlie turned to Robinson and ordered him to make the necessary arrangements for an immediate trip to Europe. Robinson obeyed although he thought his boss was out of his head—with the extras waiting on the set and the months of preparation behind him. Next night Chaplin and Robinson were on the train to New York.

Exhausted by his long work on "The Kid," the Harris divorce suit, and an attack of influenza, Chaplin was in a depressed, stagnated, and "what's the use" mood. He was also homesick for England which he had not seen in eight long years. He needed an emotional holiday and, quite frankly, wanted to bask in the spotlight of his recent success. Perhaps "The Kid" would be his last hit! He actually feared, in 1921, that his popularity would not last. At the Los Angeles station, Chaplin sidestepped reporters with the explanation that he was off on "a secret mission." Sid's parting warning to Carl, "For God's sake, don't let him get married," gave the crowd a laugh. In Chicago—more crowds, reporters, photographers, and a reunion with his poet-friend, Carl Sandburg.

Douglas Fairbanks met him at the Grand Central station in New York and escorted him to the Ritz where the gentlemen of the press fired the usual ungentlemanly barrage of questions: "Why are you going to Europe?" "What do you do with your old mustaches?" "Do you ever expect to get married?" "Do you want to play Hamlet?" "Are you a Bolshevik?"

Douglas Fairbanks and Mary Pickford knew that Chaplin wanted and needed a rest from pictures, but they insisted upon showing him their new releases, "The Three Musketeers" and "Little Lord Fauntleroy." They were anxious to get his criticism. However, his suggestions for some slight changes and cuts were politely ignored. Shortly after, Chaplin attended the riotous premiere of "The Three Musketeers," at which Doug, escorting Mary, was forced to carry her on his shoulders through the crowd. Chaplin, who was with them, was mauled and his clothing torn—but without a moment's dislocation of what he has called his "prop" smile. It was a thrilling evening and he was glad of the success of his friend—yet a little envious, too. He had never had an "opening," his films having made their debuts for him in Los Angeles projection rooms. One reason for the trip to Europe was to let him, finally, really taste his success.

His few days in New York were hurried ones. There was business to attend to at his lawyer, Nathan Burkan's, office; a visit to "Liliom," then the Broadway smash. Both as a play and in the performance by the leads, Joseph Schildkraut and Eva Le Gallienne, "Liliom" made a deep impression on Chaplin. Next morning, at the Coffee House Club, he met Heywood Broun, Frank

Crowninshield, Condé Nast, Alexander Woollcott, and other writers and artists. Later that day he missed a meeting with Ambassador Gerard through a car breakdown. The next evening he attended a "Greenwich Village" party given by Max Eastman, poet and radical, then editor of *The Liberator,* whom Chaplin had met in California and whom he found interesting company although he did not always agree with his doctrines.

As host in his turn, Chaplin brought together a mixed group at the Elysée Café: Woollcott, Broun, Eastman, Edward Knoblock, Mme. Maeterlinck, Rita Weiman, Neysa McMein, and Doug and Mary. The famous movie couple performed charades on top of the table. Chaplin and Mme. Maeterlinck did a hilarious burlesque of the dying scene in "Camille." Camille coughed but it was Chaplin, playing Armand, who was racked by convulsions and died in Camille's stead. There was singing, dancing, talk, and impromptu speeches to provide a great evening in which Chaplin was able to lose himself entirely in friendly play.

Edward Knoblock, who was also sailing, became Chaplin's companion-guide on the crossing. Knoblock, author of "Kismet" and other successful plays, had written the screen adaptation for Fairbanks' "The Three Musketeers."

The voyage had its trials. At the very start there was an unpleasant incident. A news photographer asked Chaplin to throw kisses at the Statue of Liberty. Chaplin refused to make this cheap and obvious gesture and the refusal became food for malicious gossip. The Olympic, on which the crossing was made, had its quota of autograph hunters and people who would not forego an opportunity to brush elbows with the great. Even in the Turkish bath men wanted to know was Chaplin friendly with Theda Bara and Louise Glaum and asked other idiotic questions. On his exercises around the deck he was embarrassed by people staring and pointing at him. He wanted to meet the interesting people on board but the situation made meetings on an equal footing impossible.

Finally Chaplin tried another group, the ship's fireman and stokers, who had invited him down for a game of cricket. He warmed up to the men but he was still looked upon as a celebrity, not a cricket player. And even this relaxation was spoiled by the intrusion of a motion-picture cameraman assigned to cover him on the crossing! The rest of the trip Chaplin spent partly in eluding him. Realizing he could not be himself on the ship Chaplin did not try to mingle further. However, he met one interesting couple, Guy Bolton, author of the musical "Sally," and his wife Marguerite Namara, the opera singer.

At the close of the voyage, there was another jarring note. Chaplin was requested to perform at a seamen's fund concert. He begged off, explaining that he was tired, that he had nothing prepared and, lacking his costume, the illusion would be spoiled. It was understood that he would not be called upon but in the course of the entertainment, which Chaplin attended, people in the audience turned toward him and the chairman, Herman Metz, announced that Chaplin had refused to contribute an act. He added, no matter, they could see him on the screen, anytime, for a nickel. Chaplin departed for the smoking room in a fury, leaving Robinson to tell off M. Metz. A few shuffling steps or one of his inimitable take offs might have been an easier price.

The boat stopped at Cherbourg. Chaplin's knees began to shake at sight of the attacking army of reporters and cameramen. He complained that he had not come to Europe to be interviewed but to rest. Since Chaplin knew no French, the mass interview did not last too long. One reporter, who appeared to be a Russian, asked whom he considered the greater man, Lenin or Lloyd George; to which Chaplin quipped, "One works and the other plays." His horrified publicity man, Robinson, hurried him back into his cabin. As the boat neared Southampton, Chaplin's nervousness returned. The mayor was scheduled to greet him in the morning, when the ship docked. There were consultations on how he was to be addressed and Chaplin spent a sleepless night rehearsing a speech before the mirror. Opening his door in the early morning, he was swept back by the invading task force of English reporters, looking for a little man with a little mustache. The same questions, over again. Now, however, Chaplin had recovered his ease: He gave patient answers and in the meeting with the flustered mayor he proved the better poised.

A group of friends came on board: Tom Geraghty, Hollywood scenario writer who had authored Fairbanks' "The Mollycoddle" and "When the Clouds Roll By"; actor Donald Crisp, then directing movies in England; his cousin Aubrey Chaplin; Sonny Kelly, a friend from his music-hall days and brother of Hetty, the sweetheart of his adolescence; and others who claimed they knew him "when."

We have Chaplin's published reactions to the trip. Despite his discomfort in crowds and his weariness with his fixed "prop" smile, at public occasions, he did not deny being "a little shocked" that "somehow the crowds here are not as large as I had anticipated." On being informed that the boat was a day late and the crowd had had no way of learning the hour of arrival, his disappointment was assuaged.

The train ride to London thrilled him with the views of the English countryside. He also enjoyed reminiscing with Sonny and his cousin Aubrey. Casually he asked about Hetty. "Hetty? Why she died two years ago," replied Kelly. Chaplin was profoundly moved. He had been too busy with his career to follow happenings in far-off

England. Amiable cousin Aubrey, who now operated a saloon, had not seen Charlie in ten years and was surprised how American he had become.

To compensate for the smaller than expected crowd at Southampton, the crowds welcoming him to London surpassed all expectations. He was literally extracted from the train and carried on people's shoulders to a car amid ringing cries: "There he is!" "Good luck, Charlie!" "Well done, Charlie!" "God love you!" The police could not handle them and Chaplin feared people would be trampled or run over as he was driven to the Ritz. Placards announced "Charlie Arrives," and crowds lined the streets all the way to the hotel. It was indeed a triumphal return. Somehow he was lifted and projected into the hotel, from a balcony of which he threw down roses until the police requested him to stop as a precaution against accidents. Chaplin later declared: "Thinking over what I have done, it has not been very much. Nothing to call forth all this. 'Shoulder Arms' was pretty good, perhaps, but all this clamor over a moving-picture actor!"

As soon as it became possible Chaplin used the back doors to begin a visit to his childhood haunts alone. A taxi took him to Kennington where he got out for a stroll that ended in Lambeth Walk. There he was recognized; a crowd collected; and he had to have the help of a policeman to extricate himself.

Chaplin was buried under mountains of mail (73,000 letters in three days). They included invitations, requests for money, and vilifications and threats because he had not served in the war. Six secretaries had to be hired to handle it.

During a thunderstorm Chaplin, attending a party at Knoblock's suite in the Albany, played a grisly joke. Knoblock had observed that this was the apex of Chaplin's career. Tom Geraghty, whose drinks had put him in a maudlin mood, agreed that it would be impossible to attain greater success and asserted that to live after such an ovation would be an anticlimax. The artistic thing to do would be to die. What a magnificent end! Chaplin's answer included some characteristic, blasphemous remarks which shocked the Catholic Geraghty.

Chaplin then let some of the others in on his intentions before he went to the window. Opening it he hurled defiances at the sky. There was a lightning flash and a crash of thunder; Chaplin screamed, stiffened, and fell. "My God! It's happened!" exclaimed Geraghty, dropping his whiskey glass. Chaplin was carried into the next room, from which Donald Crisp emerged to announce that he was dead. Geraghty walked slowly toward the window and had to be restrained from jumping out. Then Charlie appeared in a sheet, with pillowcases on each arm for wings, to end his little farce.

Knoblock suggested a call on Bernard Shaw whom he knew well. When Chaplin and he reached Shaw's house, which overlooked the Thames Embankment, Chaplin hesitated, in a revealing reaction, as Knoblock was about to lift the knocker. He exclaimed that movie actors, abroad, invariably visited Shaw. "I do not desire to ape others. And I want to be individual and different. And I want Bernard Shaw to like me. . . . I don't want to force myself upon him. . . . No, I don't want to meet him." Knoblock was surprised and annoyed. "Some other time. We won't call today." Not until ten years later was Chaplin to meet the great playwright.

Chaplin made a number of sentimental journeys through London. Almost every step revived memories. He found some remembered old peddlers still hawking their wares; old derelicts still at their favorite stands. He revisited Baxter's Hall where he had gone to see penny magic-lantern shows, forerunners of the movies; Kennington Gate, his meeting place with Hetty; and various houses where he had lived. He was on the very site of his youth, yet he was apart from it—he no longer belonged there. "A man cannot go back."

At a reception tendered to him at the Garrick Club, he met E. V. Lucas, Walter Hackett, James M. Barrie, Squire Bancroft, and other notables of literature and the theatre. The aging Barrie, sitting beside him, suggested that he play Peter Pan and followed with a discussion of "The Kid." Later, at Barrie's apartment, Gerald du Maurier joined them.

Chaplin was an admirer of Thomas Burke, author of "Limehouse Nights," and after their meeting in London the two prowled through that romantically sinister section of London which first reached fame in Burke's book, then acquired perhaps even greater celebrity in the Griffith films, "Broken Blossoms" and "Dream Street." Perhaps the greatest thrill of his London visit was his meeting with H. G. Wells of whose work Chaplin was a devotee. He first met Wells at a screening of "Mr. Kipps," surrounded by reporters. The English picture was embarrassingly bad, but nice things were said about George K. Arthur, the nervous and eager young star. Wells invited Chaplin to visit him in the country where they could have a proper talk.

Suddenly Chaplin decided to visit France. The Paris crowds equaled London's, only here they called him "Charlot." Among others whom he met there were Dudley Field Malone and Waldo Frank, the French cartoonist Cami, Sir Philip Sassoon, confidential secretary to Lloyd George, and the boxer Georges Carpentier. In a party including Malone and Iris Tree he visited the Montmartre night spots, observing the habitués. In Le Rat Mort he met a sensational young blonde Russian singer named Moussia Sodskay. He offered to try to find her a niche in Hollywood, but it turned out impossible for her to get a passport. She was an émigrée—a woman without a country. She had arrived recently by way of

Turkey and was not even aware of the position and prestige of the man who showed such interest in her career.
Chaplin did not forget her and years later he was glad to
hear that Moussia had married well.

Together with Robinson, Chaplin next visited Germany. From the train window he noticed the people
busily working and rebuilding. In Berlin he went about
unrecognized. His films had not been shown during the
war and had only just begun to penetrate into Germany.
He had a mixed reaction to this of relief, surprise, and
annoyance. The Adlon Hotel had no rooms available and
just as Chaplin and Robinson were about to try elsewhere, a newspaper man, Karl von Wiegand, recognized
Chaplin and offered him his rooms. On being apprised of
the importance of the new guest, the owner offered apologies—and the royal suite.

That night, visiting the Palais Heinroth, then Berlin's
chief night spot, his lack of a reputation in Germany
was again brought home to him when the headwaiter led
him and Robinson to a dim corner table. Soon, however,
he heard a voice, "Charlie!" It was Al Kaufman, Paramount's Berlin representative. Then, as Robinson and he
were led to Kaufman's table, the players in the American
jazz band shouted and waved at him. At Kaufman's table
was Pola Negri, Germany's most popular star and known
to America by the films Lubitsch directed her in, "Passion" and "Gypsy Blood." Although the Polish actress
knew no words of English and Chaplin not a word of
German they managed with their eyes. Chaplin was smitten with her beauty and vivid charm—her jet black hair,
white skin, and her soft voice. She, in turn, kept mur-
muring, "Jazz boy, Charlie." More specific compliments
were exchanged with Kaufman's aid and one, in a deliberate, joking mistranslation by Kaufman, earned him a
playful slap on the wrist. The interchange was not to the
liking of a young German at the table, a rich merchant

and Pola's fiancé. He kept stepping on her toes and pinching her arms to no effect. Robinson feared it might lead to a duel.

Pola and Charlie were inseparable for a week. They rode and dined together alone. Chaplin had expectd to stay no more than forty-eight hours in Berlin but decided each day to prolong his visit.

Among the highlights of this Berlin visit, was a party at which Pola and he did a classic dance. Then, as a solo, Chaplin interpreted and burlesqued a Russian ballet dancer. The guests happened not to have the slightest notion who he was; by the end of the evening they were bursting with admiration for him. He had built a reputation from scratch.

During his Berlin trip he twice visited the poorer sections and took note of the many war cripples. Gradually Berliners discovered what an important person was in their midst. It was with regret that Chaplin left Berlin and Pola Negri. The following year he was to meet her again in Hollywood.

Chaplin's party flew back to England from Paris. Among other visits he was conducted through a hospital for wounded soldiers by Philip Sassoon and was impressed by the spirit of some of the hopelessly crippled men. Then came his week end with H. G. Wells and discussions of politics and world affairs; and, with St. John Ervine, the dramatist, a discussion of the possibilities of talking pictures. It was the period of De Forest's Phonofilms and similar German developments. Chaplin was not interested, claiming that the voice was superfluous in films, which were essentially a pantomimic art. He would as soon rouge the marble cheeks of a statue. For relaxation, amidst the talk, charades were played, that favorite game among the well-to-do in the pre-radio, pre-record-player, pre-home-movie era. There were also long walks and some outdoor games including one invented by Wells and an effort to initiate Wells and his young son in American baseball. This visit to Wells' country place in Essex was in some ways the most enjoyable of his trip.

Chaplin flew back to Paris to attend the premiere of "The Kid," proceeds of which were to be given to a fund for war-devastated France. Doug and Mary were also then in Paris. Paris declared a holiday for the occasion. This proved to be the biggest demonstration of the voyage. Ambassador Herrick introduced Chaplin to the French Cabinet. On hand were most of the notables of France, variegated royalty and nobility including George of Greece and Princess Xenia, diplomats, etc. Among notable women were Mrs. W. K. Vanderbilt, Elsie De Wolf, Cecile Sorel, Elsa Maxwell. Chaplin's box was draped with American and British flags. The two hundred and fifty programs he autographed in the afternoon immediately sold out at a hundred francs apiece.

"The Kid" itself drew laughter and tears and stormy applause. At its close Chaplin was called to the box of the Minister of Instruction of the Public and Beaux Arts to be decorated. He went to the box "feeling like a man approaching the guillotine" and barely murmured his "Merci" as he was made an "Officier de l'Instruction Publique." Dazed, he managed to get through an acceptance speech on the importance of the motion-picture industry and how privileged he was to contribute to such a worthy cause.

In the flood of congratulatory messages, many from famous people, none pleased him so much as a note, scribbled on a program, that he received from Moussia. She had seen the picture from the gallery and had at last discovered in its completeness the identity of her world-famous friend. "You are a grand man. My heart is joy. . . . I laugh—I cry."

Chaplin's last night in England was spent with his cousin Aubrey. As his car rolled up to the latter's house

in Bayswater, Chaplin noticed a number of people standing in the shadows. His cousin explained they were
friends who just wanted to have a look at him. Though he
had stipulated that this visit was not to be made the occasion for a party, he relented and invited them all in.
For more efficient hospitality he transferred the party,
later, to Aubrey's saloon, or hotel, as he called it. The
guests were simple souls, clerks and tradesmen. Many of
them wouldn't believe they were actually seeing the
world-famous star and thought they were being hoaxed
by Aubrey.

On his way back to the Ritz at 4 A.M., Chaplin hailed
a Ford marketing truck. Its driver proved to be an impoverished young aristocrat back from the war and determined to do useful work. He seemed happy in his job
and Chaplin was inspired by this contact with "real nobility."

At Southampton close friends saw him off. The crowd
that had welcomed him gathered to bid him goodbye.
There was mutual deep feeling in the farewell. He received a touching parting gift from Sonny, a picture of
Hetty.

On his return to America, at the end of October, he
spent a few days in New York. Its highlight was a visit to
Sing Sing, with the writer, Frank Harris, noted for his
strange combination of social interest and ribaldry.

Chaplin's expenses had been heavy on this European
tour. He was not averse to recouping when he received
bids for his account of his trip, from news syndicates
and magazines.

In Thomas Burke's opinion "My Trip Abroad" is quite
a clear reflection of Chaplin's personality. The eternal
actor is frankly exposed in this comment on his reunion,
after ten years, with his cousin Aubrey. Chaplin wrote: "I
want to shock him; no, not exactly shock him, but surprise him. I find myself deliberately posing and just for

him. I want to be different, and I want him to know that I am a different person. This is having its effect. Aubrey is bewildered . . . I become radical in my ideas. Against his conservatism. But I am beginning not to like this performing for him. One feels so conscious. I am wondering whether he will understand. . . . I shall have a long talk with Aubrey later and explain everything."

The account was dictated to Monta Bell, a newspaperman hired for the purpose, during the railroad trip to the coast. The recital was finished by the time they reached Salt Lake City. Chaplin got twenty-five thousand for "My Trip Abroad," which more than covered his expenses. It was republished in book form by Harper's after its serialization. Chaplin was so satisfied with Bell that he added him to his staff. Bell later went ahead to become a director on his own.

It had been truly an emotional holiday; it had also been a triumphal progress, almost without precedent, for the little "nickel comedian." In Hollywood his return was received with joy by his little group of associates and indifference by most of the rest. He came back refreshed, inspired by the brilliant people he had met and filled with the desire to bring smiles to the tired faces of the less fortunate he had also encountered. This renewal of vitality was to reflect itself in his work.

XVII

new friends

After his divorce Chaplin's name was linked with several girls, among them May Collins and Claire Windsor. The newspapers repeatedly reported engagements. The idyl with May, a young stage actress, did not last long because, after her film appearance with Frank Mayo in "The Shark Master," she was obliged to leave for New York to fill a stage engagement. There had been no marriage proposal as some of Chaplin's intimates feared.

His association with Claire Windsor was more complicated and dramatic. Her real name was the less euphonious Olga Cronk and she hailed from Kansas. Now she was gambling on a movie career. Her stakes were a tall, slender figure and a blonde, delicate beauty. She was ten years older than the proverbial sixteen and the mother of a son whose existence she did not attempt to conceal, in the manner of the day, from the fan magazines.

Photogenic and talented enough to get by, all she needed was a little publicity to put her over. What would serve better than to be reported "engaged" to Charlie Chaplin? She smiled at him in a restaurant and they were introduced.

Soon after the papers carried sensational news! The reported fiancée of Charlie Chaplin had been kidnapped! Her horse had returned to a riding academy riderless; her handbag had been found in the hills! The police sent out an alarm. Chaplin offered a thousand dollars reward for her return. Crowds gathering in front of the police station were at lynching tension. Sirens screamed and rumors spread. Vigilantes scoured the hills and woods above Hollywood. Airplanes were held ready to fly to the rescue if she were located at any distance.

The unconscious form of Miss Windsor was finally found in brush on a hill that had already been searched over. She was now in a hospital but not yet in a condition to see anyone. It was given out that she had fallen from her horse and had suffered an amnesic shock.

The next day the young couple who had found her called at the Chaplin studios for the reward. Chaplin was ready to pay but Carl Robinson decided to consult Miss Windsor first. Pale, and with dark circles under her eyes, Miss Windsor could hardly talk. But her pantomime was better than her dialogue. She told conflicting stories and Robinson noticed that her riding boots were unmarked. On closer inspection her wan appearance turned out to be make-up. Robinson suggested that it would be better if she told the truth.

Miss Windsor finally admitted that the kidnapping was a stunt arranged by a young publicity man, who, incidentally, was in love with her. For two days and nights she had hid in the attic of a house from which she could watch the searching parties. When it was judged best for the publicity she allowd herself to be "discovered." The young couple were talked out of the reward. The publicity agent left town. The public, however, swallowed the story whole and Miss Windsor went on to stardom.

In his rented new home on Beechwood Drive and Argyle, a garish palace in Moorish style, Chaplin entertained mainly intellectual people—"free thinkers," writers, and artists. Max Eastman was a frequent visitor, as were Dudley Field Malone, the lawyer, Upton Sinclair, the novelist, and Clare Sheridan, the sculptor. A new Chaplin, visioning new horizons, emerged from these contacts. It was, in a sense, a belated education for Chaplin whose formal schooling had been sketchy.

In this period charades and similar games were enjoyed, among them one in which a player, impersonating a chosen character, was called upon to make a speech on some incongruous subject. Charlie, as "A Toothless Old Veteran," would be asked to discourse on "The Benefits of Birth Control" or, dressed as Carrie Nation, to express "Some Doubts as to the Origin of Species." In one Chaplin preached the sermon on David and Goliath which he was later to incorporate into "The Pilgrim." In fact, the film was probably built around this skit. Party groups would also draw titles and then be asked to improvise a one-act play. All this was valuable training as well as fun.

Not long after the premiere of "The Kid" Chaplin arranged to have his mother brought over from England. The mission was entrusted to his secretary, Tom Harrington. This gave rise to fresh slanders. Gossip had it that Chaplin had refused to pay the passage and that she had been forced to travel steerage! Because of her mental condition, there were difficulties in securing her admission into the United States. The elderly, broken-minded woman, carefully coached by Tom Harrington, almost passed the immigration tests but irritation over the cross-examination produced an outburst. A medical committee judged her inacceptable and detained her at Ellis Island. But on Chaplin's guarantee that his mother would be under the care of specialists and would never become a public charge she was finally admitted.

According to the Chaplin publicity releases "she was brought here so she may overcome the nervous mental condition that she is now suffering as the result of shell shock" during the Zeppelin raids. While resting at the Hotel Flanders in New York, Mrs. Chaplin was quoted as saying, "I never saw Spencer in the cinemas."

The meeting of mother and son in California was very moving. They had not seen each other in nearly ten years. But not then, nor afterward, did Mrs. Chaplin comprehend the rank that her son, whom she addressed as "The King," occupied in the world. Nor could she understand that the years of struggle were over. Frightened by the evidence of her son's wealth, she felt that such grandeur could not belong to him. She feared that his work might not be honest.

When she saw him in his makeup she protested: "Why do you want to make yourself look hideous, you who are so beautiful?" A special screening for her of one of his films merely confused her. Her only reaction was the complaint, why were they working her poor boy so hard!

Chaplin installed his mother in a house at Santa Monica overlooking the sea. She was provided with a companion and a nurse and received the best of care. Nevertheless this, too, proved grist for the gossip mill. Chaplin was criticized for not taking his mother into his own home. Unless it be considered good to torment oneself this would have been useless. His mother's condition depressed Chaplin; and all that could be done for her was to assure her comfort.

She enjoyed long drives and trips to the zoo with Kono. At times she would brighten and do a little song and dance for company.

Chaplin met Clare Sheridan at a dinner given by Abraham Lehr, an associate of Sam Goldwyn. Miss Sheridan, a sculptor and a "free thinker," was a cousin of Winston Churchill and the widow of a descendant of the great dramatist, Richard Brinsley Sheridan. As a woman who had traveled everywhere and was at home on all social levels, Chaplin found her an interesting personality. She had just returned from Russia where she had had interviews with Lenin and Trotsky. She had made busts

of many notables including Lord Birkenhead, Count Keyserling, and Mussolini. At their first meeting she proposed doing a bust of Chaplin.

She and her seven-year-old boy were invited to a showing of "The Kid" at Chaplin's studio. Later, as the two
discussed life and art, Miss Sheridan started work on his
bust. When it was completed, Miss Sheridan reports in
her book, "My American Diary," Chaplin studying it,
commented, "It might be the head of a criminal, mightn't
it?"—Theorizing that criminals and artists are psychologically akin, both have a burning flame of impulse, a vision,
and are psychologically outlaws. Miss Sheridan concluded
that in Chaplin she had met a man with "a great soul."

Their friendship came to a bizarre ending after a camping trip. Chaplin, Miss Sheridan, and her son in one car
were followed by a truck carrying complete camping
equipment and by a Ford carrying a chef. The little caravan drove up the coast to an isolated spot between Ven-
tura and Oxnard. After an enjoyable week of recreation
in the open they were spotted. Chaplin was identified
and the curious appeared from nowhere to gape at him.
When two reporters arrived, the party broke çamp and
returned to civilization.

To ward off reporters nosing a new "romance," Carl
Robinson half jokingly made the crack that Clare Sheridan was old enough to be Chaplin's mother. The next
day's headlines proclaimed that there would be no marriage with Miss Sheridan, Chaplin having declared her
"old enough to be his mother." Miss Sheridan moved
from Chaplin's mansion to a hotel. Robinson was ordered
to explain his faux pas to the lady. The next day Chaplin
saw mother and son off to New York. The interlude was
over and he went back to work on "Pay Day."

Pola Negri followed. She arrived in America, in September 1922, to fill a Paramount contract. Chaplin had
prepared the ground for her by his tributes to her beauty

and charm, on which a big advance publicity build-up had been erected. To reporters Miss Negri immediately confided how she had been looking forward to her reunion with Chaplin. With her marriage to Count Dombski dissolved, newspapers broadcast her engagement to Chaplin.

Chaplin's praises were fulsomely sung by the exotic actress who loved the limelight off the screen as well as on. Some of her statements embarrassed her fiancé. It was obvious to all, however, that a romance was in progress. At one time a report of their marriage was circulated.

About this time Chaplin met Elinor Glyn, discoverer of "It" and author of "Three Weeks," "Six Days," "One Hour," and other temporal hits. When Elinor Glyn met him she exclaimed, "Why, you don't look nearly as funny as I thought you would." His quick retort was "Neither do you."

Chaplin bought a tract of land near Pickfair, the home of his friends Mary Pickford and Douglas Fairbanks, in the exclusive hilly section of Beverly Hills. Here he built the house which is still his home—a large, square, tiled-roof, stucco structure of some forty rooms. The high-ceilinged living room contained a pipe organ and concealed projection equipment. Looking forward to the time when she would share it Pola Negri transplanted large trees to the value of seven thousand dollars, because she liked to hear the sound of wind rustling in the leaves while she slept.

But the romance between the tempestuous Polish actress and the temperamental comedian began to founder. In a press statement Chaplin professed to be "too poor" to marry. As her explanation of the broken engagement, Miss Negri handed a statement to the press, averring that she also was "too poor to marry Charles Chaplin. He needs a wealthy woman." With tears rolling down her cheeks and with trembling lips, she announced dramatically, "Now I will live only for my work." But they made up again and the now radiant actress announced: "He told me he loved me and could not live without me."

There was too much drama and temperament in the affair. Pola Negri's emotions were a torrent the little comedian could not control. The Polish tigress went tooth and nail after a rival, a Mexican girl who had entered the house by a ruse and secreted herself in Chaplin's bedroom. In the middle of 1923 the match was definitely declared off. "I am glad it is over, for it was interfering with my work. . . . I am sure I could not be a great actress as Mrs. Chaplin." The papers soon noted that Chaplin was seen escorting Leonore Ulric, while Pola, at a tennis championship match, was attended by William Tilden and Manuel Alonzo.

Chaplin seems to have been humiliated by the affair and was chagrined to hear that another actor, Rudolph Valentino, had supplanted him. "That ham," he said in disgust. In later years one of Chaplin's favorite parlor acts was his impersonation of a certain fading actress courting publicity with a great emotional scene at the funeral of a certain famous actor!

Chaplin's loves, real or gossip-created, filled the columns during the twenties. Before his marriage to Lita Grey, he was reported seen in the company of Lila Lee, Thelma Morgan Converse, Anna Q. Nilson, Josephine Dunn and others.

two minor comedies

After the enormous success of "The Kid" the two short comedies which followed seemed let-downs. Chaplin was already in Europe when "The Idle Class," made in May 1921, was released on September 21. "Pay Day," the film interrupted by his sudden vacation, was finished a few months after his return and released in April 1922. Neither "flopped" like "Sunnyside" and "A Day's Pleasure," but they caused no commotion. Produced for laughs by tried-and-true methods, they achieved their purpose. Each, besides, contained some brilliant bits and some exceptional gags, but neither ranks with his previous hits or the longer features to come.

"Pay Day" was Chaplin's last two-reeler. After 1922 he produced only feature-length pictures. This was partly a falling in with the trend of the period. Lloyd was making feature comedies in 1922—"Grandma's Boy" and "Doctor Jack"; Keaton, the following year, made the feature-length "Three Ages" and "Our Hospitality." Only the minor comedians were still turning out two-reelers.

In some ways this was unfortunate. Most slapstick comedians did not have enough to sustain a full-length picture. Two reels was an ideal length for thăt product; and, at that length, it continued to be a staple of the industry for many years—until sound killed it off with the animated cartoon.

In "The Idle Class," originally entitled "Vanity Fair," Chaplin plays a dual role—two members of the "idle class," a wealthy fop and a foppish tramp. Influenced by his new intellectual friends Chaplin was perhaps attempting social significance but the contents were less significant than the title promised. Actually, "The Idle Class," introducing nothing new, was something of a throwback to the Mutual days—smoother in production but with slower pace and fewer laughs than those classic two-reelers. Its rather thin story line is reminiscent of "The Count" and "The Adventurer"; but it provides pegs for a number of amusing gags. Though the ending is somewhat abrupt and disappointing, the picture is generally entertaining and often rises to hilarious levels. Incidentally, it was then something of a novelty to see Chaplin attired in the height of fashion. Edna Purviance, too, is fashionably dressed, a change, excepting the last part of "The Kid," from her recent appearances as a country gawk or a lower-middle-class drab. Mack Swain, whom a quarrel with a producer had banished from the screen for a while, returned to appear with Chaplin for the first time since Keystone days.

As the picture opens the Wife, a wealthy woman, descends from a Pullman car, attended by maids and porters, at the railroad station of an exclusive community. She looks around, in obvious disappointment, for her missing husband, whom she had wired to meet her. As she steps to her waiting limousine, another passenger, the Tramp, dismounts from his "berth" in the tool box under one of the coaches. He calmly adjusts his baggage, which includes a bag of golf sticks, and reaches the Wife's automobile in time to ride off with her—on the rear bumper.

After a night of celebration the Absent-Minded Husband gets started on his meeting with his wife, but is delayed by a variety of mishaps. Still in evening clothes and a high silk hat, he makes their suite at the hotel just as his wife arrives to find it empty. Crawling in on his hands and knees he suddenly darts through the room and lands upright on the bed, to turn an innocent smile at his wife. But such a reception does not go down with her and she flounces out with her maids to engage separate rooms.

Left alone the alcoholic husband broods at a table where his wife's photograph stands among other loved objects—liquor bottles. He picks up the portrait and gazes at it tearfully, turns around to put it down again, still shaken by convulsive sobs. From the rear his shoulders move up and down more rapidly, as if in an intensification of his grief. But when he turns forward it is with a bland expression and we find that the accelerated shoulder movements come from the manipulation of a cocktail shaker. (A variation, of course, on the opening gag of "The Immigrant.") Later he receives a note from his wife promising forgiveness if he will attend a masked ball that evening.

Meanwhile the Tramp has wandered to the golf course adjoining the hotel and goes into a sequence burlesquing the game, then at its peak of popularity. Not finding the sand on the course to his liking, he sprinkles his own brand, dredged from one of his pockets. Walking nonchalantly past another golfer, poised for a shot, he kicks the ball along, as though by accident, while the puzzled but suspicious golfer follows. Kicking the ball into a bush he quickly bends down to pick it up, only to face the owner who has circled around the other side and beats him to it. Wandering off Charlie sees a ball land in the open mouth of a sleeping hobo. As his snoring lifts the ball Charlie hits it out of this "trap." During the game he catches a glimpse of the Wife on horseback, on a canter through the woods. Smitten with the beautiful woman, he daydreams of what might be, in vision after vision, starring himself as romantic hero—until he reawakens to the lonely Tramp reality.

The inevitable brush with the police follows—this time innocently. His neighbor on a park bench has his pocket picked from behind and the Tramp is blamed. In the ensuing chase he takes refuge at the masked ball in the hotel ballroom.

Here the Tramp—the husband's double in appearance —is taken for the latter in masquerade disguise. The Wife in an eighteenth-century Watteau costume with a powdered wig, makes affectionate demonstrations of her forgiveness, and the puzzled Charlie thinks his dream has come true. Her stout and humorless father, a veritable gargoyle in Scottish kilts and bare legs, is also deceived, and uses the occasion for a further demonstration of his dislike for his "son-in-law."

When the real Husband arrives, unrecognizable in a suit of medieval armor into which he is locked tight, he becomes infuriated over the Tramp's liberties with his Wife and, like a knight of old, charges at the intruder. In the free-for-all that follows, the Wife's Father takes a heavy hand. Finally, with the assistance of the puzzled Tramp, the Husband is "opened" with a hammer and can-opener, and the doubles are revealed. With a quick kick to square accounts with his temporary "father-in-law," the agile Tramp takes to his heels again.

"Pay Day" is a realistic little film—a slice of the life of a building laborer before, on, and after pay day. This film, too, was probably influenced by Clare Sheridan and other social-minded friends. If so it hardly succeeds in its aim. For all its sympathy for the working man in his tribulations, its social overtones do not achieve much sonority. In fact, lacking the genuine pathos of "A Dog's Life" or the brilliance of "Shoulder Arms," "Pay Day" is closest to the Essanay films.

Technically, however, "Pay Day" is a noticeable advance. For the first time in a Chaplin film backlighting is used in the interiors. Night scenes, such as the rain and the trolley-car sequences, were photographed at night with the aid of rather skillful artificial lighting. The sets are designed with an almost stylized simplicity. Some of the key action turns, as with the escalator in "The Floor-walker" and the recalcitrant Ford in "A Day's Pleasure," on the workings of a blind mechanical force, in this case an unpredictable elevator and inaccessible street cars. Much of the action gains point as illustrations of life's little ironies. The accent is on comedy but frustrations are the normal course as the tough foreman and his haughty daughter, the workman's own menacing wife, and even the elusive street cars keep him from fulfillments, great and small. "Pay Day" was accorded a rather tepid reception here and Chaplin himself was quoted as saying that he did not consider it the equal of "The Immigrant." Some French critics, however, consider it one of his best.

"Pay Day's" opening title, "Hard Shirking Men," is followed by a scene of laborers on a building construction. Charlie, late for work, makes his entrance with a lily in his hand, with which he tries to pacify the tough foreman, like a schoolboy making up to a teacher. The first swing of his pick loosens a workman in a trench. When he feebly digs dirt by the ounce, the exasperated foreman transfers him to a high scaffold for bricklaying, which appears to be his natural forte for (with the help of a speeded up and reverse-action camera) he juggles and lays the bricks with such speed and dexterity that they cannot be tossed up to him fast enough.

The foreman's pretty daughter, who brings her father's lunch, has won Charlie's admiration. He rides up the little elevator to adore her shyly; when she notices him he goes down. One soulful upward look toward her is diverted by strong cheese set near his nose and he hurriedly descends. At another time the elevator ascends under him just in time to prevent him from sitting down on empty space. Then Charlie turns it into a restaurant dumbwaiter serving him an unexpected variety of luncheon dishes. Thus the foreman, above, lays a frankfurter on the elevator which descends to serve the meat to Charlie, who places it in a whole loaf of bread. The foreman is next surprised to find only an empty banana skin beside him.

When pay day comes Charlie believes he has been cheated. By a corner fence we see him in eloquent pantomime arguing with an off-scene person for more money. But his own fingers, as they figure, show him to have been overpaid. He hides part of his pay in his hat to keep it from his wife, but in vain, for the hefty shrew has been shadowing him. She grabs the money but he manages to pick her pocketbook before ducking away from her.

Night finds him with cronies outside the closing saloon from which they have just been ejected into the rain. They form a quartette for some sour harmonizing. When their rendition of "Sweet Adeline" is applauded with a pitcher of water from an irate woman above, Charlie nonchalantly opens an umbrella and continues singing. A drunken mix-up of coats and umbrellas follows. Charlie and a companion each get one arm in a sleeve of the other's coat and Charlie finds himself suddenly whisked around the corner, but has the presence of mind to tip his hat to a cop as he is pulled down the street. There is further comic confusion with Charlie's cane held up as a fat companion's umbrella and difficulties crossing a large puddle.

And now the struggle to board a trolley car for home. Dozens storm ahead and crowd Charlie out. On his third attempt a flying overhead dive lands him near the rear entrance, only to be pushed all the way through the car to the front entrance, and out, by the crowd swarming in after him. The last car is packed and Charlie tries to get transportation via another passenger's suspenders. These give way and down goes Charlie and part of the man's pants with him. Then, in a state of confusion, he climbs into a hot-dog wagon and starts strap-hanging from a large sausage suspended from the ceiling. He opens his newspaper in the belief that he is properly embarked for home when the proprietor forcibly disillusions him and sends him home, afoot.

Back home he oils his shoes in the hope of getting to bed unnoticed by his wife who lies with a rolling pin cuddled to her breast. As he starts to undress the alarm clock goes off. Charlie rises to the occasion and promptly dons his coat again—but doesn't fool his hard-hearted wife. Rolling pin in hand she drives him off to work again. The henpecked husband flees to the bathroom, lies down in the seemingly empty tub—to pop up dripping. A close-up of the scolding wife irises out and the camera irises in on a close-up of Charlie's bare shivering feet, with his clothes drying on a radiator in the background.

Considered rather slight fare in 1921 and 1922 "The Idle Class" and "Pay Day" would be welcomed as extremely pleasant entertainment today when comedy of this genre is so rare.

"The Pilgrim"

With the completion of "The Pilgrim" on September 25, 1922, Chaplin finished up his First National contract. He made his next films for United Artists, a company which he had helped to form in 1919, with Mary Pickford, Douglas Fairbanks, and D. W. Griffith. Its origin has been traced to a remark made by Oscar Price who became the company's first president. Price, then in charge of public relations for William C. McAdoo, Secretary of the Treasury, had remarked to the three stars while on their Liberty Loan tour: "Why don't you folks get together and distribute your own pictures? You are big enough to do that." The casual suggestion bore fruit.

In their United Artists company the three stars and the great director planned to invest their own money, produce their own pictures and distribute them themselves, thus assuring a higher rental fee and better returns. They pitted the box-office value of their names against the theatre domination of the big corporations. The United Artists Corporation of Delaware was incorporated in April 1919 with Price as president and McAdoo as counsel. The two were soon to resign and Hiram Abrams was to head the organization. Because of Chaplin's slow fulfillment of his First National contract for eight pictures, he was not effectively in the new company until he produced "A Woman of Paris" in 1923. From then on all his films were to be handled by United Artists.

"The Pilgrim" is a short feature—four reels in length. Not so well remembered as "Shoulder Arms" and "The Kid," it is one of Chaplin's masterpieces. It is highly characteristic of Chaplin, full of his irreverent nose-thumbing at pomp and convention, in an expansive nothing-is-sacred mood. Not as hilarious as "Shoulder Arms" and lacking the sentiment of "The Kid" the picture, nevertheless, has considerable comedy and tenderness. The chief butts of its satire are rural types and small-town puritanism.

Here again Chaplin reveals his minute observation and perfect mimicry. Just as in earlier pictures he was a super-policeman, super-fireman, or super-doughboy, here, as an escaped convict in ministerial disguise, he becomes a super-clergyman, assuming all the mannerisms of the typical minister in a clever caricature. Trade critics at the preview worried over the reaction of the church-going public. Again their worries proved unfounded. It was taken goodhumoredly and was generally popular. The strict Pennsylvania censors alone barred "The Pilgrim" because "it made the ministry look ridiculous."

At least three of its scenes equal anything Chaplin did: the famous pantomime sermon on David and Goliath, the encounter with the obnoxious boy (played by Dinky Dean, son of "Chuck" Riesner), and the concluding booting across the Mexican border.

Charlie, escaping from prison, borrows the clothes of a minister who is in swimming. At the railroad station he studies the list of towns, wondering where to go. Shutting his eyes, he decides to buy a ticket for whatever town his pin hits. His first try lands him in Sing Sing; his second try in a neighbor who is also studying the board; his third try in Devil's Gulch for which he buys a ticket.

On board the train he discovers that the man reading the paper beside him is a policeman and what he is reading is the account of the prison break. Charlie decides to hurry off that train.

At the small-town station where he alights a church reception committee is awaiting the arrival of a new minister. From force of habit, Charlie holds out his hands to the local sheriff to be handcuffed. With the gesture perhaps interpreted as a benediction, the "new preacher" is made welcome by the simple country folk. A telegram from the real minister explaining his delay is received by the pompous deacon who, being without his glasses, asks Charlie to read it. Hearing from Charlie that the telegram concerns a delayed package, the deacon tears it up.

Unwilling to accept the alternative of returning to prison and unable to elude his escort, the ex-convict is forced to continue the impersonation. In the pulpit of the little rural church, he prepares to conduct the services. Charlie imitates every gesture of the sacristan—even coughing in unison. At one point, to relax himself from the strain, Charlie pulls out a cigarette and is about to light up when the black looks of the congregation remind him such things are not done in church. The collection boxes are brought up and Charlie hefts them carefully to see which contains the most money. When the time comes for the sermon, a touch of "stage fright" immobilizes him. Getting over it he goes into his impromptu pantomime "act"—the highlight of the film. The introductory title, "Goliath was a big man," is all the help the spectator needs. Enacting both David and Goliath, he jumps from one side of the platform to the other—as David, stooping down to pick up the imaginary stone and slinging it; as Goliath, threatening and tottering down, etc. The "performance" wins the applause of a boy in the audience but the response of the rest of the congregation is not so favorable. This does not faze the new minister who refuses to be stared out of his curtain calls.

Following the service Charlie is escorted by the deacon to the house where he is to live. Passing a bar the women lower their eyes and Charlie pantomimes his regrets he cannot enter. He is to stay at the home of Mrs. Brown and her pretty daughter whom he had already noticed at the station and again at the church organ. Charlie patiently endures the showing of the family album. Among other comic moments is the plight of the deacon when he smashes a bottle of homemade "hootch" in his pocket.

Visitors arrive, among them a garrulous lady, her subdued husband, their obnoxious child, and a crook who recognizes the Pilgrim as a former cellmate. The pugnacious brat is the very antithesis of the Kid. As they try to converse, the father and the Pilgrim are used as stepladders and punching bags by the brat who then tries to see what nuisances can be committed with flypaper and live goldfish.

A suggestion to the brat to go and play elsewhere gets the parents nowhere. Another suggestion to "go play with the gentleman" precipitates a mauling of Charlie who, restrained by his supposed position and the dignity of the occasion, endures it with super-Christian patience. But when the others troop to the dining room and Charlie is left alone with the brat clamped to his heels, his inhibitions are released and he sends the pest flying with a deftly delivered kick in the stomach.

In the kitchen the brat's next feat is to set his father's derby over the plum pudding in such a way that Charlie does not see it when he turns to cover the pudding with sauce and whipped cream. The father, declining an invitation to tea, searches for his hat. The lost headgear finally turns up when "the pastor" struggles to slice the derbied plum pudding. As the infuriated owner looks on, the brat licks gobs of the sweet goo off the remains of the hat.

In the evening, in the garden, the new pastor seeks better acquaintance with the charming daughter of the house. The crook, ignoring Charlie's warnings not to try anything here, sets out to rob the deacon. Charlie foils him twice by amazing feats of legerdemain. The crook watches the hostess opening a drawer where her mortgage money is kept, and when the family retires Charlie keeps watch. The crook steals in and a battle follows in utter silence. As the crook opens the drawer, Charlie closes it with his foot. Finally the crook gooses Charlie with a lighted candle, grabs the money, and gets away. As the girl, hearing the commotion, rushes in, Charlie tells her the mortgage money has been stolen but, "Don't worry, I'll get it back."

The crook repairs to the saloon and gambling house which is held up immediately after his arrival. Charlie arrives in time to steal back the mortgage money. The sheriff, meanwhile, enters the Browns' home to search it for a convict posing as a minister. Charlie comes in to hand over the mortgage money retrieved heroically at great risk. Despite the girl's pleas the sheriff arrests Charlie who bids the somewhat disillusioned girl a gallant and apologetic farewell.

The sheriff has been touched, however, and he leads his prisoner to the Mexican border informing his charge that he can gain his freedom by crossing the line. Charlie laughs at what he thinks is a "joke." Then he is ordered to go pick some flowers across the line, but the super-honest prisoner returns with a bouquet with which he pursues the sheriff who is riding away. Finally the officer dismounts and, leading the prisoner to the border, kicks him over the line. At last Charlie catches on. With the United States to the left and Mexico to the right he hesitates until some bandits make their appearance in Mexico. With the "law" on one side and lawlessness on the other, Charlie runs down the boundary line, hopping from one side to the other according to circumstances. Finally, straddling the border with one foot in each country, but with both feet ready to take the easiest way at the first indication of danger from either side, he rapidly waddles off into the distance. In this humorous and eloquent ending some have seen a symbol of the eternal pilgrim on the tragic roads of the world.

"A Woman of Paris"

"A Woman of Paris," the straight dramatic picture which Chaplin directed but did not star in, is a milestone in the history of the screen and appears on almost every list of ten best pictures of all time. It did not matter to Chaplin that it was not a financial success. It fulfilled an old ambition and brought him further prestige. "A Woman of Paris" initiated a new school of film art—sophisticated, intimate drama—and exerted a great influence on motion-picture style in general.

One day, in the late summer of 1922, when Chaplin was casting about for a subject for his first film for United Artists release, Marshall Neilan rushed into his office to tell him he had Peggy Hopkins Joyce outside in his car. Chaplin, idly fingering his violin, invited them in for a drink. The much-married and bejeweled Peggy gave him a grande dame greeting; but as the drinks took effect, her affected accent dropped away and she became quite natural. Chaplin was fascinated by this woman of the world, a type so removed from his previous loves. For two weeks, which included a trip to Catalina Island, they were inseparable. Then she departed for a New York stage engagement, Peggy with pleasant memories and Chaplin, in addition, with the idea for his next picture.

When he announced to his staff that he would not be making a comedy, but a tragedy in which he would not appear, they were dumbfounded. Back in 1915, however, while at Essanay, Chaplin had started the serious film

"Life," which he had never completed because of the demand for comedies. It was his ambition to do at least one big dramatic feature to show the world that he could be something else besides a clown. To this end, in 1917, he purchased the rights to Hall Caine's "The Prodigal Son" intending to cast himself in the title role. That picture was never even started.

The story of his new film was built around some chapters in the early life of Peggy Hopkins Joyce. It also has suggestions of "Camille" and a pessimistic flavor à la Hardy. It ran through three titles—"Destiny," which was discarded, then "Public Opinion," under which it was known in Europe, and "A Woman of Paris," its title in this country.

In "A Woman of Paris" Chaplin also fulfilled his promise to Edna Purviance to make a dramatic actress of her. Indeed, the film was made partly for this purpose, his reward to his loyal leading lady, who had appeared in all his comedies for nine years, a total of thirty-four films. For the male lead Chaplin picked Adolphe Menjou. Reputedly Peggy Joyce pointed him out as resembling a certain wealthy bon-vivant of Paris. After some dickering he was hired at five hundred dollars a week—a much higher salary than Chaplin usually paid. The impression many have that Menjou was discovered by Chaplin is mistaken. Menjou had a not inconsiderable reputation, already, as a "villain" and character actor and had appeared in Pickford's "Through the Back Door," Fairbanks' "The Three Musketeers" (as Louis XIII), Valentino's "The Sheik," Wallace Reid's "Clarence," and other features. However, "A Woman of Paris" launched him in the new suave and cynical philanderer role in which he was to win great success in many subsequent pictures.

Ironically Edna Purviance's career, instead of being advanced, was virtually brought to an end by "A Woman of Paris." The public had become accustomed to seeing her in sympathetic roles. Her worldly new role of a demi-mondaine confused many people. So good was her portrayal that she managed to arouse considerable sympathy in spite of a role in which she brought tragedy to others. Nevertheless Adolphe Menjou "stole" the picture from her. In France, later, Miss Purviance made "The Education of a Prince," directed by Henry Diamant-Berger, which was not released in this country. And in 1926 Chaplin, seeking to bring her out of retirement, put Josef von Sternberg under contract to direct her in a film, variously entitled "The Sea Gull" and "The Woman of the Sea." It did not turn out well although Chaplin, in an effort to salvage it, himself directed some additional scenes. After one preview he decided not to release it. The reason gossip gives for its withdrawal is that Eve Southern, in the second lead, again stole the film from Edna who, by the standards of that period, had become too "mature."

For directorial and script assistants on "A Woman of Paris" Chaplin had the ambitious Eddie Sutherland and the clever Monta Bell. To be assured of authentic French atmosphere he hired Jean de Limur and Harry d'Abbadie d'Arrast. All four later became directors on their own. Production began in December 1922, in a by now completely enclosed studio equipped with the best lighting and production installations. In some nine months of shooting, Chaplin used nearly half a million feet of film and spent $800,000.

"A Woman of Paris" opened at the Lyric Theatre, New York, on October 1, 1923. Presented twice a day at advanced prices, it was Chaplin's first United Artists picture. Chaplin himself was not billed, but he appeared in it briefly, and almost unrecognizably, as a porter.

Although a great critical success, the fact that both Chaplin and his type of comedy were lacking, went against it and the "big audience" was lukewarm to it. It was a courageous experiment which, however, Chaplin never repeated. It seemed to be too adult for the general film audience which, according even to present surveys, is concentrated in the adolescent-age range. It went over only in the biggest cities. However, it was very popular —almost a cult—with the intelligentsia, and the twenties saw frequent revivals of the film.

The story itself, a variation of the old triangle, was not unusual; but the imaginative and brilliant handling, the significance carried by its details, its indirect and subtle style, its laconic touches, won it the admiration of sensitive audiences. It reflected Chaplin's deep insight into human nature and especially his understanding of feminine psychology. It is probably the first film which consciously attempted to express complexity in human character and in human relations. To present the human mixture of good and bad in a film's principal characters was, in itself, quite unprecedented, on a screen whose "heroes" and "heroines" were usually elemental symbols painted either white or black.

"A Woman of Paris" is subtitled "a drama of fate" and fate's hand moves throughout the film. We see it in the death of the father as Jean sets out to elope with Marie; in the interrupted telephone call at the station; in their accidental meeting years later in Paris; in the failure to see each other as Pierre and Marie pass each other at the end of the film. This ending has a symbolical significance besides being a human irony. Pierre is in a speeding automobile; Marie rides on the tail of a hay cart. The separation of their paths is social and moral as well as geographical. (There was an alternative ending for Europe in which Marie, after Jean's suicide, is forced to return to Pierre.)

The foreword to the film, which may be taken as a Chaplin credo, runs as follows: "Humanity is composed not of heroes and villains, but of men and women, and all their passions, both good and bad, have been given them by God. They sin only in blindness, and the ignorant condemn their mistakes, but the wise pity them." Some highbrows found such moralizing objectionable. Similar forewords, however, were indispensable to the big silent productions of the period. In "A Woman of Paris" a foreword was necessary to set the tone for such a departure from the usual.

Theme, characters, and atmosphere were all very daring for the time. The film was realistic and made no concessions to sentiment or moral codes. Humanity itself was indicted. Virtue was not shown in any self-reward nor vice as a self-punishment. He comments on problems of life without attempting to solve them, on human frailties without attempting to reform them. His is no preacher's viewpoint but one of half-sympathetic, half-cynical psychological understanding. Pennsylvania banned the film as ". . . indecent, immoral, and deals with prostitution in Paris and indecent love affairs." But except, possibly, for one gay studio-party scene, there was nothing in it to compete with the permitted "jazz" films or De Mille orgies of the period.

Simplicity marked the presentation of action and the treatment of emotions. The heavy emotionalism, standard for that day, was avoided. For the first time on the screen a triangle plot was presented in a straightforward and casual manner. In the past that embarrassing reality of life was treated either in heavy melodramatic or in farcical style.

Even the sets were simple. In the opening scene, roofs and a lighted window are enough to suggest a small French town at night. The railroad station is created by light and shadow. Many other scenes are mere stylized corners.

Ever consistent on economy in expression and achieving much with subtle suggestion, the film provided a post-graduate course in screen technique for directors and producers. One celebrated bit is the scene where Marie leaves the small station waiting room to entrain for Paris. As she looks up, the reflections from the lighted windows of the train pass over her and along the wall behind her. The train itself is not shown. This device has been so often imitated since that it is now a cliché absorbed into the general body of cinematic technique. But in 1923 this approach was breathtaking.

Considerable use is made of ellipsis or abridgment in time and action—the skipping over of unessential details. Marie is shown, following the misunderstanding with her lover, as a wealthy bachelor's mistress. The circumstances involved in her transformation from a simple country girl to an elaborately gowned "woman of Paris" are left entirely to the beholder's imagination. Again, toward the end of the picture, the former lover is shown in the lobby of the cafe after he has been ejected for picking a quarrel with Marie's escort. We do not see him shoot himself, but the cafe crowd reacts to a "shot," then we see a man falling into a fountain. Applications of this device have been innumerable, particularly in the talkies where sound can readily suggest off-stage action.

Typical subtle touches are achieved by the use of objects—handkerchiefs, collars, chocolate candy, musical instruments. When Pierre visits Marie's apartment, their relationship is clearly established when he goes to her bureau drawer for one of his handkerchiefs. Later the relationship is made clear to her artist admirer when, picking out a dress for Marie to pose in, one of Pierre's collars falls to the floor as a gown is lifted out. Thus censorship was neatly sidestepped.

The picture's restraint and casualness are vivid in the scene where Pierre discovers Marie with her artist friend. None of the customary frenzied gestures or furniture-

smashing. Pierre merely suggests that perhaps the gentleman in the next room might like some chocolates. At a
later meeting of the two rivals Pierre's suavity is high-
lighted by his offering and lighting a cigarette for the
other man.

In possibly the outstanding sequence in the picture, a
succession of images and movements take the place of
dialogue. As Marie bemoans her lot Pierre points out
the window to a mother trying distractedly to manage a
brood of dirty, quarreling, bawling children. When he
fingers her diamond necklace significantly she rips it off
and tosses it angrily out the window. But when a tramp
picks it up Marie darts down after him while Pierre
blandly plays his saxophone.

Another interesting sequence of shots irised in and out
contrasts the activities of the principal characters at a
certain hour of the night.

Tragic though it is "A Woman of Paris" is not without
Chaplinesque humor, satire, and irony. The obsequious
head-waiter is played by Henry Bergman in customary
Chaplin comedy style. The comedian himself contributes
a comic bit when, as a porter, he nonchalantly drops a
heavy trunk to the floor. While a boisterous girl is paw-
ing him, Pierre telephones to Marie that he is having
"just a quiet little party with friends." When Marie first
visits Jean's studio, the embarrassment of his poverty is
heightened when a napkin, unfolded, reveals holes.

Possibly the most humorous sequence is the massage
episode. While Marie is being massaged (below camera
range), a stony-faced masseuse mechanically goes about
her work, clearly revealing which part of the body she
is at, and pretends to be paying no attention to Marie's
gossiping girl friends, yet absorbing every remark. The
pantomime of this scene could have found a place in any
of Chaplin's comedies.

"A Woman of Paris" introduced the comedy of manners to the screen, and showed how to circumvent the censors by subtleties and laconic touches. It may truly be called the first "Lubitsch" picture, for the great German director, taking his cue from "A Woman of Paris," abandoned the historical spectacles which had made him famous and embarked on the series of modern social comedies, "The Marriage Circle," "Forbidden Paradise," "Kiss Me Again," etc. These were to bring him greater fame and start a new school. The impact of "A Woman of Paris" was also perceptible in Monta Bell's "Broadway After Dark" and "The Torrent" (Garbo's first American film), d'Arrast's "Service for Ladies" and "A Gentleman of Paris," Mal St. Clair's "The Grand Duchess and the Waiter," etc. And its influence was diffused through the whole of subsequent movie-making. But the depth and irony of this Chaplin classic has seldom been equaled.

Perhaps "A Woman of Paris" was overpraised. Chaplin himself is said to have become bored by the eulogies. There were a few critics who complained that the story was banal, the ending too moralistic. Chaplin himself once quipped to a critic, "How can you be sure Marie will stay on the farm more than an hour after the end of the film?" No doubt such famous "touches" as the train shadows were dictated by economy (it would have been expensive to reproduce a French train). Possibly some of the indirection and "restraint" in the emotional scenes may have been adaptations to the placid disposition of Miss Purviance. Sometimes the titles, despite their brevity, are too numerous for "pure" cinema.

The film has not been revived since the twenties and might seem rather tame today. What was then new has long been absorbed into the general technique of picture making; and what was then skating on thin ice is now accepted as a matter of course, morals and customs changing as they do. The long potato-sack dresses and coiffures of 1923 would in themselves date the film.

No matter what it may look like today, the importance of "A Woman in Paris" in motion-picture history is unquestionable. It takes a place among the landmarks of the screen along with "The Birth of a Nation," "Intolerance," "Broken Blossoms," "Greed," "The Last Laugh," "Potemkin," "The Passion of Joan of Arc," "The Informer," "Citizen Kane," "The Bicycle Thief," and other greats. And in Carol Reed's "The Third Man," one of the biggest hits of 1949-1950, a different type of film altogether, we find three scenes which trace back, directly or indirectly, to this pioneer Chaplin classic.

The opening scene is "a small village somewhere in France," at night. A girl is seen waiting at an upper lighted window of a stone house. Dissolve to a medium shot, then to a closer shot of "Marie St. Clair, a woman of fate, a victim of the environment of an unhappy home." Her father, out in the hall, turns on the gas light, peers into her room, then locks the door. To her art-student sweetheart Jean, who has arrived in the street below, she cries down, "I'm locked in!" He climbs up to her window over the sloping roof and helps her down. The father, seeing them, locks the window and bars the front door.

Midnight. The couple return. In the cold night air, they finish discussion of their plans. "We'll get to Plymouth and be married." They kiss and Jean helps Marie climb back. "He's locked my window!" They also find the door barred. Jean knocks and the father slams the door after telling Marie, "Perhaps he will provide a bed for you for the night.

Jean comforts her. "Mother will put you up for the night." They walk through the drizzling rain to his parents' house. In the hall Marie hesitates. Jean reassures her. "Don't worry. Tomorrow we'll forget all these tears."

The father, turning on the light, angrily asks to see his son alone, then demands, "Get that woman out of this house!" He refuses to hear any explanations. Jean claims his mother will understand. "She's been locked out. That's all." In the hall Marie says, "I'd better go," covers her face with her hands. The mother comes downstairs and another quarrel starts. Jean leaves with Marie, rebuffing his mother's pleas.

The couple go to the railway station, where a porter carrying a large trunk on his back offhandedly dumps it on the floor. A train for Paris is due in thirty minutes and Jean gives Marie money to buy their tickets while he rushes home to pack. "Don't be long," she pleads.

Back home, as the father turns away from Jean, the mother pleads: "Father's determined; why not make the best of it?" Jean angrily: "I never want to see him again!" In the parlor the father offers Jean money through the mother as intermediary, but ignores her pleas to say goodbye to him. Jean, coming downstairs with his bag, refuses to take the money or to say goodbye to his father whose back is turned and hidden by the large chair he is sitting in. As the mother weeps, the son calls out a farewell to the father but, receiving no reply, he starts away. Then he notices his father's pipe on the floor, and rushing back finds his father motionless. Jean calls his mother; the two, distraught, loosen the stricken man's clothing. Jean calls the doctor.

From the station the impatient Marie telephones: "Jean, haven't you left yet?" He replies, "Oh, is that you, Marie? We'll have to postpone our trip." There is an interruption; he asks her to wait "just a-moment." He leaves the telephone to open the door for the doctor. Marie, believing he has changed his mind, hangs up with an embittered expression. She comes out of the station door and as she looks up (in a semi-close-up), the reflections from the lighted windows of the unseen train pass over her and across the wall behind. Jean fails to get her on the phone.

"A year later. Paris—the magic city, where fortune is fickle and a woman gambles with life." A cabaret. At the tables decadent types: an elderly woman with a gigolo, military officers, turbaned Orientals, European debauchés.

A grand entrance is made by Marie St. Clair. "Time brings many changes." And in a few short months life has made of her "a woman of Paris," the beautiful toy of Pierre Revel. The wealthiest man in the gayest city in the world, his whims have ruined many. He suavely bows to acquaintances.

After descending the steps to their table Pierre bows to a man who returns the bow. Marie asks, "Who's that you bowed to?" Pierre replies, "The richest bachelor in Paris." An elderly woman is shown with a polished young man. "Who is that?"—"One of the richest old maids in Paris."—"Who's the man with her?"—Pierre merely smiles and raises his eyebrows.

"Pierre makes a study of eating as he does of living." He enters the kitchen to pick a fowl and supervise the preparation of his order, the waiter standing in obsequious attention. Back at his table the couple are first served champagne truffles ("a delicacy for pigs—and gentlemen"). The headwaiter pours the wine himself with fawning smiles and brusquely gives orders to other waiters who compete for the privilege of the other services.

"Marie's apartment early the next morning." Her friend Fifi enters, "young and vivacious, hungry for excitement." Fifi teases and kisses Marie who is still in bed. "Why, Marie, of all the lazy people." She flings open the window and tells Marie to get up—not to waste her life in bed. When asked what she is doing up so early, Fifi, taking off her coat, reveals an evening dress.

chapter XII

62   64

63   65

2-69 Eight scenes from "Shoulder Arms":

  62 "The Awkward Squad."
  63 In the dugout, Sid Chaplin on right.
  64 "Over There."
  65 "Over the top."

66   68

67   69

Eight scenes from "Shoulder Arms" (cont.)

66   Discovered by the French girl.
67   Disguised in a German uniform.
68   Charlie routs the Germans.
69   Charlie pretends to be severe with Sid before he captures the Kaiser.

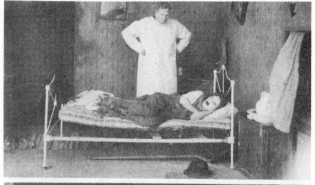

chapter XIII

70 The Hired Man and the Hardhearted Employer
in "Sunnyside."
71 Charlie admires the Village Belle in "Sunnyside."
72 The dream ballet from "Sunnyside."

73 Chaplin and Jackie Coogan in "The Kid."

74　The Tramp and the Kid plying their trade.

75   The Policeman (Tom Wilson) is suspicious
of the Tramp and the Kid.

76   The Tramp rescuing the Kid from the orphanage truck.

77   Chaplin directing Jackie Coogan.

78   Chaplin amusing Jackie Coogan between scenes.

79 Chaplin in 1921.

80 Portrait of Claire Windsor, 1922.
81 Claire Windsor in a Goldwyn picture of 1923.

82   Pola Negri, the tempestuous Polish actress who came to America in 1922 after great success in German films.

83   Chaplin romping by the swimming pool of his Beverly Hills estate with Dinky Dean, son of his associate director Chuck Riesner.

84 "The Idle Class."
85 **Edna Purviance** believes the Tramp to be her husband in disguise.

86   Charlie and the foreman's daughter in "Pay Day."

Charlie's wife follows him on pay day.

88 Charlie believes he is riding a trolley home. Sid Chaplin as
the food-stand owner is more sober.

"I haven't been to bed yet!" This earns a playful spank from Marie.

"The business office of Pierre" turns out to be his bedroom. He watches ticker tape unwinding at his bedside while his secretary stands near. Soon tiring of this "work," he picks up a magazine where he sees an announcement of his engagement to a woman of social prominence. "The wedding will unite large fortunes." The secretary leans over, "Won't this complicate matters?" —"What do you mean?"—"The other lady—does she know?"—"Let's call her up."—"Who?"—"The other lady." . . . Marie answers the telephone. "Hello, Marie dear, shall I see you tonight?" "Why, of course." Pierre turns slyly to his secretary. "She doesn't know yet."

Paulette, another friend of Marie's, enters. The women kiss. Aside, Paulette shows Fifi the magazine. "Has Marie seen this?" Paulette doesn't know. When Marie asks what's up Paulette shows her the magazine. Marie glances at it casually and laughs it off—lights a cigarette to cover her emotion—tosses the magazine aside—picks it up again and shrugs, "Well, such is life." The girls assure her everything will be all right. After they leave, Marie snatches up the magazine, studies it in obvious agitation.

In the evening Pierre calls to take Marie to dinner. Among other familiarities he gets one of his handkerchiefs from Marie's bureau drawer. When Marie enters, he plants a "husbandly" kiss, takes a drink, and offers her some. She refuses, "It's no use, Pierre, I can't go out tonight." Is she depressed? Then he sees the magazine. "You're not worried about that? It will make no difference." She is angry. "How can you talk like that—as if I had no feelings at all," and starts to weep. He leaves her, saying, "I'll see you tomorrow when you are in a better mood."

That evening, at a party in the Latin Quarter, Pierre, reclining on a chaise longue, telephones Marie. He tells her he is in the studio of an artist friend. "What's going on?" As a boisterous girl beside him tousles him, he replies, "Oh, just a quiet little party with some friends," and gives an address, but is uncertain which side of the hall the studio is on. A Master of Revels enters carrying a girl swathed only in a veil. She strips by unwinding her veil upon a man who serves as a human spool. All the audience sees at the end is a close up of scampering bare feet.

Marie drives to the Montmartre address in her car, and knocks, by mistake, on the door of a studio now occupied by Jean, her old sweetheart, who has come to Paris to continue his art studies. Marie, Jean, and his mother (entering from the kitchen) each in turn exclaim, "Well!" They are stiff with embarrassment. "Time makes strangers of erstwhile friends and formality covers their real emotions." As Marie explains her accidental knocking, Jean asks her to sit down. Tea is brought by the mother. The talk is stiff, Jean comments upon her appearance, Marie comments on his paintings. (While here formality and small talk cover their emotions, in the other studio Pierre "fights" his way out of the revel.) At tea, as Marie unfolds her napkin, it turns out to be full of holes, causing further embarrassment. "Then it's understood you are to paint my portrait." Jean shows her to her luxurious limousine and, as it rolls away, Jean's agonized expression reveals his realization of what Marie has become.

The following morning Jean calls on Marie, to be studied by the departing Paulette. Marie tells Jean, "I have several dresses to choose from" and displays some of her gowns. As she lifts one, a collar of Pierre's falls out on the floor. As Jean examines the gown, Marie notices his mourning band. "Why, Jean, who are you in mourning for?"—"My father."—"When did he die?"—"The night you left."

Pierre comes in and is informed by the maid that
Marie is busy. He is announced and Marie comes out.
Nonchalantly he helps himself to some chocolates, offers
the box to Marie, and when she refuses, he suggests:
"Ask the gentleman in the next room if he would care
for some." Marie replies, "Why should I explain? You
wouldn't understand."—"You jump at conclusions. I
understand perfectly." Marie smiles, "You're too clever."
As they kiss he warns, "Only be careful," pats her, and
leaves. Jean comes out, with his choice, among her gor-
geous gowns, of the one she is to wear for her portrait.
They part with a formal handshake.

"And the passing days brought about the final touches
to Marie's portrait." Weary of posing in her beautiful
evening gown and feathered headdress, Marie stretches
and smilingly asks Jean if he too is tired. Jean shakes his
head and goes on painting. Finally when he too yawns,
Marie steps down off the platform. Covering the canvas
Jean reminds her: "Now you promised not to look at it
until it is finished." She playfully remarks that she means
to see it when she has changed her dress. When, finally,
she does look she sees that Jean has painted her as she
used to be—a country girl in simple country clothes.
"Why bring up the past?"—"Because I knew you better
then." As she starts to leave, Jean stops her. "I love you,
Marie, in spite of everything." His mother, entering with
packages, hears Jean's avowal: "We can marry and begin
a new life." She sits down dejectedly in the other room.
Marie, saying it can never be, bids him goodbye.

The following scene is in Marie's apartment. Pierre,
who has been toying with a saxophone, declares, "It isn't
such a bad way. You have everything." Marie retorts,
"Not everything." Pierre, raising his eyebrows, pats her
head. "Poor little woman." As she goes to the window, he
follows her. "The trouble is you don't know what you
want." Below in the street, they observe a dismal family

scene—quarreling, squalling children, one of whom is being spanked by the harassed, impoverished mother. Pierre laughs, "Now then, what on earth is wrong?"—"Everything! What do I get out of life?—Nothing." Significantly he fingers her diamond necklace. On an angry impulse she brushes him away and throws it out the window. Pierre, smiling, returns to his saxophone, oblivious of Marie's tantrum.

Down in the street a tramp picks up the necklace. Marie excitedly informs Pierre, who refuses to budge and keeps calmly tooting on his saxophone. So Marie goes on the chase, snatches the necklace from the puzzled tramp, then runs back to give him a reward. All this evokes amazement from a policeman and amusement from Pierre watching from the window. Hurrying back, Marie breaks one of her high heels and, limping and panting, she returns, finds Pierre laughing, and hurls her broken shoe at him. "Idiot!" Pierre: "Why all this temperament? What does it all mean?" As she sulks, he asks, "Who is it, this young artist?"—"It doesn't matter. He loves me and is going to marry me."—"Do you love him?" She nods. Pierre's expression manifests his disbelief. In a close-up, sitting on the bed, she repeats "I love him." He bends down, kisses her on the forehead. "I'll see you tomorrow night for dinner." She mutters, "Never again." As he leaves. Pierre says, "Why not phone me sometime?"

"An eternal problem—mother and son." Wearied by his mother's reproaches, Jean says "All right, I won't marry her. I told you I'm not going to."—"My boy, I'm thinking of your future." Angrily he retorts, "Yours! you think only of my future when it concerns your own!" But, just as Marie enters the other room, the contrite Jean declares to the weeping mother, "You take too much for granted. Of course, I shouldn't marry her." He admits he proposed, but "in a moment of weakness." Marie walks in. "Perhaps it was a moment of weakness," she says with a shrug, and refuses to stay to hear any explanations. The son turns angrily to his mother, "See what you have done. Damn you, keep out of my affairs!"—and rushes out of the studio.

"That night at the cafe Pierre dines as usual," but not with Marie—with her gay friend Paulette. Fifi spies them. There is whispered gossip. But the evening ends with a disappointment for Paulette. Pierre does not invite her up to his rooms but orders his chauffeur to drive her home. Angrily she gets out and walks.

Three contrasts:

"And that night Marie dined alone"—and at home. She knows Jean is below, in the street, pacing under her window. She refuses to see him.

At Pierre's. He has just returned. He orders his valet to call Marie just as she is ordering her maid to call Pierre. "Did you call?" "No, did you?" "Let's stop this nonsense," says Pierre. "When shall I see you?" And, after some further exchanges, Pierre has his way. She will go to dinner with him.

At Jean's studio. His mother sets food and a candle beside her son's empty bed. He is keeping his vigil under Marie's window.

There follows another series of contrasting shots, each irised in and out: the mother, who has been waiting up for Jean, asleep holding a rosary; Jean distraught on a bridge; Marie asleep; Pierre, drinks at hand, sitting up with a copy of *La Vie Parisienne*. Jean returns home, in a state of exhaustion and despair.

The following morning as Marie, stretched out on a table under a sheet, is being massaged, Fifi rushes in and kisses her: "My dear, I've got so much to tell you!" Then she begins informing on "that cat Paulette." The poker-faced Swedish masseuse, wearing severe bobbed hair, goes about her work seemingly oblivious of the gossip of the two girls—even turning her head away—but taking in everything. The sheet is removed from Marie (now below camera range) and the masseuse rubs and pats her entire body, which is unmistakably outlined in the massage motions. Paulette enters, and also kisses Marie. But in the outer room she warns Fifi—who agrees—not to breathe a word about last night. Then Paulette confides that Pierre has invited her out again, but declares that she is worried about Marie.

As Paulette fixes her make-up, Fifi rushes in to Marie. "What do you think she said? She's going out with Pierre again!" Then she rushes back. The deceit and heartlessness under the honeyed talk of the three girls is beautifully emphasized as it registers on the stony face of the masseuse. Marie, now dressed, telephones Pierre. "What time do we dine tonight?" He replies, "Seven thirty." The girls listen raptly. "Sure you have no other engagement?" asks Marie. "No." Paulette then kisses Marie sweetly. "Well, I must be running along. Goodbye, dear." She departs, exchanging meaningful glances with Fifi.

"Remorse and despair control the fate of Jean." He is shown at home loading a revolver, which he puts aside as his mother enters with a bag of biscuits. She offers him some. He refuses. "You look tired, dear. Don't stay out too late," she pleads as he leaves.

Marie's apartment. Pierre helps her into her coat. Gaily she puts a flower in his buttonhole. He says: "I don't know which mood amuses me the most." Marie silences him with a hand over his mouth. Even the maid smiles as they depart affectionately. In the street, Jean follows them.

Cabaret gayety. Dancing girls float in with balloons. Marie and Pierre toy with a balloon at their table. From the lobby Jean sends a note in to Marie: "I must see you for the last time. J." Pierre, shown the note, exclaims, "Bring him in." The two men shake hands. Affably Pierre seats him beside Marie, gives him a cigarette, lights it for him, all very suavely. But Pierre significantly puts the note in his pocket and Jean lunges at him. A waiter comes up and hustles Jean out.

In the lobby Jean stands beside a fountain near a nude statue of a woman who appears to mock him. Inside, the revelers suddenly hear a shot; Jean is glimpsed falling into the fountain. A crowd gathers. He is pronounced "Dead." Marie, grief-stricken, sinks on a sofa.

Jean's mother is in her kitchen when men arrive with a body. "Your son, madame. You must be prepared for the worst." A man with a notebook fires questions at the woman, numbed with grief. "What was your son's age?"—"Was he a resident of Paris?"

Marie is prostrated. Pierre tries to comfort her and telephones for a doctor.

Jean's mother turning from her son's note pinned over the bed, to the portrait of Marie, grimly puts on her coat and hat and places a revolver in her bag—"Pursuing the wild justice that costs us so much to fulfill." At Marie's door she is told by the maid, "She left for your son's studio."

Marie, in tears, prays beside the body of Jean. The mother enters from behind, holding the revolver. Touched by Marie's grief, the revolver is lowered. She sits beside the younger woman. Sadly she puts her hand on Marie's.

"Time is a great healer, and experience teaches us that the road to happiness is in the service of others." A country cottage is shown. Inside, Jean's mother is setting the table while a new, simply dressed Marie is taking care of some children, combing the hair of one, cleaning the ears of another, wiping smears off the face of a third who suddenly points, "Mother, here comes Father."

A jolly priest enters, "I see you have another addition to the family." Distributing some toys he turns playfully to Marie. "Young lady, when are you going to marry and have children of your own?" Laughing goodnaturedly, she shrugs her shoulders. When Jean's mother hands her a milk pail, a child joins her.

A roadmarker: "To Paris, 90 km." Pierre, in the back seat with a male friend, orders his chauffeur to drive on. A haywagon, with an accordion player riding on the rear, rumbles along the road, followed by Marie and the little boy on foot. In the car, Pierre's friend asks, "By the way, whatever became of Marie St. Clair?" Pierre merely shrugs. At the accordion player's invitation Marie and the kid climb on the cart tail. Pierre's car approaches and speeds past. A close shot shows Marie singing and contented. The auto disappears into the distance; the cart down the road in the opposite direction.

"The Gold Rush"

"The Gold Rush" is probably Chaplin's most celebrated picture. For many years it was considered his masterwork, although some preferred "Shoulder Arms." Chaplin himself characterized "The Gold Rush" as "the picture I want to be remembered by."

In part a satire on Far Northern yarns and an ironic commentary on man's greed, "The Gold Rush," subtitled "a dramatic comedy," is also a portrayal of human suffering and frustrated hopes. The Donner party disaster, with its hint of cannibalism, was its gruesome inspiration.

Its realistic plot is episodic in form, each well-constructed sequence containing "O. Henry twists." Chaplin again put something more into the film than comedy. It plumbs profound depths of pathos. Its laughs, drawn out of tragedy, have a magnified force and meaning. Its principal character symbolizes the good, kind, and pitiful core of humanity. Moments of the film reach the sublime.

In "The Gold Rush" Chaplin portrays a hard-luck prospector who chases rainbows of the heart and soul in the midst of frenzied gold-seekers. His pantomime is more subtle and effective than ever. With his back to the camera, in the dancehall sequence, he expresses more with his shoulders than many actors with their eyes and mouth. A mere wistful raising of his eyebrows or a touch of his derby can carry an amazing change of emotion.

For dramatic pathos the New Year's Eve dinner sequence has seldom been surpassed in any medium. It is here that Chaplin performs the famous dance of the rolls with incomparable grace and dexterity. The clever bit is made poignant by the knowledge that he is only imagining it—it is for guests who never come. This dinner scene is one of the memorable peak moments in screen creativeness, ranking with such different but vividly remembered highlights as the Homecoming and the Ride of the Clan in "The Birth of a Nation," the closet scene in "Broken Blossoms," Douglas Fairbanks' gymnastic flight in "The Mark of Zorro," the dream of the porter in "The Last Laugh," the moving up to the front in "The Big Parade," the cream-separator sequence in "Old and New," the money ballet in "A Nous la Liberté," the shell-hole scene in "All Quiet on the Western Front," the Titanic sequence in "Cavalcade," the shooting of Frankie in "The Informer," the Indian attack in "Stagecoach," etc.

The close to hysterical suspense of the scene of the cabin half over the cliff may show the influence of Harold Lloyd who had started a vogue for comedy-thrill sequences in his "Safety Last" and other skyscraper pictures. It is Chaplin's first use of such effects but, imitated or not, his inimitable touches make it his own. The happy ending of the film, which in some ways breaks the mood, may have been inspired by the epilogue of Murnau's "The Last Laugh," which was then influencing picture-making all over the world.

Such criticism as was leveled against "The Gold Rush" at the time held it to be sometimes slow and overserious as compared with the briskly humorous "earlier" comedies. It is an odd fact, however, that through the years, each new Chaplin film has seemed more serious and less funny than the preceding one—until seen in retrospect. When revived in 1942, with music by Chaplin and a commentary spoken by him, "The Gold Rush" scored again, winning a new generation of devotees and proving itself a timeless masterpiece. Except for the titles, almost nothing was cut. Chaplin's pleasant commentary kept referring to the leading character as "the little fellow." The musical effects were valid contributions. The shoe dinner was eaten to typical "dinner music" and the roll dance was performed to perfectly synchronized dance music.

For the production the company went on location in the snow-covered mountains of Nevada. A pathway was cut through the snow for several thousand feet up a mountain, to represent the Chilkoot Pass in Alaska. Crowds of extras were used in this scene which is reminiscent of similar "long shots" of pioneers in "The Covered Wagon" and "Grass." Not all the scenes shot in Nevada were used. Other sequences were filmed against snowfields of rock salt against not too obvious back drops constructed in the studio; and plaster mountains were erected on the lot behind the town set.

Reports of the production costs of "The Gold Rush" range from "about the same as 'The Kid'" ($300,000) to $1,000,000. The actual cost was probably midway between these two figures. Begun in the spring of 1924, production of "The Gold Rush" lasted fourteen months. Cut and previewed in Hollywood in June, when more than a reel was pared, it had its New York premiere on August 16, 1925, at the Strand Theatre, where all Chaplin's films since "A Dog's Life" had opened. Chaplin attended the premiere and responded to an ovation with a modest speech.

Chaplin had conquered again after a two-and-a-half year absence from the screen, topping in artistry and popularity "The Freshman," Harold Lloyd's hilarious, gag-filled hit which opened about the same time, and Buster Keaton's droll "The Navigator" and fantastically brilliant "Sherlock, Jr."

"The Gold Rush" was one of the big money-makers of

the twenties, earning between two and a half million, which is on record as the domestic gross, and a total of five million in all. Chaplin himself profited more than two million on it.

For the feminine lead in "The Gold Rush" Lita Grey was first chosen and then withdrawn. The girl who finally received the assignment was Georgia Hale, whom Chaplin discovered in Josef von Sternberg's "The Salvation Hunters." This was a low cost experimental film which Chaplin sponsored after it was brought to his attention by the actor George K. Arthur. Probably referring to Miss Compson's striking performance in the prostitute role in "The Miracle Man" (1919), Chaplin hailed Miss Hale in "The Salvation Hunters" as "better than Betty Compson."

In "The Gold Rush," impersonating a hard, impulsive, and fiery-tempered dancehall girl—a Chaplin heroine quite different from the pretty and agreeable Edna Purviance—Georgia Hale gives a performance of considerable verve although there are moments when she slips into some stilted acting conventions of the period. After an appearance in Paramount's "The Rainmaker," "The Last Moment," and a few other films, she faded out and today is a Los Angeles dancing teacher.

Mack Swain, as the humorless and much suffering Big Jim, gave his top performance. Hired at the comparatively low salary of $250 a week, Chaplin foretold that "The Gold Rush" would bring him big offers from other producers. The prophecy came true and Swain prospered in outstanding pictures until his death in 1935.

For his assistants Chaplin had the reliable Chuck Riesner again as associate director. He also carried the Frenchman, d'Arrast, over from "A Woman of Paris" as an assistant director. Eddie Sutherland, becoming impatient with delays, left for a directing post at Paramount, arranged through Tom Meighan who was married to his aunt, Frances Ring. Jim Tully, hobo author of "Beggars of Life," was hired at fifty dollars a week, to help with the script and serve as a sort of court jester. And, of course, faithful Henry Bergman was around to double as actor-director.

"The Gold Rush" opens on an unending procession of footsore prospectors through the snowy Chilkoot Pass in the Klondike gold rush of 1898. "A Lone Prospector," flourishing a cane, appears on a narrow ledge, nonchalant despite spills and one-footed skids around corners and unaware of the huge bear following behind. Climbing down rocks, a slip sends him sliding in the snow all the way to the bottom where, pausing to lean on his cane, it sinks up to the handle. To set his course, the little fellow takes out a map and follows the arrow pointing North.

In the meanwhile Big Jim McKay, another prospector, stakes a claim, promptly finds a nugget, and basks in bliss.

"Then came a storm." Charlie seeks refuge in the cabin of the desperado, Black Larsen. Ordered out, the wind blows so hard through the door that Charlie can't buck it and keeps sliding in one spot. When the wind pushes him out through another door, he crawls back.

Big Jim, in the meanwhile, is picked up by the wind, together with his tent, and blown right through the Larsen cabin, along with Charlie. Each opening door blows someone out through another. The famished Jim snatches a bone away from Charlie, biting his finger in the process. Charlie pats the big man as if he were a mad dog.

Larsen reenters with a rifle to drive out his uninvited guests. Jim grapples with him for possession of the gun. Charlie has a desperate time keeping out of range. Every move of the wrestling men manages to keep him covered. Finally there is a shot and Charlie feels himself for blood.

Larsen is subdued, and Jim takes over the cabin. Charlie, at his side, seconds Jim's words and actions. The unappreciative Jim glares at the little man who, with a meek smile, again gives him the bone and puts his arms around him.

The three famished men and a dog are snowbound. As Jim raves, Charlie samples a candle, salting it as if it were a stalk of celery. When Jim returns from the back room, picking his teeth, Charlie whistles for the dog and is relieved to find him alive. The three men cut cards to see who is to go out foraging. Larsen is picked. Coming across two mounted police, who have been trailing him, the outlaw shoots them both and goes off with their sled.

Thanksgiving Day finds the two men so hungry they cook up one of Charlie's shoes. With all the nuances of a French chef, Charlie lifts the shoe from the smoking pot, expertly tries a fork in it to see if it is done, places it on a dish, bastes it with "gravy," sharpens his knife, carves it, separates the uppers from the sole, passes the nail-studded sole to Big Jim who rejects it and takes the tenderer uppers. Charlie attacks the sole with a gourmet's relish, twists the shoe laces around his fork like spaghetti, and sucks the nails as if they were marrow bones. Discovering a nail bent in the shape of a wishbone, he holds it out to his bewildered companion.

Later, their hunger still unappeased, Charlie returns empty-handed from a foraging expedition and warms his now burlap-wrapped foot in the oven. At his suggestion of dining on the other shoe Jim becomes hysterical. In Jim's ensuing delirium Charlie is transformed into a chicken who, in the dissolve upon this transformation, struts about and roosts at the table. When the fowl dissolves back to Charlie, Jim, with a lunatic laugh, explains that he thought his friend was a chicken. A second transformation occurs while Charlie is bending over the stove and the hunger-maddened Jim chases him around the table with a knife, and out of the cabin. When Jim fires a gun the flapping wings dissolve to the frightened arms of Charlie. The big man is remorseful, but for safety Charlie buries the gun in the snow. Back inside, Jim reverts to chicken noises. Charlie rushes out for the gun and Jim follows with an axe. There is a chase which ends with the frightened Charlie laid out by the falling door bar, and the delirious giant collapsed in bed.

Next morning we see Jim and Charlie in bed, Charlie at the foot, his hands in his protruding shoes, Jim opening one scouting eye. Rising together the two men grapple for the rifle, knocking it to the floor. While they are wrestling, Jim trying to smother Charlie under a blanket as Charlie hangs on to his leg, a bear wanders in. When Charlie extricates himself from the blanket he finds himself gripping the bear's leg. When the bear wanders out again Charlie gets the rifle, fires after him, and, as Jim goes out for the carcass, gaily starts setting the table and sharpening the carving knife.

"Then came the parting of the ways." The two shake hands and wander off in opposite directions. Jim finds Black Larsen working his claim. In the ensuing struggle, Jim is hit over the head with a shovel, and Larsen rides off. Then Nature takes a hand and finishes off the desperado in an avalanche.

In one of the boom towns created by the gold rush, we are introduced to Georgia, a saucy dancehall girl, as she comes out of a photographer's studio. Proud and independent, she disdains Jack Cameron's offer to join some other dancehall girls he is taking out on a sleigh ride. Then "a disappointed prospector" wanders into town.

That night, in the dancehall, people crowd around Georgia to see the picture the photographer has just brought her. Insolent Jack Cameron snatches it; Georgia snatches it back; and the picture is torn. Sauntering in, the little fellow goes unnoticed in the reveling crowd.

The piano and violin strike up a dance tune. Georgia turns and smiles and Charlie's face lights up, ecstatically, only to discover, as the girl nears, that her smile was for the man behind him. For consolation he goes to the bar, snatches a drink from a passing waiter, and pats his chest and rear as the drink goes down. Sitting alone and bored, Georgia looks right past Charlie who picks up her torn photograph. But when Cameron comes up to claim her as partner she shows her contempt by dancing off with the enraptured Charlie.

Bad luck, however, follows to trip him up. Hooking up his slipping pants with his cane is not quite enough. Seeing a rope on a table, he uses it as a belt. Unfortunately the other end of the rope is attached to a large dog, who complicates the dance steps and brings his brief and troubled bliss to an end as sight of a cat takes him away—and Charlie contacts the floor—to the crowd's great amusement.

Georgia finds Charlie too useful a foil against Cameron to give him up. She picks up a rose and, to mock Jack, gives it to Charlie. Cameron decides the matter has gone far enough and starts to pummel Charlie to keep him from following Georgia. Cornered against a post Charlie does some resourceful kicking. Cameron fools Charlie by offering his hand and, as Charlie's guard is lowered, pulls his derby down over his eyes. A chance punch by the little fellow hits a post, jarring the balcony clock down on Cameron's head to score a knockout. With a hitch at his capacious trousers, Charlie struts triumphantly through the awed crowd.

The following morning Charlie, peering through the window of the cabin of a man named Hank, sees him cooking beans. He lies down in the snow and when Hank comes out he finds a man frozen "stiff." Carried in, Charlie thaws back to "life." When Hank is not looking Charlie sugars and stirs his coffee, then shuts his eyes again. The invalid's appetite astounds the goodnatured Hank.

Big Jim McKay wanders into town, recovered but with his memory gone, searching for, and missing Charlie, the one man who can help him relocate his cabin and claim.

Hank's partner also arrives, and Charlie agrees to look after the cabin while they are gone prospecting. As the sled moves up hill, Charlie, standing on one of the hauling ropes, takes a tumble.

Georgia and three other girls, sliding in the snow and playfully snowballing each other, smack one in Charlie's face as he watches them from the cabin door. He uses the incident as an opportunity to invite the girls in to warm themselves. As Charlie skips out for firewood, Georgia finds her torn photograph under his pillow. The girls giggle, as Georgia brushes the snow off Charlie and holds his hand. He knows she is fooling but makes the most of it. One of the girls gives him a hotfoot by dropping a match on his burlap foot. Unconsciously he pays her back by crossing his burning leg under her chair. On leaving, Georgia accepts his invitation to New Year's Eve dinner. While, outside the door, the girls giggle, the enraptured Charlie jumps about, swings from a beam, does handsprings, and juggles a pillow until the feathers fly like snow.

To earn the money for the dinner, Charlie shovels snow, making work for himself by piling the shoveled snow successively on the next neighbor's sidewalk. The racket ends when the next neighbor turns out to be the jail.

New Year's Eve. High jinks in the dancehall. In the cabin, Charlie prepares for the party. A newspaper, cleverly torn in a pattern, becomes the tablecloth. He arranges place cards, follows the progress of the chicken roasting in the stove, lays out presents and favors on the table, lights candles. There is a stir at the door. Charlie brushes his hair and opens the door—on a donkey who consumes one of the paper favors before he is chased out.

Eight o'clock. A shot of Charlie, leaning on his elbow, patiently waiting, dissolves to one with the room crowded and festive, the merry girls at the table opening their presents, Georgia thanking him and letting him kiss her hand. The girls call for a speech and Charlie, modestly begging off from oratory, offers to dance the "Oceana Roll" for them. Spearing a couple of bread rolls on two forks, he has them step like feet. Photographed seated at the table in semi-close-up, the scene is so arranged and lighted as to make him appear like a caricature—a huge head and tiny body. He performs a sort of Highland Fling with the bread-feet. With each change of steps or rhythm his expression undergoes corresponding changes, and his eyes follow as he high kicks, slides from side to side, turns, hops sideways, does splits, dribbles off to the "wings," and returns for bows.

As the girls applaud, Charlie bows, and is so overcome when Georgia kisses him that he sinks to the floor. But the scene dissolves back to Charlie asleep at the table —and alone. In the dancehall the clock hand nears twelve. Georgia and Cameron have made up. Standing on the bar, Georgia fires off revolvers—the boom town equivalent of New Year's chimes. The sound rouses Charlie who goes to the door, to feel his disappointment and loneliness redouble as all in the dancehall join together in singing "Auld Lang Syne." Then the Virginia Reel is started. Georgia suddenly remembers her promise. She is not a mere adventuress after all. While Charlie gazes into the window of the dancehall, then wanders off, Cameron takes the girls to the cabin. Touched by the dressing of the table, the remorseful Georgia repulses and slaps the persistent Cameron.

In the Recorder's Office, Big Jim describes his claim, but can't remember its location. The clerks consider him cuckoo. Outside in the street, Charlie and Jim pass each other, but Charlie's head is turned away and they do not recognize each other.

That night, in the dancehall, Cameron trips Charlie who suffers a mishap when, after contemptuously flipping his cane toward Cameron, a further attempt at nonchalance comes to grief when he leans against a hot stove. He is comforted by a note from Georgia. "Please forgive me for not coming. I'd like to see you and explain." Suddenly he is sighted by Big Jim, whose vigorous handshake sends him sprawling. Big Jim promises to go halves on his claim if Charlie helps him find it. Charlie rushes to the balcony, climbs up, and bids an excited farewell to Georgia, with vows, protestations of love, regrets, promises—until Big Jim yanks him away.

'After a long, tedious journey" the pair reach the cabin, this time, however, plentifully supplied with food and drink. In fact, Charlie brings in a large frozen animal carcass—"Man proposes but storm disposes." As our heroes sleep a storm rises, loosens the cabin from its foundations, and blows it to a precarious perch half over an abyss. When Charlie wakes he can't see out of the iced-over window. At every step the cabin tips. Jim comments on the rocking and Charlie assures him it is his stomach rocking from last night's feast. Then he plucks icicles from the ceiling for their breakfast water. More slipping and jolting makes Charlie question the stomach explanation. As they move to either side the cabin slants with them, see-sawing on the edge of the precipice. Feeling something is missing underneath, Charlie forces the door open—to find himself hanging in space. He barely manages to climb back in.

The cabin slips further over the edge. Neither man can stand any longer on the steeply slanting floor. In fact, the cabin would go down but for a frayed anchoring rope caught between two rocks. As the cabin teeters Jim warns his companion not to get excited, to be still. The cabin's plight is so delicate that a cough jolts it. There is frantic comedy as the two clamber over each other in the effort to escape. Charlie slides out the door again; Jim reaches the top only to be slammed back by the door. Finally Jim, climbing over Charlie, reaches safety and simultaneously finds his claim. Charlie is then pulled up by a rope just as the anchor breaks and the cabin plunges into the chasm. As the men embrace, Charlie "faints."

We next find Charlie and Jim on a ship returning home to the States. They are now millionaires with fur coats and toppers to show it. Still unaccustomed to fortune, however, Charlie stoops for a cigar butt, to be scolded by Jim and supplied from a gold case. Reporters swarm around them for interviews for which Charlie poses with top hat held to one side. In their de luxe cabin, Charlie peels off two fur coats while Jim has his calluses treated by a manicure girl.

To Charlie, however, wealth does not bring happiness as he gazes wistfully at Georgia's picture. She was gone when he returned for her. Actually Georgia is on the steerage deck below. There she hears an officer speak of a search for a stowaway.

For a reporter's human interest story, Charlie puts on his tramp's outfit; and there is comic business directed at Jim with the big shoes and cane. Posing for a camera, he steps back for focus and falls down a staircase into a coil of ropes near Georgia. Believing him the stowaway, she pushes him back into the ropes and shields him with a blanket. Georgia pleads with the officer who goes for him. The captain identifies him as one of the two multimillionaires. There are apologies and orders for de luxe accommodations for the girl. A reporter asks who's the lady. His wife to be, Charlie whispers, and the two walk up together, to the upper deck, to pose in an old tintype embrace.

X X I I

Lita Grey—second marriage and divorce

After "A Woman of Paris," Chaplin felt it would not be fair to Edna Purviance, with her new standing as a dramatic actress, to ask her to play the comparatively unimportant feminine lead in his next comedy. Moreover she had matured and her type had gone out of fashion. The bold "Flapper" had displaced the demure and lady-like heroine. Chaplin began to try out new girls. He preferred an unknown, perhaps as a salary saver, but still more because it gave him pleasure to mold inexperienced, fresh talent. The tryouts left him unsatisfied until Lolita McMurry appeared at the studio with her mother.

Lolita was not unknown to Chaplin. She lived with her Mexican mother and grandparents in a bungalow near the studio. When she was seven years old she caught his attention. At the age of twelve, with her hair worn up, she played the flirting angel in the heaven sequence in "The Kid." Both she and her mother played maids in "The Idle Class." Now, at the age of sixteen, she was suddenly quite grown-up, attractive though of rather ordinary looks, with a broad face and a low forehead. Her charm lay in her animal spirits and carefree nature. She was backward in school; she lacked sensitivity and showed little signs of talent. She did not photograph well and when taught acting, showed little capacity to learn. Yet Chaplin was enthusiastic about the test. His "yes men" promptly agreed, with the exception of Jim Tully who would not commit himself.

Under the professional name of Lita Grey, she was
signed, in March 1924, at a salary of seventy-five dollars
a week. Lita jumped up and down exclaiming "Goody,
goody!" while her ambitious mother exulted. The publicity mill ground out typical Hollywood announcements
of the new leading lady, blurbing her beauty, her talents,
her "aristocratic Spanish forebears," her accomplishments
in sports, etc. Edna Purviance's dressing room was cleared
out and refurnished to Mrs. McMurry's taste.

Lita and Chaplin began to appear together in public.
He was obviously smitten with her although he, himself,
had heard her admit that she liked him the better because of his name. Suddenly, that fall, Lita's family,
which included a lawyer uncle named Edwin McMurry,
demanded that Chaplin agree to an immediate marriage
or face legal consequences. Chaplin, apparently forced to
comply, sought the dreaded wedding without benefit of
the press. An elaborate ruse was planned. He announced
a change in the locale of his new film from the Far North
to Mexico. Together with a technical crew, Chaplin's
party entrained for Guaymas, Mexico. Some reporters
with a hunch entrained as fellow-travelers. Others turned
up in Mexico.

In Guaymas the technical crew was ordered to hire a
fishing boat and stay out all day to give the impression
that they were shooting sea scenes. Kono kept reporters
away from Lita and her mother. With the newspaper men
thrown off their guard, Chaplin, Riesner, Lita, and her
mother drove to Empalme, in the state of Sonora, where,
on November 24, 1924, Lita Grey became Mrs. Chaplin. After the ceremony Chaplin went fishing.

The "happy" couple started back for Hollywood with
numerous relatives of Lita, the technicians, and about
fifty reporters in tow. While Chaplin remained alone in
his compartment, the McMurry clan celebrated in the
dining car. Lita was later to quote her husband as say-

ing to friends on the train, "Well, boys, this is better than the penitentiary but it won't last"—which Chaplin denied.

History repeated itself. The actor again found himself with a wife with whom he was completely incompatible. In addition, Lita's mother, on the grounds that Lita was still a child and could not manage, moved in with them and took over the household. Chaplin fled the house, leaving Lita to revel in her position as mistress of the Beverly Hills mansion, which became the stamping ground of the clan and their friends.

It was given out to the press that Lita Grey had retired as leading lady of "The Gold Rush" because she preferred to devote all her time to being Mrs. Chaplin. Approaching motherhood may have had something to do with it; but still more was Chaplin's resolve to return Lita to oblivion and frustrate his ambitious mother-in-law. This merely turned the mother's drive toward a new goal—to make the comedian pay for ruining her daughter's career. She was to make him pay plenty!

There was one humorous side to the marriage. Lita, being only sixteen, the Los Angeles school system forced her to continue her education. Tutors were hired and the mistress of the forty-room mansion and an army of servants made a desperate effort to complete the required schooling.

A son—Charles Spencer Chaplin, Jr.—was born June 28, 1925. An attempt to keep the event out of the papers proved futile. Just two days after nine months later on March 30, 1926, a second son was born, named Sydney Earle Chaplin after Charles' brother, who by now had achieved success on his own in "Charley's Aunt" and other pictures. The spelling with the two "y's" caused another quarrel between the couple. Lita believed it more "chic."

For sympathy and escape Chaplin often went to Marion

Davies' palatial hundred-room beach mansion at Santa Monica where a virtually continuous party went on. Marion Davies, herself a zestful mimic, Chaplin, and d'Arrast put on impromptu acts and played practical jokes on the other guests.

The inevitable rumors that all was not well between Chaplin and his wife began to circulate. There were quarrels over the bills Lita ran up. One night, returning fatigued from a long day's work on "The Circus," Chaplin found his house overrun with drunken guests. After an angry exchange the guests cleared out to be followed by Lita and the two babies. It was all over the newspapers the next day (December 2, 1926) that Lita Grey and the children had gone to live with her grandparents.

Attorneys tried to keep the separation case from reaching the courts while the two principals fired headlines at each other. Chaplin charged Lita with extravagance; Lita charged that her husband was holding trunks full of hers and the children's clothing. Chaplin claimed that he had surrounded her with luxury; Lita that he had subjected her to "cruel and inhuman" treatment. Denying this, Chaplin complained that she had made no efforts to share his friendships; Lita charged that he had rebuffed her friends as "common." And so it went.

Finally, on January 10, 1927, Mrs. Chaplin filed suit for divorce. Her forty-two-page complaint contained sensational charges against the comedian, including infidelity, threats upon her life, lack of affection for the children, and a variety of "inhuman" acts. The complaint was framed to permit service on the actor himself, the Chaplin Studios, Inc., Toraichi Kono, Alfred Reeves, the United Artists Corp., and seven Los Angeles and Hollywood banks. An order restrained Chaplin or any of his associates, from transferring or withdrawing any funds, or transporting any of the comedian's motion-picture properties out of the state.

Production on "The Circus" having been stopped, the studio was closed, and Chaplin fled with Kono to New York where he stayed at the home of Nathan Burkan, his New York attorney. Lita's battery of attorneys was headed by her uncle. With all his property seized, the future of his nearly finished production in doubt, and accusations against him a daily news feature, Chaplin was further burdened by a government process for income-tax shortages totaling $1,133,000. (He blamed his aids and four years later was fully paid up.)

Lita Grey's charges went on: that Chaplin had said the marriage was one of compulsion; that he had said he did not believe in marriage; that he had handed her a loaded revolver in her bedroom suggesting "there is one way to end it all"; that, on another occasion, he had threatened her with a revolver; that he had called her "a little Mexican gold-digger"; that he had read to her from books on distasteful subjects. She further charged him with "abnormal, unnatural, indecent acts" and "conduct tending to undermine, demoralize and distort the plaintiff's character in unnatural ways" (*New York Times*, January 11, 1927).

"During the first month of their marriage"—so ran her complaint—she "was made aware that the defendant was spending a great deal of time in company with a certain prominent motion-picture actress. The plaintiff asked her husband if this were true and he bluntly and boastingly said, 'Yes, it is true and I am in love with her and I don't care who knows it. I am going to see her when I want to and whether you like it or not. I don't love you and I am only living with you because I had to marry you.' "

Lita was ready to name, it was announced, no less than "five prominent motion-picture actresses" who had "publicly and privately" associated with Chaplin. Lita even dragged in Merna Kennedy, her childhood friend, whom she herself had picked as leading lady for "The Circus." Edna Purviance's pension of $250 a week from Chaplin was also made the subject of insinuations. Mrs. Chaplin estimated her husband's fortune at sixteen millions, of which ten millions could be classified as joint property to which, by California law, the wife was entitled to an equal share. Chaplin disputed her estimate, claiming that even three million would be an exaggeration.

The Chaplin divorce case proved sensational enough to displace the Hall-Mills murder from the headlines. Copies of Miss Grey's petition sold by the thousands for twenty-five cents apiece. Chaplin's countercharges accused his wife and her family of "a money plot." He attributed his love for young girls to a "parental feeling" they inspired in him. He explained that "you can have the same companionship and love for them as for your children." Admittedly, not an intellectual companionship: "I don't think anyone can be deeply intellectual at their age. But I love many people, and there are some friends whom I love deeply. I love some men friends, for example, as dearly as my women friends."

Women's clubs began to agitate, as they had in the Fatty Arbuckle and Mabel Normand tragedies, for the barring of Chaplin's pictures, they succeeded in a number of cities and states. Will Hays maintained a watchful silence.

Chaplin suffered a collapse and was confined to his bed at the Burkan home. It was described as "a nervous breakdown" by Dr. Gustav Tieck, a nerve specialist. Burkan denied published reports that the comedian was under guard against suicide attempts. "There is nothing in Mr. Chaplin's condition to warrant such a report. He is a highly strung man, as most actors are, or they wouldn't be good actors, and yesterday morning his condition was such, after the strain to which he has been subjected the last few weeks, that it seemed advisable to call in a physician. He will remain in bed for a week or ten days at least and get needed rest."

Meanwhile, because Alfred Reeves, who knew the combinations of the safes at the Hollywood studio, was conveniently "ill at home," Lita's clique threatened to drill the safes open. With the government liens against more than one million dollars of Chaplin's funds and property in California, Lita Grey could not collect the alimony awarded her. (Chaplin's New York funds were released when he posted bond.) Lita claimed she needed four thousand dollars a month. Attempts to ferret out information of her husband's assets produced a deposition by Henry Bergman that his restaurant was his business sideline, that Chaplin had no share in the ownership and had never deposited any of his assets with him.

Hollywood and Los Angeles clubwomen actually got together and pledged to raise funds for Chaplin's "penniless wife and children." The actor's answer to the interfering clubwomen was that it was a manufactured lie and that the plaintiffs "do not want milk for the children. They want to milk me." His California lawyer, Lloyd Wright, had been offering Lita a temporary $25 a week, but the other side was pushing for a big cash settlement.

The battle went on and on. It was stated that Chaplin would finish "The Circus" in New York. Police guarded the Lita Grey domicile after the receipt of anonymous death threats. Among other communications were marriage proposals! Not all the sentiment was on Lita's side. There were editorials scoring the comedian's critics who lived in glass houses themselves. H. L. Mencken, in the *Baltimore Sun* wrote: "The very morons who worshipped Charlie Chaplin six weeks ago now prepare to dance around the stake while he is burned; he is learning something of the psychology of the mob. . . . A public trial involving sexual accusations is made a carnival everywhere in the United States. . . ."

In France, intellectuals and artists protested against the boycott of Chaplin's films and the public pillorying of the star. Among the signers were Germaine Dulac, Louis Aragon, Man Ray, Robert Desnos, and René Clair. They inveighed against private moral judgments in the judgment of art and called the proposal to prohibit Chaplin's pictures "a stupid blunder." Chaplin himself pleaded that domestic affairs of an artist should not be allowed to clash with his creative work. (Press agents and columnists continue their disproportionate "buildups" on the private lives and tastes of "stars"; yet, when things go wrong, the industry wonders at the disproportionate public reaction.)

Claiming insolvency, Lita asked and received permission from the courts to move into the Chaplin mansion "to save rent."

After Chaplin recovered from his illness and while waiting in New York for a settlement of the case, which he feared might cost him his public and his career, there was a turn in the tide and invitations began to pour in. At the annual Old Timers' Night of the New York Newspaper Club, he received an ovation for one of his famous skits. The *Telegraph* reported, "A great hush fell over the audience as the master pantomimist squared his shoulders and, flinging back an imaginary cloak, stepped into a phantom arena and created a throbbing, vibrant image of an unlucky toreador outwitted by a vile trick on the part of the bull." This skit and one on a wife and a French lover discovered by the husband were usually reserved for his private parties.

Whether it was the effect of strategy, attributed to his lawyer who accompanied him, or another evidence of the turning tide, Chaplin won over the newspapermen present. Chaplin was entertained by the Atwater-Kents in Philadelphia; he went fishing with Frances Alda, the opera singer; at parties given by William B. Leeds, Jr.

and his wife, Princess Xenia of Russia, he met Long Island socialites. In New York he took long solitary walks about the city.

On June 1, 1927, Lita and her lawyers decided to force action. They threatened to name, in court, the five women with whom Chaplin had allegedly been intimate during his married life with her. Though Douglas Fairbanks, Jr., in a 1931 thumbnail sketch of his friend, declared that Chaplin "likes nothing better than to be referred to as a Don Juan," Chaplin shrank from this opportunity to indulge himself. According to Carl Robinson, Chaplin gave in mainly to protect these actresses, whose careers, in the then prevailing public temper, would have been ruined by the scandal. He agreed to a cash settlement. Lita withdrew her sensational complaint and asked for an interlocutory decree on the single charge of cruelty. Chaplin's cross complaint was dismissed by the court.

After twenty minutes on the stand, Lita received a six hundred thousand dollar settlement, the custody of the children, and a two hundred thousand dollar trust fund for them. Chaplin was allowed to see his sons. Lawyers on both sides received plenty. The divorce was granted August 22, 1927.

To finish the Lita Grey saga. After European trips with the children, she entered vaudeville and filled nightclub engagements billed as Lita Grey Chaplin. At various times she was reported engaged to Roy D'Arcy, Phil Baker, and Georges Carpentier. In 1936 she married Henry Aguirre, Jr., and two years later Arthur F. Day. There were further court skirmishes over the handling of the children's trust fund. In 1932 Chaplin prevented her from putting the boys in the movies. They were in uniform in World War II and have since sought stage careers.

"The Circus"

On his return from New York in October, 1925, after launching "The Gold Rush," Chaplin cast around for a new picture idea. After successive plans to film Stevenson's "The Club of Suicides" and "The Dandy," he hit upon "The Circus." For some years the role of a Pagliacci-like clown had understandably intrigued this twentieth-century counterpart of Arlequin, Arlecchino, Grock, and Grimaldi.

Most of his collaborators on "The Gold Rush," weary of the long periods between pictures and anxious to shape their own careers, had left Chaplin for other companies. A new acquaintance, Harry Crocker, of the wealthy San Francisco family, was engaged to assist with the scenario and serve as actor-director. He played the part of Rex.

Georgia Hale having gone to Paramount to do "The Rainmaker," a new leading lady was necessary. Lita Grey conspired to get the part for one of her childhood friends, Merna Kennedy, whom she felt she could trust. Lita managed it cleverly, inviting Merna to dinner, and tactfully letting Chaplin "discover" her. The seventeen-year-old Merna Kennedy who was then appearing in a musical comedy in Los Angeles naïvely confided that she would like to play in the movies. Chaplin was impressed with her charm and her possibilities for the part he had in mind. She was small and would pair well with him.

The little dinner was a success; Merna became Chaplin's new leading lady.

In making "The Circus," Chaplin spared no pains—or costs—to achieve complete realism. The costs, reputedly, ran to $900,000. A complete circus,—tent, equipment, wagons, a small zoo, trainers and the rest—was set up and maintained for more than a year. Special high platforms were built to photograph action on the high wire. Chaplin himself practiced wire-walking for several months to become quite expert, and Merna Kennedy trained herself to ride bareback.

"The Circus" was produced during the most trying period of the Lita Grey divorce proceedings with its protracted litigation and scandals. Not only were there frequent interruptions but his domestic troubles prevented full concentration on his work. However, by the end of 1926, most of the picture was shot and edited. He hoped to finish it by March of the following year and to open it in New York soon after, but was balked by the litigation which attached the film. Work was stopped; Chaplin went to New York; and for some time it was not certain that the film would ever be finished. With the divorce settlement negotiated, Chaplin, after nearly a year of troubled inactivity, returned to the studio and with great effort, finished the picture. It finally opened January 7, 1928.

"The Circus" added nothing to Chaplin's reputation but the general public found it entertaining. It employed the old comedy tricks, improved here with new twists. The more captious missed the poetry, brilliance, and feeling of "The Gold Rush." The new comedy did not seem as inspired; at times its slapstick is dragged out and mechanical. The story line, though it offers and takes advantage of opportunities for broad humor and clever gags, is rather contrived and slips into some dull moments.

The scenes between the cruel circus owner and his step-daughter are melodramatic both in concept and in the actions. But there are flickers of pathos in those scenes and also in the Tramp's relations with the little bareback rider. Pathos is also rather neatly blended with humor in the conception of the tramp-clown who is funny when he doesn't intend to be, and pathetic when he tries to be funny. The tragic ending of the film is a variation of the classic "Tramp" fade-out.

The Circus" is probably the first Chaplin film to show directly the influence of the intellectual critics. Slapstick, by now, had become "highbrow"; and Chaplin's pathos had been much praised. So it is possible he overdid both in this picture.

"The Circus," however, had enough comedy moments to make it a success. Its background offered many natural comic situations. Scenes like the chase in the fun house, the locked-in-the-lion-cage sequence and the high-wire episode where Charlie's safety appliance becomes detached, though no novelties in themselves, were made so by the originality of his treatment. Amusing and authentic are the bits where the older circus clowns try to teach the tramp how to be funny. And Chaplin makes the traditional circus clowning even funnier by capping it with novel twists. A virtue of the picture is the authenticity of its circus lore and atmosphere.

One interesting scene graphically illustrates the essential dualism in the Chaplin screen character. When Rex, the handsome tight-rope walker, joins the circus, Charlie, seated in a corner, appears melancholy and resigned as he watches the newcomer and the love-smitten Merna. But Charlie's "spirit" (thanks to double exposure) rises out of his body, knocks Rex down, and returns to inhabit the sorrowful creature in the corner (the "Strange Interlude" technique in terms of the silent film).

Chaplin himself played his tramp character in his

chapter **XIX**

89 Chaplin as the Pilgrim.

90 The new minister about to deliver his sermon on David and Goliath.

91 Edna Purviance and Adolphe Menjou in "A Woman of Paris,"
the dramatic picture which Chaplin wrote and directed but
did not appear in.

92 Edna Purviance as Marie St. Clair.

93 Edna Purviance and Adolphe Menjou in "A Woman of Paris."

94 Edna Purviance, Carl Miller and Adolphe Menjou in "A Woman of Paris."

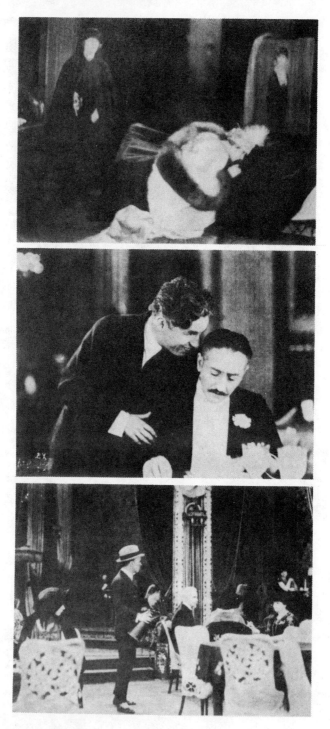

95 Lydia Knott and Edna Purviance.
96 Chaplin directing Adolphe Menjou in "A Woman of Paris."
97 Chaplin directing "A Woman of Paris."

98 "The Gold Rush."
99 With Mack Swain in "The Gold Rush."

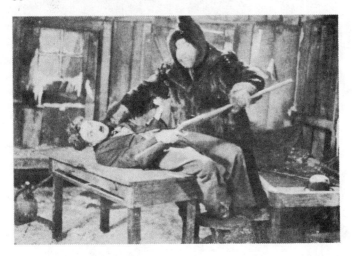

chapter XXI

100   The Thanksgiving Dinner—eating the cooked shoe.
101   The Lone Prospector and the dance-hall girl (Georgia Hale).

102   "The Gold Rush."

103 The dance-hall girl ignores Charlie.

104 The New Year's Eve Dinner which Charlie celebrates alone.

105 (*opposite*) Frame enlargements of the Roll Dance from "The Gold Rush."

106 Charlie gazing in at
the festivities.

107 "The Gold Rush."

108   The cabin balancing on the edge of a cliff.

109   Georgia and Charlie in the final scene.

110 Chaplin directing "The Gold Rush." D'Arrast at left,
Riesner at right.

111 Lita Grey signing contract to appear as Chaplin's leading lady. Instead she married him.

112

chapter XXIII

112-115 Scenes from "The Circus."

113

114

115

116 Rex, the new tightrope walker, fascinates
     Merna Kennedy.
117 The substitute high-wire walker performs
     under difficulties.

118 The circus moves on.

chapter **XXII** cont.

old manner, using his most characteristic tricks and pantomime. Toward the close of the film, he had the daring
to turn his personal troubles to advantage before the
camera. The last scene was deliberately photographed in
the harsh, early morning light to bring out the careworn
lines of his face. This adds great poignancy to his repre-
sentation of the tragic emotions of the eternal frustrated
misfit.

Merna Kennedy, slightly reminiscent of Mabel
Normand, though lacking her talent and personality, is
merely competent. Later she appeared in "Broadway,"
the early Universal talkie, and "Hell's Highway." After
an indifferent career, she died of a heart attack, in 1944,
at the age of thirty-five.

During Chaplin's two-and-a-half-year absence from the
screen, 1925 to 1928, his popularity had again been
threatened by Harold Lloyd with "For Heaven's Sake"
and "The Kid Brother," and by Buster Keaton with "The
General" and "College." Moreover, three clever new-
comers emerged: Raymond Griffith, a cross between
Chaplin and Adolphe Menjou, but with an individual
style of his own; Lupino Lane, an English acrobatic
comedian with a wistful personality; and Harry Langdon, a clown rather similar in appeal to Chaplin but not
an outright imitator. During 1926 and 1927 Langdon
came nearest to stealing Chaplin's crown. His "The
Strong Man" and "Long Pants," directed by Frank
Capra, were almost up to Chaplin's best. The baby-faced
Langdon had an individual, hesitant style, clever pantomimic "routines," and a natural pathos.

Many comedy "teams" were formed during this period:
Wallace Beery and Raymond Hatton, W. C. Fields and
Chester Conklin, Karl Dane and George K. Arthur, Edmund Lowe and Victor MacLaglen (in a new type of
"comedy" stemming from "What Price Glory," namely,
that of a pair of tough soldier "buddies" outwitting each

other and competing for the same girl); and the greatest team of all—Stan Laurel and Oliver Hardy, screen
veterans who never really caught on until they joined
forces.

Despite all this competition, Chaplin held his own. It
may be remarked, parenthetically, that Chaplin maintained his position for many more years, while most of
his competitors have long disappeared. After "The Gold
Rush" he was at the very height of his fame and popularity. Hence "The Circus," although not one of his best
pictures, was a box-office success.

The setting of "The Circus" is "somewhere in the
sticks." The film opens with a paper star in a hoop which
a bareback rider rips through, disclosing a circus framed
within its jagged rim. The little equestrienne misses a
hoop but takes her bows anyway. The Circus Proprietor,
her stepfather, bawls her out, and knocks her down
through another hoop. "For that you don't eat tonight!"
The clowns, back from their turns, come in for their
share of abuse. The empty house and the tepid applause
are blamed on them.

A Tramp joins the carnival crowd before a funhouse,
taking a place next to a pickpocket who has just snatched
a wallet and a watch. As the victim turns toward the
crook, the latter slips the loot into the Tramp's pocket,
then shows that his pockets are empty. Meanwhile the
tramp ambles to a hot-dog stand. Hungry and without
funds, he makes friends with a baby, possessed of a
frankfurter. The child, hanging over its father's shoulder,
is induced to hold out the roll. The hungry tramp takes a
bite, and manages to have mustard added before a second
bite.

A cop nabs the crook in an attempt to retrieve his
loot; and the tramp is startled to receive money from the
law. He doesn't enjoy his affluence very long. As
Charlie is preparing to dine, the pickpocket's victim sees

his watch and chain adorning Charlie. At the same time the crook gets away and Charlie and he are chased by two policemen down the midway, Charlie politely tipping his hat to his fellow-fugitive, running beside him.

Escaping into the "Mirror Maze" in the fun house, Charlie runs into himself and starts a series of comical collisions as he tries to pick up his hat, etc. The hilarity of this scene redoubles when the crook enters to demand the money and the mirror images multiply. Charlie finally eludes the crook only to encounter the cop; and the chase takes a faster tempo over turntables and other carnival paraphernalia—with one mirthful pause as Charlie freezes into a wooden statue among other figures on a Noah's Ark, as the cop dashes past.

The chase takes Charlie under the big tent itself, and the audience, mistaking it for one of the acts, gives him a big hand. From then on Charlie plays an unintended stellar role. In the magician's box he emerges in the place of the truly "Vanishing Lady."

By the time the cop arrives to nab Charlie, next exposed under the black cloth, the Vanishing Lady reappears in his stead while Charlie slips nimbly out of the box to get another big hand from the audience.

Outside he bumps into crook and cop and Charlie is glad to surrender the money and take a needed rest in a chariot. Back under the circus tent, the audience boos the regular clowns and clamors for the new "funny man." The owner hunts Charlie, yanks him out of his nap, and offers him a tryout in the morning.

Early next morning we find Charlie cooking in a tin can over an open fire. With a spoon fished out of one pocket, he dips sugar from another vest pocket and samples the brew. An important-looking hen happens along. Charlie follows her and returns with an egg. Merna, the supperless bareback rider, steps out of her wagon and, as Charlie goes for wood, she picks up a piece of bread near the fire, which she eats greedily. Charlie berates the hungry girl but ends by sharing his meal with her. In pantomime he chides her for eating so fast—bad for the stomach! Take it easy! When she has hiccups, he reminds her of his warning. But, overcome by hiccups himself, he gives the girl the rest of his meal.

At his tryout, the tramp's repertoire, a flip of his feet, gets no response. He is told to watch a team of clowns in the William Tell act and see if he can do it. The lesson starts with a mishap when Charlie pulls up a chair. It happens to be the one from which the boss has momentarily risen and seeks to sit down on again—with disastrous results.

In the course of the elaborately pantomimed William Tell act, the old clown and his victim each take bites of the target-apple until there is nothing left to shoot at. Charlie, first taught how to gesture floridly and smile, then reviews the act. After he bites the apple, he crooks his finger to indicate a worm, then spits it out. The apple gone, Charlie substitutes a banana and juggles it on his head, only to win the circus owner's disapproval.

Next the "barber-shop act" is put on. Charlie replaces the owner's chair just in time to avoid another fall. Two barbers compete for a customer who, when finally seated, is submerged in lather applied with a painter's brush from a pail. Following this the two barbers plaster each other to a messy finish. Charlie, in his tryout, vainly dodging the brush, gets well lathered and staggers around "blind." He ends by plastering the owner—and getting the boot.

Outside Merna helps him wash the suds off his face. As the signal is given for the start of the show, Charlie explains his departure as a failure to agree on terms. Merna's fond goodbye makes Charlie change his direction; he hops after her, only to return with a donkey at his heels.

When the unpaid property men quit, the frantic Head Property Man hires Charlie and hands him a pile of dishes. The donkey, who has taken a dislike to him, chases him into the ring where, in a grand dish-spill, a fall into a woman's lap, and a shove into a barrel, he again blunders into circus stardom, winning roars of laughter from the audience.

Charlie is about to toss some food up to the ill-treated Merna, practicing on the rings, when the boss enters. Charlie pretends to be practicing juggling. When Merna fails to catch a pie and it messes the giant prop-ertyman's face, Charlie sidesteps blame by locking his thumbs in a gesture implying that a bird did it.

It is kept from the new prop man that he is the hit of the show and he is given menial cleaning tasks to per-form. The resulting comedy bits include the wiping of live goldfish; the accidental exposure of the magician's bag of tricks and the release of his menagerie of rabbits, birds and pigs; his frantic efforts to put things in order again; and a veterinary sequence in which he is to blow a large pill down the throat of a sick horse, only to have the horse blow first and get the pill down the "doctor's" throat.

In another sequence the unfriendly donkey chases him into the cage of a sleeping lion. As Charlie reaches out for the gate handle, the outside latch falls and he is locked in. Timidly waving his handkerchief for help, he tiptoes to another door which opens into a tiger's cage. Knocking a tray of water off the wall, he catches it just in time. Then a little dog begins to bark at him. Charlie orders him off, and when that fails, tries tearful pleas.

At this point Merna appears and seeing his plight she faints. Through the bars Charlie sprinkles water on her and, as he does so, the lion yawns, rises, goes over to Charlie, apparently finds him not to his taste, and lies down again. Charlie feels himself to see if he is really in-tact. When Merna revives and opens the door for him, Charlie lingers to take a few heroic poses as conqueror, cockily approaches the lion, only to have a roar from the beast send him flying out of the cage and up a high pole. Pretending it was just a trick to amuse Merna, he slides down flapping his hands like a bird.

Caught idling, a kick from the property man brings up the pill stuck in Charlie's throat. Merna then explains to him that he need not take the abuse, that he is the hit of the show. The owner overhears her and is about to whip her when Charlie grabs the end of the quirt. "If you strike that girl, I'll quit." He follows this with a demand for a raise and gets it.

"The success of the Tramp made life easier for the girl and himself." Charlie now dresses nattily and, as the star clown, is treated with respect. In the next dressing room, Merna has her fortune read. "I see love and marriage with a dark, handsome man who is near you now." Charlie, on the other side of the curtain, is ecstatic, and prances in giddy horseplay with the Old Clown.

A new added attraction joins the circus—Rex, a tightrope walker. Merna meets and falls for the handsome Rex just as Charlie is buying a ring from a clown. Charlie is crestfallen to hear Merna tell the gypsy she is in love—with the tightrope walker. This blow affects Charlie's work; he hardly gets a laugh. Spying Merna and Rex, his "spirit" (through double-exposure) rises up to smite his rival. In some wonderful pantomime Charlie simultaneously registers disdain for the tightrope walker's act, envious jealousy of his daring and skill, and hope that he will fall and break his neck.

Charlie's new ambition is to become a tightrope walker. He practices on a rope close to the ground—takes bows, etc., until he is interrupted by the boss who threatens to fire him if he doesn't become funny again.

One day Rex does not show up and Charlie is pressed to substitute for him. Merna pleads with him not to do it. Noting a prop man with a halter and wire, Charlie bribes him to fasten it to him. In a prophetic trial

Charlie is pulled off the ground and lands on his head.

On the high wire, knowing the safety appliance is on, Charlie does reckless and amazing stunts. Unfortunately the halter becomes detached. The prop man tries to warn him but he goes on. Suddenly he sees the halter loose above him and tries to grab it. His situation is made more ticklish by some escaped monkeys who crawl over his face and tear off his trousers while he is balancing. He falls, catches the wire, climbs underhand to the bicycle for the "ride for life," misses the catch below and lands in a store across the street from which he staggers out, dazed, to take a bow.

On his return to the circus he finds the owner mistreating Merna again. Charlie attacks the boss and the scene dissolves to his booting out of the tent.

"That night" Charlie, on the road again, huddles by his fire in the moonlight. Merna appears out of the darkness and tells him she has run away. "Can't you take me with you?" Charlie slips back to the circus to find Rex. Charlie explains to him the one way out, gives Rex his ring, takes him to Merna, sees the couple married in a country church, and showers them with rice.

The three return to the circus. The owner threatens his stepdaughter until Rex informs him, "You are now speaking to my wife." Forced to forgive them, he shakes hands but not with Charlie. The couple then refuse to go on with the show unless Charlie is rehired and the owner gives in. As Merna and Rex enter their wagon and ask Charlie to join them, he pantomimes that three is a crowd and shuts the door on the happy couple.

The circus moves on. Charlie stands in the empty ring as the wagons pass. Finally he is alone in the circle. Seated on a box, he sadly watches the caravan depart. Then he crumples up a piece of tissue paper with a star printed on it, kicks it away with his heel, and waddles jauntily toward the horizon as the scene irises out.

"City Lights"

"The Circus" brought in three times its cost, but Chaplin himself never considered it one of his best films and was anxious to start another. Less than a month after completing "The Circus" he began work on an idea for his next film. It was only an idea. Whatever the picture was to be, its heroine was to be a blind girl!

Chaplin may have been inspired by Raquel Meller's singing of "La Violetera" (Who'll Buy My Violets). He was certainly much taken by the Spanish diseuse on her 1926 tour and at one time there was talk of her playing Josephine to his Napoleon. In fact, publicity pictures were taken of Chaplin costumed as the little Emperor. But the singer was happily and undetachably married to Gomez Carrillo, Ambassador to France, the man who had exposed the famous spy, Mata Hari.

At any rate, nothing came of the Napoleon plan. Nor of another rumored plan to play Christ in a new interpretation which would shift from an emphasis upon His meekness to an emphasis on His virility, His commanding qualities as a leader of men.

The image of the blind girl displaced Napoleon and Christ. Around that bare idea, Chaplin began building a scenario. His collaborators were Harry Crocker, who had assisted as collaborator, director, and actor in "The Circus"; Henry Bergman, who had been with him since 1916; his public relations man, Carl Robinson; and

Henry Clive, Australian artist and a newcomer in the "clique." Production started in March 1928.

No sooner had work got under way when panic struck Hollywood. The talkies had arrived to stay!—after a succession of failures to win the public from as far back as 1900. Improved amplification techniques and the spread of radio had made the public more receptive. By the summer and fall of 1928 the major companies were turning to talkies, though many in the industry still looked upon it as a passing fad. Talkies started a new migration of actors—and singers—from Broadway to Hollywood, as many old screen idols faltered in the new medium. New technicians and techniques came into the field. The sound "revolution" was on!

Chaplin halted his picture.

Chaplin had two advantages for a try at talkies had he wished it—a good voice and stage experience. But he considered pantomime a superior and more universal art, and better suited to the screen than the talkie, which he regarded as a mere imitation of the stage. He himself was essentially a pantomime artist and he considered the silent screen best, not only for himself, but for the character he had built up. Spoken dialogue, he feared, might destroy the illusion of the universal little-man character he had spent years perfecting. Moreover, many of his best effects were gained by "under-cranking" the camera, thus speeding up the action—an effect impossible with the sound camera which was run by motor, at a set speed of twenty-four frames a second.

The most practical objection was that English dialogue would limit his enormous foreign market. (It was simple to translate titles.) He usually earned his production costs from Japan alone.

When Chaplin resumed production of "City Lights," it was as a silent picture.

On his small lot, elaborate sets began to go up—elaborate at least for Chaplin. Actually the entire "city" was just one "T" shaped set, with a theatre entrance and cabaret on one side, the flower shop and a couple of stores on the other, and the monument at the crossbar of the "T," before a mere suggestion of a public building. This one set, photographed from a variety of angles, gave a remarkable illusion of vastness. There was also a corner, backed by a drop with painted windows, where the blind girl sits with her basket of flowers (juxtaposed, for the sake of economy, to the millionaire's house and garden).

Chaplin filled the sets with a swarm of extras (mostly pretty girls under 25!) and scudding automobiles to give an almost abstract impression of a synthesized metropolis—New York, London, and Paris, in one. For interiors, two arch pieces served in the millionaire's living room, bedroom, and dressing room.

It took some time to find the actress he needed for the blind girl. None of his tests had turned up a girl who fitted the one in his mind. He had given up hopes of finding her in Hollywood when, at a boxing match, one night, he thought he saw her in a girl sitting at the ringside. She reminded him of Edna Purviance as she had looked of old—the same blonde hair, the same classic features, the same radiant smile. He sought her out, after the match, and next day Virginia Cherrill, who had never appeared on stage or screen—who, at least according to her own statement, had no Hollywood ambitions at all—was Chaplin's new leading lady. Her salary was a mere hundred a week, no great sum in those halcyon days. However, all she brought to the part was good looks and near-sightedness, the latter a deficiency in general, though an asset for the particular role she was cast in. The flower girl was full grown in Chaplin's mind; all he needed was this girl's physical frame, as a sculptor needs clay of a certain consistency.

Miss Cherrill was vacationing in California after a long

divorce suit in Chicago from Irving Adler. She submitted herself, with bewilderment, to Chaplin's coaching.

At this point Chaplin suffered a bereavement. His mother, whom it had been necessary to move from her seaside home to a Glendale sanitarium, died there. The finest care had failed to arrest the clouding of her mind. After visits to her Chaplin would sink into melancholy for days and he had a long fit of depression after her death. He had her buried near the "little mouse." At the funeral, Lita Grey and her mother appeared in elaborate mourning down to the black-bordered handkerchiefs. Only the tact of Carl Robinson, who kept Chaplin from seeing them, prevented a violent scene. Lita probably wanted to figure in the press reports and pictures; or may even have hoped to star in a big "reconciliation scene at grave of mother."

Work resumed on "City Lights." Chaplin shot thousands of feet, in his usual fashion, improvising and retaking with no thought of time, and began, too, to indulge in his familiar inexplicable whims.

First he fired Harry Crocker, who had been with him for three years. The next victim was Henry Clive, playing the millionaire. Clive had done his scenes well but refused to do the drowning scene in the river (Chaplin's studio pool) until the water had been warmed a while in the sun—claiming that he had a cold. Chaplin had been working all night; the rest of the crew were exhausted; but he insisted that they go on with the scene. On Clive's continued refusal, Chaplin left the set in a rage and ordered Robinson to fire him. After a break of several days, Chaplin hired Harry Myers, fondly remembered for his lead in the 1921 version of "A Connecticut Yankee in King Arthur's Court." Myers was more robust and inured to cold water. He made an excellent foil for the little tramp, but it took six months of reshooting for Chaplin to reach the scenes again where Clive was fired!

Then, suddenly, Chaplin expressed dissatisfaction with Virginia Cherrill. Half a million feet of film had been shot, much of it with Virginia; yet Chaplin suddenly found her unsuitable.

She had given him trouble from the beginning. Living on alimony, she felt no compulsion to work. She was a party girl given to staying out most of the night. Many mornings she would appear on the set somewhat the worse for wear, unfit for the camera which magnifies the slightest sign of dissipation. Chagrined by a lecture from the puritanical Kono on her drinking and the strain on Chaplin, she promised better behavior. She was, in fact, more serious in her work and improving remarkably under Chaplin's coaching when he suddenly took a violent dislike to her.

Chaplin sent her word that she wouldn't be needed for a few days, and as soon as she had left Georgia Hale, heroine of "The Gold Rush," with whom Chaplin was still on intimate terms, flounced into the studio with an assortment of blonde wigs. Chaplin began making tests. Though it seems impossible that the fiery prostitute of "The Gold Rush" could have effected a believable transformation into the sweet blind girl, Chaplin's "yes-men" nodded to his judgment that her tests were successful— all but Carl Robinson, who bluntly asserted that she was awful. Chaplin said nothing at the time; but he later rejected Georgia and the search went on.

One day a sixteen-year-old appeared at the studio with her mother. She was beautiful and intelligent, and Chaplin, after playing some scenes with her, was on the verge of drawing up a contract. In a panic over the potentialities for disaster in another sixteen-year-old and her mother, Robinson had Reeves dismiss the one remaining secretary in the office. With no typist available, the signing of the contract was postponed till the following day. By then Chaplin had changed his mind, anyway.

The girl, whose name was Marilyn Morgan, went on her way to achieve a measure of fame, later, as Marian Marsh.

Incidentally, one of the extras in the cafe scene was also to go on to fame. Chaplin had taken notice of this girl, with strikingly light hair, in the company of an older woman. They were identified to him as a Mrs. Pope and her daughter Jean. Even before "City Lights" was released, Jean Pope was whizzing on her brief, bombshell career as Jean Harlow.

After changing his mind about Marilyn Morgan, Chaplin called back the unsuspecting Virginia Cherrill. For more than an hour the two were closeted in his office. When she came out, her face was covered with tears. But production went on.

Under Chaplin's direction Virginia Cherrill proved unusually effective as the blind girl, and certainly she is one of the most strikingly beautiful young women ever to appear in films. But apparently there was little love lost between the Svengali and his creature. After "City Lights" she went out of his life forever.

Like his other leading ladies, Virginia's career did not prosper once she was on her own. Following "City Lights" she was signed on by Fox for a minor film, "Girls Demand Excitement," released simultaneously with the Chaplin picture. After a couple of other minor pictures she returned to her first love—matrimony. She had a succession of husbands, including William Rhinelander Stewart and Cary Grant, to end, in 1937, as the Countess of Jersey. In England, she later distinguished herself in war work.

More than eight hundred thousand feet of film were shot for "City Lights," a good two years were spent on its production, and its cost ran to a million and a half.

By 1930-1931 talkies had entirely superseded the silent film and people had almost forgotten what the screen was like before it talked. Realizing that there had to be at least a musical accompaniment to the film, Chaplin spent the next three months composing a score for it. The synchronization of the "City Lights" music required weeks of work and cost forty thousand dollars.

"City Lights" had an exciting gala premiere in Los Angeles, Chaplin attending with Albert and Mrs. Einstein. The public, however, did not flock to it after the big opening. It was feared that Chaplin, too, had been forgotten in the eventful three years since "the birth of sound." Popular Broadway comedians appeared to have taken Hollywood over. The big names now were Al Jolson, Eddie Cantor, Wheeler and Woolsey, and the Marx Brothers, who had brought a new musical-comedy humor to the screen. Gone was the "pure" screen comedy originated by Mack Sennett.

Chaplin decided to enhance the New York and London opening with an in-person appearance; in fact, to travel around the world with the film and "re-sell" himself. Kono and Robinson were to accompany him on the tour. When he left Hollywood, Georgia Hale was at the train to see him off.

In New York, Chaplin was conducted in stately fashion to the Ambassador Hotel by A. C. Blumenthal, a close friend of Mayor Jimmy Walker; but almost at once, fresh difficulties arose. There was a conflict between Chaplin and United Artists about the distribution rights. Chaplin demanded what they considered far too high a rental —fifty percent of the gross, an unheard-of figure at the time. He finally decided to exhibit the picture independently and rented the old George M. Cohan Theatre for the premiere. United Artists were to regret their action. Chaplin netted over $400,000 from the Cohan run alone.

The "City Lights" premiere, on February 6, 1931, was

one of the most distinguished in Broadway history.
Chaplin attended the opening, escorting Constance Collier, the veteran English actress. In the audience were
Peggy Hopkins Joyce, Grace Moore, and other notables.
The film was received with cheers and tears. Some pronounced it Chaplin's masterpiece—the climax of his art.
This may be considered not merely a tribute to the film
itself, but an indirect comment on the quality of talking
pictures people had been subjected to in the past four
years. It may be that "City Lights" reminded them of
something valuable they had lost. After the publicity,
and the enthusiastic reviews, the New York public
crowded the theatre.

Those who had shaken their heads when Chaplin began "City Lights" now had to admit that he had done the
seemingly impossible. He had made a financially successful silent film three years after the supposed demise of
the silent screen. Their astonishment would have been
even greater could they have foreseen the year 1950,
when its revival on Broadway outgrossed many new films.

"City Lights," subtitled "A comedy romance in pantomime," is one of Chaplin's cleverest and most original
story ideas. Actually it is a tragi-comedy, the accent as
much on the love story as on the humor; and its prevailing attitude one of sharp irony. Critics who had de-
plored the "vulgarity" of his previous films changed
their tune. Though many of his old slapstick gags re-
appeared, he had now become an accepted tradition, a
king who could do no wrong. Some critics even complained that the film was too slow!

There is, in fact, little of the old slapdash knockabout
that distinguished his early films. The approach to the
story is a straight, realistic one with none of the fantastic
elements contained in "The Pawnshop," "Shoulder
Arms," "The Gold Rush," etc. No one scene in "City

Lights" comes up to the brilliant virtuosity of the roll dance in "The Gold Rush" or the sermon in "The Pilgrim." However, as a blend of comedy and pathos, "City Lights" is perfect.

The equivocal ending of the film, ironic and vibrant with the tragic sense of life, seldom fails to bring tears. The terrified smile of the tramp at the girl who has recovered her vision through him, and through that recovery is lost to him, is one of the most poignant scenes ever photographed.

After "City Lights," in many ways his greatest film, Chaplin possibly let his "intellect" run away with him at the expense of his creative gifts. At any rate, his three films made since, brilliant though they are in many respects, suffered, in progressive degree, from the absence of the older qualities in which he stood unique. Significantly, "City Lights" showed a profit of some $5,000,000, while "Monsieur Verdoux" (1947) was withdrawn from the American market at a loss.

Technically, "City Lights" is Chaplin's most polished production. As a rule he was more interested in the effect than the manner. The "City Lights" sets, photography, and lighting show considerably more finish than is usually the case in the Chaplin films, and approached the standard of the best work of the period. At this time panchromatic film and incandescent lighting, neither perfected yet, and just gaining general acceptance in pictures, caused a certain grayness and flatness. This sacrificed much of the "snap" of productions like "The Gold Rush." In recent years, pan stock has improved and a new type of strong arc light supplements the soft incandescents.

This lack of contrast in the images is a minor fault of "City Lights," however. To those of us who have suffered through the duped and scratched prints of Chaplin's early films, "City Lights" is a joy to behold.

The picture opens with the words "City Lights" spelled out in electric bulbs over a city square at night. The scene fades into daytime with a crowd gathered for the unveiling of a monument: "To the people of the city we donate this monument: Peace and Prosperity." It consists of three figures, a seated woman and two standing male figures below, one with a sword. In a burlesque of the talkies, a saxophone jabbers in accompaniment to the speaker, resuming on a higher note, behind the next speaker, an elderly clubwoman. Then the monument is unveiled—to reveal a little tramp asleep in the stone woman's lap. Dignitaries yell at him to climb down immediately, which he does, only to impale himself on the sculptured sword. As he attempts to regain his footing when the national anthem is played, he blunders into a position where a statue's upheld hand thumbs Charlie's nose. Finally, with an apologetic tip of his hat, he steps off and disappears over a fence.

"Afternoon." At a busy street corner he has trouble with a jeering newsboy who snatches his cane from under his arm, then plucks a ragged glove end off Chaplin's chiding finger. The tramp has to remove the glove end again to snap his fingers in the boy's face. Then he gets in trouble with a sidewalk elevator while admiring some art objects, including a nude statuette, in a store window. His eyes keep returning to the nude but with all the pretenses of the esthete appreciating subtleties of molding and proportions. Each time he steps back, for perspective, the elevator rises just in time; but eventually he finds himself taken down. He climbs back to the sidewalk and from there starts bawling out the man coming up who, as the elevator completes its ascent, towers over him and sends the little tramp scuttling.

On his way he avoids a traffic cop by slipping through a limousine parked at the curb. A pretty flower girl, hearing the limousine door open and believing a millionaire has just alighted, tries to sell him a flower. Charlie discovers she is blind when she gropes for the flower he accidentally knocks out of her hand. The little tramp gives her his last coin and tiptoes away. Smitten by this lovely girl, who has mistaken him for a millionaire, he steals back to sit near her in adoration, only to have her, unaware of his presence, douse him with water as she rinses her bucket at the corner fountain.

"Evening." The blind girl returns to her slum room where she lives with her grandmother. She turns on a victrola and, hearing a fellow whistle to his girl, she wistfully waves out the window at the couple.

"Night." Under a bridge by the river, a drunken, manic-depressive millionaire, in a moment of drunken remorse, resolves to drown himself. He ties a rope, weighted with a rock, around his neck, to make the drowning sure. Lost in dreams of the girl, with the dearly purchased flower still under his nose, and in a mood to save all humanity, the tramp comes on the scene. He dashes forward to stop the suicide. "Tomorrow the birds will sing," he reminds the drunkard. "Be brave, face life!" But the millionaire, not to be dissuaded, places the rope around both heads—and slips out himself. In their struggles, one to die, the other to save his life, it is the tramp who goes overboard when the stone is tossed into the river.

There follows a hilarious sequence as they alternately pull each other in and rescue each other, until they stand safe, but dripping and panting, at the edge. The cold water cures the millionaire's depression, but brings on the manic phase. He invites the Tramp to his home to warm up.

Informed by the butler that his wife has sent for her baggage, he replies, "Good." He then pours Charlie a drink, but misses Charlie's glass and sends it down the oversize trousers. More comic drink pouring, with Charlie surreptitiously disposing of unwanted liquor down his vest. It is brought to an end by a return of the millionaire's depressive phase. Grabbing a gun, he puts it to his temple, but this time the tramp's frantic suasions work. The millionaire decides to live and "burn up the town!"

In a crowded night club, the drunken pair cause mirthful havoc. The Tramp's old nemesis, the slippery floor, gets in its dirty work. Mistaking the menu for a hymn book, Charlie stands up to sing. The millionaire, mistaking his napkin for a shirt tail, stuffs it into his trousers. As they finally settle down Charlie keeps lighting the cigar his friend keeps waving in his face. The confusion ends with the finally lighted cigar tossed on a lady's seat and Charlie charging gallantly to the rescue, with squirts from a seltzer bottle on her smouldering rear.

In the next mess Charlie mixes ends of paper streamers with his spaghetti, munching ceilingward to encompass all the coils of one of the streamers. Ever chivalrous, he then goes to the rescue of a girl apparently undergoing mayhem in an apache dance number.

Inflamed by the shimmying movements of a girl near him, Charlie grabs a passing middle-aged woman and whirls her around. When her husband cuts in, Charlie changes to a waiter carrying a tray full of dishes. As the waiter falls (with the dishes intact), Charlie sinks back exhausted.

"Early morning—homeward bound." Driving back, bumping over curbstones and dodging vehicles, the little tramp admires the car and is made a gift of it.

At the mansion door the tramp spies the flower girl on her way to work. The millionaire gives him money to buy some of her flowers and Charlie purchases her whole day's stock. Then he drives her home in his new car. On the steps he kisses her hand and asks if he may see her home again. "Whenever you wish, sir." After she goes in, he is lost in dreamy revery, with a flower pressed to his nostrils. The revery ends when a cat above dislodges a flower pot on his head. Up on a barrel, under a rain spout, he peeps into her room. A nosy janitor puts an end to that, but gets an unexpected shower when Charlie hops off and flees to his car.

The eccentric millionaire, sober, is a different man. He doesn't remember the tramp who, returning to his new friend, is shut out of the house. Needing a smoke, he jumps into his Rolls-Royce, and follows a cigar smoker until he throws away the butt. He beats an old bum to it, then climbs back into his luxurious car, leaving the mystified bum staring.

Once more Charlie returns to the mansion. The millionaire, now cold sober, is leaving. He steps into his Rolls-Royce without so much as a glance at the little tramp, and drives off. And the bewildered tramp shuffles away, drawing disconsolately at his cigar butt.

In a later encounter, the same day, the millionaire, roaring drunk again, embraces the tramp like a long-lost brother and proffers a party in his honor. There Charlie, in an alcoholic daze again, confuses a bald head with a cream pudding. A toy whistle, received as a party favor, goes down his throat when a girl gives him a playful nudge. With every hiccup he now emits a toot, much to the annoyance of a pompous singer who has been invited to perform. Seeking the seclusion of the millionaire's garden, his whistle draws first a taxi, then a pack of dogs.

Next morning again the millionaire, as his sober self, remembers nothing of what happened to his drunken self. He stares at the stranger sharing his bed, and orders him thrown out, while he begins packing for a trip to Europe. In the course of the booting out, which involves some delightful foolery with the butler, the little tramp snatches a banana which, when he is shut out, he non-chalantly peels as he stalks off in unperturbed dignity.

At the familiar corner the blind girl is missing. The little tramp hurries to her home, where, peering through a window, he sees that she is ill and hears the doctor say she needs special care. Determined to help the girl, he finds work as a streetcleaner, and is promptly appalled by the threat of work for him in a procession of circus animals, including an elephant.

At lunch, as Charlie washes his hands, his soap cake interchanges with his neighbor's block of cheese. The bawling out he gets is enlivened with the soap bubbles, issuing with the curses.

"To play the part of a gentleman without the million-aire was difficult, but he did his best." He brings the girl food and reads her an article about a Viennese doctor who has a cure for blindness. "Wonderful! Then I'll be able to see you," exclaims the girl. He is pleased at first, then pauses, realizing the risk in that. In a wool-winding episode he loses his underwear by degrees as an unravel-ing thread is wound into the ball. Learning that she and her grandmother are to be evicted for non-payment of rent, he promises to bring her the money next morning. The girl, tears in her eyes, thanks him for his generosity, while he, with a snap of his fingers, acts every inch the millionaire.

Returning to work late, he is fired. A boxer, seeing him discharged, takes him aside, asks him if he wants to make some easy money.

That night, in the dressing room of the boxing arena, the little tramp waits to go on. He is to fight a fixed match with his new acquaintance; they will split the purse fifty-fifty. After warming up a bit, Charlie whispers something in his friend's ear, and his friend points off right, presumably to the lavatory. Charlie goes off, but returns to have his gloves removed. Then he goes off to the—water fountain for a drink!

The friendly, broken-down boxer gets a telegram warning him the police are on his trail and to get out of town. Before Charlie knows what has happened, his friend has vanished and he is face to face with a real tough fighter, one who has no intention of splitting the purse and who misinterprets the little man's somewhat coy overtures for friendship.

Charlie is beside himself with fear. Seeing a husky Negro boxer rubbing himself with a rabbit's foot, he borrows the charm to use on himself. When a few minutes later the Negro is carried back unconscious, Charlie frantically tries to rub off the "charm."

In the ring, he seeks safety from the tough guy behind the referee. The fight turns into ballet as the two boxers sidestep around the referee. He ducks and hugs his opponent at every swing. Later (with the aid of an invisible wire) he dives across the ring into his opponent's and the referee's stomachs. In a one-two-three punch by his opponent, the first sways him in one direction, the second in the other direction, but the third, instead of putting him out, gives him extra pep. The fight is crowded with more ineffable funny business, including simultaneous knockouts and counts, first on one of the boxers, then on the other, an entanglement with the bell rope, and an unexpected but logical end—Charlie out for the count.

"Still hoping to get money for the girl," Charlie wanders the city. In a theatre crowd the millionaire, back from Europe and drunk to the point of recognition, sees the little tramp, pushes him into his car, and takes him home.

There a pair of robbers are at work when they hear the car drive up. They hide behind a curtain as the befuddled millionaire gives Charlie the money to pay for the blind girl's operation. As the millionaire goes into his depressive state, one of the crooks slugs him while the other heads for Charlie. There is an elusive chase which ends with Charlie in the hands of a cop, accused of robbery by the butler and confronted by the reviving millionaire. Unfortunately the millionaire revives cold sober, and instead of recognizing Charlie, asks his butler, "Who is this man?"

In despair Charlie snatches the money, turns out the lights, and gets away. He brings the money to the blind girl and persuades her to go for the operation. He must go away for a while, he tells her, but promises to see her again, but he dreads what will happen when she regains her sight and sees him for what he is.

Nabbed on a street corner by detectives, he is hustled off to jail. At its gates he disposes of his cigarette by batting it into the air with a philosophical back kick.

Months pass. Autumn comes around. The girl, now cured, runs a swanky florist shop. Whenever a handsome, wealthy man comes into the shop her heart leaps with the hope that he is her benefactor. But every hope is dashed.

Meanwhile, the little tramp, released from prison, wanders the streets, a ragged derelict. He fails to find the girl at her old station. A flower he picks up from the gutter reminds him of her. Jeering newsboys torment him with a pea-shooter.

Despite his tatters he remains the impeccable gentleman. When one of the boys pulls a rag end out of his trouser pocket Charlie reproves him, blows his nose on the rag, folds it neatly, and tucks it into his vest pocket.

The commotion between the tramp and the newsboys amuses the girl, watching from behind her shop window. The tramp turns and sees her and stands transfixed. The girl, noticing his expression but not knowing who he is, giggles to her assistant, "I've made a conquest." She holds a fresh flower and a coin out to the little tramp.

The tramp comes to his senses and starts away in panic. But the girl comes out of the shop and calls after him. He shyly hesitates, then lets the girl press the flower and the money into his hand. The touch of his hand tells her who he is.

"You?" she asks falteringly. And the little tramp, her flower in his hand, nods, with an embarrassed smile.

"You can see now?" he asks.

She looks into his eyes, her own eyes dulled by the shattering truth. "Yes, I can see now," she says slowly, and presses his hand.

And so they stand, looking into each other's eyes. In the final close up, the tramp, his finger in his mouth, still holding her flower, smiles painfully at her, with a mixture of tremulous hope and terror, as the scene fades out.

Chaplin as a composer

The credit title on "City Lights," "Music composed by Charles Chaplin," brought a surprised and indulgent raising of eyebrows. Because of the occurrence of phrases, here and there, from some familiar melodies, inserted, in most cases, for comic effect, and the use of "La Violetera" (Who'll Buy My Violets) as a theme for the blind flower girl, Chaplin was assumed, by some, to be stretching his claim to everything in the film.

Attitudes changed with the subsequent appearances of Chaplin scores in "Modern Times," "The Great Dictator," and "Monsieur Verdoux" (the two latter talkies with occasional musical interludes and "background" music), and with the full score for the reissued "The Gold Rush." A quality, which can only be described as "Chaplinesque" was discerned and commented upon in this music, despite the fact that it was arranged and orchestrated by other hands. Those who still believe that Chaplin merely hummed a tune or two and that "real musicians" did the rest have only to listen to the scores of several of his films. The style is marked and individual. It shows a fondness for romantic waltz hesitations played in very rubato time, lively numbers in two-four time which might be called "promenade themes," and tangos with a strong beat.

It can now be seen that Chaplin's music is an integral part of his film conceptions. In similar fashion D. W.

Griffith also composed some musical themes for his pictures. But perhaps of no other one man can it be said that he wrote, directed, acted, *and scored* a motion picture. Incidentally, Chaplin even conducted the orchestra, himself, during recordings, an added reason for the satisfying impression of wholeness in the Chaplin films.

Although musically untrained, Chaplin nevertheless had the advantages of a musical inheritance from his ballad-singer father, the natural endowment of a quick ear, and a superb sense of rhythm, a taste for the art, experience with it on the stage, and an amateur performer's devotion to it. In "My Trip Abroad" there is a passage describing his first consciousness of music. As a boy, in Kennington Cross, he was enraptured by a weird duet on clarinet and harmonica, to a tune he later identified as the popular song, "The Honeysuckle and the Bee." "It was played with such feeling that I became conscious, for the first time, of what melody really was."

According to Fred Karno's biography, young Chaplin spent much of his leisure time between shows picking out tunes on an old cello. When Chaplin was signed by the Essanay Company, he bought a violin on which he scraped for hours at night, to the annoyance of less wakeful actors when they all lived next to the studio at Niles, California.

While he was being feted during the negotiations with the Mutual Company in New York, Chaplin, appearing at a benefit concert at the old Hippodrome (February 20, 1916), led Sousa's band in the "Poet and Peasant" overture and his own composition, "The Peace Patrol." That same year Chaplin published two songs, "Oh that Cello" and "There's Always Someone You Can't Forget," which was a musical tribute to his first romance. In the twenties he made records of his "Sing a Song" and "With You, Dear, in Bombay," both later used in the sound version of "The Gold Rush." Subsequent years saw the publication of a theme from "The Great Dictator" to a lyric entitled "Falling Star," and three numbers from "Monsieur Verdoux": "A Paris Boulevard," "Tango Bitterness," and "Rumba."

After Chaplin made his first million, he installed a pipe organ in his Beverly Hills mansion. In certain moods he is known to have fingered this expensive instrument for hours at a time. Realizing the importance of musical accompaniment to the silent film, Chaplin sought to have it reproduced in every theatre exactly as he wished it. He supervised the cue sheets (lists of numbers to be played, sent free to all theatres booking a film) of his pictures from "The Kid" (1921) up to "City Lights" (1931)— when it was possible to have the music recorded on the film itself. Then it also was commercially expedient to claim at least "music and sound effects" since by 1931 the silent picture had been superseded by the talkie.

Arthur Johnston and Alfred Newman arranged and orchestrated the music for "City Lights," Chaplin's outstanding score. But the melodies, with the exceptions noted above, used for the associations they would evoke, were composed by Chaplin. At least twenty numbers in the score could be published as separate and original works. As was customary in the scoring for silent pictures, the Wagnerian *leitmotiv* system was followed—a distinctive musical theme associated with each character and idea. The musical cues in "City Lights" come to some ninety-five, not counting the passages where the music follows or mimics the action in what is generally known as "mickey-mousing," from its use in the scoring of animated cartoons.

A fanfare on trumpets, over a night scene, opens the picture proper. It is heard again as a sort of fate theme at moments of crises, such as the count over Charlie in the boxing ring, and his capture and imprisonment. Saxophone bleating, in slightly off synchronization with the lips, mimics the speakers at the unveiling of the monument. This shrill squeaking is used not only as a comic note in itself, but as a burlesque of the talkies. When Charlie is ordered down, a bustling "galop" number in G minor, played in fast tempo, accompanies his scrambling over the statues. The tramp's wanderings through the city streets are accompanied by a gallant bitter-sweet melody mostly on the cello. The theme is repeated seven times when he is in hopeful moods. The flower girl's principal theme is "La Violetera," and phrases of it are played behind the tramp, when it is pertinent to indicate that his thoughts dwell on her. She had two subsidiary themes, one a pathetique for scenes in her slum room, and the other a violin caprice, for her wistful moments.

The music behind the tramp's meeting with the eccentric millionaire is an amusing burlesque of opera. A dramatic theme introduces him and is followed by an over-dramatic agitato as he ties the suicide noose. Charlie's dissuasions are musically rendered in burlesqued opera recitative. Another kind of music is kidded in the accompaniment to Charlie's promise that "Tomorrow the birds will sing"—the "April-showers, silver-lining, rainbow-round-my-shoulder" sort of "theme song" that echoed through early talkies, particularly in the Al Jolson films. In later sequences the tramp has only to point upward in mock-heroic fashion; no title is necessary, the music "tells" what he is saying.

The nightclub music for the "burning up the town" is a hectic jazz theme with a long sustained high note and marked rhythm. A rumba-like number accompanies the party scene where the tramp swallows the whistle. When the millionaire wakes sober, to find a stranger sharing his bed, there is a snatch of Rimsky-Korsakov's ballet "Scheherazade"—played in duet form—in low register for the perplexed millionaire and high for the tramp. In like manner bits of "How Dry I Am," "I Hear You Calling Me," etc., are called upon for comic comments.

There are two love themes—one a light romantic waltz played very rubato to action, and a tragic piece associated with the tramp's hopeless love. Played also behind the tragic close of the picture, with its grim and fateful chords, the second has a distinct Puccini flavor. A sprightly theme on the bassoon accompanies many of the tramp's more humorous moments, such as his mishaps behind his streetcleaner's cart; and there is a singularly amusing use of a tango during the boxing sequence. The fight itself is underlined by a feverish musical "hurry," also used behind other fast action.

It is true that one or two of the minor numbers are reminiscent. A short dance piece resembles "I Want To Be Happy." The famous apache dance is a paraphrase. The crooked-fighter theme sounds a bit like "Look out for Jimmy Valentine." Some Debussy chords herald the morning, and the "Second Hungarian Rhapsody" is cleverly jazzed up for a little chase scene. Nevertheless, the principal themes are Chaplin's. A film eighty-seven minutes long calls for a score of about a hundred and fifty pages and a little "borrowing" here and there can be overlooked.

"City Lights" ends with the following music. The tramp, let out of prison, searches for the blind girl.

Sequence	Music
Cue 91. Tramp comes to corner where girl used to sell flowers	"La Violetera" (played slowly)
Cue 92. Tramp wanders the streets	Tramp theme (played slowly and tragically)

Sequence	*Music*
Cue 93. Tramp finds flower in gutter	"La Violetera" (normal tempo)
Cue 94. He turns to the girl in window of her shop laughing at him	Violin Caprice (secondary girl theme)
Cue 95. Girl touches hand of tramp	Tragic love theme

Incidentally, sound effects are sparingly used, and then only for deliberately pointed effects, like the swallowed whistle, bells, the firing of revolvers, etc. Falls and blows are not accented by traps, nor are there the other taste-less noises by ratchets, etc., that have feaured so many "revivals with sound added," copied from the distracting technique of sound cartoons. Above all, the human voice is not employed, an artistic mistake too often made in at-tempts to bring old silent pictures "up to date."

The haunting and pleasant Chaplin melodies in "City Lights" are pleasing in themselves, but the picture is one of the few extant examples of the silent medium's power when wedded to a musical score which properly inter-prets the action and heightens the emotion. The legend has grown that silent pictures were accompanied by a tinkling piano, either played thumpily in the so-called "nickelodeon" manner, or in a more dignified, but es-sentially neutral style. Actually, from 1914 on, every town of five thousand or over had at least a three-piece orchestra—or an organ. The Griffith and Fairbanks films, specials like "The Covered Wagon" and "The Big Parade," all had orchestras traveling with them, playing scores as carefully worked out as "City Lights."

By strict musical standards Chaplin's score may not equal those of Virgil Thompson, Max Steiner, Georges Auric, or William Walton. Thompson's scoring for "The River" and "Louisiana Story," with extremely clever arrangements of old folk tunes, is far more sophisticated and intellectual. Nor does Chaplin possess the virtuosity and present grandiose manner of Steiner, where too often sheer bombast attempts to make up for the emotional vacuity in the picture itself. But who, better than Chaplin, could point up musically the tragi-comic adventures of the tramp character he himself created?

trip around the world; Paulette Goddard

To sell his latest picture was not Chaplin's sole reason for his trip to Europe and around the world in 1931. Other reasons were touched on in an article ghost-written by his secretary, Catherine Hunter ("A Comedian Sees the World," published in the *Woman's Home Companion*, 1933). "The disillusion of love, fame and fortune left me somewhat apathetic. . . . I needed emotional stimulus . . . like all egocentrics I turn to myself. I want to live in my youth again."

At the last minute, Chaplin invited his artist friend, Ralph Barton, famous for his caricatures of theatre celebrities, to accompany him. Barton, unable to work, was in a depressed state of mind. His wife had left him and he had recently attempted suicide. "Life could never defeat me," Chaplin told him. "Nothing matters, only physical pain. Our tragedies are only as big as we make them. . . . All artists experience a lull in their work. . . . What you need is adventure, so come to Europe."

Chaplin's entourage, consisting of Barton, Carl Robinson, and Kono, sailed on the Mauretania. As on the 1921 crossing, Chaplin avoided the other passengers. He and Barton hardly ever left their cabin. After all the hubbub surrounding the New York opening, Chaplin needed a rest.

London repeated its riotous welcome of ten years ago but there were some unpleasant incidents, particularly sieges by reporters whom Chaplin at first refused to see. Finally, persuaded by Carl Robinson, he gave the demanded press interview.

There were showers of letters and invitations. The first of a continuous procession of receptions was a dinner at Sir Philip Sassoon's house in Park Lane. There followed a luncheon at Cliveden, the famous salon-home of Lady Astor, the former Nancy Langhorne of Virginia and then a member of the House of Commons. Bernard Shaw was a fellow guest. Chaplin diffidently broached the subject of art and propaganda, relieved that Shaw did not take it up. Shaw had been quoted as saying that all art should be propaganda, and Chaplin, at that time at least, considered "the object of art is to intensify feeling, color, sound—if object it has—for this gives a fuller range to the artist in expressing life." But Chaplin did not feel equal to a controversy with Shaw. Politics from all angles and by members of all parties was discussed at Cliveden.

After visiting his old haunts in London, Chaplin accepted an invitation from Alistair MacDonald, whom he had met in California, to meet his father, Ramsay MacDonald, then Prime Minister, at Chequers, his country home. After mentioning the changes he had observed in England since 1921, Chaplin tried to draw the Prime Minister into a political discussion, which the latter evaded. In this evasion and in other ways, MacDonald failed to impress Chaplin favorably.

The following day, after a lunch at the House of Commons, Sir Philip Sassoon took him to tea with Lloyd George, who made a better impression. Lloyd George was patient and indulgent with the comedian's suggested projects for relief of the unemployed and London slum clearance. Later, at Cliveden, Chaplin made a speech proposing solutions for the depression. He touched on world trade, abolition of the gold standard, a reduction of working time, minimum wages, etc. His talk was received goodnaturedly. In Lloyd George's analysis of everyone's arguments, including Chaplin's, he gave proofs of his powers of leadership.

Visiting the school where he had spent two unhappy years of his childhood, Chaplin decided to do something for its children. A motion-picture projector was ordered to be presented the next day, together with candies and gifts for each child, to be handed out by Chaplin himself. The next day, however, at the scheduled time, Chaplin could not be persuaded to leave the luncheon party he was at, to make the presentations. Robinson and Kono officiated in his place. The children made their disappointment known. Reporters were present and there was unfavorable publicity.

At last the day of the "City Lights" opening arrived. To avoid the crowds, Chaplin and Barton slipped into the Dominion Theatre at three in the afternoon. Their dinner was sent in to them and they dressed for the occasion, back stage. Seated between Shaw and Lady Astor, Chaplin dreaded some caustic comments from the playwright who, it turned out, enjoyed the picture and made favorable comments. When the showing ended, Chaplin was called upon to make a speech and was "so thrilled and excited that nothing seemed to come out."

Afterwards he slipped out a back door to a party he had arranged at the Carlton Hotel for about two hundred people. Winston Churchill made the toast of honor. In reply Chaplin began, "My lords, ladies, and gentlemen" (the opening of Churchill's speech)—"my friend, the late Chancellor of the Exchequer—" and heard Churchill laugh. "Pardon me, I mean the Ex—the Ex-Chancellor of the Exchequer"—more laughter. Finally Chaplin stammered, "My friend, Mr. Winston Churchill—" The ice was broken and everyone had a good time.

In Carl Robinson's circle, that evening, were the actresses Sari Maritza and Vivian Gaye. The former afterwards had a brief career in Hollywood and the latter was to marry Ernst Lubitsch. Chaplin indicated to Robinson that he would like to dance with Sari. He found her adept in the tango, his favorite step, and the rest of the evening he monopolized her, in spite of Robinson's warnings that the press would report him engaged. A new romance began and Robinson was forced to squire Sari in public in order to keep the reporters off the track.

By this time Barton had tired of the excitement. He was moody and insisted on sailing home. Soon after his return, he committed suicide.

Then another sudden Chaplin *faux pas.* He failed to keep a dinner engagement with the Prime Minister. The explanation given to the son was that he was required to attend the Berlin opening of his picture. Then, to make matters worse, he was on the point of delaying his departure, to have another day with Sari. Carl Robinson virtually dragged him to the train, leaving young MacDonald stupefied and Sari Maritza furious.

Since his last visit the Germans had become Chaplin fans and the Berlin ovation outdid London's. Among the first to welcome Chaplin was Marlene Dietrich, whom he had met a year or so before when she was brought to Hollywood by his former protégé, Josef von Sternberg. Later, there was an afternoon reception with several members of the Reichstag who expressed pessimism over Germany's economic future. Theatre-going and night-clubbing with Karl von Vollmueller and others, Chaplin was impressed by an exotic dancer named La Jana. On being informed that she was the favorite of the old Crown Prince, he switched his interest to Betty Amann, a German movie actress with a reported San Francisco origin.

Chaplin returned Einstein's earlier visit. The comedian found the great scientist a simple and congenial man. At his modest home Einstein's son quipped, "You are popular because you are understood by the masses. On the other hand, the professor's popularity with the masses is because he is not understood."

Conversation dealt largely with the depression. Modern machines need less men. This has cheapened the cost of commodities. Money must cheapen, too. Chaplin launched into his attack on the gold standard. "These two mediums of exchange—credit and gold—will never stabilize prices, for credit is more elastic than gold. Therefore the value of all our enterprises built up on credit will always be at the mercy of the gold standard which can reduce those values at will." Einstein smiled, "You're not a comedian. You're an economist." Chaplin was pleased. The Barrymores, similarly, used to be delighted by compliments on their musical or artistic talents, their acting being taken for granted. Chaplin's solution for nearly everything was: "Reduce the hours of labor, print more money, and control prices."

After visits to Vienna and Venice, Chaplin returned to Paris for a meeting with M. Briand. The latter did not speak English and was weighed down by responsibilities. While awaiting word of the impending ceremonial award to him of the Legion of Honor, King Albert of the Belgians expressed a desire to meet the actor. The encounter was rather formal. Chaplin's seat was set considerably below the king's. This may have suggested one of the comic scenes in "The Great Dictator." Chaplin accepted the Duke of Westminster's invitation to a boar hunt in Normandy. He had reason to rue it. All the way to the south of France, he was under the care of a masseur.

Frank Jay Gould, who owned the Majestic Hotel and the Casino at Nice, and had once been married to Edith Kelly, a sister of Arthur and Hetty, invited Chaplin to visit him. Gould did not hesitate to exploit the publicity value of Chaplin's visit. At Nice Chaplin had a reunion with his brother Sidney and Sidney's wife, who had been living in Nice to get out of American income tax difficulties.

In order to handle the large amount of correspondence in several foreign languages, a multi-lingual secretary was necessary—and—the mysterious May Reeves enters the picture. A friend of Sid's, May was introduced to Robinson at the Casino. She has been variously described as "French-English," "an exotic Latin beauty," and "a pretty Czech." May knew six languages and had been an efficient secretary—until Chaplin discovered her. He found her "adorable." She was a rather naïve girl in spite of her seeming sophistication. Chaplin danced the tango and played tennis with her every day.

Meanwhile the meetings with celebrities continued: Mary Garden, the Duke of Connaught, Elsa Maxwell, Emil Ludwig (biographer of Napoleon, one of Chaplin's heroes), H. G. Wells, Churchill, Harry d'Arrast, and the Prince of Wales. He met the latter through Thelma Morgan Converse who later was to introduce the Prince to Wallis Simpson. In a single dinner the actor and the prince achieved the intimacy of "Charlie" and "Eddie."

May Reeves accompanied Chaplin on a trip to Algiers and Morocco, although she sailed on a later boat to evade reporters who had wind of the romance. Both Sidney, who again began to take over his brother's affairs, and Carl Robinson tried to break up the affair, and this was partly the reason for Chaplin's firing Robinson after sixteen years of service. On his way to May, waiting for him in Paris, Chaplin at Marseilles was greeted by Aimee Semple McPherson. Chaplin twitted Aimee about her success as an evangelist, attributing it to her magnetic personality and her showmanship. She was an actress, he said, performing to people who frowned upon the real theatre. Aimee, refusing to argue, admitted their worlds were "vastly different." The incongruous couple made several pleasant excursions around the city before the evangelist journeyed on to the Holy Land.

Back in London, May Shepherd, the busy secretary hired by Robinson to handle the Chaplin correspondence, filed suit, claiming compensation over and above the twenty-five dollars a week of her salary. The British United Artists were willing to accede to her demands for five times that amount, but Chaplin was stubborn and drew more unfavorable publicity until the suit was settled. Chaplin had also ignored an unofficial command to appear at a benefit vaudeville performance, graced by the presence of the King and Queen of England. The explanation seems to be that, during the illness of Kono, at Juan les Pins, Chaplin, unaccustomed to handling his correspondence, had laid the invitation aside. Another press furor resulted, which Sir Philip Sassoon patched up as best he could.

On a return trip to London Chaplin met Mahatma Gandhi. Before the meeting Gandhi asked, "Who is Mr. Chaplin?" The Indian leader had never heard of him although his films were popular in India. They met at the home of Dr. Chuna Lal Katial, a Hindu, who lived close to the Limehouse district of London. At the meeting, of which cameramen who were present took a photographic record, machinery was discussed. Chaplin defended the use of machinery because it lightened men's burdens and represented a common inheritance of mankind. "I understand the occidental viewpoint, but your viewpoint is not suited to application in India," said Gandhi. He then looked at his dollar watch, and discovered it was time for evening prayers. "A tremendous personality," Chaplin remarked as he departed. Other meetings included a reunion with Douglas Fairbanks at St. Moritz, the Swiss winter playground. With May and Sid, Chaplin joined Fairbanks in December for the winter sports.

Later in Rome Chaplin almost met Mussolini, but Il Duce was engaged. May was still in the picture and, by now, very much in love with the actor. Chaplin had promised to star her in a film about a gypsy. Several people believed that May would have made him a good wife.

However, she was left behind on the Naples dock when the actor, Sid, and Kono sailed for the Orient. Her romance with Chaplin is recorded in her book, "Charlie Chaplin Intime," which was published in France.

After a tour of Ceylon, Singapore, Java, and Bali, the party arrived in Japan in May 1932. Here Chaplin was welcomed like a king. An escort of hundreds of policemen was assigned to guide him through the cheering Tokyo crowds to his suite in the Hotel Imperial, designed by the American architect Frank Lloyd Wright. The next day, the son of Tsuyoki Inukai, the Premier of Japan, invited Chaplin to attend a wrestling match.

On leaving the stadium, Kono learned that the Premier had been assassinated while his son was away arranging for Chaplin's attendance at the match. Precautions were taken to protect the actor. Chaplin revealed, ten years later, that his death had also been planned by the assassins—members of a militarist clique—in the hope that the act would precipitate a war between Japan and the United States. His name was found on the roll of intended victims prepared by Japanese extremists for the terroristic outbreak of May 1932. It was this act of terrorism, reputedly organized by the Black Dragon Society, which intimidated popular opposition to imperialism in Japan and launched the country on the aggressive road that ended in Japan's subjugation.

Interested in the Japanese drama (he had admired Japanese performances in Los Angeles), Chaplin attended several plays. He also showed interest in other phases of Japanese culture. Then negotiations for the distribution of his new film, for which he asked a high price, were completed, and Chaplin and Kono sailed for Seattle while Sid returned to Nice.

On the boat Chaplin began making notes. After a fifteen months' tour of the world, observing the effects of the depression and hearing the opinions of men reputed

as world spokesmen, he had his idea for his new picture—
eventually entitled "Modern Times." On his return to
Los Angeles he dictated a few articles on currency reform
as a cure for the depression, expanding his theory that a
shortage of money, and not any disparity between supply
and demand, was the cause of the world depression. Then
he set to work on "Modern Times."

While preparing the script of his new film ("Modern
Times" was his first film to be produced from anything
but rough notes), the producer, Joseph Schenck, then
president of United Artists, invited the actor to relax for
a week end aboard his yacht. Schenck invited two extra
girls to join the party. One of them was Paulette Goddard, who had appeared as a chorus girl in Eddie Cantor's
"A Kid from Spain" and in some Hal Roach shorts. Born
Pauline Levy, in New York City, around 1911, Miss Goddard had appeared in a "Peaches" Browning skit in the
Ziegfeld show "No Foolin'" (1926). The following year
she appeared as a chorine in the same producer's "Rio
Rita." Later she played a small part in Archie Selwyn's
"The Conquering Male." The year 1931 found Miss Goddard in Reno receiving a divorce from Edgar James, a
wealthy playboy whom she had married in 1927. It was
but a step to Hollywood.

Chaplin bought up Paulette Goddard's Roach contract
and had her change her platinum-blonde hair back to its
original brown. Then he engaged voice and dancing
teachers for her. He himself, now and then, coached her
in acting. All this led up to her appearance as leading
lady in the new Chaplin film. He called his new protégée
"absolutely unique" as a screen personality. In fact the
part of the gamin in "Modern Times" was built around
her and for her. Ambitious and intelligent, Miss Goddard
lived up to Chaplin's expectations, and she is, of course,
the only Chaplin leading lady who succeeded on her own,
after leaving his wing.

More mature and understanding than most of Chaplin's loves, and yet possessing youthful zest, Paulette, for some years, seemed to be the perfect companion for him. It was always a matter of speculation when, where, and if they were married, since they were living together without concealment in the Chaplin Beverly Hills home. There were stories that Paulette had been married to the actor aboard his yacht in 1932 and that they had been married in Singapore during their later trip to the Orient, following the opening of "Modern Times." Neither would make any public confirmation or denial.

Her unwillingness or inability to publicly define her status cost Miss Goddard one of the dramatic plums of the decade. At one time she was cast as Scarlett O'Hara in "Gone with the Wind." However, women and women's clubs all over the country barraged the studio with their objections because of her equivocal relations with Chaplin, although an objection on this ground seemed ridiculous, considering the character of Scarlett. Miss Goddard would not produce the nuptial details even to obtain the coveted role. In 1940, at the opening of "The Great Dictator," Chaplin referred to Miss Goddard as "my wife." Immediately afterwards, however, they separated, leaving many with the impression that they may have gone through a ceremony just in time to obtain a divorce.

Before "The Great Dictator" was produced, there were rumors that Chaplin was going to star Miss Goddard in "Regency" by D. L. Murphy, "White Russian," the story of a Russian refugee girl in Shanghai who stows away to this country, and also in a talkie remake of "A Woman of Paris." These plans came to naught as Paulette began her active career with other companies.

"Modern Times"

Started in October 1934, the shooting on "Modern Times" took ten months, a trifle less than Chaplin usually spent on a feature. Perhaps the prepared script accounted for the comparative speed. A million and a half dollars went into it. Altogether 215,000 feet of film were exposed, and two of the largest sets Chaplin ever used in a picture were constructed for it. One was the interior of the factory built on his own lot. Its wood and rubber machinery, painted to look like steel, cost fifty thousand dollars to build. It actually worked; but not even the actor-producer knew what it manufactured, sausages or cars. Another set, constructed to simulate the factory area of a large industrial city, covered five acres of ground which Chaplin leased near the Los Angeles harbor. The film was shot at sound speed with motor-driven cameras.

"Modern Times" was the second name chosen for it, the first, "The Masses," having been discarded. It was the first Chaplin film in five years. Once again he took the risk of producing a silent film, years after its supposed final demise. The only concessions were a musical accompaniment and sound effects and a few spoken sentences, allowed because they issued as television or loudspeaker voices. Except for the song at the end of the picture, Chaplin's voice was not heard.

A disappointing preview in the West, before its New

York opening on February 5, 1936, led to some revisions. Its New York reception was mixed. The critics welcomed back the well-loved figure and paid tribute to his undiminished pantomimic skill, but found the film uneven. On the whole, the critical reception may be called a case of damning with faint praise.

As Chaplin's foreword characterizes it, " 'Modern Times' is the story of industry, of individual enterprise—humanity crusading in the pursuit of happiness." Its opening suggests satire on modern mass production, its regimentation, and the cruelty of machinery to man. Unemployment and other problems of the day are touched on. It starts off with hints of social satire but these promises are not quite fulfilled. It soon gets back to the old Chaplin comedy pattern. There is fuzziness in the form, drag in the pace, breaks in the continuity, and lack of climax. The last two-thirds of the picture is a sort of an anticlimax to the opening idea.

In this reversion to type, Chaplin produces a sort of Chaplin anthology, as he works his celebrated gags over again. It is a nostalgic repetition of a great tradition, in disconnected episodes involving oil cans, threatening cops, roller skates, waiters' trays, swinging doors, etc., done this time with little of the old inspiration. The only new element was his song to the tune of "Titina," which he accompanies with genuinely amusing pantomime, a song mixing all languages and gibberish and, perhaps, symbolizing the confusion of our times.

"Modern Times" *has* several clever and moving scenes, but not enough to bring it up to "The Gold Rush" or "City Lights," in comedy or pathos. Some critics perceived a failure to keep up with the general advance in films. This may have been due to his attempt to merge his old technique with a little of the new. There is an excessive number of sub-titles, some clearly unnecessary. There is even the title "Dawn." The silent technique seems somehow clumsier and more antiquated here than in "City Lights," suggesting that, in the intervening years, Chaplin himself may have lost familiarity with the old style, without the constant reminders of other silent films, and was now merely making "a silent talkie."

To some people Chaplin now seemed like a creature from another world. His comedy was so remote from the new types—the new realistic comedy of such films as Frank Capra's "It Happened One Night" (1934) and W. S. Van Dyke's "The Thin Man" (1935). Slapstick had become streamlined in this so-called "haywire" or "screwball" school, featuring fast American humor that fused the old Sennett slapstick with hardboiled modernism. In these, laughs were built on unusual situations, wacky dialogue, mildly eccentric characters, and sudden slapstick in straight scenes. Its climax was reached in Wellman's "Nothing Sacred." The later Preston Sturges comedies belong to the same category.

During the middle thirties, W. C. Fields attained great popularity. His drawling comments and bibulous pantomime in the role of henpecked husband or pompous faker made him regarded by many as "the funniest" of comedians. However, he did not create a type as universal as Charlie. Neither comedian would acknowledge the existence of an equal. Fields contemptuously dismissed Chaplin as the "ballet dancer" and himself records an amiable conversation with Chaplin in which the latter failed to make a single reference to Fields' work on the screen. Animated cartoons—especially those of Disney—had also contributed a new concept of comedy, a combination of violence, speed, and the sort of fantasy possible to pen creatures freed from the restrictions of gravity or human limitations. It is significant that one New York critic found the Donald Duck curtain raiser to "Modern Times" funnier than the feature.

It is therefore remarkable that Chaplin, with this film,

nevertheless retained his position as the King of Comedy, despite his five years' absence, the fickleness of audiences, and the changing comedy styles. While not a complete success, "Modern Times" made a deep impression and its scenes were discussed for years, whereas "City Lights" came, conquered, and was virtually forgotten until its recent revival. "Modern Times" is still fondly remembered; but what average movie-goer recalls or expresses an urgent desire to see again "The Lives of a Bengal Lancer," "Becky Sharp," "The Dark Angel," or "The Plainsman" —so-called "polished" Hollywood productions of 1935-1936?

With the actor regarded by many as a "parlor pink," the opening of "Modern Times" was awaited with considerable titillation in some quarters. It was rumored that the film would dramatize "the class struggle," that it would portray the tragedy of the "petty bourgeois" under capitalism, that it would spread leftish social messages and propaganda. But, while it obviously reflects the depression and the confusions of that time, particularly in the opening sequences, Chaplin remains the artist foremost and propandist only incidentally.

More social significance was read into it, by some, than Chaplin intended; while others dismissed the social elements as a mere new and timely background for the old rough-and-tumble farce. Brooks Atkinson, in the *New York Times,* commented that in "the scene in which he unwittingly carries a red flag at the head of a parade of bellicose strikers, the social significance of the new film is more technique than philosophy." Critics of the left found the same scene a "bitterly satirical cartoon on red scares." Similar critics took the humorous feeding-machine scene as a bitter comment on the machine age and even as satire on Soviet efficiency. To Robert Garland, critic for the *World Telegram,* the picture was "neither fish, flesh, nor good red propaganda."

Most significant perhaps was the Russian reaction. At its Moscow showing, according to an article in the *New York Times*, the film was not considered much of an aid to the cause of revolution. The Moscow public greeted the conveyor-belt scene in stony silence (perhaps because of the turn to conveyor-belt production in Soviet industry and the new speed-up order). The incident of the red flag failed to get over and the automatic feeding machine did not appear to them to be a practical idea.

Chaplin himself is quoted as saying: "There are those who always attach social significance to my work. It has none. I leave such subjects for the lecture platform. To entertain is my first consideration." When informed of the ban on the picture in Germany and Italy, he said: "Dictators seem to believe the picture is communistic. It's absolutely untrue. In view of recent happenings, I am not surprised at the ban. But our only purpose was to amuse. It was just my old Charlie character in circumstances of 1936. I have no political aims whatever as an actor. . . .

"It started from an abstract idea, an impulse to say something about the way life is being standardized and channelized, and men turned into machines—and the way I felt about it. I knew that was what I wanted to do before I thought of any of the details."

A social parable perhaps, but in it Chaplin champions individualism against the mechanized life rather than government ownership and the abolition of capitalism. The tramp escapes from the world of machinery and regimentation into the freedom of the open road.

Once more the musical score was Chaplin's own composition. As used here it often deftly characterizes action. There is a memorable waltz theme as well as novel machine music. Alfred Newman, hired to do the arrangement and orchestration, found Chaplin too intense, critical, and erratic to work with, and walked out on him. David Raskin finished the job.

Paulette Goddard, different both from the old, passive Chaplin heroine, and the tempestuous Georgia, played the role of the gamin with vitality and spontaneity. The rest of the cast shows the familiar faces of the other Chaplin comedies.

"Modern Times" grossed but $1,800,000 in this country, a large sum for the depression period but a disappointment to the comedian. The deficiency was made up abroad. Chaplin's fortune, in 1932, was estimated at $8,-000,000 and he led the tax rolls in Hollywood for many years.

Two plagiarism suits were filed against Chaplin in connection with "Modern Times." One was entered by Michael Kustoff, a former officer in the Imperial Russian Army, who claimed to have submitted the story through an agent only to have it rejected. On Chaplin's testimony that he had never seen the agent, the judge dismissed the suit.

In 1937 the French film company, *Filmes Sonores Tobis*, filed suit for plagiarism, claiming that Chaplin borrowed the conveyor-belt sequence from René Clair's "À Nous la Liberté," released in 1931. René Clair himself declared, when informed of this, that he was flattered, having himself borrowed so much from his teacher, Chaplin. "À Nous la Liberté," also a satire on the machine age, may have influenced Chaplin. On the other hand, the Clair picture is full of Chaplin touches. One of its principals, Emil (played by Henri Marchand), is modeled closely on the wistful Charlie character. The hero's mistaking a girl's smile toward another man as intended for him is characteristically Chaplinesque as is the wife's tossing of the money given by her husband to the floor and then grabbing it from the butler. The picture also has a Chaplinesque chase, the classic walking-down-the-road finish,

and other bits direct from Chaplin. Yet, despite the bor-
rowings and its lack of a strong character lead "À Nous la
Liberté" is the greater film—one of the wittiest and most
brilliant ever produced. Perhaps because of Clair's attitude, *Tobis* dropped its plagiarism suit.

The opening scene of "Modern Times" shows sheep
rushing through a gate, and is immediately followed by
shots of workers rushing out of the subway on their way
to work. Among the many is Charlie who works in a huge
factory, his task to tighten bolt after bolt on an endless
conveyor belt. With two monkey-wrenches he makes light-
ning-like swoops at the gadgets racing by. The slightest
error causes havoc. In pursuit of one neglected bolt he
knocks other workers over, upsets the whole belt line
routine, and ends a captive in the machinery.

In another sequence Charlie and a fellow-mechanic get
lost in an enormous dynamo-like machine they are repair-
ing. Caught in its cog wheels, they are whizzed about on
different levels and go riding up and down chutes.

The boss gets the idea of cutting down lunch time by
the use of a feeding machine. Chosen to try it out,
Charlie is seated inside it and is administered an automatic feeding. Spoons jab into his mouth, a typewriter-
roller sort of gadget revolves a corn cob against his
teeth, while a mechanical napkin wipes his face after
each course. Something goes wrong, however, and Charlie
(in Keystone slapstick, modernized) is fed steel nuts,
soup is tipped down his shirt, pies are flung in his face,
and he is unable to get out of the contraption as he is
inundated with floods of food.

The monotonous routine of the endless nut tightening
finally drives Charlie "nuts." The screen-projected face
of the boss ordering him to hurry follows him even into
the washroom when he retires for a smoke. He goes berserk. Holding wrenches to his head like horns, he per-

forms a faun-like dance, upsets the fences with a long-stemmed oil can, pulls switches at random. He tears through the factory and into the street tightening everything in sight that looks like a nut the nose of the foreman, fire plugs, and finally strategically placed bodice buttons on a woman's dress; and ends up in a psychiatric ward.

Cured of his nervous breakdown—but jobless—he leaves the hospital to start life anew, only to face the nerve-wracking unemployment problem. After working a few short hours on his first job in months, a strike is called. Police forbid the workers to congregate. As one policeman gets tough with the protesting Charlie, he backs away upon the end of a board which tips up a brick that conks the cop. Stealing a ride on the back of an explosives truck, Charlie is jolted off, together with its red danger flag. Picking it up and waving it to attract the truck driver's attention, he suddenly finds himself at the head of a communist demonstration. Mistaken as the leader of the Reds, he is arrested and tossed into the patrol wagon.

In prison, Charlie inadvertently salts his food with "joy powder." The drug imparts superman strength to him. He stops a jail break and is rewarded with a cell fixed up with "all the comforts of home." These include a formal tea at which his gargling noises and other "table manners" disconcert the prim old ladies. To his dismay, he is pardoned just as he was settling down to a life of ease.

Meanwhile, at the water front, "the gamin," who had stolen some bread and bananas, escapes from the juvenile officers who take her younger orphan sisters into custody.

Charlie's next job is in a shipyard where he "launches" and sinks an unfinished ship. Fired, he decides to return to the security of the jail. He runs into the gamin and sympathizes with her. When she is arrested, Charlie unsuccessfully tries to take the blame. Then he enters a restaurant, orders everything in sight, and unable to pay the bill, achieves his purpose of getting arrested. On the way to the jail he encounters the girl again, becomes interested, and decides to stay out of jail. The two break out of the patrol wagon together.

After a search they find a shack on the water front with a kennel beside it.

Though a beam falls on Charlie's head and a table collapses when he leans on it, they dub the place "Paradise." Charlie sleeps outside in the dog house. In the morning he poises gracefully and dives into his "swimming pool" —which turns out to be a six-inch puddle.

More or less accidentally, Charlie gets a job as a department store night watchman—a job that is finally to his liking. He admits the shivering girl, wraps her in an ermine coat borrowed from a mannequin, and puts her to sleep in a store bed. Among other comic business is a skating act performed blindfold for the girl's amusement and instruction, that ends in near neck-breaking teetering before a broken railing. He sees the yawning abyss in time and hobbles away in panic.

Burglars—unemployed factory workers break in and find a sympathetic watchman. But his sympathy earns him another jail term.

While he is in, the girl gets a job dancing in a cabaret. On his release she gets him a job there as a waiter. Then follows: "Now we'll get a real home" parody of smug suburban domesticity with the husband returning from work to be welcomed by his little housewife in their ideal home. But it is only a vision. In one of the restaurant scenes, Charlie, trying to bring a roast duck to an impatient and irate diner across the crowded dance floor, is pushed about by the dancers and held back from his destination. Tossed through the mob like a football, the duck becomes a chandelier ornament before the customer finally receives it.

In the cabaret a song is to be introduced. Forced to substitute for the male singer, Charlie has the girl write the words of the song on his cuff. The cuff comes off at the wrong moment and Charlie sings a jabberwocky, mixing several languages and double-talk. He is a hit, but his triumph is cut short by juvenile officers coming for the girl. The pair make a getaway.

Sitting at a country roadside, the two, depressed by their bad luck, finally perk up as they decide, "We'll get along." The final scene shows them, with undiminished courage, walking arm in arm down the road toward the horizon.

"The Great Dictator"

It was only natural that Chaplin should capitalize on his screen resemblance to Hitler (or was it vice versa?). After a period of secret preparation, Chaplin started on the script January 1, 1939, and completed it in three months. Work on miniatures and sound tests began in June.

The outbreak of war in 1939 brought a halt to the production. There were rumors that the picture would be abandoned, that Hitler jokes had ceased to be funny, and so on. Deciding that ridicule is a powerful weapon and that laughter is a tonic, a release from pain, Chaplin resumed production.

With the final shooting script ready and casting completed by September 5, the actual shooting began on September 9 and continued for 127 days until March 9, 1940. Retakes, editing, and scoring delayed its release till October 15, 1940. Its cost ran over two million dollars and half a million feet of film were shot.

Critics and first-nighters at "The Great Dictator" opening found too much grim reality in the picture and thought that Chaplin had overstepped his field. The situation needed a Voltaire rather than a charming little clown. The final long speech (six minutes) surprised and embarrassed some as out of place, tacked on rather than integral to the film. Other elements in the ending were thought to be propagandistic and banal.

Later audiences, however, thrilled to it. Its sheer histrionic virtuosity is amazing, and it demonstrated Chaplin's capacity for other roles besides the one he had nailed down as his own.

Reports had it that Steinbeck had been called in to help with the final speech but that Chaplin had returned to his own version. In defense of the speech (and the picture in general) Chaplin declared, "I had to do it. They had their laughs and it was fun, wasn't it? Now I wanted them to listen. . . . I did this picture for the Jews of the world. . . . I wanted to see the return of decency and kindness. I'm no communist . . . just a human being who wants to see this country a real democracy and freedom from this infernal regimentation which is crawling over the rest of the world."

The tendentious and controversial aspects of "The Great Dictator" are balanced by its drollery and satire. The old "Charlie" character is virtually abandoned although the Jewish barber retains some of his traits. Chaplin speaks, for the first time on the screen, and in two voices. As the little barber he speaks in meek monosyllables (easily understood in foreign countries). But as the dictator he shouts in fake Teutonic gutturals and double talk, in perfect mimicry of Hitler's mannerisms, poses, gestures, and choleric rantings.

This, Chaplin's first talkie, falls more or less in the modern talkie comedy style. Its humor rises more from dialogue and situation than from pantomime and gags. The pace is slower than before and the easy spontaneity is gone. Everything is calculated in talkie fashion. There is a little slapstick, and when it appears it is almost a shock. The boisterous scenes between Hynkel and Napaloni constitute the funniest, if not the only truly funny, scenes in the old tradition. The laughs depend largely on mimicry and occasional wit. But in scenes like the shaving of the customer to the rhythm of Brahms' "Hungarian Dance," and Hynkel's ballet with the world-balloon we rediscover the traditional Chaplin at his best.

The supporting cast is much stronger than his usual one. For the first time it features established stage and screen actors. Jack Oakie, a natural for the part, brilliantly, if superficially, caricatures Mussolini. Paulette Goddard is effective in her part which, according to Chaplin, "typifies the whole Jewish race, their strength, their resentment against senseless persecution, their hope for a better future." Clever performances are also given by Reginald Gardiner, Henry Daniell, Billy Gilbert, the late Maurice Moscovich, and others.

In the interview already quoted from, Chaplin observed that in the playing, his part seemed like a merging of Napoleon with Nijinsky. "All my repressed desires are fulfilled in writing, directing, and playing such a picture. With the dictator and myself, one of us a tragedian, the other a comedian, I don't know which is which."

Karl Struss, one of the best cameramen in the industry, joined forces with Chaplin's own veteran, Rollie Totheroh, in photographing the picture. Traveling and crane shots are used and the lighting is good. Some of the sets are elaborate and solid though others are rather flimsy. Trick work, such as projected slides and rear projection, is used for the Nazi mass mobilizations and similar scenes. Such "process shots" are seldom completely convincing, but are understandably used here for the big effects.

The financial return on "The Great Dictator" is reported to have fallen below Chaplin's expectations. The picture was banned in a number of European countries and in Argentina. After the war, it enjoyed a postponed success throughout Europe, Germany included. Chaplin, nettled by the New York critics, refused their award for what was indeed the best performance of the year 1940.

The closing long speech and the poetic concluding scene of the distant and prostrate Hannah rising to the word of hope are straight drama. But "The Great Dictator," on the whole, is satire—and a brilliant one. Had it been directed by Lubitsch or René Clair, critics would have raved; for too much is always expected of Chaplin. The picture will probably serve an additional documentary function since, like "Shoulder Arms," it caught the people, events, and social attitudes of the era in its accurate though oblique focus.

The picture's opening titles are: "Note:—Any resemblance between Hynkel the dictator and the Jewish barber is purely coincidental."—"This is a story of the period between two World Wars—an interim in which Insanity cut loose, Liberty took a nose dive, and Humanity was kicked around somewhat."

"The World War 1918." The camera pans over a battlefield, over soldiers, trenches, and barbed wire; takes in artillery firing, stops and edges toward a "Big Bertha." A radio voice explains that Tomania's armies, though weakened in the last year of war, fought on, training their big guns on Notre Dame, Paris, seventy-five miles away. The new conscript, a barber, in an oversize helmet, waits for the signal to fire. His mumbled, "Yes sir," are Charlie's first words. At the command he sets the big guns off and grabs his field glasses—to see the shell hit an outhouse. At another try the shell dribbles out of the cannon's mouth, making strange noises. Charlie is ordered to check the fuse. No matter where he turns the shell faces him, sputtering fire. . . .

A new danger—enemy aviation overhead! Charlie is sent to man the anti-aircraft gun which he has never handled before . . . He gets a shoot-the-chutes ride on the balky mechanism. . . . Still another danger—an enemy breakthrough—all men to the trenches!

Hand grenades are distributed. Charlie asks, "Pardon me, sir, but to work this. . . . ?" He follows instructions in concentrated pantomime, gets the grenade down his sleeve, and in attempts to extricate it, loses it down his pants. It is extracted just in time. In the counterattack, the barber, lost in the smoke and calling out "Cap-i-taine!—Woo, woo!" finds himself advancing between two American soldiers. Exclaiming, "Oh, excuse me," he runs back.

In the airplane scene, Schultz, the wounded aviator, has important dispatches to deliver and Charlie loyally steps to the wheel. Flying upside down, he observes that "The sun seems to be shining upwards!"—He takes his watch out, to find it pointing upward too. Conveniently, the water from the canteen also flows up toward his face. But it is not Charlie's piloting but their running out of gas that leads to the inevitable crash. Just before the crash landing the delirious Schultz launches an ode to spring: "Ah, Spring in Tomania! Hilda would be in her garden now with her daffodils—she could never bear to cut the daffodils—it is like taking life to cut them—sweet, gentle Hilda. . . ." and continues, after the crash—"A beautiful soul and she loved animals and little children, too."

As Charlie's head emerges from a mud hole, two soldiers come up to tell them the war is over. Tomania is vanquished.

Montage sequence: Newspaper Armistice extras; celebrations; Charlie being taken to the hospital; soldiers marching home. Headlines: "Peace," "Dempsey beats Willard," "Lindbergh flies the Atlantic," "Depression," "Riots in Tomania," "Hynkel party takes power."

Charlie is then shown as a convalescent in the hospital. The commentator explains that the little barber has suffered amnesia and has no knowledge of the events of the intervening years.

Next we see Adenoid Hynkel on a platform haranguing the sons and daughters of the Double Cross, in German-English double-talk. "Wiener Schnitzel, lager beer, und sauerkraut. . . ." It is marvelous mimicry of the Hitler delirium, particularly the pursed-lip rendering of the German gutturals—"mit der ach hic," etc., ending in a coughing spell. The tirade continues. (The official radio translator's rendering: "Yesterday Tomania was down but today it has risen.")

Hynkel pauses to moisten his gullet, also pouring a glassful down his pants. Silencing the crowd with a limp salute, he goes on, "Democratia shtunk!" (Translator: "Democracy smells.") "Libertad shtunk!" ("Liberty is odious.") "Frei sprachen shtunk!" ("Free speech is objectionable.") Tomania has the greatest army and navy in the world but, "we must sacrifice, tighten der belten."

The plump Herring rises to do so only to have it split wide open when he sits down again. Garbitsch, on the other side of the stand, impatiently scans his watch as Hynkel slobbers over his early struggles shared with his two comrades, wiping his eyes on his tie, and climaxing with a coughing fit. From that, to rhapsodies (with gestures) over the beautiful Aryan maiden, who must be strong to produce many "kinder katzenjammer. . . . soldiers for Hynkel!"

Then his tirade becomes more violent and completely unintelligible and the microphones recoil. The translator explains that the fuehrer has just referred to the Jewish people.

Flourishes of hands, raising of his fist, gorilla drumming on his chest, cursing of every country in the world . . . "all shtunken," but Tomania, this the urbane translator renders as an offer of peace to the rest of the world.

At the end of the speech Herring, bowing to a lady, butts Hynkel down a flight of stairs. Hynkel bawls him out, strips the medals off his chest, and gives him a poke which visibly indents his paunch. At Hynkel's car there is the prepared greeting with little flower girls and the pose holding a baby. The baby fails in proper respect. Hynkel has to wipe his hand after he returns the infant to his mother.

Hynkel's auto passes statues of Venus and The Thinker, each with an arm raised to hail him. Garbitsch tells him his tirade against the Jews was a shade too restrained. Violence against the Jews might take people's minds off their stomachs. "Perhaps you're right. Things have been quiet in the ghetto lately."

The camera moves down from the Ghetto sign and up the street to a courtyard. "Good morning," Mr. Mann greets old Mr. Jaeckel—"What's good about it?" grumbles Jaeckel. "Conditions could be woise," answers Mann but Jaeckel remains sour. They talk about Hannah who lost mother and father (killed in the war), can't get a job, and can't pay her rent to Jaeckel, who can't throw her out. Hannah comes down with a basket on her head to deliver some laundry. Marching storm troopers singing: "The Aryans, the airy, airy Aryans, as we go marching by," break windows, rob a fruit stand, hold up a truck. Hannah, exclaiming "Pigs!" as they toss tomatoes at her, gets her clean washing messed up.

In the hospital two doctors discuss the barber's amnesia. Unaware of what has been happening, he is only concerned to get back to his barber shop, which he thinks he left a few weeks ago. When he runs away from the hospital no effort is made to find him. He is considered a harmless case.

In the Ghetto the barber comes briskly round the corner, and opens his shop door to be greeted by departing cats. He opens the shutters, puts on his barber's jacket, pulls up the shade, and shakes his head, amazed at the dust and cobwebs. Outside two storm troopers begin painting "Jew" on his window. He goes out, washes it off, and is kicked and pushed around. He smears one trooper with the paint brush and orders the other to arrest the first, but is put under arrest himself. As he ducks, one trooper hits the other. From her window, Hannah conks one on the head with a frying pan, then the other, then hits the barber by mistake. Dazed, he dances up the street and back, "tacking" and stumbling. One conked trooper, rising, is conked again and slumps on the barber. The two do a staggering dance together until the trooper collapses. "Sorry mister," Hannah tells the barber, explains that his conking was an accident, and pulls him into the house. As other troopers arrive, she shushes him. The fallen troopers are taken away in a car. "That did me a lot of good. That's what we should do," explains Hannah. "We should all fight back—we can't fight alone. We can lick them, together."

A new irruption of storm troopers into the shop; "Heil Hynkel." The barber follows their saluting hands in amazement. "Who's he?" A beating is the reply. Before being handcuffed, he is ordered to repaint the window. He throws the pail of paint in a trooper's face and runs, while the trooper is conked again by Hannah from the window. Soldiers surround the barber and he is strung up on a lamppost.

Schultz, now a Nazi big shot, drives by and stops to look into the fracas. As the troopers stand at attention, the rope is released and down comes the barber. Noting the mess, Schultz demands, "What the devil goes on here?" He is told, "A Jew was attacking storm troopers." Looking at the prostrate barber—"You!—Don't you remember me—the war—you saved my life—strange, and I always thought of you as an Aryan." "I'm a vegetarian," pipes up the barber. Schultz assures him he will not be molested again. When Hannah downs another storm trooper with a chimney pot the barber saves her by explaining she is his friend.

The camera moves forward, in the great throne room in Hynkel's palace. As he stuffs a folded letter into an envelope, a flunkey bends, sticks out his tongue, and Hynkel seals the envelope. He goes into another room to pose for a few seconds for an artist and a sculptor.

The bell rings. Herring has a bullet-proof suit to demonstrate, "made of material as light as silk." Hynkel tests it by shooting at the inventor. As the man falls dead, Hynkel casually remarks, "Far from perfect."

He goes to another room, tripping over raised insignia on the floor, and sits at the piano. The notes he produces have a gargling sound and he sprays his throat. Then he yells into a concealed microphone in a fruit bowl, summoning a man whom he orders to summon his secretary.

A bugle is blown, the girl enters, heils, and is ordered to "take a letter." Hynkel stares at her, snorts, bends her back in a passionate embrace and snorts as she pipes "No! No!" but the telephone rings . . . he drops her. . . . Herring has a parachute hat to demonstrate.

Herring brings in the inventor. Wearing the contraption the inventor heils and jumps out the window. The two men lean out and Hynkel exclaims testily, "Herring, *why* do you waste my time like this?"

The dictator darts in for another two seconds of posing, then confers with Garbitsch. Too much money is being spent on the concentration camps. Garbitsch exclaims they have to accommodate the five or ten thousand people arrested daily. Moreover the prisoners complain of the quality of the sawdust in the bread. Hynkel is indignant. "It's from the finest lumber our mills can supply!"

As Hynkel admires himself in the mirror, Garbitsch says, "The people are restless. . . . We might go further with the Jews." Hynkel disagrees, "We must do something more dramatic, like invading Austerlich." Garbitsch explains that this will require a loan from Epstein (a

Jew). They decide on a change of policy toward the Jews; persecution must cease until the loan is negotiated.

The scene changes to the barber shop. The barber is at work on Jaeckel as Hannah scrubs the floor. The absent-minded barber sharpens a comb on the razor strop, opens the cash register, but puts the money in his pocket, etc. On his way out, Jaeckel suggests he give Hannah a beauty treatment.

As she sits in the chair, Hannah comments on the new conditions. "It's funny how they've left us alone lately." Then she speaks of their resemblances to each other—both are so absent-minded. And she chatters on as he lathers away at her face and shaves her, remarking, "I wonder why women never grow whiskers." . . .Then they both realize the mistake. . . .

After a shampoo, a new coiffure, and a facial treatment, Hannah looks in the mirror. "Gee, ain't I cute? How'd you do it?" She suggests he would be handsome, too, with a treatment. He takes a glance at the mirror and shakes his head.

Outside Hannah, buying potatoes, stumbles, and is astounded as storm tropers help her up and salvage the potatoes. She turns toward the camera: "Something's happened! Wouldn't it be wonderful if they would leave us alone—if we didn't have to go to another country. Wouldn't it be wonderful if they'll let us live and be happy again."

The scene shifts to a comic Hynkel dictation: a long speech is followed by a couple of clicks on the typewriter; a short speech by many. Herring breathlessly announces a marvelous poison gas: "It will kill *everybody!*" Garbitsch explains the loan is bound to go through; all the members of the Board are now Aryans. A woman secret agent reports a strike: "The leaders were shot." This does not satisfy Hynkel. He orders all three thousand strikers shot. "I don't want any of my workers dissatisfied." He is finally persuaded to spare them to keep up production.

Since the leaders were brunettes, Garbitsch advises elimination of brunettes also. "We will never have peace until there is a pure, blue-eyed, blond race—with you as dictator of the world." "Dictator of all the world!" says Hynkel. "They will worship you as a God!" continues Garbitsch. "No, no, you mustn't say it. You make me afraid of myself," Hynkel simpers, leaps across the room, and shins up a window curtain. "Nation after nation will capitulate!" promises Garbitsch. "Leave me, I want to be alone!" says Hynkel.

With Garbitsch gone, Hynkel slides down the curtain and, to the strains of the Prelude to Wagner's "Lohengrin," begins toying with the globe. Rapaciously studying countries to be conquered, he embraces the now balloon-like globe, lifting it, spinning it, bouncing it, kicking it, butting it with his head, dancing with it, jumping (in slow motion). It is a scene that enthralls one, simultaneously with its wit, its irony, its fantasy, and its ballet grace. An overclose embrace finally bursts the balloon. Breaking into tears, Hynkel sobs on the desk.

To lively (radio) strains from Brahms' "Hungarian Dance No. 5," the barber shaves an elderly customer. In strict time to the music, he rinses his hands, wipes them, pulls out a hair to test the razor, strops the razor, lathers the customer's face, shaves him, wipes the razor, wipes the face, rips off the sheet, puts the customer's hat on the customer's head, holds out his hand for the fee, all exactly in time to the musical beat.

Epstein refusing to deal with a "medieval maniac," the invasion of Austerlich is delayed. Hynkel says, "First I will deal with his people" and ominously cracks nuts. He answers Schultz's protests with the remark that Schultz needs "a vacation—fresh air—outdoor exercise" and orders him to a concentration camp. As he is led out, Shultz exclaims, "Your cause is doomed to failure!" Hynkel shouts "Traitor, Democrat!" and goes into a tantrum which ends when a voluminous cape is thrown over him, which acts like a strait jacket. He cannot extricate his hands even to receive some notes.

The barber, all spruced up, equips himself with a toothpick from the cash register, shines his nails on the barber chair, and watched by all the neighbors, strolls out with Hannah. Their gayety ends when the radio starts blaring Hynkel's latest speech. The street loudspeaker dissolves to a closeup of Hynkel raving before the mike. The ghetto folk start running. As the raving intensifies ("rouse mitter," etc.), the barber dives into a barrel head first.

The radio blast continues; the camera moves very close to Hynkel's face. The march of the storm troopers is heard . . . people running . . . shots. . . . Hannah becomes hysterical. Jaeckel says, "Lock the doors, we've got to make a stand. We might as well die as go on like this."

Troopers break in and the barber gets a beating until he is identified as Schultz's friend. He feels safe until he hears the news flash announcing Schultz's arrest. The troopers break in again.

The camera moves into a closeup of a bird cage as there is a rush up the stairs. The troopers chant, "We want the barber!" The couple escape to the roof top in time to see the barber shop burning. Hannah says, "Never mind; we can start over again in Austerlich." Jaeckel announces, "The coast is clear." As they go back Schultz is found hiding in the cellar.

At a midnight meeting in the cellar, Schultz calls for an uprising against the tyrant. Mrs. Jaeckel and Hannah are worried. "We Jewish people shouldn't get mixed up in such business." The conspirators decide to blow up Hynkel's palace, the bomb thrower to be signified by a coin in a cake.

There is amusing foolery as each conspirator, finding a coin in his cake, passes it furtively to his neighbor. The barber swallows three coins in this sequence, hiccups, to a clinking of coins at each hiccup. Finally, old Jaeckel dramatically announces "Gentlemen, the coin is here!" As the barber coughs his three coins up and pockets them, Hannah admits she has put one in each cake. "It is wrong to blow up a palace and kill people. There's enough trouble."

Next morning the papers announce Schultz's escape and that a certain Jewish barber is wanted for questioning. Jaeckel muses, "Meyerburg was also wanted for questioning but we never heard of him since." As the troopers are heard marching, Schultz and the barber are helped to escape. Loaded with baggage and golf bags and an empty hat box over the barber's head, they seek escape over the rooftops.

Unable to see through the hat box, the barber walks out on a pole high above the street. He is warned, "Look where you are!" and drops the golf bags. When he removes the hat box to see, he drops everything.

The escaping pair run up and down a gable roof. Slipping on a loose shingle, the barber falls through a skylight, lands on a bed, politely says, "Pardon me" to the husband and "Sorry" to the wife and runs out to be nabbed by the troopers on the roof. We next see Schultz and the barber goose stepping in a concentration camp.

In a series of dissolves (silent action with music), Hannah and Jaeckel pull a wagon over a bridge and escape into Austerlich. . . . They work in the vineyards. . . . They set a table outside a farm cottage. . . . Hannah writes to the barber, "We are anxiously waiting for your release so we can all be together again. . . ."

119

120

chapter **XXIV**

119-128 Scenes from "City Lights." Virginia Cherrill as
the flower girl. Harry Myers as the eccentric
millionaire.

121

122

"City Lights."

chapter **XXIV** cont.

123

124

126

125

127

"City Lights."

128

chapter XXV

129   Chaplin playing his favorite instrument, the cello, during
the scoring of "The Gold Rush," 1942.

131   London crowds greeting Chaplin, 1931.

132 Chaplin in 1931.

133 Chaplin with Bernard Shaw at the London opening of "City Lights."

134 "Modern Times."
135 With Chester Conklin in "Modern Times."
136 Charlie goes mad from the factory routine.

137 Charlie and the gamin (Paulette Goddard).

138 Henry Bergman is persuaded to give Charlie a job.

139 The finale of "Modern Times."

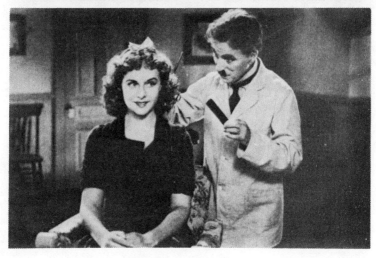

140 Chaplin as Adolph Hynkel in "The Great Dictator."
141 Hynkel with Napaloni (Jack Oakie).
142 The Jewish barber, who resembles Hynkel, gives Hannah (Paulette Goddard) a beauty treatment.

143 Hynkel embracing the world-globe.

144 Verdoux, the suave Bluebeard, preparing to "liquidate" his wife Lydia (Margaret Hoffman).

145 Verdoux with Annabella (Martha Raye).

146 Verdoux prepares to step out with the indestructible Annabella.

147 Verdoux's past catches up with him. Lena (Almira Sessions) recognizes him as the murderer of her sister.

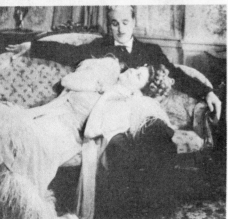

148 Chaplin with Mary Pickford and his wife, the former Oona
O'Neill, at the première of "Monsieur Verdoux," 1947.

He is shown reading the letter in prison. Through double-exposure his thoughts are registered.

A banquet in Hynkel's palace. Hynkel announces the march on Austerlich. As Herring weeps with adoration Hynkel rewards him with another medal, but has difficulty finding a place to pin it. As they are toasting each other a telephone call announces that Napaloni has 60,000 men on the Austerlich border.

In a rage Hynkel rips the medals, one by one, off the protesting Herring, rips the buttons off, tears the coat, snaps his suspenders, and slaps his face. Then Hynkel signs a declaration of war, muttering, "Napaloni!—The grosse peanut—the cheesie ravioli." A telephone call from Napaloni. Garbitsch answers. At Hynkel's instructions Garbitsch invites Napaloni to a conference in Tomania. A show of strength is expected to convince Napaloni not to interfere with the invasion of Austerlich. The declaration of war is torn up. "Peace is declared!"

The reception at the station. Hynkel salutes—and scratches under his arm. A carpet is unrolled, but the jolting train keeps missing it. "Hey! whatsa alla disa mixup?" The carpet must be placed before Benzino Napaloni, dictator of Bacteria, will condescend to alight. Finally ("You gottama carpet. Well putama down!") the carpet and the train manage to come together. Napaloni exits with his jaw protruding.

Alternate saluting complicates the ceremonial handshakes. Then the rival dictators shoulder each other out of focus as the frantic news cameramen follow them.

The two dictators appear together before a great crowd. Napaloni sneers at a clock tower adorned with a statue of Hynkel saluting: "Two minutesa slow." But as kisses are blown at him, he observes, "Verra nize pipple."

In the throne room, Garbitsch explains to Hynkel how to make Napaloni feel inferior by "applied psychology." Napaloni is to be seated on a low chair from which he will have to look up to Hynkel; while, additionally, a bust of the Tomanian dictator will glower down at him. He will also have to enter from the far end of the room and have the embarrassment of walking the entire length toward Hynkel.

Napaloni frustrates this plan by entering boisterously from behind Hynkel's desk, slapping him on the back and knocking him off his chair. When Napaloni is seated in the low chair he changes to a seat on the desk, scratches a match on the glowering bust, and outglowers him with an out-thrust of his chin and lower lip.

The conference ends in the suggestion to take a shave together. In the barber chairs they compete for the higher position, raising their chairs higher and higher. As they hit the ceiling, Hynkel crashes down.

At a military display in the stadium, only the spectators are shown. Passing tanks, planes, and other equipment are identified by their noises: Hynkel and Napaloni dispute whose planes are flying above them, and the spectators' heads are shown rotating together. As crashes are heard, Napaloni says, "You're right! They're yours."

A ball in the palace. On the balcony Garbitsch and Hynkel discuss invasion plans. Hynkel will go duck hunting until the appointed time in order to avoid suspicion.

Garbitsch urges Hynkel to dance with the plump and neglected Mme. Napaloni. "It will carry weight." "You mean *I* will carry weight." A comedy dance with Mme. Napaloni leading, and Hynkel bent back, etc. Hynkel and Napaloni decide to have a bite and talk things over in the buffet room.

Over limburger and strawberries the two dictators argue and eat, with the text of the treaty between them. Comic business includes dousing of a flunkey with strawberries and whipped cream, tongue-cooling as they absentmindedly overdo the mustard, getting the treaty by mistake into a sandwich, tossing ingredients in the punch, not called for by any recipe, some tricks with rubber spaghetti, absent-minded turning of the conference into public harangues, both dictators haranguing in unison, threatening each other with platters of food, etc.

Finally the treaty is signed. "After he removes his troops, we can move in without losing a man," Garbitsch whispers to Hynkel. The two dictators embrace.

The barber and Schultz, escaped from the concentration camp, walk along a highway in uniform. Hynkel, in Tyrolean costume, is duck hunting nearby in a small boat. "Invasion of Austerlich, now or never," he mutters. "Ha, ha" calls a duck. Firing up at it, Hynkel loses his balance, falls overboard. Prison guards searching the woods find him, capture him, hit him over the head, and drag him off, demanding "Where's Schultz?"

The two escaped men near the village of Pretzelburg. Troopers approach. The barber is taken for Hynkel. The troops line up and terrify the barber as they present arms. As the barber and Schultz are led into a car, they are told everything is under control. "Where are we going?" the barber timidly asks Schultz. When told, "You are invading Austerlich," he collapses.

Tanks appear out of haystacks and the invasion starts. . . . "Ghettos are raided" . . . "property confiscated" . . . the son of a resisting storekeeper is shot. . . . Hannah on the farm is knocked down and troopers take possession.

Austerlich thousands await the conqueror. "Your excellency, the world awaits your word." Drums beat as the barber, bowlegged and toes out, is led up the steps of the platform. Garbitsch and others wonder at Hynkel's strange appearance and Schultz's presence. They assume Schultz has been pardoned.

The "conqueror's" chair collapses. When he is re-seated, Garbitsch declares that Liberty, Equality, and Democracy are but words to fool the people. In the future each man owes all his duty to the state. He then introduces the dictator of Tomania, conqueror of Austerlich, "the future Emperor of the World!"

"You must speak," Schultz tells the nervous barber. "I can't!"—"It's our only hope." The other repeats the word "hope" as he thinks of Hannah (musically portrayed).

The barber rises; goes to the microphones; the thousands are in suspense. He begins simply and quietly: "I'm sorry, but I don't want to be an emperor. That's not my business. I don't want to rule or conquer anyone. I should like to help everyone—if possible—Jew, Gentile, black man, white. We don't want to hate and despise one another. In this world, there is room for everyone. And the good earth is rich and can provide for everyone. The way of life can be free and beautiful, but we have lost the way. Greed has poisoned men's souls. . . . Machinery that gives abundance has left us in want. Our knowledge has made us cynical. . . . We think too much and feel too little. More than machinery, we need humanity. . . . Even now my voice is reaching out. . . ." (Hannah is shown weeping on the ground). "To those who can hear me I say, do not despair. . . . The hate of men will pass and dictators die and the power they took from the people will return to the people. And so long as men die, liberty will never perish. . . . Soldiers! Don't give yourselves to these brutes—men who despise you— enslave you—regiment your lives—treat you like cattle and use you as cannon fodder—You are not machines! You are men! You have the love of humanity in your hearts—don't hate. . . ." (Camera moves closer to his face, revealing real perspiration as he builds to a climax) ". . . The Kingdom of God is within man . . . in the name of democracy let us all unite. Let us fight for a new world—a decent world that will give men a chance to work. . . . Dictators enslaved the people. . . . Now let us fight to free the world—to do away with national barriers—to do away with greed, with hate and intolerance —jobs for youth—security for old age.—Let us fight for a world of reason—a world of science—where progress will lead to the happiness of us all. Soldiers!" (he shouts) "In the name of democracy, let us *unite!*"

The crowds cheer. Hannah rises slowly from the ground. The barber runs his hand through his hair, whispers, "Hannah can you hear me?"

Hannah is shown listening as his voice continues, "Wherever you are, look up, Hannah! The clouds are lifting—the sun is breaking through—we are coming out of the darkness into a new world—where men will rise above their hate, their greed, and their brutality. Look up, Hannah! The soul of man has been given wings and at last he is beginning to fly. He is flying into the rainbow—into the light of hope—into the future, into the glorious future that belongs to you—to me—and to all of us.—Look up, Hannah, look up!"

Jaeckel at the door exclaims, "Did you hear that!" "Listen!" commands Hannah. In the final closeup of her, against the clouds with the wind blowing her hair and mystic music playing, she turns and smiles hopefully through her tears.

law suits and another marriage

The forties brought Chaplin law suits, violent
press attacks, general unfavorable publicity, and failure
for his only film of the decade. Following the opening of
"The Great Dictator" in October 1940, Chaplin spent
some time in New York, in an apartment overlooking the
East River. He was variously reported to be planning a
film about a refugee in New York, to be considering the
lead in "The Flying Yorkshireman," which Frank Capra
was preparing to make, to be negotiating a picture version of the play, "Shadow and Substance," with Joan
Barry. He decided on "Lady Killer," which became
"Monsieur Verdoux" in 1947.

True or not, the following note in Sheilah Graham's
gossip column is typical of the snide turn comments on
the comedian took during this period. Chaplin, Miss
Graham wrote, was so sure he would win the 1941
Academy Award that he had prepared a rejection speech
which he practiced before friends. Its keynote was to be,
"How can anyone decide which member of a picture is
the person responsible for its success?" It seems doubtful
that he would make such a speech considering the way his
films are made—though it might apply to the average
Hollywood picture. Like almost everything in the industry, whatever truth there was in this was magnified
out of all proportion.

Income tax difficulties vexed him most in the first
years of the decade. Finally the government's claim for a

large additional sum was ruled out in court while his contention that he had overpaid $24,938 was upheld.

In 1942 Paulette Goddard, after nearly ten years together, obtained a divorce in Mexico. The *New York Times* reports that "so secretive was the action that an entry of the decree has been ordered removed from the record by the jurist who issued it." Miss Goddard, now an established actress, was soon to marry Burgess Meredith.

On July 22, 1942, Chaplin made his premature demand for a second front. Speaking from Hollywood over a long distance wire to a meeting in Madison Square Garden, in New York, he said: "On the battlefield of Russia democracy will live or die." He demanded that England and the United States attack from the West while Russia had her back against the wall. Such a move might bring victory by the following spring. Otherwise, he warned, Hitler might overrun Asia. Many people considered the speech ill-timed and rather presumptuous on his part. Military leaders, better versed in these matters, were at that very moment maturing their own plans.

In October, in Carnegie Hall, Chaplin again called for a second front: "This is the time for action and I want to do what I can. Right now is the best time for a second front while the Hun is so busy in Russia." In another address, at a dinner of the "Arts in Russia Week" committee of the Russian War Relief in the Hotel Pennsylvania, he urged elimination of anti-communist propaganda in the interest of winning the war, "since our Allies do not object to our own ideals and form of government." This, however, was more or less in line with the policies of the day.

In 1943 and 1944 the tabloids had a headline festival over Joan Barry's paternity suit against Chaplin. A rather mousy but screen-struck girl from Brooklyn, she arrived in Hollywood in 1940. She had to be content with non-acting jobs, including that of a waitress, until the millionaire oil man, J. Paul Getty, included her in a party of girls to go to Mexico for the inauguration of Avila Camacho. In Mexico, Joan Barry was given a letter of introduction to Tim Durant, United Artists agent and long a friend of Chaplin. Durant suggested that she meet the actor, who was looking for a leading lady for his new picture.

They met in June 1941, and Chaplin, "telling her that she had all the qualities of a new Maude Adams," gave her a contract for seventy-five dollars a week. She was sent to Max Reinhardt for dramatic instruction and also received coaching from Chaplin himself. While grooming her for "Shadow and Substance," Chaplin, according to Miss Barry, "became interested in her as a woman." She underwent two illegal operations, she said, while preparing for her promised movie debut.

In October 1942, along with signs that the actor was tiring of her, her salary was cut to twenty-five dollars a week. Just before Christmas Miss Barry, in a desperate mood, went to Chaplin's house where she threatened to shoot him and then end her own life, using a pistol she had bought in a pawnshop. Evidently Chaplin was more amused than frightened, for then and there he wooed and won her again. When, a week or so later, she made another scene, Chaplin, whose interest had turned elsewhere, called the police. The girl was given a ninety-day suspended sentence and ordered to leave town. As she left the courtroom, she was handed a railroad ticket and a hundred dollars. In May, she returned to the Chaplin mansion. She was caught after crawling in through a rear window, was arrested for vagrancy, and sentenced to thirty days in jail. Most of the sentence was spent in a sanatorium by court permission, "because of the physical condition of the defendant."

When the paternity suit was filed, Chaplin, through his attorneys, denied that he was the father of the child his former protégée expected in three months, but agreed to pay the costs of the confinement and submit to a blood test. By the terms of a temporary settlement, the twenty-three-year-old girl received twenty-five hundred dollars and a hundred dollars a week until further court order and four thousand dollars for medical expenses.

Meanwhile on June 16, 1943, Chaplin, then fifty-four, married his fourth bride, eighteen-year-old Oona O'Neill, daughter of Eugene O'Neill. She, too, had studied drama with Chaplin and had been seen in his company frequently during the previous eight months. She had been given a part in "The Girl From Leningrad," which she now gave up, abandoning her acting ambitions.

According to Miss Barry's lawyers their client collapsed on hearing the news. There followed Chaplin's indictment by a Federal grand jury. There were four separate counts including violation of the Mann Act and conspiracy to deny Miss Barry her civil rights. The F.B.I. was appealed to. At the hearing the Mann Act charge was dismissed and Chaplin was acquitted of the other counts.

On October 2, 1943, Joan Barry gave birth to a daughter. In a subsequent paternity suit the jury found against Chaplin despite blood tests that proved he was not the father. In May 1946, Chaplin was ordered to continue to support the child.

While press photographers were flashing Chaplin being fingerprinted and the papers seethed with lurid details of the case, a Chaplin festival was ordered in Russia. At a gala showing of "The Gold Rush," *Time* magazine reports that Solomon Mikhoels, director of the Jewish Art Theatre, pinned Chaplin's troubles on the Trotsky-

ites. "Who are these . . . mercenary tricksters of the
Hearst and McCormick tabloid press . . . who started
slinging mud . . . morally to discredit Chaplin's name
so as to weaken the force of his ideology? . . . Trotsky-
ites!"

Then came Konrad Bercovici's five-million dollar plagiarism suit against Chaplin which reached trial but was
settled out of court for ninety-five thousand dollars.
Bercovici claimed that he had submitted a rough sketch
of a satire on Hitler and a nonentity who resembled him
and took his place; that the actor had returned it, de-
claring that production of such a picture was not feasi-
ble; and that " 'The Great Dictator' was identical in all
substantial respects" with Bercovici's sketch. On the
stand Chaplin denied that he had made an agreement
with Mr. Bercovici and asserted that he had originated
the plot. Both sides seemed glad of an opportunity to
settle the suit out of court.

Chaplin continued to issue statements such as: "I am
not a Jew! I am a citizen of the world!" and "I am an
internationalist, not a nationalist, and that is why I do
not take out citizenship." When informed that he might
be called to Washington to appear before the House
Un-American Activities Committee, he asserted, "I am
not a Communist, I am a peacemonger."

Chaplin was criticized for introducing Henry Wallace
to a Los Angeles rally at which several other prominent
motion-picture people appeared. The actor was also active in the movement to prevent the deportation of
Hanns Eisler, Vienna-born composer and acknowledged
former communist, who had been admitted to the United
States through the intercession of Eleanor Roosevelt.
Chaplin also cabled Pablo Picasso, the French artist
and an avowed communist, asking him to head a committee of French artists to protest the deportation pro-

ceedings against Eisler to the American Embassy in Paris.

Westbrook Pegler, on December 3, 1947, devoted a whole column to anti-Chaplin vituperation. On the Eisler incident, Pegler fulminates: "This was an attempt by an alien, resident here for more than thirty-five years, guilty of a degree of moral turpitude which disqualifies him for citizenship, caught in the act of cheating the government of an enormous debt for taxes, a slacker in both World Wars, although he clamored with the Communists for a second front in the latest one—an attempt by this alien . . . to foment an artificial political demonstration against the United States by Communists in Paris in reprisal for certain legal action taken by the elected Representatives of the American people in Congress."

1947 seems to have been the lowest point in Chaplin's popularity. He was even attacked in Congress. On June 12, Representative John E. Rankin demanded his deportation, asserting that the film actor's Hollywood life "is detrimental to the moral fabric of America" and, that he has refused to become an American citizen. By deporting him, "he can be kept off the American screen and his *loathsome pictures* can be kept from the eyes of American youth." A variety of other organizations and individuals participated in the attacks. Probably no performer in the history of the theatre has had to weather such extremes of adulation and hate.

On the other hand, transgressions sometimes help at the box office. It is a strange commentary on our times that the public forgives transgression that is in keeping with the actor's screen portrayals; others are punished with mud-slinging and loss of attendance. It seems impossible for the public to separate a screen actor's work and private life.

For a London publication, Chaplin wrote that he had had enough of Hollywood. "Before long, I shall perhaps leave the United States, although it has given me so many moral and material satisfactions. I, Charlie Chaplin, declare that Hollywood is dying. Hollywood is now fighting its last battle and it will lose that battle unless it decides, once and for all, to give up standardizing its films —unless it realizes that masterpieces cannot be mass-produced in the cinema, like tractors in a factory. I think, objectively, that it is time to take a new road, so that money shall no longer be the all-powerful god of a decaying community." Apparently Chaplin's bitter mood had not been helped by the failure of."Verdoux."

After the premiere of this film a producer telegraphed Hedda Hopper, the columnist, that he had just witnessed an historic event. "I have seen the last film of Chaplin."

During the mid-forties, most of Chaplin's old friends drifted away or died. King Vidor and Harry Crocker, once his cronies, were no longer seen in his company. Henry Bergman, who had been with him on all his films since 1916, died in 1946. Bergman had been a sort of Chaplin trade-mark and good-luck charm, and Robert Florey, associate director on "Verdoux," had sought to have him appear as a judge in the courtroom scene but Chaplin did not want to disturb his ailing friend. Dr. Cecil Reynolds, the actor's physician, adviser and friend for many years, committed suicide. Alfred Reeves, his manager and associate since 1910, when he was with Karno, also passed on. Many other of Chaplin's old associates had been dropped or lost through quarrels but a few of the technical crew still remained. Edna Purviance still visited the studio, but only occasionally.

One gets the impression that Chaplin must sometimes feel alone. However, his present marriage has lasted several years. A daughter, Geraldine, was born in 1944 and a son, Michael John, two years later.

X X X

Chaplin and politics

Chaplin has often been attacked on political grounds. As early as 1921 reporters were asking him if he was a "Bolshevik." Twenty years later he was denounced in Washington for his "communistic connections." To this Chaplin has made several public denials that he is a communist. What are the facts? Let us examine the actor's own statements and activities and the statements of those intimately associated with him.

Having seen poverty in his own childhood, Chaplin was naturally interested in any plans for social betterment. A rebel and non-conformist in private life, he was drawn to any doctrine which seemed to promise or vaguely connote "freedom."

Max Eastman appears to have been the first political intellectual to influence him. Eastman, when he met Chaplin in 1919, was a radical poet and editor of the *Liberator,* a left-wing magazine. Today Eastman is an editor of *Reader's Digest* and his writing is anti-communist and anti-Soviet. At that time, however, he was, in his own words, "the only Socialist agitator who opposed the World War and supported the Russian revolution, and yet managed to stay out of jail." Chaplin, who heard him in the Philharmonic Auditorium in Los Angeles, admired his "restraint." Through Rob Wagner he later met the speaker. Personable and not much older than Chaplin, Eastman hit it off well with Chaplin.

Eastman was then raising money for *The Liberator.* He put the touch on Chaplin but received only twenty-five dollars. In "Heroes I Have Known," Eastman writes: "As it was, I learned right there never to try to drag Charlie in, as I did most of my rich friends, on various schemes of social reform. Charlie likes radical ideas; he likes to talk about transforming the world; but he doesn't like to pay for the talk, much less the transformation."

Chaplin was all praises for Eastman's radical speech, yet the following day, according to Eastman, he heard the actor "express a glowing belief in slavery as an immortal institution, backing it up with arguments and illustrating it with a pantomime that left his hearers breathless if not convinced."

If this were true Chaplin was probably not referring to Negro slavery. At another time, speaking of Negroes, Chaplin said, "I never laugh at their humor. They have suffered too much ever to be funny to me." He never used Negroes as comic relief in his films, though in the 1914 Keystone comedy "The Rounders," there is a white man, in blackface, playing a bit part as a doorman and others appear in the background of some Essanays.

This cannot be taken as an example of race prejudice any more than Griffith's use of blackface for some of the leads in "The Birth of a Nation." It was simply the custom of the time. There were few Negro actors available for regular dramatic roles. Strangely enough, along with other stock national types, there are several examples of Jewish stereotypes in the Mutual comedies, with long beards, hooked noses, and low-fitting derbies. This again can be attributed to then-current conventions.

Chaplin's friendship with Eastman was a lasting one. In "My Trip Abroad," the actor calls Eastman "a charming and sympathetic fellow who thinks. All of his doctrines I do not subscribe to, but that makes no difference in our friendship. We get together, argue a bit, and then agree to disagree and let it go at that and remain friends."

His classic reply to reporters who, in 1921, asked if he was a Bolshevik was: "I am an artist. I am interested in life. Bolshevism is a new phase of life. I must be interested in it."

On his 1921 trip to Europe he met H. G. Wells and others who took a strong interest in social problems. His next intellectual influence after Eastman, however, was the sculptor Clare Sheridan. She had just returned from Russia and had met leaders of the new regime. In her frank "My American Diary," she thus characterizes Chaplin: "He is not Bolshevik nor Communist, nor Revolutionary, as I had heard rumored. He is an individualist with the artist's intolerance of stupidity, insincerity and narrow prejudice"; adding, "he was rather scornful about the sentimentalism of my revolutionary ideals." Chaplin advised her, "Don't get lost on the path of propaganda. Live your life as an artist . . . the other goes on—always. . . ."—advice he himself failed to follow in the forties.

In the early twenties, as the actor began to make fewer pictures and became more leisurely, he had gatherings of artists and intellectuals, Upton Sinclair among them, in his home. Except for his succession of girl friends and Mary Pickford and Douglas Fairbanks, Chaplin mingled little with the movie crowd.

According to his publicity man, Carl Robinson, the actor liked to call himself a socialist. Sam Goldwyn, in his "Behind the Screen," records that mention of a new "ism" or "ology" brought Chaplin loping from the farthest corner of the room. "His prejudice is against anything which interferes with his own personal freedom. The censor, the income tax, any supposed obstruction— these are hateful to him in the degree to which they infringe upon that coveted sense of power."

During the filming of "The Gold Rush," the writer Jim Tully worked in close association with the comedian. Tully "exposed" his employer in several articles and sketches. He has this to say about Chaplin's political leanings: "He was often criticized by radicals who wanted him to be more revolutionary. . . . On no political fence longer than a bird, those citizens who would make a better world often caused him amusement. . . . If he did not agree entirely with the social system, he saw its many good points, and though talkative of changes he would make them slowly, or rather, leave them to others. He caught things quickly, the snob in Karl Marx—the hypocrisy of Napoleon; and the confusion within himself." Tully added this observation: "If Chaplin pitied the poor in the parlors of the rich, it was often hurt self-interest instead of compassion." When the Mexican artist Diego Rivera told Jim Tully that Chaplin had given fifty thousand dollars to the Communist cause, an item never verified, the writer quipped, "It must have been money of the Madera regime" (meaning that it was worthless).

According to "A Comedian Sees the World," one of his few (and ghost-written) articles, Chaplin was at one of Lady Astor's Cliveden salons in 1931. Each guest made a speech on ways of dealing with the depression in England. A reduction of the role of government in the life of the nation was put first in Chaplin's speech.

"The world is suffering from too much government and the expense of it. I would have government ownership of banks and revise many of the laws and those of the Stock Exchange. I would create a government Bureau of Economics, which would control prices, interests and profits. . . . I would issue scrip to alleviate the expense of the budget. . . . My policy would stand for internationalism, world cooperation of trade, the abolition of the gold standard, and world inflation of money. . . . My policy would stand for the reduction of the hours of

labor and for a minimum wage of no less than a comfortable amount to all men and women over the age of
twenty-one. I would stand for private enterprise so far
as it would not deter the progress or well-being of the
majority."

When Churchill jibed that the actor should go into
Parliament, Chaplin replied, "No, sir. I prefer to be a
motion picture actor these days. However, I believe we
should go ahead with evolution to avoid revolution, and
there's every evidence that the world needs a drastic
change."

"Modern Times," both before and after its release, gave
rise to speculations and rumors about his politics. Karl
Kitchen, interviewing him for the *New York Times* while
the film was in progress, brought up the touchy question
of Chaplin's citizenship, to be answered, half-jokingly,
"If I were ever to take out citizenship papers it would be
in Andorra, the smallest and most insignificant country in
the world." Kitchen added: "Whether Chaplin is sincere
when he discusses certain phases of socialism is dubious.
He long has had the reputation of being a 'parlor pink.
. . . But the years and the responsibilities of wealth . . .
have made him more conservative."

Following his ill-timed plea for a second front to help
Russia, his support of Henry Wallace, and the production
of his controversial "M. Verdoux," Chaplin was openly
referred to as a communist. This he again denied in a
press interview following the "Verdoux" opening. To the
direct question, "Are you a communist?" he produced an
unequivocal, "No!" To the question, "Are you a communist sympathizer?" Chaplin replied, "During the war I
was sympathetic with the Russians who were holding the
front. I believe we owe her thanks and in that sense I
was sympathetic."

The comedian said it was because he was an internationalist that he had not become an American citizen;

that he was a believer in no system of politics, had never voted, and was a member of no political party; that his ideology consisted of a defense of "the little man—his right to have a roof over his head and to work and raise a family." This interview with seventy-four reporters and photographers, was recorded and later broadcast. As *Variety* reported: "Press 'wolves' yap at Chaplin's politics, but get little of his hide."

Hollywood and theatrical people have long felt that Chaplin's interest in "isms" is a pose to be classed with his once-publicized desire to play Hamlet. To a friend Chaplin said, not long ago, that he subscribed to no "ism," that if he could be labeled at all it would be as a "social anarchist."

Chaplin's understanding of and love for the type of underdog he portrays on the screen and for humanity in general is obvious from his many motion pictures. He himself wrote: "I find unsuccessful people much more likable and interesting. They haven't lost something human and impulsive and warm, especially if they have always been poor and unsuccessful. . . ."

On another occasion he said: "I've known humiliation. And humiliation is a thing you never forget. Poverty— the degradation and helplessness of it! I can't feel myself any different, at heart, from the unhappy and defeated men, the failures."

An individualistic and even anarchistic personality, Chaplin has shown his resistance to regimentation, beginning with the type practiced in Hollywood itself.

"Monsieur Verdoux"

"Monsieur Verdoux" is the most controversial and, financially, the least successful of Chaplin's films. Suggested by the career of Landru, the French Bluebeard, it was based on an idea by Orson Welles. Chaplin worked two years on the script alone. The first title, "Lady Killer," was abandoned. Production was delayed until June 1946. Then the film was shot in the record time—for Chaplin—of twelve weeks. Despite its more than fifty sets, its several established and high-salaried actors, and increased general costs, it is unlikely that its production outlay reached the advertised two million dollars.

In "Verdoux" Chaplin finally and completely abandons his famous tramp, of whom there had been some surviving traces in "The Great Dictator." Verdoux's make-up and character are entirely different. Gone are the baggy trousers and the famous mustache. Outwardly Verdoux is a dapper, middle-class bank clerk, fashionably attired and sporting a little French mustache. And the character is no pathetic, blundering underdog now, but a cynical modern businessman whose line happens to be murder for profit. The picture is intended to be, not so much a comedy about a modern Bluebeard, as a satire on the modern business- and war-minded world.

In an advance interview Chaplin remarked: "The picture has moral value, I believe. Von Clausewitz said that

war is the logical extension of diplomacy; M. Verdoux
feels that murder is the logical extension of business. He
should express the feeling of the times we live in—out of
catastrophe come people like him. He typifies the psychological disease of depression. He is frustrated, bitter, and
at the end, pessimistic. But he is never morbid; and the
picture is by no means morbid in treatment. . . . Under
the proper circumstances, murder can be comic." His
treatment of the subject he felt was in "good taste."

When "Monsieur Verdoux" opened on April 11, 1947,
more than six years after the last Chaplin film, its critical
reception was divided and its box-office reception disastrous. Critical comment ranged from blast to eulogy: "It
has little entertainment weight, either as somber symbolism or sheer nonsense. . . . It is also something of an af-
front to the intelligence" (Howard Barnes in the *Herald
Tribune*); "The film is staged like an early talkie with
fairly immobile camera, self-conscious dialogue, acting
that looks like the late twenties . . . an old-fashioned
production, almost quaint in some of its moments" (Eileen Creelman in *The Sun*); "It is permanent if any
work done during the past twenty years is permanent
(James Agee in *The Nation*); and "Totally successful. . .
a landmark not only in Chaplin's long career but in the
progress of the American screen" (Lewis Jacobs in *Cinema*).

The picture became a cause célèbre for a small group
of intellectuals who found much depth and significance
in it, but the general public was not entertained. It had a
very short New York run and in many other places it
was banned. Ohio theatre owners proposed to make their
ban nation-wide. The Memphis Tennessee Board of Censors barred it as "a comedy that makes murder a joke."
Catholic War Veterans picketed it in several cities.
Loew's, Inc., however, in barring it from their circuit,
denied having been swayed by pressure from any group.

Joseph Vogel, general manager of the Loew's chain, explained that the picture lost money: "It's amazing how little the Chaplin picture could do. . . . Maybe what they want is the old clown."

In this reception to "Monsieur Verdoux" many felt that the man was being attacked through his film. Chaplin ordered United Artists to withdraw the picture from further distribution after a disappointing two years in which it played only 2,075 dates and grossed a mere $325,000 in domestic rentals. Normally a Chaplin film could count on between twelve thousand and thirteen thousand dates and an average of $150 an engagement. In Europe the picture was better received and was awarded prizes.

Except for three scenes, in which the obstreperous Annabella participated (Chaplin created the part with Martha Raye in mind), and occasional flashes of droll wit, there is little in "Verdoux" of the sort of comedy associated with Chaplin. Nor is its social criticism new or revolutionary. As Parker Tyler points out in the *Kenyon Review*: "One might, from the broad view, even call it paltry. In certain radical circles, not necessarily politically denominated, 'War' as 'a business,' which is Chaplin's chief indictment of modern society in 'Monsieur Verdoux,' is a hoary platitude and in itself not heating to the blood. But patently it is a considerable novelty on the movie screen, where it is stated verbally by Chaplin in the bluntest possible terms and with a bitterness of intonation carrying with it, astonishingly enough, a grain or two of smugness. Monsieur Verdoux's death-cell justification is to assert that his crimes of having murdered some fifteen innocently bigamous wives for their money has been only a small private enterprise compared with the wholesale murder of wars. A certain naïveté, naturally, appears amid the coarse integument of the comic murderer's too serious 'last words.' "

Yet Chaplin must be commended for attempting something different and for speaking his mind about some of today's problems as he sees them. Some of his own bitterness and despair went into it. The scene in court is not unlike some of his own experiences. Granted that the film is not uproariously funny or entirely successful, it reflects an individuality. As Archer Winsten points out, "That's like the old, fine days of the American movies when everyone tried to be a genius and some succeeded. Not like today's smooth, mindless, faceless products of the group."

Chaplin's new character is perhaps the logical extension of the Tramp who might have turned into a Verdoux had he lived today. As the actor said, "Things are in just as much of a mess now [as during the war] and I could hardly come on again in baggy pants, pretending that life is still all Santa Claus." Impersonating the difficult role of a man who is both a ruthless killer and a person of delicate sensibilities, Chaplin performed with his usual finesse. Super-waiter, super-skater, super-boxer, super-policeman, super-tightrope walker, and now super-bank clerk, Chaplin's best effects have been gained through super-expert professional dexterity. In "Verdoux," the super-bank clerk counts his victim's money and leafs through directories with machine-like speed.

In the supporting cast, in addition to the antic Martha Raye, Isobel Elsom, a recruit from the stage, was effective as the society woman (Edna Purviance made tests for this part); Ada-May Weeks, former musical comedy star, was amusing as the maid who dyed her hair with poison; but Marilyn Nash, the much-publicized "find," was rather amateurish as The Girl whom Verdoux freed. The rest of the cast, including some old faces, had little to do other than serving as foils for the star.

The Verdoux script, too, is uneven. In places the dialogue rises to almost Shavian wit; but elsewhere, in the opinion of many, the writing, as well as the ideas, is pretentious and muddled and sinks to almost sophomoric levels.

The production itself and the technique are not of the best. Some sets have a flimsy appearance; the lighting is not always perfect; rear projection was used ineptly. And train wheels as a transition device was already a cliché in Garbo's "Susan Lennox" (1931). The film gets off on a bad foot, technically speaking, in the rather long first scene with the Couvais family. Directed as though performed on a stage, all the players faced forward and were photographed full length. Although Chaplin himself prefers playing to the camera for intimate effects, it was unnatural here; and modern camera angles were seldom used.

Robert Florey, the Frenchman who has directed many pictures in America and a friend of Chaplin's of long standing, gives an interesting account of his hectic experiences as associate director of "Verdoux," in his book "Hollywood d'hier et d'aujourd'hui" (Hollywood Yesterday and Today). Chaplin acts with his feet and indeed with his whole body. Therefore he insisted on having his scenes photographed mostly in full length as he had been doing for years. He did not care for trick angles or "Hollywood chichi." He once declared: "I am the unusual and I do not need camera angles. . . ."

In this stand Chaplin was probably the wiser. His old methods were probably better suited to his style than Hollywood's modern methods.

Chaplin also ordered closeups for himself in a scene but often restricted them for others, even where they were needed for cross-cutting in dialogue. He had an inadequate knowledge of camera lenses. He couldn't understand how his feet would show when the camera came close, apparently not aware that a lens of short focal length has a wide angle of view. He would jump from a long shot to his close scene without a transition. At all times he was impatient with or contemptuous of the technical end—the sound, the moving camera, the lighting, etc.

But in his perfectionist way, once he got into his scene, he was never too tired for the endless retakes that he considered necessary. Unfortunately he never did the scenes twice in the same manner, which confused the script girl and later made cutting and matching difficult.

Florey had a hard time getting authentic French atmosphere. He was forced to turn the ghetto set of "The Great Dictator" into a French town. He had a fight on his hands eliminating obsolete "apaches" and fin-de-siècle costuming of some of the extras. Chaplin was not too concerned over authenticity in atmosphere detail, feeling that the story he was telling was a universal one.

A dynamo of energy, Chaplin was obstinate and arrogant during work. In relaxed moments between scenes he could be very gracious and charming, playing his violin or entertaining with one of his inimitable bits of mimicry.

Florey considered the script on the macabre side, objected to some repetitious ideas, and advised that some of the dialogue be converted into cinematic action. Once Chaplin began to talk, he overdid it, even resorting to one or two soliloquies. Despite all this, Florey enjoyed the experience, observing that some day he would like to see "Charlie" once more on the screen. Many others concur in the wish.

Lately Chaplin has begun to feel that the moviegoers may have been right to reject "Verdoux." He realizes that he did not rouse the sort of sympathy that has made his other pictures so successful.

However, "Monsieur Verdoux" is one of those controversial pictures which will be discussed and revived for years to come. Time alone will tell whether its importance is innate or merely transitory agitation over a daring but unsuccessful experiment by the veteran comedian.

Subtitled "A comedy of murder," "Monsieur Verdoux" opens with a closeup of a tombstone inscribed: "Henri Verdoux, 1880-1937." Verdoux's voice is heard: "Good evening. I was a bank clerk until the depression of 1930." Casually, he explains how he then went into the business of marrying women with money and then liquidating them. He did it to support home and family. He never loved the women; it was strictly business. The camera then moves across the cemetery.

"The home of the Couvais family," a quarrelsome menage ruled by the spinster Lena. The postman brings a letter from the Paris National Bank. All Thelma Couvais's money was drawn out two weeks ago. A woman of fifty, she had left for Paris sometime ago and had not been heard from in three months. She had gone off to marry a man of whom young Jean says, "I'd like to have his technique." "We ought to go to the police," one of the old women insists. Pierre says wait a day or two. Jean brings out a picture of Verdoux: "Funny-looking bird, isn't he?"

"A small village somewhere in the South of France." Henri Verdoux is introduced fastidiously cutting roses in a garden; in the background, an incinerator smoking with his latest victim. (Verdoux's gay musical theme continues in counterpoint to the implications of the scene.) He avoids stepping on a worm, picking it up and placing it on a bush, with a shudder.

The doorbell rings. The postman holds out a letter for Thelma Varnay to sign. Verdoux goes upstairs, tells the no longer extant Thelma not to bother getting out of her tub, just dry your hands and sign. "There, that's it." Verdoux opens the letter, dated June 6, 1932. . . . the transaction "terminates your account." Verdoux, the super-bank clerk, moistens his fingers and counts sixty thousand francs, very fast. Pocketing the money, he calls long distance; then rubs his hands and sits down to the piano to render the last part of the "Second Hungarian Rhapsody." Knocks, which Verdoux first thinks come from the piano, turn out to be the tapping on the window pane of a new cook bringing references. After giving her some orders, he telephones a broker and buys some stock.

At the "Police Judiciaire," Lena Couvais explains that no sooner had their sister married than she disappeared. The police inspector explains that twelve other women have similarly disappeared recently, each a middle-aged woman with property. The man is "a Bluebeard—a mass killer."

The snobbish Marie Grosnay calls at Verdoux's house with a real estate agent. Verdoux, his arms full of roses, meets her. When she admires the flowers, he calls the maid to wrap them up for her. Like a slick floorwalker, Verdoux shows Mme. Grosnay around the house.

Upstairs she drops the remark that her husband has been dead several years. "Indeed!" and at once his wheels start turning. As he explains that this was his late wife's bedroom, he pushes an ample dressmaker's dummy behind a screen. Mme. Grosnay's eyes, he declares, are "deep pools of desire." It is destiny that they have come together. But Mme. Grosnay protests it is too late now. "Nonsense, what difference does age make? You have ripeness, luxuriousness, more experience, more character now—more everything!" He grabs her hand, "This is inevitable."

As he pursues the middle-aged woman around the room, the real estate agent enters. Verdoux pretends to have been chasing a bee, claps his hands by the window, loses his balance, and somersaults out on the roof. "I must have slipped!" On leaving, Mme. Grosnay is presented with his bouquet of roses.

Train wheels (this shot, a sort of leitmotif, recurs during the pictue as a symbol for a transition to another locale or for lapse of time.) Verdoux in a Paris street cafe meets two men, former bank clerk associates. When Verdoux pulls a roll of bills out of his pocket, one exclaims, "You must have made a killing!" Verdoux replies, "Yes!" When he leaves, one of the men explains that Verdoux got a raw deal—was with the bank over thirty years, but with the depression, was one of the first to go.

Verdoux enters his office, goes upstairs to the telephone. The market has dropped. Unless he produces fifty thousand francs he will be wiped out. Pulling out his address book, he comes across the name of Lydia Floray. He mutters to himself that the banks in her town close at four. Train wheels.

At the door he is greeted by the acidulous Lydia: "I thought you were in Indo-China! What do you want?" The clock strikes quarter to four. "Let us not argue. We are not young. In the sunset of life we need tenderness." Looking at his watch, he takes her hand. She repulses him, "I'm getting too old for all that." Then he explains that he was tipped off that the banks are on the point of collapsing; tomorrow there will be a run on them. "Good heavens," she screams, "get the money out—seventy thousand francs!" He hurries out.

The scene dissolves to Verdoux at the piano as Lydia stuffs her money in a box. As they retiré upstairs, Verdoux, from the balcony, exclaims, "What a night! How beautiful this pale Endymion hour. . . . Our feet were soft in flowers!" Lydia snarls, "Get to bed." He enters the bedroom.

The camera remains on the hall as night changes to morning. Verdoux comes out with the box. Downstairs he counts the money and calls long distance. In the kitchen he prepares breakfast, sets two places, then stops to remove one. Train wheels.

In a beautiful cottage in the country, Verdoux, relieved to get away from "the jungle fight," greets his little son. His wife has forgotten it was their tenth wedding anniversary, but Verdoux has a sentiment for such things. As she exclaims, "Ten wonderful years!" the camera moves down to her foot in a brace. The present he gives her is a deed to the house and garden. "They'll never take that away from us." With better luck, in a few more years, he'll retire.

When his wife speaks of the strain he has been under in recent years and that he seems so desperate, Verdoux replies, "These are desperate days. Millions are starving and unemployed. It is not easy for a man of my age." In moments of trouble he thinks of this other world. "You and Peter are all I have on this earth," he says, as he wheels his wife inside. When his son pulls the cat's tail, he remarks, "There's a cruel streak in you. I wonder where you got it . . . violence begets violence, remember."

Train wheels . . . Verdoux in a coach. The raucous Annabella Bonheur is entertaining some guests. Just as Annabella remarks, laughing, that her husband comes home for one week and is away six—he enters. It is Verdoux in a naval uniform. "Pigeon," he shouts.

The guests leave, and there is an amatory scene on the sofa with Annabella reclining in his lap. It is interspersed with a business discussion—her investments in the Pacific Ocean Power Co., her purchase of a diamond from one of the guests who has just left. To prove that she can't manage money affairs, Verdoux examines the phony diamond. "Glass, you silly ass. Glass!"

Putting on a large, feathered hat, Annabella with Verdoux visits a nightspot. There he runs out to a druggist's to pick up a vial of chloroform, having learned that Annabella has just withdrawn her money from the bank. While he is making the purchase, the president of the "Salt Water Fuel Co." (which transforms salt water into gasoline) tries to sell stock to Annabella, but Verdoux manages to get back in time to drag her away. She is enraged and that night he sleeps alone. In the morning Verdoux takes his departure. Train wheels.

In his office Verdoux rapidly turns the pages of the directory. He calls on Mme. Grosnay and is rebuffed. In a florist shop he orders the girl to send three dozen roses and orchids to be delivered to Mme. Grosnay— twice a week for two weeks.

Back home Verdoux discusses poisons with the local druggist, dwelling on a formula which leaves no trace in the body. "Think what an arch criminal could do with it. . . ." Train wheels.

Back at his Paris office, Verdoux prepares to experiment with the new poison. In the rain he meets a young girl, offers her his umbrella, invites her to his place, and learns her story. She is from Belgium, has been up against it, has done a turn in jail for pawning a rented typewriter. "Nothing is permanent in this world—not even our troubles," he assures her. In the kitchen he prepares refreshments and the poison.

She continues her story and he learns that her husband, a disabled war veteran, died while she was in jail, but she still holds to her ideals. He is deeply touched. Removing the poison glass, he gives her money and sends her on her way. "This is a ruthless world and one must be ruthless," he advises her. It is "a blundering world" and "a little kindness goes far." She retorts, "Goodbye and thank you." Verdoux shrugs.

Detective Morrow arrives to ask a few questions. Verdoux pours him a drink. "Do you know Thelma Varnay?" "Lydia Florey?" Verdoux denies any acquaintance with them. The detective tells him that he has been shadowing him for two weeks and charges him with bigamy and fourteen counts of murder.

Verdoux is relieved when the detective takes a drink. "We'll find the bodies." "I don't think you will," counters Verdoux. Train wheels. On board the train the detective is sleeping. Slapping the detective to see if he is "awake," Verdoux gets the key and slips out of his handcuffs. Opening the detective's wallet, he finds a ticket and money. Then he steps off the train.

Newspaper headlines: Inspector Morrow found dead on train. Verdoux, reading them in a Paris cafe, is not displeased. The young girl he helped warmly greets him, but with noble abnegation he pretends he doesn't remember her and orders the puzzled girl about her business as he steps into a street car.

Train wheels. Verdoux returns to his "pigeon," who holds up baby socks she is knitting. Verdoux is startled until she explains it is for the pregnant woman next door. The maid, about to bleach her hair, uses a bottle marked "peroxide" into which Verdoux had poured some poison—and her hair comes out in handfuls. She drops the bottle and replaces it with another from which Verdoux fills Annabella's glass.

After a patient wait on Verdoux's part, Annabella sips the drink and spits it out, roaring in disgust, "That's sarsaparilla!" Verdoux, alarmed that he might have drunk the poison, rushes to the kitchen for some milk as an antidote. As he screams, "I'm dying. Tell my wife I'm here," the maid enters with her few remaining tufts of hair standing on end.

Verdoux next takes the indestructible Annabella out in a rowboat intending to drown her, after first putting her out with chloroform. Approaching her as if she is fishing, he is tipped back in the rocking boat and chloroforms himself. On reviving he tries to slip a rope

weighted with a rock around her and push her overboard, but tumbles in himself and is rescued by Annabella.

Flowers arrive for Mme. Grosnay. She tells a friend
they are from "that awful man who is pursuing me."
Verdoux, calling from the florist shop, tells Mme.
Grosnay, "Your eyes—they're beautiful" as he ogles the
young flower girl. His persistence finally wins him an
invitation from Mme. Grosnay. She playfully calls him a
"wicked man" as he kisses her hand. Verdoux's technique begins to work.

At the big reception when Verdoux finally wins Marie
Grosnay, Annabella's loud laugh is suddenly heard. Verdoux dodges her by ducking into the greenhouse, under
tables, into various rooms, and out windows. Finally he
disappears over the garden wall, abandoning Mme.
Grosnay.

Montage sequence: "Stock Crash" . . . "Panic in the
Stock Exchange" . . . "Banks fail" . . . "Riots" . . . "Suicides" . . . Verdoux is informed he was wiped out hours
ago. . . . "Crisis in Europe" . . . 1933 . . . crowds
. . . Mussolini and Hitler . . . soldiers marching . . .
"Nazis bomb Spanish Loyalists" . . . "Thousand of civil-
ians killed." . . .

Verdoux, now older and slightly bent, stepping away
from a cafe table, is almost run over by an automobile.
The car belongs to the girl he once befriended. "Don't
you remember me?" She offers him a lift and they drive
to the Cafe Royale. He finally recalls her and she goes
on with her story. Her fortunes have improved. She has
married a munitions manufacturer. Verdoux smiles ironically and replies: "That is the business I should have
been in. It will be paying big dividends soon!"

Of himself Verdoux says: "Business is a ruthless business." He gave up the fight—soon after the crash he lost
his wife and child. What followed was a monotonous

dream world. "Despair is a narcotic: it lulls the mind into indifference." But life must go on.

Into the cafe come Lena Couvais and her nephew Jean. As they pass Verdoux, Lena recognizes him. Realizing that he is trapped, Verdoux manages to elude Jean by going in and out of a revolving door and locking him in a room. He uses the interval of liberty he has won to bid goodnight to the girl. "I'm going to fulfill my destiny." He follows the detectives inside. After the fainting Lena points and gasps, "That's him!" Verdoux calmly lifts her off the floor, bows sardonically: "Henri Verdoux, at your service."

Train Wheels. In court the spectators are asked by the prosecutor to look at the "cruel and cynical monster." . . . Verdoux turns toward them obligingly. . . . The prosecutor decries his lack of "decent instincts" . . . demands that the criminal who made a "business" of killing . . . be punished "for the protection of society," etc. . . . Wheels. . . . "Verdict expected soon." Asked if he has anything to say, Verdoux remarks, "Mass killing —does not the world encourage it? . . . I'm an amateur in comparison." After the verdict of guilty, he states ominously, "I shall see you *all* soon—very soon!"

Train wheels. In prison Verdoux, accepting his fate, offers philosophical explanations: "We can't have good without evil; shadows are cast by the sun." He refuses to be photographed. A reporter interviews him, "You'll have to admit crime doesn't pay." "Not in a small way," replies Verdoux. His statements confound the little group. Reporter: "What's this talk about good and evil?" Verdoux: "Arbitrary forces, my good fellow! Too much of either would destroy us all." Reporter: "We can never have too much good in this world." Verdoux: "The trouble is we've never had enough. We don't know." The reporter tries to get a "story" but Verdoux goes on expounding. "Wars, conflict—it's all business.

One murder makes a villain; millions, a hero. Numbers sanctify!"

A priest enters. Verdoux, after asking him somewhat fliply what he can do for him, claims that he is at peace with God; his conflict is with man. Priest: "Have you no remorse for your sins?" Verdoux: "Who knows what sin is—born as it is from heaven—from God's fallen angel? Who knows what ultimate destiny is served?—After all, what would you be doing without sin?" The priest asks Verdoux to let him pray for him. "As you wish." Priest: "May God have mercy on your soul." Verdoux: "Why not? After all it belongs to Him."

Men enter to carry out the sentence. Offered rum, Verdoux at first refuses, and then, "Just a minute. I've never tasted rum." He relishes it before his hands are tied. When the door to the courtyard opens, Verdoux takes a deep breath. The priest mumbles as the cortège marches toward the guillotine. The music swells as the picture fades.

postscript

There have been many rumors about Chaplin's plans. During the past two years he has been working on the script of a film to be called "Footlights," thereby scotching rumors that he will retire. The new picture, apparently with an autobiographical overtone, will deal with an aging English music-hall comedian who fears he is losing his ability to make people laugh. He falls in love with a young ballet dancer disillusioned with life. In the process of encouraging her to go on, he makes his own "comeback." The picture will have all the familiar Chaplin ingredients except the tramp character.

Early in 1950 his composition of a ballet, entitled "Death of Columbine," for Alicia Markova and Anton Dolin, was announced. Apparently nothing came of it.

In July 1950, after several years of negotiations, United Artists was reorganized. Mary Pickford and Chaplin surrendered their control of the company; 3,600 of their 4,000 shares were bought by a group headed by Paul V. McNutt and Frank L. McNamee. With 400 shares between them, Miss Pickford and Chaplin will still have a voice in the company they helped found in 1919.

With some trepidation "City Lights" was revived on Broadway on April 8, 1950. The releasing company feared that a new generation had grown up that had never heard of Chaplin. They also feared possible demonstrations or picket lines. "City Lights," wiping away any possible bad taste left by "Verdoux," confounded

the Chaplin detractors who in 1947 predicted that the
public had permanently soured on him. Moreover, a
new generation that had grown up without ever having
seen Charlie Chaplin took "City Lights" to their hearts
as if it had been made only yesterday. *Life* magazine
proclaimed the twenty year old film "the best picture of
the year." And *Time* magazine remarked that it will
probably last as long as anything on film. "Its storytell-
ing is so eloquently visual that it makes most sound
movies seem like the stunted products of a half-forgotten
art." More reissues are promised.

Even if Chaplin does not make another film, his old
pictures will continue to be revived. And with their
timeless comedy and humanity they will doubtless continue to be shown in theatres, auditoriums, and on television so long as celluloid holds out.

an index to the films of Charles Chaplin

and

biographical sketches of the people
professionally associated with Chaplin

an index to the films of Charles Chaplin

When this index was published in 1945 as a supplement to *Sight and Sound,* the magazine issued by the British Film Institute, it was the first time that the Chaplin films had been completely and accurately listed, exact information on the Keystones, in particular, being nonexistent. As no cast lists were printed on the Chaplin films or in newspapers until "The Kid" (1921), all the early ones are by the author, with names and relationships noted when possible.

Keystone Films (1914)

MAKING A LIVING

Released by Keystone, February 2, 1914. (1 reel)

Directed by Henry Lehrman. With Henry Lehrman, Virginia Kirtely (girl), Alice Davenport (mother), Minta Durfee, Chester Conklin (cop and bum). Reputedly photographed by E. J. Vallejo. Most other Chaplin-Keystones were photographed by Frank D. Williams. (Reissued as *A Busted Johnny, Troubles,* and *Doing His Best.*)

See p. 30, 37, 39

KID AUTO RACES AT VENICE

Released by Keystone, February 7, 1914. On the same reel with

a factual film: Olives and Their Oil.

Directed by Henry Lehrman. With Henry Lehrman.

See p. 30.

MABEL'S STRANGE PREDICAMENT

Released by Keystone, February 9, 1914. (1 reel)

Directed by Henry Lehrman and Mack Sennett. With Mabel Normand, Harry McCoy, Alice Davenport, Hank Mann, Chester Conklin, Al St. John. (Also known as *Hotel Mix-up.*)

See p. 31

BETWEEN SHOWERS

Released by Keystone, February 28, 1914. (1 reel)

Directed by Henry Lehrman. With Ford Sterling, Chester Conklin (cop), Emma Clifton. (Also known as *The Flirts, Charlie and the Umbrella,* and *In Wrong.*)

Comic byplay prevails as Charlie and Ford compete to help a buxom girl over a large puddle caused by a shower. Also a misunderstanding all around as to the ownership of an umbrella.

A FILM JOHNNIE

Released by Keystone, March 2, 1914. (1 reel)

Supervised by Mack Sennett. With Virginia Kirtley, Fatty Arbuckle, Minta Durfee, other Keystoners. (Also known as *Movie Nut* and *Million Dollar Job.*)

Charlie follows the actors going into the Keystone studio. Inside he ruins several scenes, finally spoiling a thrilling rescue staged at a real fire. Outstanding scene: Charlie, after having the fire hose directed on him, twists his ear and a stream of water spurts out of his mouth.

TANGO TANGLES

Released by Keystone, March 9, 1914. (1 reel)

Supervised by Mack Sennett. With Ford Sterling, Fatty Arbuckle, Chester Conklin. (Also known as *Charlie's Recreation* and *Music Hall.*)

An impromptu picture, taken in a real ballroom and featuring the dance rage of 1914. Chaplin and Sterling both appear without their make-up. The men compete for the hat-check girl with much chasing, sliding and falling among the dancers.

HIS FAVORITE PASTIME

Released by Keystone, March 16, 1914. (1 reel)

Directed by George Nichols. With Peggy Pearce, Fatty Arbuckle. (Also known as *The Bonehead.*)

Charlie's favorite pastime is drinking highballs and annoying people in the saloon. He follows a girl home. The husband returns and a wild melee ensues.

CRUEL, CRUEL LOVE

Released by Keystone, March 26, 1914. (1 reel)

Supervised by Mack Sennett. (Also known as *Lord Helpus.*)

Disappointed in love, Charlie (here portraying a man of wealth with walrus mustache and make-up similar to *Making a Living*) tries to end it all, but his butler changes the poison. He then tries several other comic means to depart this cruel world, but is unsuccessful in all his attempts.

THE STAR BOARDER

Released by Keystone, April 4, 1914. (1 reel)

Supervised by Mack Sennett. With Edgar Kennedy, Alice Davenport,

Gordon Griffith (as the kid). (Also known as *The Hash-House Hero*.) Charlie, as the favorite of the lady who runs a boarding house, arouses her husband's jealousy. At an outing, their small boy takes compromising pictures of all concerned, causing general havoc when they are displayed at a magic-lantern show. Outstanding scene: Charlie and the landlady playing tennis.

MABEL AT THE WHEEL

Released by Keystone, April 18, 1914. (2 reels)

Directed by Mack Sennett and Mabel Normand. With Mabel Normand, Chester Conklin (father), Harry McCoy (boy friend), Mack Sennett (as a rube). (Also known as *His Daredevil Queen* and *Hot Finish*.)

Chaplin wears a long frock coat, high hat, and sports two tufts of hair on his chin in addition to his regular mustache. With his motorcycle he competes with Harry's snappy racing car for Mabel's favor. Charlie having tied up his rival at a race, Mabel is forced to drive the auto. Outstanding scenes: Mabel falling off the rear of Charlie's motor cycle; Charlie waters the track, causing Mabel's car to go in the wrong direction.

TWENTY MINUTES OF LOVE

Released by Keystone, April 20, 1914. (1 reel)

Supervised by Mack Sennett. With Edgar Kennedy, Minta Durfee, Chester Conklin. (Also known as *He Loved Her So, Cops and Watches,* and *Love-Friend*.)

Chester steals a watch for his girl friend from a man sleeping on a bench. Charlie, in turn, borrows it and gives it to the girl first. A brawl starts, with the cop and everyone landing in the lake.

CAUGHT IN A CABARET

Released by Keystone, April 27, 1914. (2 reels)

Directed by Mabel Normand and Charles Chaplin. With Mabel Normand (society girl), Harry McCoy (her boy friend), Alice Davenport (her mother), Chester Conklin (a waiter), Mack Swain (a tough), Minta Durfee (dancer), Phyllis Allen, Gordon Griffith, Edgar Kennedy, Hank Mann, Alice Howell. (Also known as *The Waiter, Jazz Waiter,* and *Faking with Society*.)

See p. 32, 36, 38

CAUGHT IN THE RAIN

Released by Keystone, May 4, 1914. (1 reel)

Written and directed by Charles Chaplin. (The first film which he directed by himself. From now on he was to write and direct virtually all his Keystone pictures.) With Alice Davenport, Mack Swain. (Also known as *At It Again, Who Got Stung,* and *In the Park*.)

Following a married lady from the park into her hotel bedroom, Charlie is thrown out by the big husband. Later the wife comes sleepwalking into his room. Caught leading her back, he is thrown out of the window into the rain.

A BUSY DAY

Released by Keystone, May 7, 1914. (A split reel)

Written and directed by Charles Chaplin. With Mack Swain. (Also known as *Militant Suffragette.*)

Chaplin impersonates a woman for the first of three occasions on the screen. Still retaining his large shoes, he plays a roughneck wife who, neglected on an outing, catches her husband flirting with a pretty girl and upbraids them both violently. (Released on the same reel with a factual film, *The Morning Papers.*)

THE FATAL MALLET

Released by Keystone, June 1, 1914. (1 reel)

Probably directed by Chaplin and Sennett. With Mabel Normand, Mack Sennett, Mack Swain. (Also known as *The Pile Driver.*)

By a river Charlie and two others are rivals for the favor of the haughty Mabel. A roughhouse ensues involving people being hit over the head with bricks and mallets. Outstanding scene: Mabel being bored with the whole proceedings until she receives a swift kick from Charlie.

HER FRIEND THE BANDIT

Released by Keystone, June 4, 1914. (1 reel)

Directed by Charles Chaplin and Mabel Normand. With Mabel

Normand, Charles Murray. (Also known as *Mabel's Flirtation.*)

Charlie, a bandit, takes the Count de Bean's place at a fancy party in Mabel's house. Not knowing how to behave in society, he makes many crude blunders and causes great consternation to Mabel and the others. (Prototype of *The Count, The Adventurer*, etc.)

THE KNOCKOUT

Released by Keystone, June 11, 1914. (2 reels)

Supervised by Mack Sennett. With Fatty Arbuckle, Minta Durfee, Al St. John, Edgar Kennedy, Mack Swain, Hank Mann, Alice Howell, Slim Summerville, Charley Chase, Mack Sennett, the Keystone Cops. (Also known as *Counted Out* and *The Pugilist.*)

Actually this is an Arbuckle film with Chaplin appearing briefly for about three minutes as an officious referee at a boxing match between Arbuckle and Kennedy. Charlie gets hit in the interchange of blows, falls, becomes caught in the ropes, etc. Otherwise the picture is a typical Keystone with plenty of slapstick, the Keystone cops, and a wild chase. Outstanding scene: the recumbent Chaplin pulling himself along the slippery floor by the rope and counting "stars."

MABEL'S BUSY DAY

Released by Keystone, June 13, 1914. (1 reel)

Directed by Mabel Normand and Charles Chaplin. With Mabel Nor-

mand, Chester Conklin, Harry Mc-
Coy, Slim Summerville. (Also
known as *Charlie and the Sausages, Love and Lunch,* and *Hot
Dogs.*)

Mabel peddles hot dogs at the auto
racetrack. Charlie, after a visit to
a saloon, butts in, swipes the sausages one by one, and eventually
bankrupts Mabel.

MABEL'S MARRIED LIFE

*Released by Keystone, June 20,
1914. (1 reel)*

Directed by Charles Chaplin and
Mabel Normand. With Mabel Nor-
mand, Mack Swain, Charles Mur-
ray, Hank Mann, Harry McCoy,
Alice Davenport, Alice Howell,
Wallace MacDonald. (Also known
as *When You're Married* and *The
Squarehead.*)

Disappointed by Charlie because
he doesn't rescue her from a large
Lothario, Mabel buys a boxing
dummy hoping to make a man of
her husband. Coming home drunk,
Charlie orders the "man" out, but
the bouncing dummy overwhelms
him. Outstanding scene: Mabel
Normand's contemptuous mimicry
of Chaplin and her experimental
bout with the dummy.

LAUGHING GAS

*Released by Keystone, July 9, 1914.
(1 reel)*

Written and directed by Charles
Chaplin. With Fritz Schade (den-
tist), Alice Howell (wife), Slim
Summerville, Mack Swain, Joseph
Swickard.

(Also known as *Tuning His Ivories, The Dentist,* and *Down and
Out.*)

Charlie, as a dentist's assistant, becomes involved with people in the
office, flirts with the dentist's wife,
uses enormous pliers on a patient,
etc. It ends in a free-for-all. Outstanding scene: Charlie enters the
office, looks patients over, slowly
removes gloves, rubs his hands,
then picks up the cuspidors to go
to work as a menial assistant.
(Prototype of his *Surprise Twists.*)

THE PROPERTY MAN

*Released by Keystone, August 1,
1914. (2 reels)*

Written and directed by Charles
Chaplin. With Fritz Schade, Phyllis Allen, Mack Sennett (in theatre audience). (Also known as
Getting His Goat and *The Roustabout.*)

See p. 37, 38, 39, 75

THE FACE ON THE BAR-ROOM FLOOR

*Released by Keystone, August 10,
1914. (1 reel)*

Directed by Charles Chaplin. With
Fritz Schade, Cecile Arnold, Ches-
ter Conklin. (Also known as *The
Ham Artist.*)

A burlesque of the famous poem
by Hugh Antoine D'Arcy of the
broken-down artist who, having
lost his wife to another man, draws
her face on the floor. Charlie, at
a bar, tells his "tragic" story in
flashbacks. The sight of his former love and the other man with

half a dozen kids assuages his disappointment somewhat.

RECREATION

Released by Keystone, August 13, 1914. (A split reel)

Written and directed by Charles Chaplin. (Also known as *Spring Fever*.)

An improvised little affair in a park: Charlie waddling and skidding about, flirting, kicking, throwing bricks, and ending with everyone landing in the lake. (On the same reel with a scenic, *The Yosemite*.)

THE MASQUERADER

Released by Keystone, August 27, 1914. (1 reel)

Written and directed by Charles Chaplin. With Fatty Arbuckle, Charles Murray, Fritz Schade, Charley Chase, Harry McCoy, Minta Durfee, Cecile Arnold. (Also known as *Putting One Over, The Female Impersonator, The Picnic*, and erroneously as *His New Profession*, the title of another Keystone.)

Charlie is an actor in a movie studio. The first scene shows him without make-up. Then in his familiar garb, flirting with the girls, he misses his cue and ruins the scene. Fired, he returns disguised as a woman. Winning all with his coy charm, he is hired. The ruse discovered, he is chased down a well. Outstanding scene: Charlie as the woman picking up a cigarette and blowing the smoke in the other direction when the director enters.

HIS NEW PROFESSION

Released by Keystone, August 31, 1914. (1 reel)

Written and directed by Charles Chaplin. With Charley Chase. (Also known as *The Good-for-Nothing* and *Helping Himself*.)

A young man offers the impoverished Charlie a dollar to wheel his crippled uncle around while he sees a girl friend. After Charlie is refused money in advance for refreshment, the uncle with his gouty foot almost goes off the pier. But the girl and the angry nephew cause Charlie's downfall.

THE ROUNDERS

Released by Keystone, September 7, 1914. (1 reel)

Written and directed by Charles Chaplin. With Fatty Arbuckle, Minta Durfee (his wife), Phyllis Allen (as Charlie's wife), Al St. John, Charley Chase, Fritz Schade, Wallace MacDonald. (Also known as *Revelry, Two of a Kind*, and *Oh, What a Night*.)

See p. 36, 37, 39, 40, 48, 288

THE NEW JANITOR

Released by Keystone, September 24, 1914. (1 reel)

Written and directed by Charles Chaplin. With Al St. John, Jack Dillon (?) (Also known as *The New Porter* and *The Blundering Boob*.)

Charlie, a blundering janitor in an office building, drops a pail of water on the boss below in the street. Fired, he answers the stenographer's ring in time to capture a clerk who is robbing the safe. The boss rewards him with a roll of money which Charlie counts to one side before thanking him.

THOSE LOVE PANGS

Released by Keystone, October 10, 1914. (1 reel)

Written and directed by Charles Chaplin. With Chester Conklin, Cecile Arnold, two unknown girls. (Also known as *The Rival Mashers* and *Busted Hearts*.)

Charlie and Chester are rivals for the favor of their landlady and some girls in the park, the unresponsive Chester usually winning while Charlie "swoons" from unrequited love. It ends with a roughhouse in a movie theatre.

DOUGH AND DYNAMITE

Released by Keystone, October 26, 1914. (2 reels)

Written and directed by Charles Chaplin. With Chester Conklin, Fritz Schade, Phyllis Allen, Charley Chase, Slim Summerville, Wallace MacDonald, Vivian Edwards, Norma Nichols, Cecile Arnold. (Also known as *The Doughnut Designer* and *The Cook*. Reissued in 1923 with new, rather tasteless titles by Sid Chaplin.)

Typical Keystone slapstick, beginning a new series of longer and more elaborate Chaplin comedies.

Charlie works in a combination bakery and restaurant. There are gooey fights between him and Chester. The picture ends in an explosion when strikers place dynamite in a loaf of bread.

GENTLEMEN OF NERVE

Released by Keystone, October 29, 1914. (1 reel)

Written and directed by Charles Chaplin. With Chaplin (as Mr. Wow-Wow), Mabel Normand (Mabel), Chester Conklin (Walrus), Mack Swain (Ambrose), Phyllis Allen, Charley Chase, Slim Summerville. (Also known as *Some Nerve*.)

Chester takes Mabel to the auto races. Charlie and Mack, without sufficient funds, sneak in through a hole in the fence, the latter getting stuck. After Mabel quarrels with Chester, she sits by Charlie. The suspicious policeman arrests Chester and Mack, leads them out as Charlie and Mabel laugh. Outstanding scene: Charlie sipping soda through a straw in the bottle a girl is holding, casually looking up at the sky and drumming his fingers whenever she turns around.

HIS MUSICAL CAREER

Released by Keystone, November 7, 1914. (1 reel)

Written and directed by Charles Chaplin. With Mack Swain, Alice Howell. (Also known as *The Piano Movers* and *Musical Tramps*.)

Charlie and Mack are piano movers. Told to deliver a piano to

Mr. Rich at 666 Prospect Street and bring back one from 999 Prospect Street, they get the signals mixed, dragging the piano upstairs to the 999 address and proceeding to remove the one at the other place until Miss Rich and her father protest. So the pair shove the piano down the street into a lake. Outstanding scene: Charlie's difficulty in straightening up after carrying the piano on his back.

HIS TRYSTING PLACE

Released by Keystone, November 9, 1914. (2 reels)

Written and directed by Charles Chaplin. With Mabel Normand, Mack Swain, Phyllis Allen. (Also known as *Family House*.)

Careless with the baby, Charlie is scolded by Mabel. In a restaurant he gets his coat mixed with Mack's. Mabel finds a note in it from a girl, chases Charlie out. Later she finds him in the park sobbing his marital woes to Mack's wife who finds a bottle in her husband's coat. There is quite a mix-up until all is explained. Outstanding scenes: Charlie carrying the baby by the scruff of its rompers; Mabel breaking an ironing board on Charlie's head and pushing him into an ash can.

TILLIE'S PUNCTURED ROMANCE

Released by Keystone, November 14, 1914. (6 reels)

Directed by Mack Sennett. Scenario by Hampton Del Ruth, based on the musical comedy "Tillie's Nightmare" by Edgar Smith (in which Marie Dressler starred on the stage). Cast: Marie Dressler (Tillie the country maid), Charlie Chaplin (the city slicker), Mabel Normand (Charlie's partner), Mack Swain (Tillie's father), Charles Bennett (Tillie's rich uncle), and in smaller parts: Chester Conklin, Edgar Kennedy, Charley Chase, Charles Murray, Minta Durfee, Gordon Griffith, Phyllis Allen, Alice Davenport, Harry McCoy, Alice Howell, Wallace MacDonald, the Keystone Cops (who include Slim Summerville, Hank Mann, Al St. John.)

See p. 6, 40, 41, 44, 124

GETTING ACQUAINTED

Released by Keystone, December 5, 1914. (1 reel)

Written and directed by Charles Chaplin. With Chaplin (as Mr. Sniffles), Phyllis Allen (Mrs. Sniffles), Mabel Normand, Mack Swain, Edgar Kennedy (cop), Harry McCoy, Cecile Arnold. (Also known as *A Fair Exchange*.)

Charlie taking the air with buxom wife (Phyllis Allen), Mabel, and her husband Mack, the policeman, and a Turk, ride a veritable merry-go-round until Charlie is yanked away by his spouse. Outstanding scene: Mabel's comic annoyance at Charlie's flirtation, changing to smiles and winks when the cop on the hunt for mashers comes up behind him.

HIS PREHISTORIC PAST

Released by Keystone, December 7, 1914. (2 reels) Written and directed by Charles Chaplin. With Chaplin (as Weak-chin), Mack Swain (King Lowbrow), Gene Marsh (watermaiden), and Fritz Schade (Cleo). Also known as *A Dream*.)

See p. 38

Essanay Films (1915)

HIS NEW JOB

Released by Essanay, February 1, 1915. (2 reels) Written and directed by Charles Chaplin. Photographed by Rollie Totheroh. With Ben Turpin, Charlotte Mineau (actress), Leo White (actor and receptionist), Gloria Swanson and Agnes Ayers (extras).

See p. 48, 55

A NIGHT OUT

Released by Essanay, February 15, 1915. (2 reels) Written and directed by Charles Chaplin. Photographed by Rollie Totheroh. With Ben Turpin, Leo White (Frenchman), Bud Jamison (head waiter), Edna Purviance (wife of the waiter).

See p. 48, 50, 52

THE CHAMPION

Released by Essanay, March 11, 1915. (2 reels) Written and directed by Charles Chaplin. Photographed by Rollie Totheroh. With Bud Jamison, Edna Purviance, Leo White, Ben Turpin, Lloyd Bacon, "Broncho Billy" Anderson (playing an extra in the stands). (Also known as *Champion Charlie*.)

See p. 47, 48, 51

Outstanding scenes: the dog refusing to eat a frankfurter until Charlie puts salt on it; Charlie showing off to Edna while training; imitating the villainous Leo's pose, Charlie scratches the wrong head; the mock farewell to his dog before the championship bout.

IN THE PARK

Released by Essanay, March 18, 1915. (1 reel) Written and directed by Charles Chaplin. Photographed by Rollie Totheroh. With Edna Purviance, Leo White (lover), Lloyd Bacon (tramp), Bud Jamison.

Pushed off the bench by a spooning couple, Charlie next falls into a baby carriage. In a brickfight with two tramps, the girl and her sweetheart are hit. Her pocketbook stolen by a tramp, the girl accuses the lover who lacks the courage to commit suicide until Charlie pushes him into the water. A policeman comes and in the fracas that follows Charlie hurls all into the lake. Outstanding scene: as a tramp picks his pocket of sausages, Charlie extracts with his cane the stolen pocketbook.

THE JITNEY ELOPEMENT

Released by Essanay, April 1, 1915. (2 reels)

Written and directed by Charles Chaplin. Photographed by Rollie Totheroh. With Edna Purviance, Leo White (the count), Lloyd Bacon.

Edna, a wealthy heiress, drops a note begging to be saved from the Count de Ha Ha to whom her father has betrothed her. Charlie, finding it, impersonates the count and receives a royal welcome until the real count appears. The couple escape and flee in a jitney (an old model T Ford). After a wild chase over rough roads and through mud puddles, Charlie backs his car suddenly and the pursuer's auto is pushed off a pier into the water. Then the couple race for a parson. Outstanding scenes: Charlie's table antics; Charlie drops a nickel in the "slot" to start the flivver.

THE TRAMP

Released by Essanay, April 11, 1915. (2 reels)

Written and directed by Charles Chaplin. Photographed by Rollie Totheroh. With Edna Purviance (farmer's daughter), Bud Jamison (tramp), Leo White (tramp), Paddy McGuire (farm hand), Lloyd Bacon (lover), Billy Armstrong (poet?).

See p. 47, 49, 50, 95

BY THE SEA

Released by Essanay, April 29, 1915. (1 reel)

Written and directed by Charles Chaplin. Photographed by Rollie Totheroh. With Edna Purviance, Billy Armstrong, Bud Jamison.

A short film evidently improvised at the seashore—a minor Essanay not without a certain impromptu charm. On a windy day by the sea, the string attached to Charlie's hat becomes tangled with belligerent Billy's resulting in a comic tussle by the two. Then Charlie tries to flirt with Edna, the wife of the giant Bud, and with another girl who turns out to be Billy's. As both couples threaten Charlie, the bench, holding all five, collapses. Outstanding scenes: Charlie tosses a banana skin in the air, bats at it with the wrong foot, slips on the skin; he amuses Edna by moving his hat with the concealed string.

WORK

Released by Essanay, June 21, 1915. (2 reels)

Written and directed by Charles Chaplin. Photographed by Rollie Totheroh. With Charles Insley (boss), Edna Purviance (maid), Billy Armstrong (husband), Marta Golden (wife), Leo White (secret lover), Paddy McGuire. (Recently revived as *The Paperhanger*.)

Charlie, as a paperhanger's assistant, pulls a heavy wagon loaded with paraphernalia through traffic and up hill. In a hectic household he spills a pail of paste on his boss's head, does a thoroughly messy job. When the wife's lover arrives there is a mad chase, in the midst of which the stove explodes. In the final close-up, Charlie emerges from the stove, smiles, is hit by plaster, and closes the stove again. Outstanding scenes: as he delicately manicures his nails with a trowel, Charlie pantomimes the "sad story" of his life to Edna; putting a lamp shade on a small statue, he makes it dance the hootchy-kootchy.

A WOMAN

Released by Essanay, July 12, 1915. (2 reels)

Written and directed by Charles Chaplin. Photographed by Rollie Totheroh. With Edna Purviance, Charles Insley (father), Marta Golden (mother), Margie Reiger (flirt), Billy Armstrong (suitor), Leo White. (Also known as *The Perfect Lady* and *Charlie the Perfect Lady*.)

Taken home by Edna and her mother, Charlie is thrown out by the father with whom he previously had been embroiled. Returning, he puts on some of Edna's clothes, shaves off his mustache. Coming downstairs with a mincing walk, the father and the suitor compete for the favor of the coy "woman"—until Charlie's slipping skirt exposes him and he is kicked out again. Outstanding scenes: Stuck to the mother's large feathered hat, Charlie resembles a large chicken until the pin is pulled out; Charlie coyly undressing a clothes dummy; dressed as a woman, he

keeps losing the upper part of his "figure."

THE BANK

Released by Essanay, August 9, 1915. (2 reels)

Written and directed by Charles Chaplin. Photographed by Rollie Totheroh. With Edna Purviance (stenographer), Carl Stockdale (the cashier), Billy Armstrong (other janitor), John Rand (bond salesman), Charles Insley (bank president), Leo White (officer), Fred Goodwins. (Also known as *Charlie at the Bank.*)

See p. 49, 52, 56, 57

SHANGHAIED

Released by Essanay, October 4, 1915. (2 reels)

Written and directed by Charles Chaplin. Photographed by Rollie Totheroh. With Edna Purviance, Wesley Ruggles (father), John Rand (ship's mate), Billy Armstrong, Paddy McGuire, and Leo White (as shanghaied men), Fred Goodwins.

Charlie is offered three dollars to help shanghai three men. He in turn is hit over the head and tossed on the ship. As assistant to the cook, he has great difficulty serving meals on the rocking ship. Edna, the shipowner's daughter, is a stowaway. Overhearing a plot to destroy the boat for the insurance, Charlie tosses the dynamite overboard just in time. Outstanding scenes: Charlie below deck juggles a ham bone while dancing the hornpipe; although falling and turning somersaults, he keeps a tray of dishes upright on the violently rocking boat.

A NIGHT IN THE SHOW

Released by Essanay, November 20, 1915. (2 reels)

Written and directed by Charles Chaplin. Photographed by Rollie Totheroh. With Chaplin in a dual role: as Mr. Pest, a gentleman in evening clothes, and as Mr. Rowdy, a bum; Edna Purviance (lady in orchestra), Dee Lampton (the fat boy), Leo White (Frenchman and Negro in balcony), May White (dancer), Bud Jamison (singer), James T. Kelly, John Rand, Paddy McGuire. (Also known as *Charlie at the Show.*)

Mr. Pest causes as much disturbance in the orchestra as Mr. Rowdy in the balcony. The former changes his seat several times and annoys the musicians. Then he proceeds to interfere with the performers on the stage. Rowdy throws icecream cones from the balcony and Mr. Pest, borrowing a fat boy's pie, squelches some sour singers. Alarmed at the Fire Eater, Rowdy turns the fire hose on the stage, also drenching the audience. Outstanding scenes: Seated next to a homely woman, Mr. Pest quickly changes his seat, turns and applauds the woman as part of the show; flirting with a girl, he accidentally takes her husband's hand; he scratches a match on an oriental dancer's bare feet; the last close-up of Charlie with a broken umbrella over his head.

CARMEN (Charlie Chaplin's Burlesque on Carmen)

Released by Essanay, April 22, 1916. (4 reels)

Written and directed by Charles Chaplin. Photographed by Rollie Totheroh. With Chaplin (as "Darn Hosiery"), Edna Purviance (Carmen), Ben Turpin (Renendados), Jack Henderson (Lilas Pastia), Leo White (Civil Guard), John Rand (Escamillo), May White (Frascita), Bud Jamison (a soldier), Wesley Ruggles (a tramp).

See p. 49, 50, 51, 52, 53, 54, 61

POLICE

Released by Essanay, March 27, 1916. (2 reels)

Written and directed by Charles Chaplin. Photographed by Rollie Totheroh. With Edna Purviance, Wesley Ruggles (the crook), James T. Kelley (the drunk and a bum), John Rand (the policeman), Leo White (as fruit vendor, flop house owner, and a policeman), Billy Armstrong, Bud Jamison, Fred Goodwins.

See p. 50, 52, 54

TRIPLE TROUBLE

Released by Essanay, August 11, 1918. (2 reels)

Written and directed in part only by Charles Chaplin. With Chaplin as "the new janitor," Edna Purviance (servant girl), Leo White (German diplomat), Billy Armstrong (cook and miser), James

T. Kelley (singer), Bud Jamison (bum), Wesley Ruggles (crook).

See p. 54

THE ESSANAY-CHAPLIN RE-VUE OF 1916

Released by Essanay, September 23, 1916.

A 5-reel mosaic made up mostly of *The Tramp, His New Job,* and *A Night Out.*

CHASE ME CHARLIE

Released by George Kleine (in England), May, 1918.

A 7-reel mosaic by Langford Reed, similarly constructed from several Essanays.

Mutual Films (1916-17)

THE FLOORWALKER

Released by Mutual, May 15, 1916. (2 reels, 1734 feet)

Written and directed by Charles Chaplin. Photographed by William C. Foster and Rollie Totheroh. With Edna Purviance (secretary), Eric Campbell (manager), Lloyd Bacon (the floorwalker), Albert Austin (a clerk), Charlotte Mineau (detective), Leo White (customer).

See p. 60, 67, 68, 115, 159

THE FIREMAN

Released by Mutual, June 12, 1916. (2 reels, 1921 feet)

Written and directed by Charles Chaplin. Photographed by William C. Foster and Rollie Totheroh. With Edna Purviance, Eric Campbell (chief), Lloyd Bacon (Edna's father), Leo White (owner of house), John Rand, Frank J. Coleman, and James T. Kelley (firemen).

See p. 68, 116

THE VAGABOND

Released by Mutual, July 10, 1916. (2 reels, 1956 feet)

Written and directed by Charles Chaplin. Photographed by William C. Foster and Rollie Totheroh. With Edna Purviance (the gypsy drudge), Eric Campbell (chief), Leo White (old Jew and gypsy hag), Lloyd Bacon (artist), Charlotte Mineau (mother), and John Rand, Albert Austin, Frank J. Coleman, and James T. Kelley (band players).

See p. 60, 70, 95, 126

ONE A.M.

Released by Mutual, August 7, 1916. (2 reels)

Written and directed by Charles Chaplin. Photographed by William C. Foster and Rollie Totheroh. With Chaplin in a solo performance.

See p. 17, 71

THE COUNT

Released by Mutual, September 4, 1916. (2 reels)

Written and directed by Charles Chaplin. Photographed by Rollie Totheroh. With Edna Purviance (heiress), Eric Campbell (tailor), James T. Kelley (butler), Leo White (count), Albert Austin (guest), Charlotte Mineau (mother), Frank J. Coleman (policeman).

See p. 60, 72, 116, 156

THE PAWNSHOP

Released by Mutual, October 2, 1916. (2 reels, 1940 feet)

Written and directed by Charles Chaplin. Photographed by Rollie Totheroh. With Edna Purviance (daughter), John Rand (clerk), Henry Bergman (owner), Albert Austin (customer), Eric Campbell (thief), James T. Kelley.

See p. 50, 73, 75, 225

BEHIND THE SCREEN

Released by Mutual, November 13, 1916. (2 reels, 1796 feet)

Written and directed by Charles Chaplin. Photographed by Rollie Totheroh. With Chaplin (as David, a stagehand), Eric Campbell (as Goliath, his boss), Edna Purviance, Frank J. Coleman (assistant director), Albert Austin (a stagehand), Henry Bergman (dramatic director), Lloyd Bacon (comedy director), Charlotte Mineau (actress).

See p. 289

THE RINK

Released by Mutual, December 4, 1916. (2 reels, 1881 feet)

Written and directed by Charles Chaplin. Photographed by Rollie Totheroh. With Edna Purviance, James T. Kelley, (her father), Eric Campbell (Mr. Stout), Henry Bergman (Mrs. Stout), Albert Austin (cook), Charlotte Mineau (Edna's friend), John Rand (waiter).

See p. 33, 76

EASY STREET

Released by Mutual, January 22, 1917. (2 reels, 1757 feet)

Written and directed by Charles Chaplin. Photographed by Rollie Totheroh. With Edna Purviance (mission worker), Albert Austin (minister and policeman), Eric Campbell (the bully), James T. Kelley (missionary and policeman), Henry Bergman (tough), John Rand (bum and policeman), Charlotte Mineau (a mother), Frank J. Coleman.

See p. 60, 61, 63, 77

THE CURE

Released by Mutual, April 16, 1917. (2 reels, 1834 feet)

Written and directed by Charles Chaplin. Photographed by Rollie Totheroh. With Edna Purviance, Eric Campbell (man with gout), John Rand (attendant), Albert Austin (tall attendant), Frank J. Coleman (head of institution),

James T. Kelley (bearded bell-hop), Henry Bergman (masseur).

See p. 60, 79

THE IMMIGRANT

Released by Mutual, June 17, 1917. (2 reels, 1809 feet)

Written and directed by Charles Chaplin. Photographed by Rollie Totheroh. With Edna Purviance (an immigrant), Albert Austin (Russian immigrant and a diner), Henry Bergman (fat woman on boat and the artist), Stanley Sanford (gambler-thief), Eric Campbell (headwaiter), James T. Kelley (the old tramp), John Rand (a customer), Frank J. Coleman (owner of the restaurant).

See p. 59, 80, 95, 123, 157, 159

THE ADVENTURER

Released by Mutual, October 23, 1917. (2 reels, 1845 feet)

Written and directed by Charles Chaplin. Photographed by Rollie Totheroh. With Edna Purviance, Eric Campbell (suitor), Henry Bergman (father and a laborer), Albert Austin (butler), Frank J. Coleman (guard), Kono (Chaplin's Japanese chauffeur).

See p. 59, 80, 95, 123, 157, 159

First National Films (1918-1922)

A DOG'S LIFE

Released by First National, April 14, 1918. (3 reels, 2674 feet)

Written and directed by Charles Chaplin. Assistant director, Chuck Riesner. Photographed by Rollie Totheroh. With Edna Purviance (the singer), Tom Wilson (the cop), Sidney Chaplin (owner of food wagon), Albert Austin (crook), Henry Bergman (a bum and the fat lady), Chuck Riesner (clerk and drummer), Billy White (Cafe owner), James T. Kelley (a bum).

See p. 86, 95-101, 102, 158, 189

THE BOND

Made for the Liberty Loan Committee and distributed without charge in the fall of 1918. (Half reel)

Written and directed by Charles Chaplin. Photographed by Rollie Totheroh. With Edna Purviance, Albert Austin.

See p. 87

SHOULDER ARMS

Released by First National, October 20, 1918. (3 reels, 3142 feet)

Written and directed by Charles Chaplin. Photographed by Rollie Totheroh. With Edna Purviance (the French girl), Sidney Chaplin (the American sergeant and also the Kaiser), Henry Bergman (German officer and American bartender), Albert Austin (American officer and a German soldier), Tom Wilson (sergeant in camp), Jack Wilson (Crown Prince).

See p. 55, 86, 188, 101-109, 126, 140, 155, 163, 187, 225

SUNNYSIDE

Released by First National, June 15, 1919. (3 reels, 2769 feet)

Written and directed by Charles Chaplin. Photographed by Rollie Totheroh. With Edna Purviance (the village belle), Tom Wilson (the hardhearted employer), Albert Austin? (the city slicker), Henry Bergman, Loyal Underwood, Park Jones.

See p. 33, 86, 109, 110-113, 155

A DAY'S PLEASURE

Released by First National, December 7, 1919. (2 reels, 1714 feet)

Written and directed by Charles Chaplin. Photographed by Rollie Totheroh. With Edna Purviance (the mother), Tom Wilson, Henry Bergman, Babe London (the fat girl), Jackie Coogan (as an extra).

See p. 109, 113-115, 155, 159

THE KID

Released by First National, February 6, 1921. (6 reels, 5300 feet)

Written and directed by Charles Chaplin. Associate director, Chuck Riesner. Photographed by Rollie Totheroh. With Jackie Coogan (the Kid), Edna Purviance (the woman), Carl Miller (the man), Tom Wilson (the policeman), Chuck Riesner (the bully). Also

unbilled: Albert Austin (a crook), Nellie Bly Baker (slum woman), Henry Bergman (proprietor of lodging house), Lita Grey (the flirting angel).

See p. 6, 12, 55, 70, 92, 110-116, 124-134, 135, 142, 145, 150, 152, 155, 156, 163, 189, 199, 237

THE IDLE CLASS

Released by First National, September 25, 1921. (2 reels, 1916 feet)

Written and directed by Charles Chaplin. Photographed by Rollie Totheroh. With Edna Purviance (wife), Mack Swain (the angry father), Allan Garcia, Loyal Underwood, Henry Bergman, Rex Story, John Rand, Lita Grey and mother (maids).

See p. 135, 155-158, 161, 191

PAY DAY

Released by First National, April 2, 1922. (2 reels, 1892 feet)

Written and directed by Charles Chaplin. Photographed by Rollie Totheroh. With Phyllis Allen (the wife), Mack Swain (the foreman), Edna Purviance (his daughter), Sidney Chaplin (friend and owner of food stand), Henry Bergman, Allan Garcia.

See p. 152, 158-161

THE PILGRIM

Released by First National, February 25, 1923. (4 reels, about 4000 feet)

Written and directed by Charles Chaplin. Associate director, Chuck

Riesner. Photographed by Rollie Totheroh. With Edna Purviance (the girl), Kitty Bradbury (the mother), Mack Swain (the deacon), Loyal Underwood (the Elder), Dinky Dean [Dean Reisner] (the boy), May Wells (his mother), Sidney Chaplin (her husband), Chuck Riesner (the crook), Tom Murray (sheriff). Also unbilled: Monta Bell (policeman), Henry Bergman, Raymond Lee, Edith Bostwick, Florence Latimer.

See p. *150, 162, 167, 226*

United Artists Films (1923-1947)

A WOMAN OF PARIS

Released by United Artists. Opened October 1, 1923 at the Lyric Theatre, New York. (8 reels, 7577 feet)

Written and directed by Charles Chaplin. Assistant director, Eddie Sutherland. Editorial direction, Monta Bell. Art director, Arthur Stibolt. Research, H. d'Abbadie d'Arrast and Jean de Limur. Photography by Rollie Totheroh and Jack Wilson, With Edna Purviance (Marie St. Clair), Adolphe Menjou (Pierre Revel), Carl Miller (Jean Millet), Lydia Knott (his mother), Charles French (his father), Clarence Geldert (her father), Betty Morrissey (Fifi), Malvina Polo (Paulette). Also unbilled: Henry Bergman (maitre d'hotel) Harry Northrup (valet), Nellie Bly Baker (masseuse), Charles Chaplin (station porter).

See p. *56, 117, 123, 152, 168-186, 257*

THE GOLD RUSH

Released by United Artists, August 16, 1925. (9 reels, 8498 feet) Opened at the Strand Theatre, New York (First shown at Grauman's Egyptian Theatre, Hollywood, June 26, 1925 in 10 reels 9760 feet). Reissued with sound track April 18, 1942, 72 minutes.

Written and directed by Charles Chaplin. Associate directors, Charles Reisner and H. d'Abbadie d'Arrast. Technical director, Charles D. Hall. Photographed by Rollie Totheroh and Jack Wilson. With Mack Swain (Big Jim McKay), Tom Murray (Black Larsen), Georgia Hale (the girl), Betty Morrissey (her friend), Malcolm Waite (Jack Cameron), Henry Bergman (Hank Curtis).

See p. *50, 55, 95-101, 187, 198, 208, 209, 212, 222, 225, 226, 237, 253, 283, 290*

THE CIRCUS

Released by United Artists, January 7, 1928. Opened at the Strand Theatre, New York. (7 reels, 6700 feet)

Written, directed and produced by Charles Chaplin. Assistant, Harry Crocker. Photography directed by Rollie H. Totheroh. Cameramen, Jack Wilson and Mark Marklatt.

Laboratory Supervision by William E. Hinckley. With Allan Garcia (Circus proprietor and ring master), Merna Kennedy (his stepdaughter, a circus rider), Betty Morrissey (the vanishing lady), Harry Crocker (Rex, tightrope walker), George Davis (magician), Henry Bergman (old clown), Stanley Sanford (chief property man), John Rand (assistant property man), Steve Murphy (pickpocket), Doc Stone (prizefighter).

See p. 70, 202, 203, 204, 205, 208-217, 218

CITY LIGHTS

Released by United Artists, February 6, 1931. Opened at the George M. Cohan Theatre, New York. (9 reels, 87 minutes)

Written, directed and produced by Charles Chaplin. Assistant directors: Harry Crocker, Henry Bergman, Albert Austin. Photography by Rollie Totheroh, Gordon Pollock and Mark Marklatt. Settings by Charles D. Hall. Music composed by Charles Chaplin. Musical arrangement by Arthur Johnston. Musical direction by Alfred Newman. General Manager, Alfred Reeves. With Virginia Cherrill (blind girl), Florence Lee (her grandmother), Harry Meyers (eccentric millionaire), Allan Garcia (his butler), Hank Mann (prizefighter). Also unbilled: Henry Bergman (official and janitor), Albert Austin (streetcleaner and crook), Stanhope Wheatcroft (distinguished extra in cafe), John Rand (old tramp), James Donnelly (foreman), Eddie Baker (ref-

eree), Robert Parrish (newsboy).

See p. 97, 117, 218-234, 235, 237, 239, 240, 244, 253, 254, 255, 308, 309

MODERN TIMES

Released by United Artists, February 5, 1936. Opened at the Rivoli Theatre, New York. (85 minutes)

Written, directed and produced by Charles Chaplin. General manager, Alfred Reeves. Assistant production manager, Jack Wilson. Settings by Charles D. Hall. Music composed by Charles Chaplin. Musical director, Alfred Newman. Assistant directors: Carter De Haven and Henry Bergman. Photographed by Rollie Totheroh and Ira Morgan. With Paulette Goddard (gamin), Henry Bergman (cafe proprietor), Chester Conklin (mechanic), Stanley Sanford, Hank Mann and Louis Natheaux (burglars), Allan Garcia (president of a steel corporation). Also unbilled: Lloyd Ingraham, Wilfred Lucas, Heinie Conklin, Edward Kimball, John Rand.

See.p. 116, 235, 250, 251, 252-261, 291

THE GREAT DICTATOR

Released by United Artists, October 15, 1940. Opened at the Astor and Capitol Theatres, New York. (126 minutes)

Written, directed and produced by Charles Chaplin. Musical direction by Meredith Willson. Assistant directors: Dan James, Wheeler Dryden and Bob Meltzer. General assistant, Henry Bergman. Directors of photography: Karl Struss, A.S.C. and Rollie Totheroh, I.A.T. S.E. Art director, J. Russell Spencer. Film editor, Willard Nico. Sound: Percy Townsend and Glenn Rominger. With Charles Chaplin (dictator of Tomania and a Jewish barber), Paulette Goddard (Hannah), Jack Oakie (Napaloni, dictator of Bacteria), Reginald Gardiner (Schultz), Henry Daniell (Garbitsch), Billy Gilbert (Herring), Grace Hale (Madame Napaloni), Carter De Haven (Bacterian ambassador), Maurice Moscovich (Mr. Jaekel), Emma Dunn (Mrs. Jaekel), Bernard Gorcey (Mr. Mann), Paul Weigel (Mr. Agar). Also unbilled: Chester Conklin (man Chaplin shaves to music), Eddie Gribbon (storm trooper), Hank Mann (his assistant), Leo White (a barber), Lucien Prival (officer). Esther Michelson, Florence Wright, Robert O. Davis, Eddie Dunn, Peter Lynn Hayes, Nita Pike.

See p. 55, 123, 235, 237, 246, 251, 262-279, 280, 284, 293, 298

MONSIEUR VERDOUX

Released by United Artists, April 11, 1947, opening at the Broadway Theatre, New York. (122 minutes)

Written and directed by Charles Chaplin. Based on an idea by Orson Welles. Associate directors, Robert Florey and Wheeler Dryden. Photographed by Curt Courant, Roland Totheroh, and Wallace Chewing. Art direction, John Beckman. Sound, James T. Corrigan. Assistant director, Rex Bailey. Editor, Willard Nico. Music composed by Charles Chaplin; arranged and directed by Rudolph Schrager. With Charles Chaplin as Henri Verdoux, Mady Correll as Mona, wife of M. Verdoux, Allison Roddan as their son, Robert Lewis as Maurice Bottello, Audrey Betz as Mme. Bottello, Martha Raye as Annabella Bonheur, Ada-May as Annette her maid, Isobel Elsom as Marie Grosnay, Marjorie Bennett as her maid, Helen Heigh as Yvonne, Margaret Hoffman as Lydia Floray, Marilyn Nash as The Girl, Irving Bacon as Pierre Couvais, Edwin Mills as Jean Couvais, Virginia Brissac as Carlotta Couvais, Almira Sessions as Lena Couvais, Eula Morgan as Phoebe Couvais, Bernard J. Nedell as prefect of police, Charles Evans as Detective Morrow. *Also unbilled:* William Frawley (police inspector), Arthur Hohl, Fritz Leiber (the priest), John Harmon, Barbara Slater (flower girl), Vera Marshe, Christine Ell, Pierre Watkin, Lois Conklin, Wheeler Dryden (bond salesman), Barry Norton (extra at party), Tom Wilson.

See p. 56, 226, 235, 237, 280, 286, 291, 293-306, 308

biographical sketches of the people professionally associated with Chaplin

The answer to the question of who were the often unbilled people who supported Chaplin through the years.

NOTE: The established players of stage and screen who appeared in "The Great Dictator" and "Monsieur Verdoux" are not included. See a recent edition of *International Motion Picture Almanac* (edited by Terry Ramsaye for Quigley Publications).

ALLEN, PHYLLIS

b. Staten Island. 5'8, 175 lbs. Early career:—vaudeville, musical comedy. Screen 1910, Selig Co., Keystone 1913–1916, Fox, Vitagraph, "Pay Day."

ARBUCKLE, ROSCOE

b. Smith Center, Kansas, 1887. 5'9, 285 lbs. Early career:—vaudeville, musical comedy, toured West with Leon Errol. Brief engagement with Selig Co., 1909. Keystone 1913, replacing Fred Mace. Fatty and Mabel series, etc. Paramount:— "The Butcher Boy," "Fatty in Coney Island," "The Garage," "Out West," "The Cook," "The Traveling Salesman," "The Life of the Party," "Brewster's Millions," "Crazy to Marry."
Retired 1921 due to involvement in unfortunate scandal, was acquitted, but barred from the movies. Tried directing under the name of William B. Goodrich:— "The Red Mill" (Marion Davies), and shorts. Died 1933.

ARMSTRONG, BILLY

b. Bristol, England, 1891. 5'8, 150 lbs. Karno Pantomime Co., Harry Tate's Co., etc. Essanay 1915, Horsley, Cub Comedies, L-Ko, and Keystone comedies, "An International Sneak," "Down on the Farm," "Love, Honor and Behave," "Skirts."

AUBREY, JIMMY

b. Liverpool, England. 5'6, 165 lbs. Karno's "A Night in an English Music Hall," Gus Hill, vaudeville and musical comedy. Pathé comedies—Heinie in "Heinie and Louie" series, Vitagraph; "Call of the Klondike," "Two Fresh Eggs," "The Light That Failed."

AUSTIN, ALBERT

b. Birmingham, England, 1885. 5'11, 160 lbs. "A Night in an English Music Hall," stock Denver two years. Joined Chaplin-Mutuals 1916. Appeared in or assisted many Chaplin films to "City Lights." Most famous non-Chaplin role that of Horace in Mary Pickford's "Suds," directed "A Prince of a King," "Trouble," (Coogan).

BACON, LLOYD

b. San Jose, Calif., 1889, 5'10, 150 lbs. Son of Frank Bacon of "Lightnin'" fame, Santa Clara College. On stage, stock, etc. Entered movies playing "heavy" to Lloyd Hamilton. Then to Chaplin, Essanay and Mutuals. After war acted with William S. Hart, directed Lloyd Hamilton comedies, then to Sennett. Directed early talkies for Warners:—"The Heart of Maryland," "The Lion and the Mouse," "The Singing Fool." Also "Moby Dick," "42nd Street," "Gold

Diggers of '37," "A Slight Case of Murder," "The Sullivans," "Give My Regards to Broadway."

BELL, MONTA

b. Washington, D.C., 1891. 6'3, 175 lbs. Reporter Washington Post, stock co., wrote "My Trip Abroad" for Chaplin. Assistant on "A Woman of Paris." Directed "Broadway After Dark," "The Snob," "The Torrent" (Garbo's first American picture), "Man, Woman and Sin," supervised early Paramount talkies, "The Letter," (Jeanne Eagels) etc. Directed "Men in White," "Aloma of the South Seas," "China's Little Devils."

BERGMAN, HENRY

Swedish extraction; 5'8, 303 lbs. Joined Lehrman's L-Ko Co., 1914, Joker Co., Chaplin players 1916; also acted as assistant director on nearly all Chaplin pictures after that. On side ran restaurant in Hollywood (Henry's). Died 1946.

BRYAN, VINCENT

b. St. John's, Newfoundland, 1877. Educated N.Y.C. Wrote plays, acts and vaudeville sketches for Nat Wills, Lew Dockstader, Montgomery & Stone, Gertrude Hoffman, etc. Co-author of "Behind the Front." Wrote songs: "He's My Pal," "Don't Take me Home," "Please Go 'Way and Let me Sleep." Screen: to Keystone, then assisted Chaplin as writer at Essanay and Mutual. Later Goldwyn.

CAMPBELL, ERIC

b. Dunoon, Scotland. 6'4, 296 lbs. D'Oyly Carte Opera Co., Karno Co. and others. Screen career in London, 2 pictures of own in N.Y. Played the "heavy" in all Mutual-Chaplins. Killed auto accident Dec. 1917.

CHAPLIN, SYDNEY

b. Cape Town, South Africa, 1885 (half brother of Charles). 5'7½, 150 lbs. Stage career in London music halls, Karno, etc. Keystone late in 1914 and 1915, "A Submarine Pirate," "No One to Guide Him." Brother's manager 1916. Appeared in several First Nat.—Chaplins. Then on his own:—"Charley's Aunt," "The Man on the Box," "The Better 'Ole," "Missing Link," etc. Now in Europe.

CHASE, CHARLEY

(Charles Parrott) b. Baltimore, 1893. 6'½ 158 lbs. Vaudeville, Irish monologue, burlesque. Universal, Keystone (1)14), appeared in and wrote hundreds of 2 reel comedies, Hal Roach, Columbia series, "Position Wanted," "Why Husbands Go Mad," "Bungalow Boobs," "All Wet," etc. "Sons of the Desert." Died 1940.

CHERRILL, VIRGINIA

b. Carthage, Ill., 1908. 5'5, 117 lbs. Chicago society girl, no previous experience before "City Lights." Appeared in talkies:—"Girls Demand Excitement," "Charlie Chan's Greatest Case," "What Price Crime." Married:—Irving Adler, William Rhinelander Stewart, Cary Grant, Earl of Jersey. Lives in England.

COLEMAN, FRANK J.

b. Newburg, N.Y. 5'11, 236 lbs. Quartette, stock. Screen:—L-K-O, Rolin, Essanay, Mutuals, Lehrman, Vitagraph, First National, "The Cave Girl."

CONKLIN, CHESTER

b. Oskaloosa, Iowa, 1886. 5'4½, 135 lbs. Circus clown, stock and road co. Screen: Majestic Co. (6 mo.) Keystone 1913—"Walrus" to "Ambrose" of Mack Swain. Sennett 5 yrs. First feature:—"Greed," "We're In the Navy Now," teamed with W. C. Fields:—"Two Flaming Youths," "The Big Noise," "Varsity." Parts in talkies:—"The Virginian," "Modern Times," "Every Day's a Holiday," "Great Dictator," "Hail the Conquering Hero," "Perils of Pauline."

COOGAN, JACKIE

b. Los Angeles, 1914. Vaudeville parents, appeared with on stage before 2, with father in Annette Kellerman vaudeville act. After "The Kid," starred in "Peck's Bad Boy," "Trouble," "Oliver Twist," "Long Live the King," "Tom Sawyer," "College Swing." Was in army. Vaudeville. "Kilroy Was Here," "French Leave." Now in business. Married Betty Grable (1937), Flower Parry, Ann McCormack.

CROCKER, HARRY

b. San Francisco, Calif., 1893. 6', 180 lbs. Son of prominent and wealthy family. Yale University. Stage, L.A.—Besides assistant on "The Circus," "City Lights," appeared in Marion Davies' "Tillie the Toiler," "Sally in our Alley," "South Sea Love."

D'ARRAST, H.

D'Abbadie. b. Argentina, 1897. Met Geo. Fitzmaurice in France. Became his technical advisor. Then assistant to Chaplin. Directed:— "Service for Ladies," "A Gentleman of Paris," "The Magnificent Flirt," "Dry Martini," "Laughter," "Raffles," "Topaze." Married Eleanor Boardman in France.

DAVENPORT, ALICE

b. N.Y.C. 1853. 5'2, 140 lbs. Member of noted stage family. Mother of Mrs. Wallace Reid. 25 years in stock, repertory, etc. Screen:—Nestor, Horsley. One of the original 6 who made the first Keystone, 1912. In over 200 pictures, Sunshine comedies, Fox.

DAVIS, GEORGE

b. New York. 5'8, 155 lbs. Educational comedies, "The Circus," Mermaid comedies. "The Kiss," "Not So Dumb," "A Lady To Love."

DEHAVEN, CARTER

Chicago, Ill., 1886. Vaudeville, Weber and Fields. Musical Comedy. With his wife on screen in "Twin Beds," "Girl in Taxi," etc. Assistant on "Modern Times," and played in "The Great Dictator." Daughter—Gloria DeHaven

DE LIMUR, JEAN

b. France. Aviator in war. Played in Fairbanks' "Three Musketeers." After assisting Chaplin on "Woman of Paris," became assistant to Rex Ingram and De Mille. Wrote "The Magnificent Flirt." Directed early talkies:—Jeanne Eagels in "The Letter" and "Jealousy." Returned to France. Co-director "Don Quixote."

DEAN, DINKY

(Dean Franklin Riesner) b. 1918, son of "Chuck" Riesner. In comedies 8 months old and in vaudeville act. After "The Pilgrim" appeared in "A Prince of a King," "Peck's Good Boy." Directed "Bill and Coo."

DRESSLER, MARIE

b. Cobourg, Canada, 1869. 5'7, 150 lbs. With Lew Fields, Weber and Fields, Lillian Russell, "Tillie's Nightmare" in which she popularized the song "Heaven Will Protect the Working Girl." "Tillie" series on screen for Keystone, Lubin, World. Later "Callahans and Murphys," "Bringing up Father," "The Patsy." After spotty career made a comeback in talkies, becoming one of the biggest stars of all time:—"Hollywood Revue," "Anna Christie," "Min and Bill," series with Polly Moran:—"Caught Short," "Politics," "Reducing," "Prosperity," "Emma," "Tugboat Annie," "Dinner at Eight." Died 1934.

DRYDEN, WHEELER

b. London, 1892. 5'8½, 155 lbs. Half brother of Chaplin. Stage career in England. Toured Orient. Screen career at Sunrise Co., Universal. Recent years assisted brother.

DURFEE, MINTA

b. Los Angeles 1897. 130 lbs. Musical comedy, vaudeville, stock. Keystone comedies 1913–16. Married Roscoe Arbuckle. Later played in "Mickey," Truart Pictures. Now owns dress shop.

FRENCH, CHARLES K.

b. Columbus, Ohio. 6', 190 lbs. Stage career; variety, minstrel show, character actor. Screen 1908; actor for Biograph, director for N.Y.M.P. Co., supported Chas. Ray and Wm S. Hart in many Ince films. "The Last Warning," "The Divine Lady."

GELDERT, CLARENCE

b. St. John, B.C., 1867. 5'11, 165 lbs. Varied career, actor, with Richard Mansfield, etc. Screen 1915 in D. W. Griffith's "Intolerance," De Mille's "Joan the Woman," "Affairs of Anatol," "A Woman of Paris," etc.

GODDARD, PAULETTE

b. New York City, 1911. (Real name Pauline Levy.) 5'4, 110 lbs. Chorus of Ziegfeld's "Rio Rita" 1927, etc. Screen:—dancer in "Kid from Spain," Hal Roach. Other than 2 Chaplin films has appeared in:—"The Cat and the Canary," "The Young in Heart," "Northwest Mounted Police," "Second Chorus," "Reap the Wild Wind," "Kitty," "An Ideal Husband," etc.

GOODWINS, FRED

b. London, 1891. 5'9, 146 lbs. Newspaper man. Stage: George Alexander, Charles Frohman. Screen: Edison, Imp. Chaplin (1915–17) Horsley comedies.

GREY, LITA

b. Hollywood, Calif. 1908. (Lolita McMurry real name.) Married Chaplin Nov. 1924. Mother of Charlie Chaplin Jr. and Sidney. Divorced 1927. Recently vaudeville, Vitaphone shorts.

GRIFFITH, GORDON

b. Chicago, Ill., 1907. Stage at 1 yr. with mother Katherine Griffith. Movies 1913-26: Sennett, "Tarzan of the Apes," "Huckleberry Finn," "Little Annie Rooney." Asst. dir. Monogram. Prod. Mgr. "The Jolson Story."

HALE, GEORGIA

b. St. Joseph, Mo. 5'4, 122 lbs. Musical comedy, stock. Films 1923.

Lead in Von Sternberg's first picture, "The Salvation Hunters." After "Gold Rush":—"The Rain Maker," "The Woman Against World," "Odyssey of North," "The Last Moment." Now dance teacher.

HALL, CHAS. D.

b. England 1899. Worked with Fred Karno's shows, Harry Day's etc. Art director, Chaplin Co. 1924–1936. Also:—"Invisible Man," "Bride of Frankenstein," "Diamond Jim," "Show Boat."

HARRIS, MILDRED

b. Cheyenne, Wyoming, 1901. 5'2, 108 lbs. Child actress at nine. Broncho, Ince, Kay Bee, Triangle, Lois Weber, First National:—"Enoch Arden," "Old Folks at Home," "The Price of a Good Time," "Borrowed Clothes," "Habit," "Fool's Paradise," "Heart of a Follies Girl," "Lingerie," "No, No, Nanette." Vaudeville, night clubs, burlesque. Died 1944.

HOWELL, ALICE

b. New York, 1892. Musical comedy, burlesque, Howell and Howell in vaudeville. Keystone 1914. ("Laughing Gas," "Shot in the Excitement.") L-Ko comedies, Century. "Ballonatics," "Automaniacs," "Neptune's Naughty Daughter," "Love is an Awful Thing."

INSLEY, CHARLES

Veteran actor and screen player, in D. W. Griffith's first film ("The Adventures of Dollie"), came to California in 1909 with the Bison Co. Chaplin-Essanays, Kalem (Ham and Bud comedies).

JAMIESON, BUD

(Wm. E.) b. Vallejo, Calif., 1894. 6', 270 lbs. Cafe entertainer and performer. 4 years vaudeville, stock. Essanay-Chaplins, Rolin (Lonesome Luke series), Pathé comedies, "Buck Privates," "The Chaser," Columbia shorts, "Slightly Honorable," "Pot o' Gold," "Li'l Abner," etc. Died 1944.

KELLEY, JAMES T.

b. Castlebar County, Mayo, Ireland. 5'3, 150 lbs. 40 years Pete Daly Co. 3 years. Tivoli Opera House, San Francisco, vaudeville, etc. Screen:—Universal, Essanay, Rolin, Lone Star, Roach.

KENNEDY, EDGAR

b. Monterey, California, 1890, 6'1, 210 lbs. 4 years vaudeville and musical comedy. Keystone c. 1914. Later 2 reel comedy series for Educational, Hal Roach. Inventor of the "slow burn." "Duck Soup," "Tillie and Gus," "Kid Millions," "San Francisco," "A Star is Born," "True Confession," "Average Man" series. Died 1948.

KENNEDY, MERNA

b. Kankakee, Ill., 1908. 5'2½, 107 lbs. Musical comedy Los Angeles. After "Circus" in "Broadway," early talkie, "King of Jazz," "Easy

Millions," "Hell's Highway." Died
1944.

KIRTLEY, VIRGINIA

b. Bowling Green, Mo. 5'5, 129
lbs. Stock, L.A. Screen:—Imp,
Keystone, Selig.

KNOTT, LYDIA

b. Tyner, Ind., 1873. 5'4, 120 lbs.
Son, Lambert Hillyer. Legitimate
stage and stock. Entered Ince pictures. "The Clodhopper," "Turn
to the Right," "Our Dancing
Daughters," "Skippy."

LAUREL, STAN

(Arthur Stanley Jefferson) b. Ul-
verston, England, 1895. 5'8, 160
lbs. Karno Pantomime Co., circus,
vaudeville, etc. Came to America
in 1910 as understudy to Chaplin
in "A Night in an English Music
Hall." Entered movies in 1917 for
Hal Roach—c. 50 comedies, some
burlesquing feature hits:—"The
Egg," "Mud and Sand," "Robin
Hood Jr.," "When Knights were
Cold," "White Wings," etc. Also
directed for a while. Never made a
real hit until 1926 when he teamed
up with Oliver (Babe) Hardy who
had a similar career. The team of
Laurel & Hardy made many successful comedies:—"Do Detectives
Think," "Brats," "Pardon Us,"
"Pack Up your Troubles," "Swiss
Miss," "Saps at Sea," etc.

LAMPTON, DEE

b. Ft. Worth, Texas, 1898. 5'4, 300
lbs. 1 year on the road. Screen:—
Essanay, "A Night in the Show,"
Keystone, Rolin, Lonesome Luke
series with Harold Lloyd, Skinny
Lampton series.

LEHRMAN, HENRY

("Pathé") b. Vienna, Austria,
1886. Screen:—Biograph, Imp,
Kinemacolor, Keystone, Sterling,
L-Ko (Lehrman-Knockout). Pro-
duced Fox Sunshine Bathing
Beauty comedies (1917–18), series
with Lloyd Hamilton and Virginia
Rappe (1919), "Wild Women and
Tame Lions," "A High Diver's
Last Kiss," "The Twilight Baby,"
Features:—"Chicken a la King,"
"Why Sailors Go Wrong," "New
Years Eve."

LONDON, BABE

b. Des Moines, Iowa, 5'8, 215 lbs.
"Merely Mary Ann," "A Day's
Pleasure," "When the Clouds
Roll By," "When Romance
Rides." Christie Comedies:—"Sec-
ond Childhood," "A Hula Honey-
moon," "Be Yourself," etc. "Flirt-
ing with Love."

MANN, HANK

(David W. Liebeman) b. New
York, 1888. 5'8½, 182 lbs. Some
stage experience. Keystone (1912)
left with Ford Sterling for Sterling Co. (1914), L-Ko, back to
Keystone, Fox. "Patent Leather
Kid," "Broadway After Midnight," "Garden of Eden," "City
Lights," "Scarface," "The Devil
is a Woman," "Great Dictator,"
"Hollywood Cavalcade," "Perils
of Pauline."

MARSH, GENE

b. San Diego, Calif., 1893. 5'3½, 119 lbs. Reliance-Majestic Co. 2½ years, Keystone, ("His Prehistoric Past"), Rolin (Lonesome Luke comedies).

McCOY, HARRY

b. Philadelphia, Pa., 1894. 5'8½, 135 lbs. Vaudeville and musical comedy. 1911 Joker comedies, Universal. 1912—Keystone (5½ years), American, Selig ("The Hoosier Romance"), Lehrman ("The Twilight Baby"), Arbuckle ("The Garage"), "Skirts," "Meet the Wife." Century comedies.

McGUIRE, PADDY

b. New Orleans, La. 5'9, 155 lbs. Kolb and Dill musical comedy and burlesque. Essanay. Nov. 1915 starred on his own for Vogue ("Sticky Fingers," "Lured and Cured"), Triangle-Keystone ("Won by a Foul," etc.).

MENJOU, ADOLPHE

b. Pittsburgh, Pa., 1890. 5'10, 147 lbs. Educated Cornell University. Italian campaign, World War I, Vaudeville and N.Y. stage. Screen:—"Three Musketeers," "The Sheik," "Clarence," etc. After "A Woman of Paris" starred in:—"The Marriage Circle," "Grand Duchess and the Waiter," "A Service for Ladies," "The King on Main Street," "Blonde or Brunette," etc. Talkies: —"The Front Page," "A Farewell to Arms," "Morning Glory," "Little Miss Marker," "Sing, Baby, Sing," "100 Men and a Girl," "Golden Boy," "Father Takes a Wife," "Roxie Hart," "You Were Never Lovelier."

MILLER, CARL

b. Wichita County, Texas (1893) 6', 160 lbs. Univ. of Texas. Stage 15 months, vaudeville. Screen:— Asst. cameraman, director, actor. "The Doctor and the Woman," "Mary Regan," "The Kid," "The Bride's Play," "A Woman of Paris," "The Extra Girl," "Why Sailors Go Wrong."

MINEAU, CHARLOTTE

b. Bordeaux, France, 1891, 5'10, 165 lbs. Selig, Geo. Ade Fables, Swedie series and Chaplin-Essanay films, "Rosemary Climbs the Heights," "Love, Honor and Behave," "Love is an Awful Thing," "Sparrows."

MORRISSEY, BETTY

Discovered by von Stroheim. Appeared in "Merry Go Round," "A Woman of Paris," "The Gold Rush," "The Circus," "The Fast Worker," "Skinner's Dress Suit," specializing in "flapper" roles. Died 1950.

MURRAY, CHARLES

b. Laurel, Ind., 1872. 6', 200 lbs. Stage 20 yrs., Murray and Mack. 2 yrs. Biograph, "Hogan" series etc., Keystone, "A Henpecked Husband," "Never too Old," "Irene," "McFadden's Flats," "The Gorilla," "Cohens and Kellys," series, "Breaking the Ice." Died 1941.

MYERS, HARRY

b. New Haven, Conn., 1882. 5'11, 176 lbs. Stock and vaudeville. Screen, 1910:—Lubin, Vim comedy series with wife, Rosemary Theby, "A Connecticut Yankee," "R.S.V.P.," "Kisses," "The Marriage Circle," "The Dove," "City Lights," "Mississippi." Died 1939.

NORMAND, MABEL

b. Boston, Mass., 1894, 5'2, 100 lbs. Lived on Staten Island. Early career:—artist's model. Screen:— 1911, Vitagraph, Biograph under D. W. Griffith, Keystone (several hundred comedies). Considered the greatest comedienne of the silent screen. Biggest success:—"Mickey" made in 1916, "shelved" because it was not a typical Sennett picture and released in 1918 to become one of the greatest money makers. (The song by Moret went with it.) Series for Sam Goldwyn:— "Joan of Plattsburgh," "The Venus Model," "Peck's Bad Girl," "Sis Hopkins," "The Jinx," "Pinto," "The Slim Princess," "Head Over Heels," etc. Returned to Sennett: —"Molly O," "Suzanna," "The Extra Girl." Involved in Taylor murder case (1922), being the last known person to see him. Women's clubs barred her pictures and unfortunate scandal forced her retirement from the screen. Tried comeback with Hal Roach shorts 1926:

"Raggedy Rose," "The Nickel Hopper." Died tuberculosis Feb. 24, 1930.

PEARCE, PEGGY

b. Long Beach, Calif., 1896, 5'4, 135 lbs. Biograph, Keystone, 1913, L-Ko, return to Sennett, "Twixt Love and Fire," "Soul of a Plumber," "Won by a Foul," etc. Triangle feature with Roy Stewart, etc.

POLO, MALVINA

Daughter of Eddie Polo, Universal serial star. Played the half-wit girl in von Stroheim's "Foolish Wives," flapper in "A Woman of Paris."

PURVIANCE, EDNA OLGA

b. Lovelock, Paradise Valley, Nev., 1894. 5'5, 140 lbs. Amateur theatricals. Stenographer. Discovered in San Francisco by Chaplin. His leading woman 1915–1923. After "A Woman of Paris," Von Sternberg's "A Woman of the Sea," French picture ("The Education of a Prince"). Now retired.

RAND, JOHN

b. New Haven, Conn., 1878. 5'7, 155 lbs. Acrobat, tumbler with Forepaugh's circus, vaudeville. Keystone, Essanay, Mutual series, "The Circus," extra in "Modern Times."

REEVES, ALFRED

b. London, 1876. Manager circus and various shows and Karno Co.

when Chaplin was a member. Since 1918 general manager and vice president Chaplin Film Corp. Died 1946.

REEVES, BILLY

b. London, England. 5'5½. Circus, Karno Co., "A Night in English Music Hall"), 3 seasons Ziegfield's Follies. Screen:—Lubin Co. Died 1945.

RIESNER, CHARLES

("Chuck") b. Minneapolis, Minn., 1887. 7 yrs. vaudeville. Keith and Orpheum circuit, songwriter and professional boxer. Musical comedies. Screen:—Salt Lake City 1910, Keystone writer. Asst. to Chaplin and actor (1918–1925). Became director:—"Man on the Box," "The Better 'Ole," "Steamboat Bill, Jr." Talkies:—"Caught Short," "Reducing," "Politics," "Flying High," "Winter Carnival."

RITCHIE, BILLIE

b. Glasgow, Scotland, 1877. 5'7½, 140 lbs. Vaudeville, musical comedy, pantomime (Cinderella), Karno Co., "A Night in English Music Hall," etc. on Broadway and over Orpheum Circuit. Screen:—L-Ko, Sunshine Comedies, "The Twilight Baby," "North of the Rio Grande."

RUGGLES, WESLEY

b. Los Angeles, 1889. Musical comedy, stock. Keystone (Syd Chaplin comedies), Essanay, Vitagraph. Directed "Picadilly Jim," "The Leopard Woman," "Uncharted Seas," "Collegians" series. Talkies:—"Street Girl," "Cimarron," "Are These our Children," "I'm no Angel," "True Confession," "Sing, You Sinners," "Arizona," "See Here, Private Hargrove."

SANFORD, STANLEY J.

b. Osago, Iowa, 1894. 6'5, 280 lbs. Stock, movies 1910 on, "The Immigrant," "The Circus," "Pardon Us," "Modern Times," "A Night at the Opera."

SCHADE, FRITZ

b. Germany, 1880. 5', 193 lbs. Stage career, vaudeville. Screen:—Universal, Christie, Sennett, Keystone-Triangle. "Laughing Gas," "Fido's Fate," etc.

SENNETT, MACK

b. Denville, Quebec, 1880. See Chapter IV.

STERLING, FORD

b. La Crosse, Wis., 1880. As Keno, The Boy Clown in circus, stock, vaudeville, musical comedy. Screen:—Biograph, in 1st Keystone 1912, Cohen Series, "Dirty Work in a Laundry," and many others. His own co. 1914 but returned to Sennett. "Yankee Doodle in Berlin," "Hearts and Flowers," "His Last False Step." Later:—"American Venus," "The Show Off," "For the Love of Mike," "Gentlemen Prefer Blondes," In talkies:—"Sally,"

"Kismet," "Alice in Wonderland."
Died 1939.

ST. JOHN, AL

b. Santa Ana, Calif. 5'8, 140 lbs.
Musical comedy. Keystone 1914,
"Fatty and Mabel Adrift," "He
Did and He Didn't," teamed with
Arbuckle, "The Butcher Boy," "A
Reckless Romeo," "Fast and Furi-
ous," "Special Delivery," "Amer-
ican Beauty," "Casey Jones,"
"Hello Cheyenne," "The Dance of
Life." Now appears in westerns,
with beard, as Al (Fuzzy) St. John.
"Hopalong Cassidy," "Arizona
Terror," "Stagecoach Express,"
"Jesse James, Jr.," etc.

STOCKDALE, CARL

b. Worthington, Minn., 1874. 5'11,
155 lbs. Stock and vaudeville. 3 yrs.
Essanay, Rolfe, Fine Arts, Bel-
shazzar's father in Griffith's, "Intolerance," in Fairbank's "Americano," "Suzanna," "While London
Sleeps," "Shepherd of the Hills,"
"Oliver Twist," "The Terror,"
"The Love Parade," "The Lost
Horizon," "Blockade," "The Devil
and Daniel Webster."

SUMMERVILLE, SLIM

b. Albuquerque, New Mex., 1892.
6'2, 164 lbs. Musical comedy,
vaudeville, stock. Keystone, 1913,
"His Bread and Butter," "A Dog
Catcher's Love," series comedies
for Fox, Universal, F.B.O. Features:—"Beloved Rogue," "Last
Warning." Biggest success in "All
Quiet on the Western Front,"
(1930). Teamed with Zasu Pitts,

"Unexpected Father," "Capt. January," "Jesse Jones," "Western
Union," "Morgan Falls." Died
1946.

SUTHERLAND, EDWARD A.

b. London, 1897, 5'8, 160 lbs. Musical comedy. Nephew by marriage
to Thomas Meighan. Screen:—
actor in Helen Holmes serial, Keystone juvenile and director, assistant on "A Woman of Paris."
Directed:—"It's the Old Army
Game," "Behind the Front,"
"We're In the Navy Now." Talkies:
—"Paramount on Parade," "Mississippi," "Diamond Jim," "Poppy,"
"The Invisible Woman," "Follow
the Boy," "Secret Command."
Television direction.

SWAIN, MACK

b. Salt Lake City, Utah, 1876, 6'2,
240 lbs. Actor and Manager of own
co., vaudeville, musical comedy,
drama, stock. Keystone 1913 on,
Chaplin's 1st National pictures.
Later:—"Hands Up," "The Be-
loved Rogue," "Torrent," "My
Best Girl," "Gentlemen Prefer
Blondes," "The Last Warning,"
"Marianne," "Finn and Hattie."
Died 1935.

TERRELL, MAVERICK

b. Indianapolis, Ind., 1875. University of Indiana Law School.
Writer of magazine fiction and
stage plays, "The Woman in the
Park," "Temperament," etc. Co-
author with Rachael Marshall of
the plays, "The Cave Lady," and
"Friday the Thirteenth." Assisted

Chaplin in writing of Essanay and Mutual comedies.

TOTHEROH, ROLLAND

b. San Francisco, Calif., 1890. Early career as cartoonist. Photographer at Essanay. Chaplin's cameraman 1915–1947 (sometimes with others).

TURPIN, BEN

b. New Orleans, La., 1874. 5'4, 120 lbs. Burlesque, 11 years vaudeville. Essanay 2½ years. Vogue, Sennett: —"The Clever Dummy," "East Lynne with Variations," "Uncle Tom Without the Cabin," "Salome vs. Shenandoah," "Yukon Jake," "A Small Town Idol," "The Shreik of Araby." Smaller parts in talkies in "College Hero," "Love Parade," "Swing High." Died 1940.

WAITE, MALCOLM

b. Michigan, 1894. Screen career: Pathé, "The Gold Rush," "The Monkey Talks," "Kid Boots," "The Vagabond Lover."

WHITE, LEO

b. Manchester, England, 1887. 5'6,

132 lbs. Operettas:—"The Merry Widow," Gaston in "Mlle. Modiste" with Fritzi Scheff. Essanay, Geo. Ade comedies., Chaplin, Billy West Co., Hal Roach, "Blood and Sand," "A Lady of Quality," "Why Worry," "A Night at the Opera." Bits in "The Thin Man," "The Great Dictator," "Yankee Doodle Dandy." Died 1948.

WILLIAMS, FRANK D.

(cameraman) b. Nashville, Mo., 1893. Essanay, chief cameraman at Keystone 4½ years. "Mickey," "Queen of the Sea," Arbuckle films, Bushman and Bayne, Sessue Hayakawa, Goldwyn, Fairbanks, etc. (Invented an early process shot technique—the traveling matt). Trick work on "King Kong," "The Invisible Man."

WILSON, TOM

b. Helena, Montana. 6'2, 220 lbs. Stage, Mrs. Fiske, etc. Screen:— "Birth of a Nation," "Americano," "Intolerance," "The Kid," "When a Man Loves," "Battling Butler," "Riley the Cop." Recently bits in talkies:—"Sergeant York," "M. Verdoux," etc.

index

The titles of films made by Chaplin are in italics to distinguish them from the titles of other films, dramas, books, etc., referred to in the text.

"À Nous La Liberté," 188
Adler, Irving, 221
Adoré, René, 118
Adventurer, The, 82, 85, 121, 156
"Adventures of Kathleen, The," 23
Agee, James, 9, 294
Aguirre, Henry, Jr., 207
Albert, King of the Belgians, 246
Alda, Frances, 206
Alexandra, Queen, 14
Alkali Ike (*see* Carney, Augustus)
"All Quiet on the Western Front," 188
Allen, Phyllis, 28, 40, 71
Alonzo, Manuel, 154
Amador, 64
Ambrose (*see* Swain, Mack)
"American Citizen, An," 23
Amman, Betty, 245
Anderson, G.M., 46
"Anna Christie," 41
Aplin, Charles (*see* Amador)
Aragon, Louis, 206
Arbuckle, Roscoe (Fatty Arbuckle), 24, 25, 28, 30, 36, 39, 40, 93, 109, 204
Armstrong, Billy, 20, 56
Arthur, George K., 142, 211
Astor, Lady, 243, 244, 290
Atkinson, Brooks, 255
At It Again (Reissue of *Caught in the Rain*)
Atwater-Kents, 206
Aubrey, Jimmy, 19, 20
Austin, Albert, 20, 61

Bacon, Lloyd, 61
Baker, Phil, 207
Bancroft, Squire, 142

Bank, The, 49, 52, 56, 57
Bara, Theda, 49, 137
Barnes, Howard, 294
Barrie, James M., 128, 142
Barry, Joan, 280, 281, 282, 283
Barrymore, John, 23
Barrymores, The, 246
Barton, Ralph, 242, 244, 245
"Battle of Gettysburg, The," 23
"Becky Sharp," 255
Beery, Wallace, 24, 211
"Beggars of Life," 191
Behind the Screen, 75
"Behind the Screen," 289
Bell, Monta, 119, 147, 170, 175
Bercovici, Konrad, 284
Bergman, Henry, 61, 77, 119, 174, 191, 205, 218, 286
Bernhardt, Sarah, 22
Between Showers, 314
Bevan, Billy, 26
"Bicycle Thief, The," 176
"Big Parade, The," 102, 118, 188, 240
Biograph (film company), 23, 25, 29
Birkenhead, Lord, 152
"Birth of a Nation, The," 23, 24, 59, 116, 176, 188, 288
Black Dragon Society, The, 249
Blumenthal, A.C., 224
Bodie, Dr. Walford, 14
Bolton, Guy, 132
Bond, The, 87
Bonehead, The (Reissue of *His Favorite Pastime*)
"Borrowed Clothes," 88
Bosser, Ernst, 65
Brenon, Herbert, 23

Briand, Aristide, 246
"Broadway," 211
"Broadway After Dark," 175
"Broken Blossoms," 127, 142, 176, 188
Broncho (film company), 21
Broncho Billy (see Anderson, G.M.), 24
Broun, Heywood, 136
Browning, "Peaches," 250
Bryan, Leota, 61
Bryan, Vincent, 61
Bunny, John, 24
Burkan, Nathan, 136, 203, 204
Burke, Thomas, 7, 8, 142, 146
Bushman, Francis X., 49
Busted Hearts (Reissue of Those Love Pangs)
Busted Johnny, A (Reissue of Making a Living)
Busy Day, A, 40
By the Sea, 48, 52

"Cabiria," 22, 60
Caine, Hall, 169
Camacho, Avila, 282
Cami, 142
"Camille," 137, 169
Campbell, Eric, 61
Canham, George, 58
Cantor, Eddie, 224, 250
Capra, Frank, 26, 211, 254, 280
"Captain Kidd's Kids," 110
Carillo, Gomez, 218
Carmen, 49, 50, 51, 52, 53, 54, 61
Carney, Augustus, 24
Carpentier, Georges, 142, 207
"Casey's Court Circus," 14, 15
Castle, Irene and Vernon, 43
"Casuals, The," 16
Caught in a Cabaret, 32, 36, 38
Caught in the Rain, 32, 48
"Cavalcade," 188
Champion, The, 47, 48, 51
Champion Charlie (Reissue of Champion, The)
Chaplin, on Chaplin, 8, 242; on comedy, 3, 120, 121; on costume, 3; on government, 290, 291, 292; on Hollywood, 285; on satire, 5; on screen character, 3, 5; on social significance, 256; on tragedy, 50; on A Woman of Paris, 175; on what makes people laugh, 45, 121

Chaplin, Aubrey (Chaplin's cousin), 139, 140, 145, 146, 147
Chaplin, Charles Spencer (Chaplin's father), 10
Chaplin, Charles Spencer, Jr. (Chaplin's son), 201
Chaplin, Geraldine (Chaplin's daughter), 286
Chaplin, Michael John (Chaplin's son), 286
Chaplin, Sidney (Chaplin's half-brother), 10, 11, 12, 15, 19, 20, 58, 86, 96, 104, 108, 135, 136, 246, 247, 248, 249
Chaplin, Sydney Earle (Chaplin's son), 201
Chaplin Classics Co., The, 65
Chaplin craze, 6
"Chaplin Festivals," 66
Chaplin imitators, 64, 65
"Charley's Aunt," 201
Charlie and the Sausages (Reissue of Mabel's Busy Day)
Charlie and the Umbrella (Reissue of Between Showers)
Charlie at the Bank (Reissue of The Bank)
Charlie at the Show (Reissue of Night in the Show, A)
"Charlie Chaplin in a Son of the Gods," 64
"Charlie Chaplin Intime," 249
"Charlie in a Harem," 64
Charlie's Recreation (Reissue of Tango Tangles)
Charlie, the Perfect Lady (Reissue of Woman, A)
Chase, Charley, 26, 28
Chase Me Charlie, 325
Chequers (see MacDonald, Ramsay)
Cherrill, Virginia, 220, 222
"Chumps at Oxford," 96
Churchill, Winston, 8, 244, 247, 292
Circus, The, 70, 202, 203, 204, 205, 208-217, 218
"Circus Days," 126
"Citizen Kane," 176
City Lights, 95, 117, 218-234, 235, 237, 239, 240, 244, 253, 254, 255, 308, 309
Clair, René, 26, 206, 257, 265
"Clarence," 169
"Clarice," 13
Clark-Cornelius Co., The, 65
Clive, Henry, 219, 221
Cliveden (see Astor, Lady)

"Club of Suicides, The," 208
Cocteau, Jean, 102
"Cohen, Sam, the Jewish Comedian," 14
"College," 211
Collier, Constance, 225
Collins, May, 148
Colman, Ronald, 96
"Comedian Sees the World, A," 242, 290
Compson, Betty, 190
Conklin, Chester, 28, 36, 40, 211
Connaught, Duke of, 247
"Connecticut Yankee in King Arthur's Court, A," 221
"Conquering Male, The," 250
Converse, Thelma Morgan, 154, 247
"Convict 13," 110
Coogan, Jackie, 116, 124, 125, 126
Cops and Watches (Reissue of Twenty Minutes of Love)
Costello, Maurice, 23
Count, The, 60, 72, 116, 156
Counted Out (Reissue of Knockout, The)
"Covered Wagon, The," 189, 240
Creelman, Eileen, 294
Crisp, Donald, 139, 140
Crocker, Harry, 208, 218, 221, 286
Crosby, Bing, 26
Crowninshield, Frank, 137
Cruel, Cruel Love, 314
Crystal Hall, 59
Cure, The, 60, 79
"Cynara," 96

"Dandy, The," 208
"Dandy Thieves, The," 16
Dane, Karl, 211
Daniell, Henry, 264
D'Arcy, Roy, 207
"Dark Angel," 255
D'Arrast, Harry d'Abbadie, 170 175, 201, 247
Day, Arthur F., 207
Davenport, Alice, 28
Davies, Marion, 202
Daw, Marjorie, 89
Day's Pleasure, A, 109, 113-115, 155, 159
Dean, Dinky, 163
"Death of a Columbine," 308
Deed, André, 24
De Forest, 144
De Limur, Jean, 170
De Wolfe, Elsie, 145

De Mille, Cecil B., 23, 49, 94, 172
Del Ruth, Roy, 26
Delluc, Louis, 6, 95, 110
Dentist, The (Reissue of Laughing Gas)
Desnos, Robert, 206
"Destiny," 169
Diamant-Barger, Henry, 170
Dietrich, Marlene, 245
"Dishonor System, The," 64
"Doctor Jack," 155
Dog's Life, A, 86, 95-101, 102, 158, 189
Doing His Best (Reissue of Making a Living)
Dolin, Anton, 308
Dombski, Count, 153
"Donald Duck," 254
Donner party disaster, 187
Doro, Marie, 13
"Doug" (see Fairbanks, Douglas)
Dough and Dynamite, 37, 39, 40
Doughnut Designer, The (Reissue of Dough and Dynamite)
Down and Out (Reissue of Laughing Gas)
D'Oyly Carte Gilbert and Sullivan Co., 61
Dream, A (Reissue of His Pre-historic Past)
"Dream Street," 142
Dressler, Marie, 6, 26, 40, 41
Drew, Sidney, 24
"Duck Soup," 67
Dulac, Germaine, 206
Du Maurier, Gerald, 142
Dunn, Bobbie, 64
Dunn, Josephine, 154
Durant, Tim, 282
Durfee, Minta, 28, 31

"Early Birds," 16
Eastman, Max, 8, 120, 137, 149, 287, 288, 289
Easy Street, 60, 61, 63, 77
Edison (film company), 23
"Education of a Prince," 170
Edward, King, 14
"Eight Lancashire Lads," 11
Eilers, Sally, 26
Einstein, Albert, 224, 245, 246
Einstein, Albert, Mrs., 224
Eisenstein, 123
Eisler, Hans, 284, 285
Elsom, Isobel, 296
Eltinge, Julian, 61, 62

Ervine, St. John, 144
"Escape, The," 23
Essanay (film company), 23, 33, 35, 46, 47, 48, 53, 54, 55, 57, 58, 59, 60, 61, 158, 168, 236, 288
Essanay-Chaplin Revue of 1916, The, 325
Export and Import Co., 65

Face on the Bar-room Floor, The, 38
Fairbanks, Douglas, 86, 87, 136, 137, 145, 153, 162, 240, 248, 289
Fairbanks, Douglas, Jr., 207
Fair Exchange, A (Reissue of *Getting Acquainted*)
"Fall of the Rummy-Nuffs, The," 64
Faking with Society (Reissue of *Caught in a Cabaret*)
"Falling Star, The," 237
Family House (Reissue of *His Trysting Place*)
Famous Players (film company), 22
Farnum, William, 61
Farrar, Geraldine, 49, 62
Fatal Mallet, The, 316
Faure, Elie, 7
Fazenda, Louise, 26
Female Impersonator, The (Reissue of *Masquerader, The*)
Fields, W.C., 26, 77, 211, 254
"Film Folk," 85
Film Johnny, A, 38
Fireman, The, 68, 116
First National (film company), 84, 85, 86, 95, 125, 134, 162
Fiske, Mrs., 6, 63
Fleckenstein, William P., 94
Flirts, The (Reissue of *Between Showers*)
Floorwalker, The, 60, 67, 68, 116, 159
Florey, Robert, 286, 297, 298
"Fly Cop, The," 110
"Flying Yorkshireman, The," 280
Folies Bergères, 18
"Fool's Paradise," 94
"Football Match, The," 16
"Footlights," 308
"For Heaven's Sake," 211
"For Husbands Only," 88
"Forbidden Paradise," 175
Foster, William C., 60
Frank, Waldo, 7, 142
"Freshman, The," 96, 189
Freuler, John R., 58

Frohman, Charles, 13
"From Rags to Riches," 13
Fuller, Mary, 24

Gandhi, Mahatma, 248
Garbo, Greta, 94, 175, 297
Garden, Mary, 247
Gardiner, Reginald, 264
Garland, Robert, 255
Gaye, Vivian, 244
"General, The," 211
Gentlemen of Nerve, 319
"Gentleman of Paris, A," 175
George, King of Greece, 145
Georgia (see Hale, Georgia)
Geraghty, Tom, 139, 140, 141
Gerard, Ambassador, 137
Getting Acquainted, 40
Getting His Goat (Reissue of *Property Man, The*)
Getty, J. Paul, 282
"Giddy Ostend," 12
Gilbert, Billy, 264
Gilbert, John, 118
Gillette, William, 13
"Girl from Leningrad, The," 283
"Girls Demand Excitement," 223
Gish, Dorothy, 63
Glaum, Louise, 137
Glyn, Elinor, 153
Goddard, Paulette, 62, 123, 250, 251, 257, 264, 281
Godowsky, Leopold, 63
Gold Rush, The, 50, 55, 95-101, 187, 198, 208, 209, 212, 222, 225, 226, 237, 253, 283, 290
Golden, Marta, 56
Goldwyn, Sam, 23, 151
"Gone with the Wind," 251
Good-For-Nothing, The (Reissue of *His New Information*)
Gould, Frank Jay, 246
Graham, Sheilah, 280
"Grand Duchess and the Waiter, The," 175
"Grandma's Boy," 155
Grant, Cary, 223
"Grass," 189
Great Dictator, The, 55, 123, 235, 237, 246, 251, 262-279, 280, 284, 293, 298
"Greed," 176
Grey, Lita, 154, 190, 200, 201, 202, 203, 204, 205, 206, 207, 221
Gribbon, Harry, 26
Gribouille (series), 24

Griffith, D. W., 23, 25, 27, 29, 59, 88, 95, 116, 118, 123, 127, 142, 162, 235, 240, 289
Griffith, Raymond, 26, 211
"Grocery Clerk, The," 110
Guaranteed Pictures Co., 66
"Gypsy Blood," 143

Hackett, Walter, 142
Hale, Georgia, 190, 208, 222, 224, 251
Ham Artist, The (Reissue of Face on the Bar-room Floor, The)
Hannah (Chaplin's mother), 10, 150, 153, 221
Hanwell Residential School, 11
Hardy, Oliver (Babe), 64, 96, 212
Harley, Lily (Chaplin's mother's stage name), 10
Harlow, Jean (see Pope, Jean)
Harrington, Tom, 62, 85, 150
Harris, Frank, 146
Harris, Mildred, 56, 88, 89, 90, 91, 93, 94
Hash-House Hero, The (Reissue of Star Boarder, The)
Hatton, Raymond, 211
"Haunted Spooks," 110
Haver, Phyllis, 26
Hayakawa, Sessue, 23
Hays, Will, 204
He Loved Her So (Reissue of Twenty Minutes of Love)
"Hearts Adrift," 23
"Heaven Will Protect the Working Girl," 40
"Hell's Highway," 211
Her Friend, the Bandit, 316
Hern Boys College, 12
"Heroes I Have Known," 288
Herrick, Ambassador, 145
"High and Dizzy," 110
"Hilarity," 16
His Daredevil Queen (Reissue of Mabel at the Wheel)
His Favorite Pastime, 36
"His Majesty's Guests," 16
His Musical Career, 319
His New Job, 48, 55
His New Profession, 318
His Prehistoric Past, 38
His Trysting Place, 37, 39
Hitler, Adolf, 262, 263, 281, 284
Hitchcock, Raymond, 60
"Hollywood, Yesterday and Today," 297
"Home from Home," 16

"Honeysuckle and the Bee, The," 236
Hopper, Hedda, 286
Hot Dogs (Reissue of Mabel's Busy Day)
Hot Finish (Reissue of Mabel at the Wheel)
"How Dry I Am," 239
Hughes, Ray, 64
Hunter, Catherine, 242
"Hypocrites," 88

"I Hear You Calling Me," 239
"I Want to Be Happy," 239
Idle Class, The, 135, 155-158, 161, 191
Immigrant, The, 59, 80, 95, 123, 157, 159
Imp (film company), 23
In the Park (Reissue of Caught in the Rain), 48, 315
In Wrong (Reissue of Between Showers)
Ince, Thomas H., 23, 88
"Informer, The," 176, 188
Insley, Charles, 56
"Intolerance," 60, 176
Inukai, Tsuyoki, 249
"It Happened One Night," 254
"It Took Nine Tailors," 117

"Jack Jones," 11
Jacobs, Lewis, 294
"Jail Birds," 16
James, Edgar, 250
Jamieson, Bud, 56
Jazz Waiter (Reissue of Caught in a Cabaret)
Jefferson, Arthur Stanley (see Stan Laurel)
"Jim, the Romance of Cocaine," or "Jim, the Romance of a Cockney," 13
"Jimmy, the Fearless," 17
Jitney Elopement, The, 48
Johnson, Arthur, 23
Johnston, Arthur, 237
Jolson, Al, 224, 238
Joyce, Peggy Hopkins, 168, 169, 225

Kalem (film company), 23
Kaplin, Charlie, 65
Karno, 16, 18, 32, 36, 48, 61, 286
Karno, Fred, 15, 236

Karno Company, 15, 16, 18, 32, 56, 64
Katial, Dr. Chuna Lal, 248
Kaufman, Al, 143
Kay Bee (film company), 21
Keaton, Buster, 109, 155, 189, 211
Kellerman, Annette, 64, 124
Kelley, James T., 56
Kelly, Arthur (Sonny), 18, 139, 246
Kelly, Edith, 246
Kelly, Hetty, 18, 139, 141, 246
Kennedy, Edgar, 26, 28, 40
Kennedy, Merna, 203, 208, 211, 213, 217
Kennedy, Tom, 26
Kennington (London slum district), 11, 140, 141, 236
Kessel, Adam, 21
Kessel and Bauman, 21-30
Keyserling, Count, 152
Keystone (film company), 20, 21, 24, 25, 27, 28, 30, 32, 33, 35, 36, 37, 38, 39, 41, 45, 46, 47, 48, 76, 258, 288
Keystone Mabel (see Normand, Mabel)
Kid, The, 6, 12, 55, 70, 92, 110-116, 124-134, 135, 142, 145, 150, 152, 155, 156, 163, 189, 199, 237
Kid Auto Races at Venice, 30
"Kid Brother, The," 211
"Kid from Spain, A," 250
King Bee (film company), 64
"Mr. Kipps," 142
Kirtely, Virginia, 29
"Kismet," 137
"Kiss Me Again," 175
Kitchen, Fred, 32
Kitchen, Karl, 291
Kline, Eddie, 26
Knoblock, Edward, 137, 140
Knockout, The, 39, 48
Kono, 62, 91, 92, 151, 200, 202, 222, 224, 242, 244, 248, 249
Kustoff, Michael, 257

L-Ko—Lehrman Knockout (film company), 32
La Jana, 245
La Verne, Lucille, 9
"La Violaterra," 218, 235, 238, 239, 240
"Lady Killer" (see Monsieur Verdoux, 280, 293)
Landru, 293

Lane, Lupino, 211
Langdon, Harry, 26, 211
Langhorne, Nancy (see Astor, Lady)
Lasky, Jesse, 23
"Last Days of Pompeii, The," 22
"Last Moment, The," 190
"Last Laugh, The," 176, 188
Lauder, Harry, 63
Laughing Gas, 37
Laurel, Stan, 17, 20, 96, 212
Lawrence, Florence, 23
Le Gallienne, Eva, 136
Leeds, William B., Jr., 206
Lehr, Abraham, 151
Lehrman, Henry, 29, 30, 31, 32, 38
Lenin, 138, 151
Leo, Dan, 17
Levy, Pauline (see Goddard, Paulette)
Liberty Loan, 86, 87, 162
Life, 54, 169
"Life of the Party, The," 110
"Liliom," 136
"Limehouse Nights," 142
Linder, Max, 24, 32, 33
"Little Lord Fauntleroy," 136
"Lives of a Bengal Lancer, The," 255
Lloyd George, 138, 243, 244
Lloyd, Harold, 52, 65, 96, 109, 110, 188, 189, 211
Loew's, Inc., 295
Lombard, Carole, 26
Lone Star Studio, 59
Lonesome Luke (see Harold Lloyd)
"Long Live the King," 126
"Long Pants," 211
"Look Out for Jimmy Valentine," 239
Lowe, Edmund, 211
Lord Helpus (Reissue of Cruel, Cruel Love)
Love and Lunch (Reissue of Mabel's Busy Day)
Love-Friend (Reissue of Twenty Minutes of Love)
Lubin (film company), 23
Lubitsch, Ernst, 25, 118, 143, 175, 245, 265
Lucas, E.V., 142
Ludwig, Emil, 247

Mabel at the Wheel, 57
Mabel's Busy Day, 316
Mabel's Flirtation (Reissue of Her Friend, the Bandit)
Mabel's Married Life, 316

Mabel's Strange Predicament, 31
MacDonald, Alistair, 243
MacDonald, Ramsay, 243, 245
MacLaglen, Victor, 211
Maeterlinck, Mme., 137
Making a Living, 30, 37, 39
Malone, Dudley Field, 142, 149
Mann, Hank, 26, 28
Marchand, Henri, 257
Maritsa, Sari, 244, 245
"Mark of Zorro, The," 188
Markova, Alicia, 308
"Marriage Circle, The," 175
Marsh, Marian (*see* Morgan, Marilyn)
Marx Brothers, 26, 67, 224
Masquerader, The (Sometimes reissued as *His New Profession,* title of another Keystone film), 38, 40
"Masses, The" (*see Modern Times,* 252)
Maxwell, Elsa, 145, 247
Mayer, Louis B., 90
Mayo, Frank, 148
McAdoo, William C., 162
McCoy, Harry, 28
McGovern, Everett T., 94
McGuire, Paddy, 56
McMein, Neysa, 137
McMurray, Edwin, 200
McMurray, Lolita (*see* Lita Grey)
McMurray, Mrs. (Lita Grey's mother), 200
McNamee, Frank L., 308
McNutt, Paul V., 308
McPherson, Aimee Semple, 247
Meighan, Tom, 191
Melba, Nellie, 63
Meller, Raquel, 218
Mencken, H.L., 205
Menjou, Adolphe, 117, 123, 169, 170, 211
Meredith, Burgess, 281
Metz, Herman, 138
"Mickey," 34
Mikhoels, Solomon, 283
Militant Suffragette (Reissue of *Busy Day, A*)
"Million Bid, A," 23
Million Dollar Job (Reissue of *Film Johnny, A*)
"Million Dollar Mystery, The," 23
Mineau, Charlotte, 56
"Mlle. Modiste," 56
Modern Times, 116, 235, 250, 251, 252-261, 291

"Mollycoddle, The," 139
Monsieur Jack, 65
Monsieur Verdoux, 56, 226, 235, 237, 280, 286, 291, 293-306, 308
Moore, Grace, 225
Moran, Polly, 26
Morgan, Marilyn, 223
Moritz (*see* Prince, Charles)
Moscovich, Maurice, 264
Motion Pictures Patents Co., 46
Movie Nut (Reissue of *Film Johnny, A*)
"Mumming Birds," 16
Murnau, 188
Murphy, D. L., 251
Murray, Charlie, 26, 28
Mussolini, 152, 248, 264
Mutual (film company), 47, 58, 59, 60, 65, 66, 76, 77, 80, 82, 84, 85, 86, 156, 236, 288
"My American Diary," 289
"My Trip Abroad," 146, 147, 236, 288
Myers, Harry, 221
Myers, Rev. James, 89

Namara, Margaret, 138
Nash, Marilyn, 296
Nast, Condé, 137
Nathan, George Jean, 68
"Navigator, The," 189
Negri, Pola, 143, 144, 152, 153, 154
Neilan, Marshal, 168
New Janitor, The, 39
New Porter, The (Reissue of *New Janitor, The*)
"New Woman's Club," 16
New York Motion Picture Co., 21
Newman, Alfred, 237, 256
"Night in an English Music Hall, A," 16, 18, 19, 29, 48, 61
"Night in a London Club, A," 19
Night in the Show, A, 17, 48, 52
Night Out, A, 48, 50, 52
Nijinsky, 6, 63, 264
Niles (Essanay studio at), 47
Nilson, Anna Q., 154
"No Foolin'," 250
Normand, Mabel, 24, 25, 28, 29, 31, 33, 34, 37, 40, 42, 204, 211
"Nothing Sacred," 254

Oakie, Jack, 264
"Oh That Cello," 236

Oh, What a Night (Reissue of *Rounders, The*)
O. Henry, 187
"Old and New," 188
"Oliver Twist," 126
One A.M., 17, 71
"One Hour" (*see* Glyn, Elinor)
"One Law for Both," 64
O'Neill, Eugene, 283
O'Neill, Oona, 283
Onesime, 24
"Our Hospitality," 155

Paderewski, 63
"Painful Predicament of Sherlock Holmes, The," 13
Paper Hanger, The (Revival of *Work*)
Paramount (film company), 84, 143, 152, 190
"Paris Boulevard, A," 237
"Passion," 143
"Passion of Joan of Arc, The," 176
Pathé (film company), 24
Pawnshop, The, 50, 73, 75, 225
Pay Day, 152, 158-161
"Peace Patrol, The," 236
"Peck's Bad Boy," 126
Pegler, Westbrook, 285
Perfect Lady, The (Reissue of *Woman, A*)
"Perils of Pauline, The," 23
Perils of Patrick, The, 45
"Peter Pan," 13, 142
Phonofilm, 144
Picasso, Pablo, 284
Piano Movers, The (Reissue of *His Musical Career*)
Pickford, Jack, 91, 93
Pickford, Mary, 23, 86, 136, 137, 145, 153, 162, 169, 289, 305
Pile Driver, The (Reissue of *Fatal Mallet, The*)
Pilgrim, The, 150, 162-167, 226
"Plainsman, The," 255
Police, 50, 52, 54
Pope, Jean, 223
Potel, Victor, 24
"Potemkin," 176
Power, Tyrone, 88
Prevost, Marie, 26
Price, Oscar, 162
"Price of a Good Time, The," 88
Prince, Charles, 24
"Prodigal Son, The," 169
Property Man, The, 37, 38, 39, 75

"Public Opinion" (*see A Woman of Paris,* 169)
Pugilist, The (Reissue of *Knockout, The*)
Purviance, Edna, 54, 55, 56, 57, 60, 62, 63, 76, 77, 78, 79, 82, 83, 85, 87, 99, 100, 111, 156, 169, 170, 175, 199, 200, 220, 286, 298
"Puss in Boots," 11, 12
Putting One Over (Reissue of *Masquerader, The*)

Quirk, James, 109
"Quo Vadis," 22

R.K.O Van Buren Corporation, 65, 66
"Rain Maker, The," 190, 208
Ramsaye, Terry, 59
Rand, John, 60
Rankin, John E., 285
Raskin, David, 257
Ray, Charles, 110
Ray, Man, 206
Raye, Martha, 295
Recreation, 318
Reed, Carol, 176
Reeves, Alfred, 20, 118, 202, 205, 222, 286
Reeves, Billy, 19, 20
Reeves, May, 247
"Regency," 250
Reid, Wallace, 49, 169
Reinhardt, Max, 282
Reliance (film company), 23
Revelry (Reissue of *Rounders, The*)
Reynolds, Dr. Cecil, 286
Riesner, Chuck, 86, 163, 190, 200
Rigadin (*see* Prince, Charles)
Rimsky-Korsakov, 238
Ring, Frances, 191
Rink, The, 33, 76
"Rio Rita," 250
Ritchie, Billy, 20, 64
Rival Mashers, The (Reissue of *Those Love Pangs*)
Rivera, Diego, 290
Roach, Hal, 250
Robinson, Carl, 123, 135, 136, 139, 143, 144, 149, 152, 207, 218, 221, 222, 224, 242, 243, 244, 245, 247, 289
Rodemich, Gene, 65
Roosevelt, Eleanor, 284
Rosza, Miklos, 241
Rounders, The, 36, 37, 39, 40, 48, 288

"Roundup, The," 110
Roustabout, The (Reissue of *Property Man, The*)
Ruggles, Wesley, 56
"Rumba," 237
Russian War Relief, 281

"Safety Last," 188
St. Clair, Mal, 26, 175
St. John, Al, 28
Saintsbury, H. A., 13
"Sally," 138
Sandburg, Carl, 136
"Salvation Hunters, The," 190
Sassoon, Sir Philip, 142, 144, 243, 248
"Saturday to Monday," 16
"Scarecrow, The," 110
Scheff, Fritzi, 56
"Scheherazade," 238
Schenck, Joseph, 250
Schildkraut, Nathan, 136
"Sea Gull, The," 170
Sechan, André, 65
"Second Hungarian Rhapsody," 239
Seldes, Gilbert, 1, 7
Selig (film company), 23
Selwyn, Archie, 250
Semon, Larry, 109
Sennett, Mack, 20, 24, 25, 26, 27, 28, 29, 30, 31, 32, 34, 36, 40, 47, 51, 59, 116, 224
"Service for Ladies," 175
"Seven Lively Arts, The," 7
"Shadow and Substance," 280, 282
Shanghaied, 323
"Shark Master, The," 148
Shaw, George Bernard, 140, 243, 244
"The Sheik," 169
Shepherd, May, 247
Sheridan, Clare, 149, 151, 152, 158, 289
"Sherlock Holmes," 13
"Sherlock, Jr.," 189
Sherwood, Robert E., 4
Shoulder Arms, 55, 86, 88, 101-109, 126, 140, 155, 163, 187, 225
Simpson, Wallis, 247
Sinclair, Upton, 149, 289
"Sing a Song," 236
Sisnette, Frank, 15
"Six Days" (*see* Elinor Glyn)
"Skippy," 126
Slippery Slim (*see* Potel, Victor)
Sodkay, Moussia, 142, 143, 145

Some Nerve (Reissue of *Gentlemen of Nerve*)
Sorel, Cecile, 145
Southern, Eve, 170
Spoor, George K., 46, 58
Spring Fever (Reissue of *Recreation*)
Squarehead, The (Reissue of *Mabel's Married Life*)
"Squaw Man, The," 23
"Stagecoach," 188
Stanley, Joseph, 13
Star Boarder, The, 314
Steinbeck, John, 263
Steiner, Max, 241
Sterling, Ford, 20, 24, 25, 28, 30, 31, 32
Stewart, Anita, 23, 91
Stewart, George, 91
Stewart, William Rhinelander, 223
Stockdale, Carl, 56
Strauss, Karl, 264
"Strong Man, The," 211
Sturges, Preston, 26, 123, 254
Sullivan and Considine (vaudeville circuit), 20
Summerville, Slim, 26, 28
"Sun Up," 13
Sunnyside, 33, 86, 109, 110-113, 155
"Susan Lennox," 297
Sutherland, Eddie, 119, 170, 190
Swain, Mack, 25, 28, 31, 36, 40, 156, 190
Swanson, Gloria, 26, 55
Swedie (*see* Beery, Wallace)
Sweet, Blanche, 29

"Tango Bitterness," 237
Tango Tangles, 40
Tartufini (*see* Prince, Charles)
Taylor, Charles A., 13
Taylor, Laurette, 13
Taylor, William D., 33, 93
Temple, Shirley, 127
"Ten Looneys, The," 14
"Terrible Turk, The," (*see* Aubrey, Jimmy)
Terrill, Maverick, 61
"There's Always Someone You Can't Forget," 18, 236
"Thin Man, The," 254
"Third Man, The," 176
"Thirsty First, The," 16
Thompson, Virgil, 241
Those Love Pangs, 39, 40
"Three Ages," 155

"Three Musketeers, The," 136, 137, 169
"Three Weeks" (see Glyn, Elinor)
"Through the Back Door," 169
Tieck, Dr. Gustav, 204
Tilden, William, 154
"Tillie's Nightmare," 40
"Tillie's Punctured Romance," 6, 40, 41, 44, 124
"Titina," 253
Tobis Filmes Sonores, 257, 258
"Torrent, The," 175
Totheroh, Roland (Rollie), 56, 60, 264
"Tragedy of Errors, A," 16
Tramp, The, 47, 49, 50, 95
Tree, Sir Herbert Beerbohm, 13, 62
Tree, Iris, 62, 142
Triangle (film company), 23, 88
"Triple Trouble," 54
Trotsky, 151
"Trouble," 126
Troubles (Reissue of Making a Living)
Tully, Jim, 33, 191, 199, 290
Tuning His Ivories (Reissue of Laughing Gas)
Turner, Florence, 23
Turpin, Ben, 50, 53, 56
"Turpin's Ride to York," 15
Twenty Minutes of Love, 38, 48
Two of a Kind (Reissue of Rounders, The)
Tyler, Parker, 295
"Typhoon," 23

Ulric, Lenore, 154
Un-American Activities Committee, 284
United Artists (film company), 162, 202, 224, 248, 250, 282, 295, 308
Universal (film company), 23, 28

Vagabond, The, 60, 70, 95, 126
Valentino, Rudolph, 154, 169
Van Brugh, Irene, 14
Van Dyke, W. S., 118, 254
Van Pelt, Ernest, 56
Vanderbilt, Mrs. William K., 62, 145
"Vanity Fair" (see Idle Class)
Vidor, King, 118, 286
Vitagraph (film company), 23
Vogel, Joseph, 295

Von Sternberg, Josef, 170, 190, 245
Von Stroheim, 118, 123
Von Volmueller, Karl, 245
Von Wiegand, Karl, 143

Wagner, Robert, 85, 287
Waiter, The (Reissue of Caught in a Cabaret)
Wales, Prince of, 247
Walker, Lillian, 24
Walker, Mayor Jimmy, 224
Wallace, Henry, 284, 291
Walrus (see Conklin, Chester)
Walton, William, 241
Weber, Lois, 88
Weeks, Ada May, 296
Weiman, Rita, 137
Wellman 254
Welles, Orson, 123, 293
Wells, H. G., 142, 144, 145, 247, 289
West, Billy, 61, 64
Westminster, Duke of, 246
"What Price Glory," 211
Wheeler and Woolsey, 224
"When the Clouds Roll By," 139
When You're Married (Reissue of Mabel's Married Life)
"Where Are My Children," 88
Whiffles (see Prince, Charles)
White, Leo, 54, 56, 60, 64
"White Russian," 251
Who Got Stung (Reissue of Caught in the Rain)
Williams, J. D., 84
Windsor, Claire, 148, 149
Winsten, Archer, 296
"With You, Dear, in Bombay," 236
Woman, A, 48, 52
Woman of Paris, A, 56, 117, 123, 162, 168-186, 257
"Woman of the Sea, The," 170
Woollcott, Alexander, 8, 137
Work, 47, 48, 50
"Wow Wows, The," 19
"Wrath of the Gods," 23
Wright, Arthur, 92
Wright, Frank Lloyd, 249
Wright, Lloyd, 205

Xenia, Princess, 145, 206

Ziegfeld, Florenz, 250
Zukor, Adolph, 22, 84